Four-Eyed Prince

3

Wataru Mizukami

Translated and adapted by
Jamie Jacobs

Lettered by
North Market Street Graphics

DEL
REY

Ballantine Books · New York

A Del Rey Manga/Kodansha Trade Paperback Original

Four-Eyed Prince volume 3 copyright © 2008 Wataru Mizukami
English translation copyright © 2010 Wataru Mizukami

Published in the United States by Del Rey, an imprint of
The Random House Publishing Group, a division of Random House, Inc.,
New York.

DEL REY is a registered trademark and the Del Rey colophon is a
trademark of Random House, Inc.

Publication rights arranged through Kodansha Ltd.

First published in Japan in 2008 by Kodansha Ltd., Tokyo, as *Megane Oji*

ISBN 978-0-345-52020-3

Printed in the United States of America

www.delreymanga.com

2 4 6 8 9 7 5 3 1

Translator/Adapter: Jamie Jacobs
Lettering: North Market Street Graphics

Contents

HONORIFICS EXPLAINED

Throughout the Del Rey Manga books, you will find Japanese honorifics left intact in the translations. For those not familiar with how the Japanese use honorifics and, more important, how they differ from American honorifics, we present this brief overview.

Politeness has always been a critical facet of Japanese culture. Ever since the feudal era, when Japan was a highly stratified society, use of honorifics—which can be defined as polite speech that indicates relationship or status—has played an essential role in the Japanese language. When you address someone in Japanese, an honorific usually takes the form of a suffix attached to one's name (example: "Asuna-san"), is used as a title at the end of one's name, or appears in place of the name itself (example: "Negi-sensei," or simply "Sensei!").

Honorifics can be expressions of respect or endearment. In the context of manga and anime, honorifics give insight into the nature of the relationship between characters. Many English translations leave out these important honorifics and therefore distort the feel of the original Japanese. Because Japanese honorifics contain nuances that English honorifics lack, it is our policy at Del Rey not to translate them. Here, instead, is a guide to some of the honorifics you may encounter in Del Rey Manga.

-san: This is the most common honorific and is equivalent to Mr., Miss, Ms., or Mrs. It is the all-purpose honorific and can be used in any situation where politeness is required.

-sama: This is one level higher than "-san" and is used to confer great respect.

-dono: This comes from the word "tono," which means "lord." It is an even higher level than "-sama" and confers utmost respect.

-kun: This suffix is used at the end of boys' names to express familiarity or endearment. It is also sometimes used by men among friends, or when addressing someone younger or of a lower station.

-chan: This is used to express endearment, mostly toward girls. It is also used for little boys, pets, and even among lovers. It gives a sense of childish cuteness.

Bozu: This is an informal way to refer to a boy, similar to the English terms "kid" and "squirt."

Sempai/
Senpai: This title suggests that the addressee is one's senior in a group or organization. It is most often used in a school setting, where underclassmen refer to their upperclassmen as "sempai." It can also be used in the workplace, such as when a newer employee addresses an employee who has seniority in the company.

Kohai: This is the opposite of "sempai" and is used toward underclassmen in school or newcomers in the workplace. It connotes that the addressee is of a lower station.

Sensei: Literally meaning "one who has come before," this title is used for teachers, doctors, or masters of any profession or art.

-[blank]: This is usually forgotten in these lists, but it is perhaps the most significant difference between Japanese and English. The lack of honorific, known as *yobisute,* means that the speaker has permission to address the person in a very intimate way. Usually, only family, spouses, or very close friends have this kind of permission. It can be gratifying when someone who has earned the intimacy starts to call one by one's name without an honorific. But when that intimacy hasn't been earned, it can be very insulting.

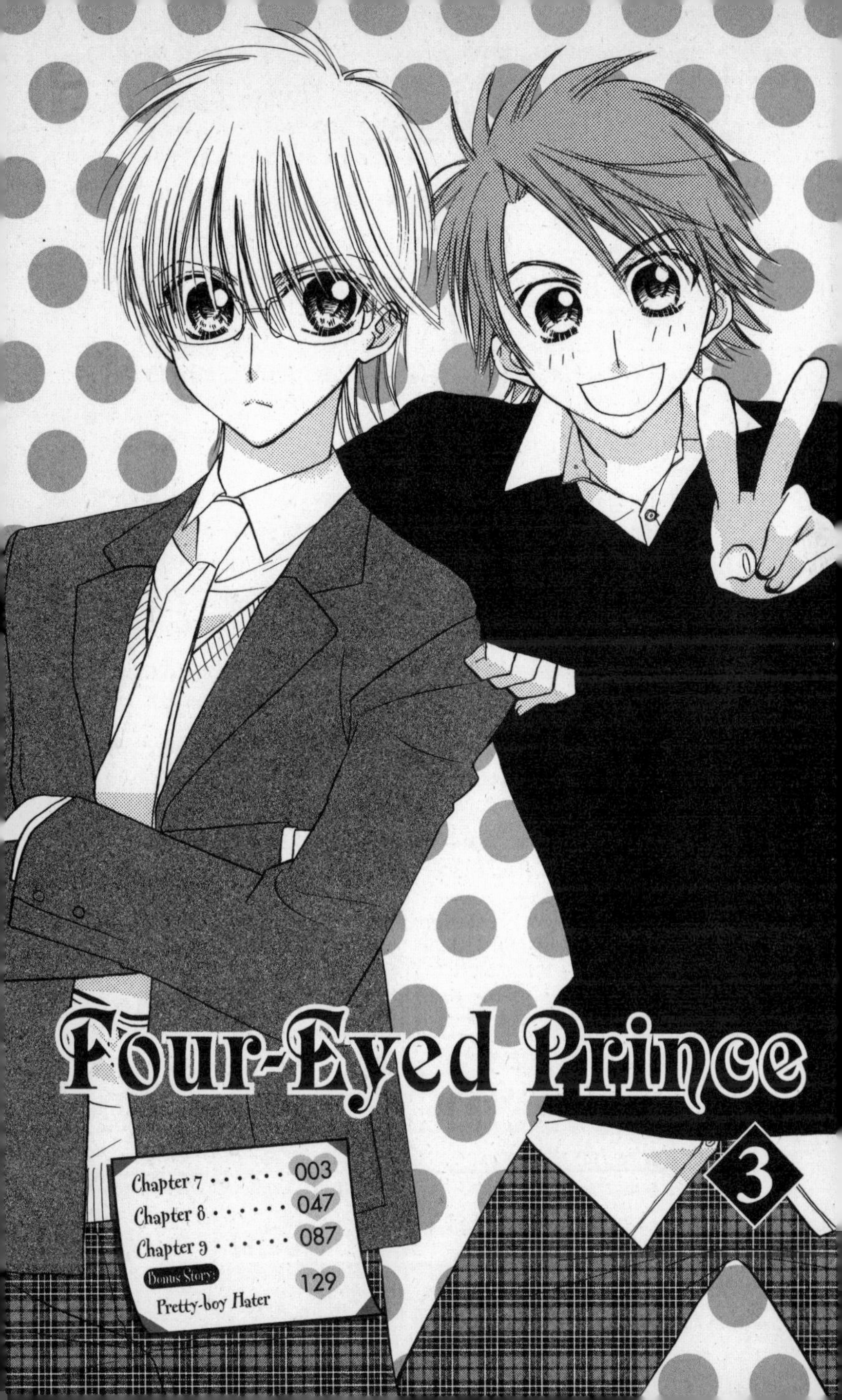

Four-Eyed Prince 3

Characters & Story

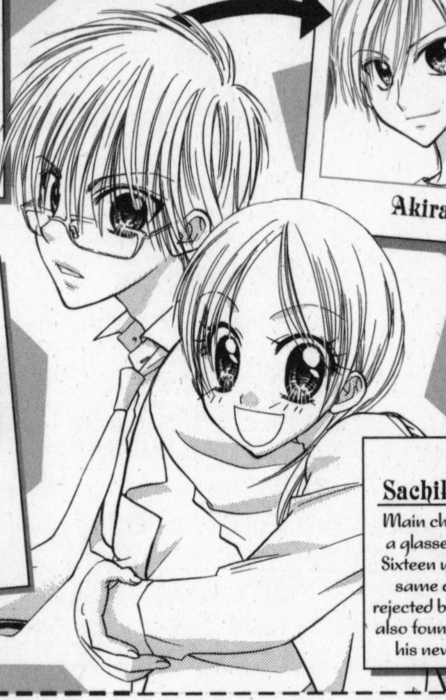

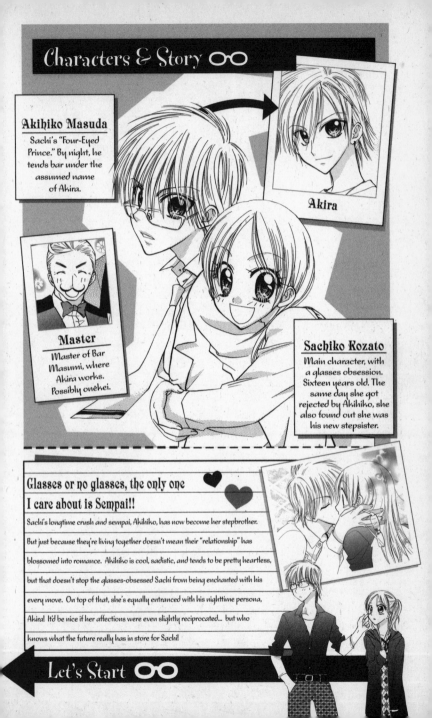

Akihiko Masuda

Sachi's "Four-Eyed Prince." By night, he tends bar under the assumed name of Akira.

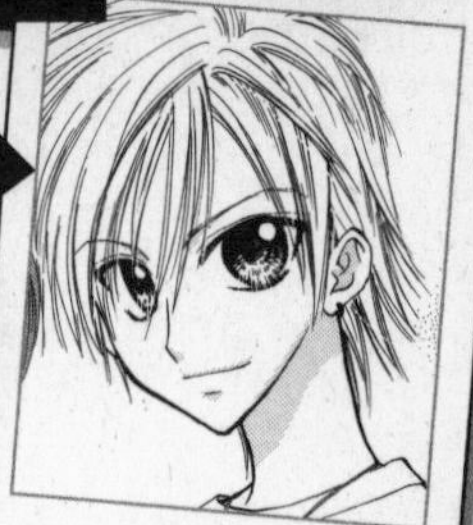

Akira

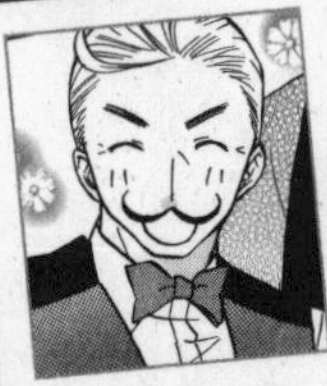

Master

Master of Bar Masumi, where Akira works. Possibly onēkei.

Sachiko Kozato

Main character, with a glasses obsession. Sixteen years old. The same day she got rejected by Akihiko, she also found out she was his new stepsister.

Glasses or no glasses, the only one I care about is Sempai!!

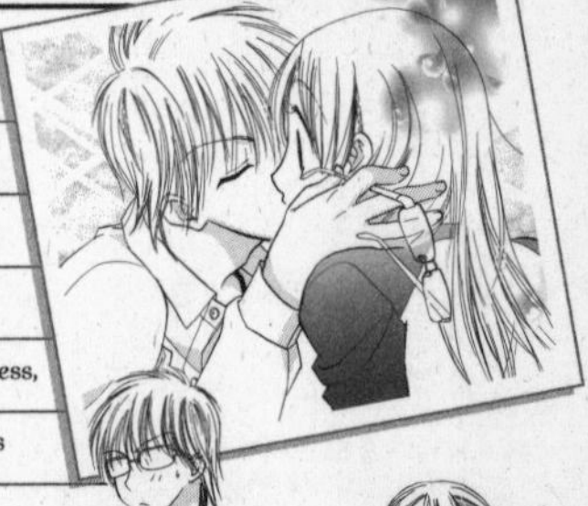

Sachi's longtime crush and sempai, Akihiko, has now become her stepbrother. But just because they're living together doesn't mean their "relationship" has blossomed into romance. Akihiko is cool, sadistic, and tends to be pretty heartless, but that doesn't stop the glasses-obsessed Sachi from being enchanted with his every move. On top of that, she's equally entranced with his nighttime persona, Akira! It'd be nice if her affections were even slightly reciprocated... but who knows what the future really has in store for Sachi!

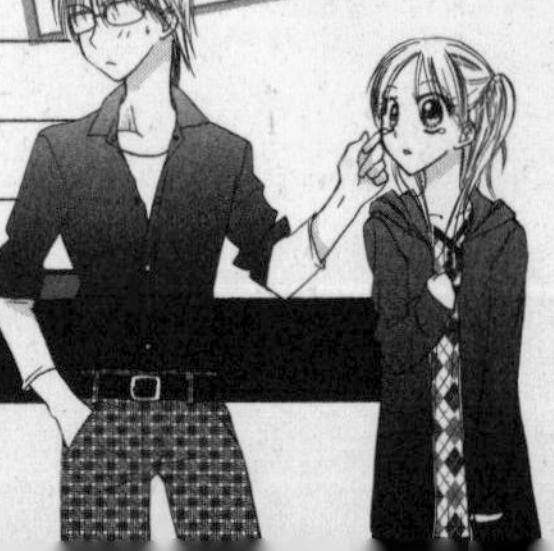

Let's Start

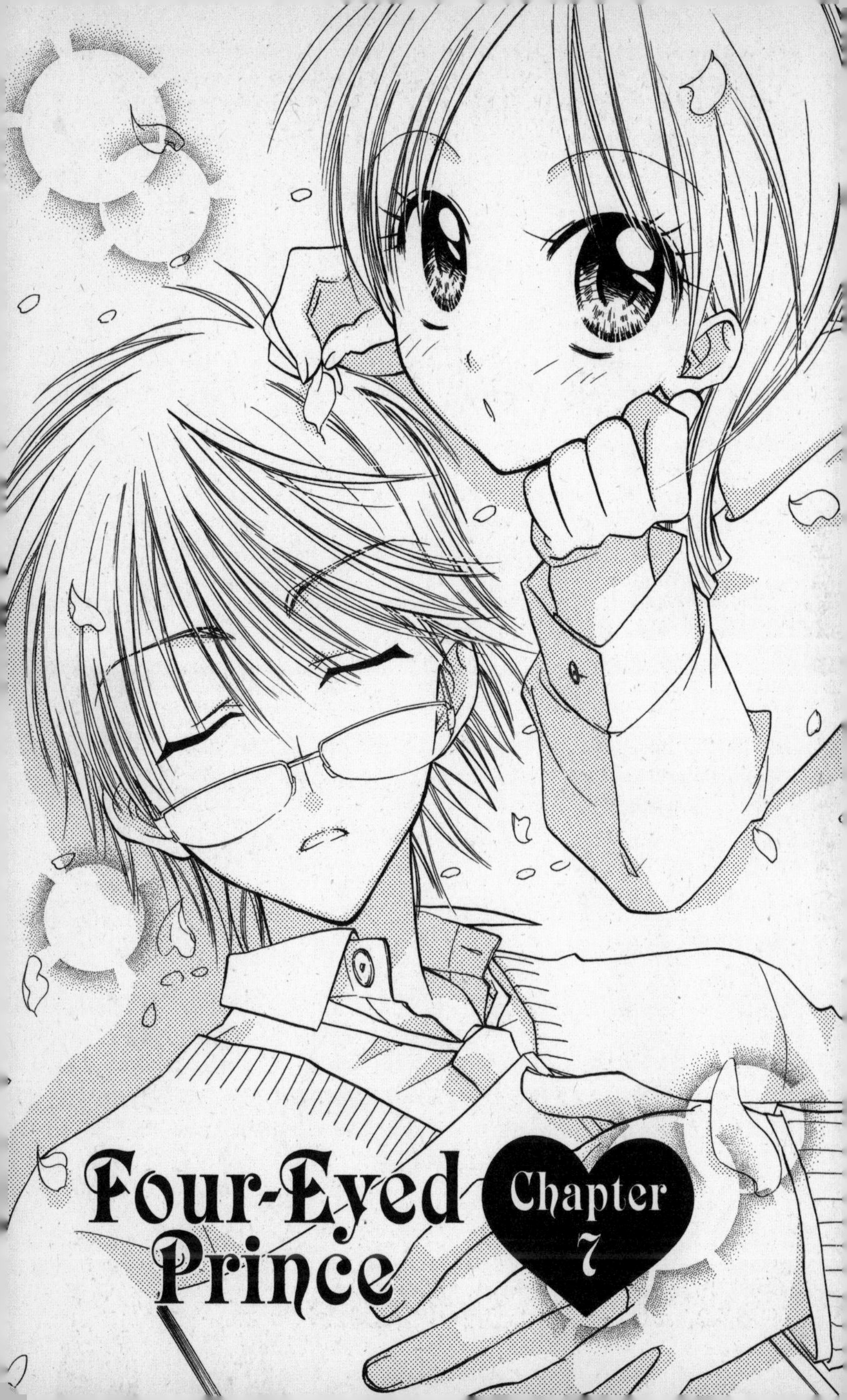
Four-Eyed Prince
Chapter 7

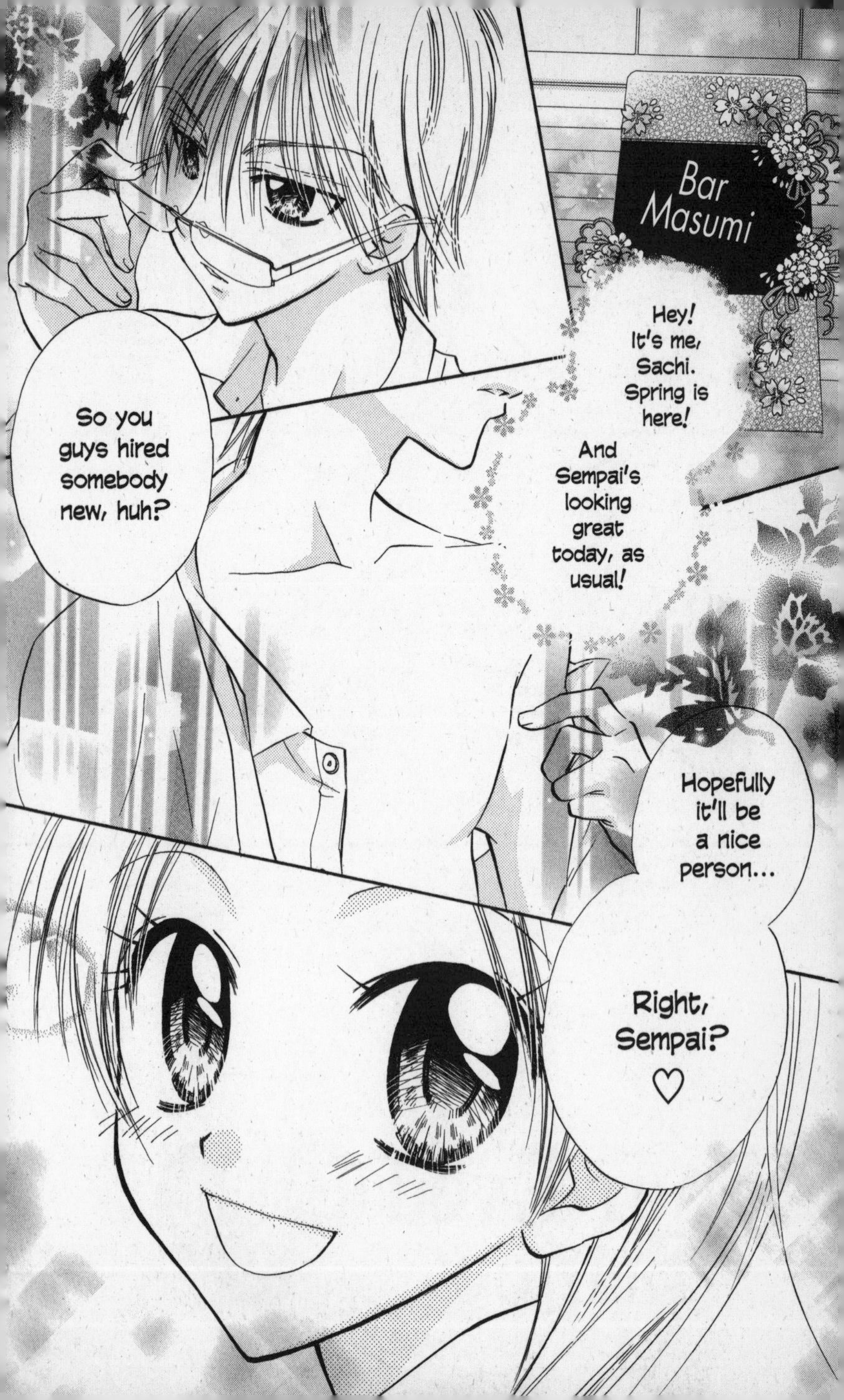
Bar Masumi
Hey! It's me, Sachi. Spring is here!
And Sempai's looking great today, as usual!
So you guys hired somebody new, huh?
Hopefully it'll be a nice person...
Right, Sempai? ♡

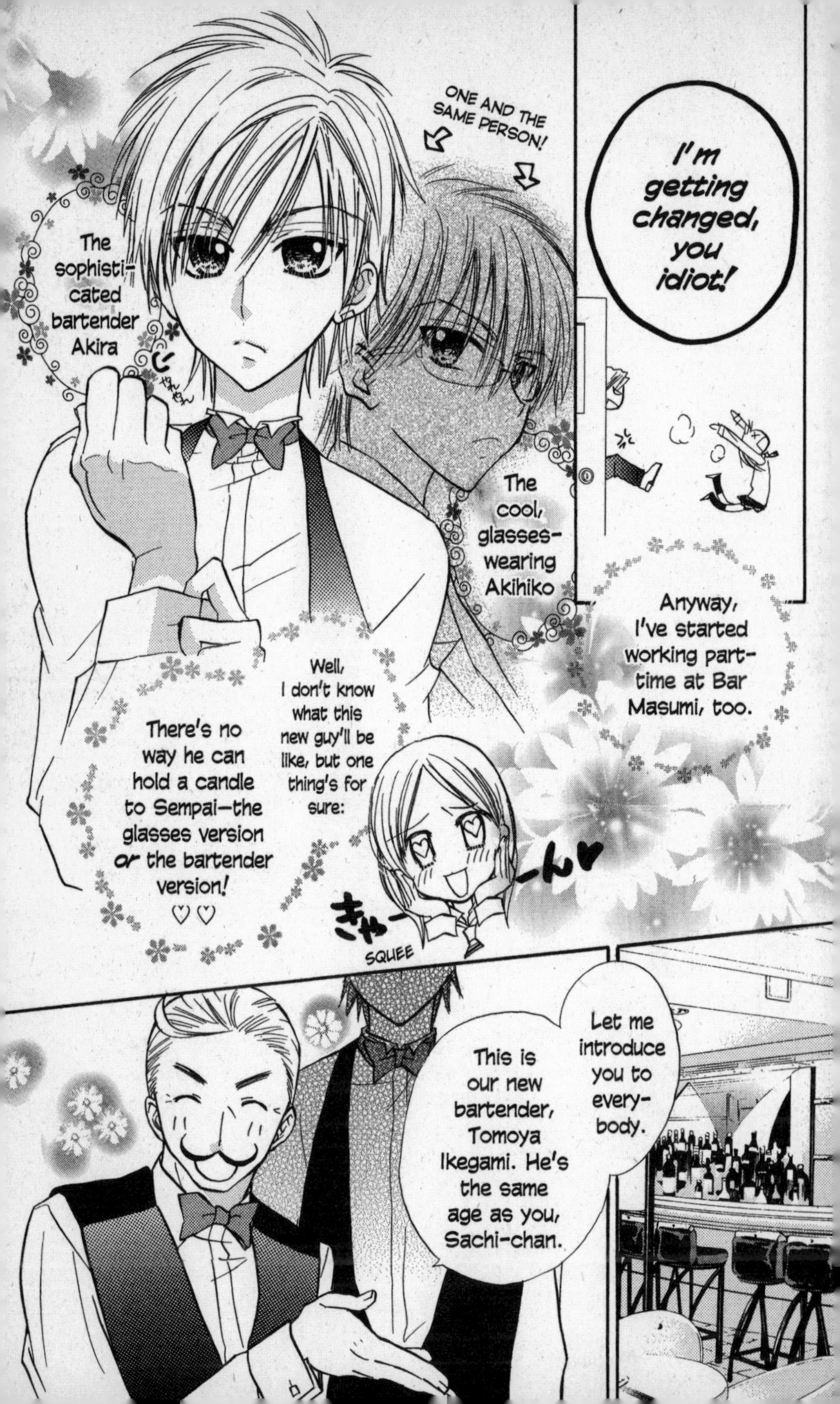

I'm getting changed, you idiot!
ONE AND THE SAME PERSON!
The sophisti-cated bartender Akira
The cool, glasses-wearing Akihiko
Anyway, I've started working part-time at Bar Masumi, too.
Well, I don't know what this new guy'll be like, but one thing's for sure:
There's no way he can hold a candle to Sempai—the glasses version *or* the bartender version! ♡♡
きゃー
ーん♥
SQUEE
Let me introduce you to every-body.
This is our new bartender, Tomoya Ikegami. He's the same age as you, Sachi-chan.

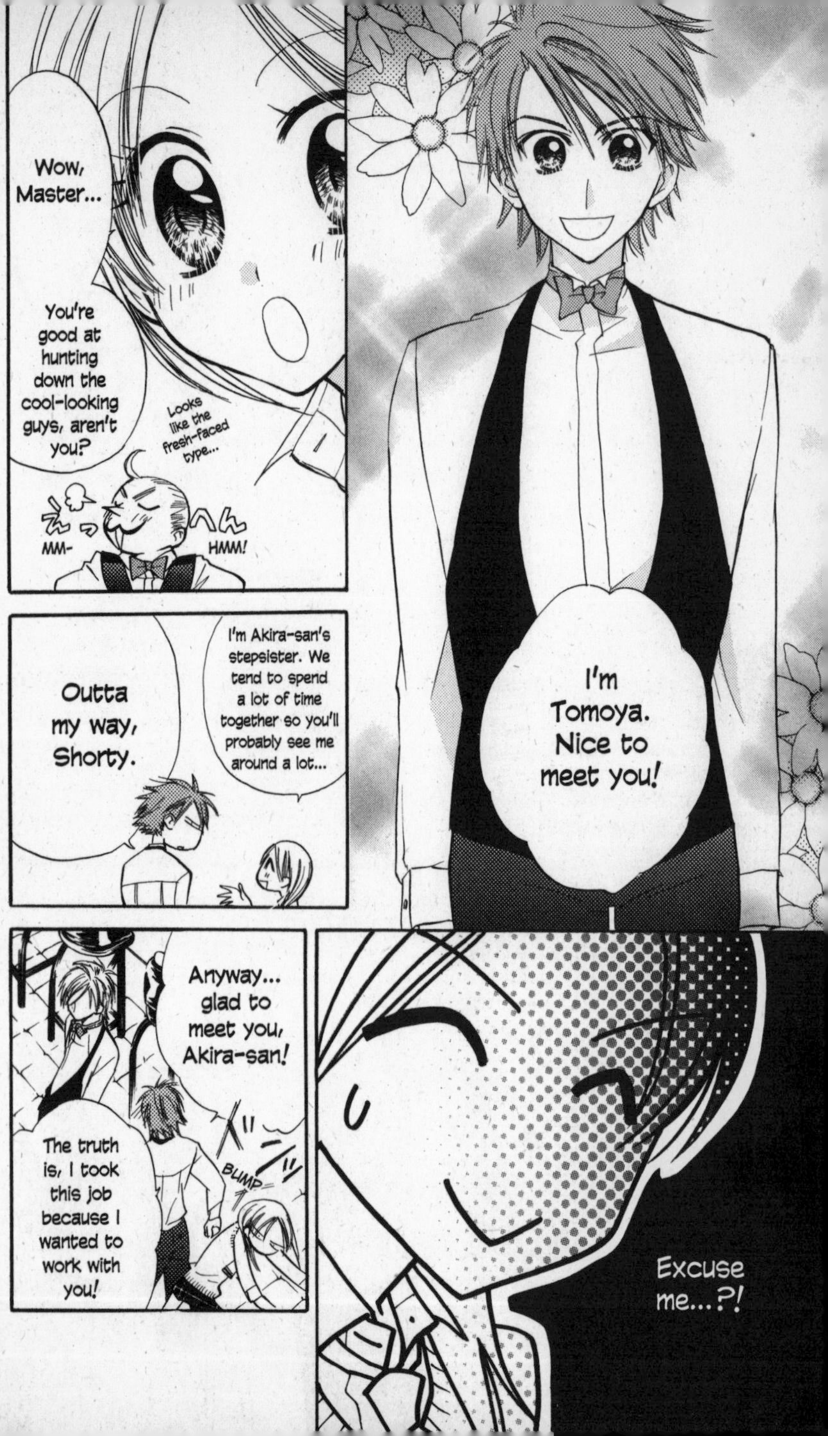

I'm Tomoya. Nice to meet you!
Wow, Master...
You're good at hunting down the cool-looking guys, aren't you?
Looks like the fresh-faced type...
MM- HMM!
I'm Akira-san's stepsister. We tend to spend a lot of time together so you'll probably see me around a lot...
Outta my way, Shorty.
Excuse me...?!
Anyway... glad to meet you, Akira-san!
BUMP
The truth is, I took this job because I wanted to work with you!

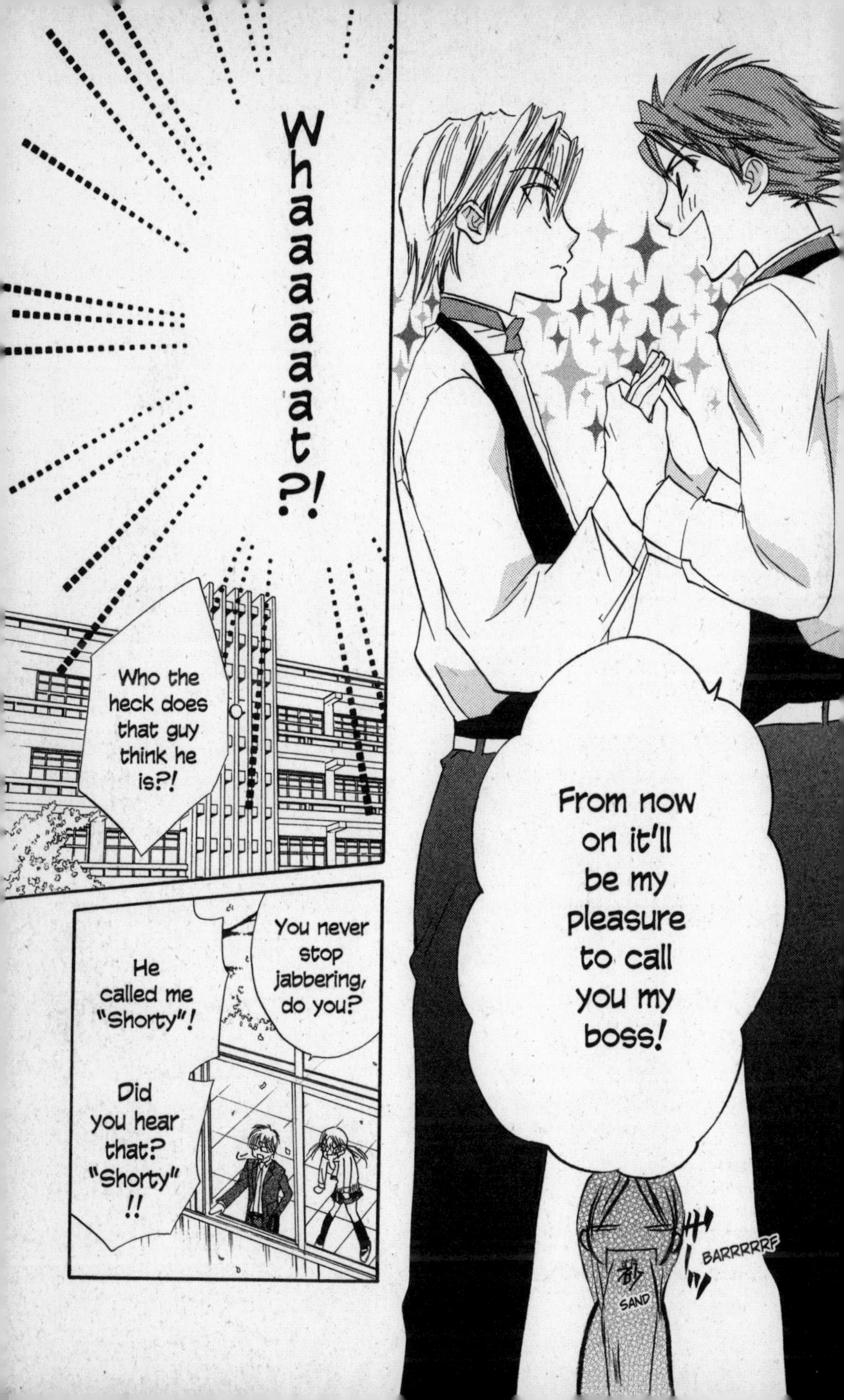
From now on it'll be my pleasure to call you my boss!
BARRRRRF
SAND
Whaaaaaaat?!
Who the heck does that guy think he is?!
You never stop jabbering, do you?
He called me "Shorty"!
Did you hear that? "Shorty" !!

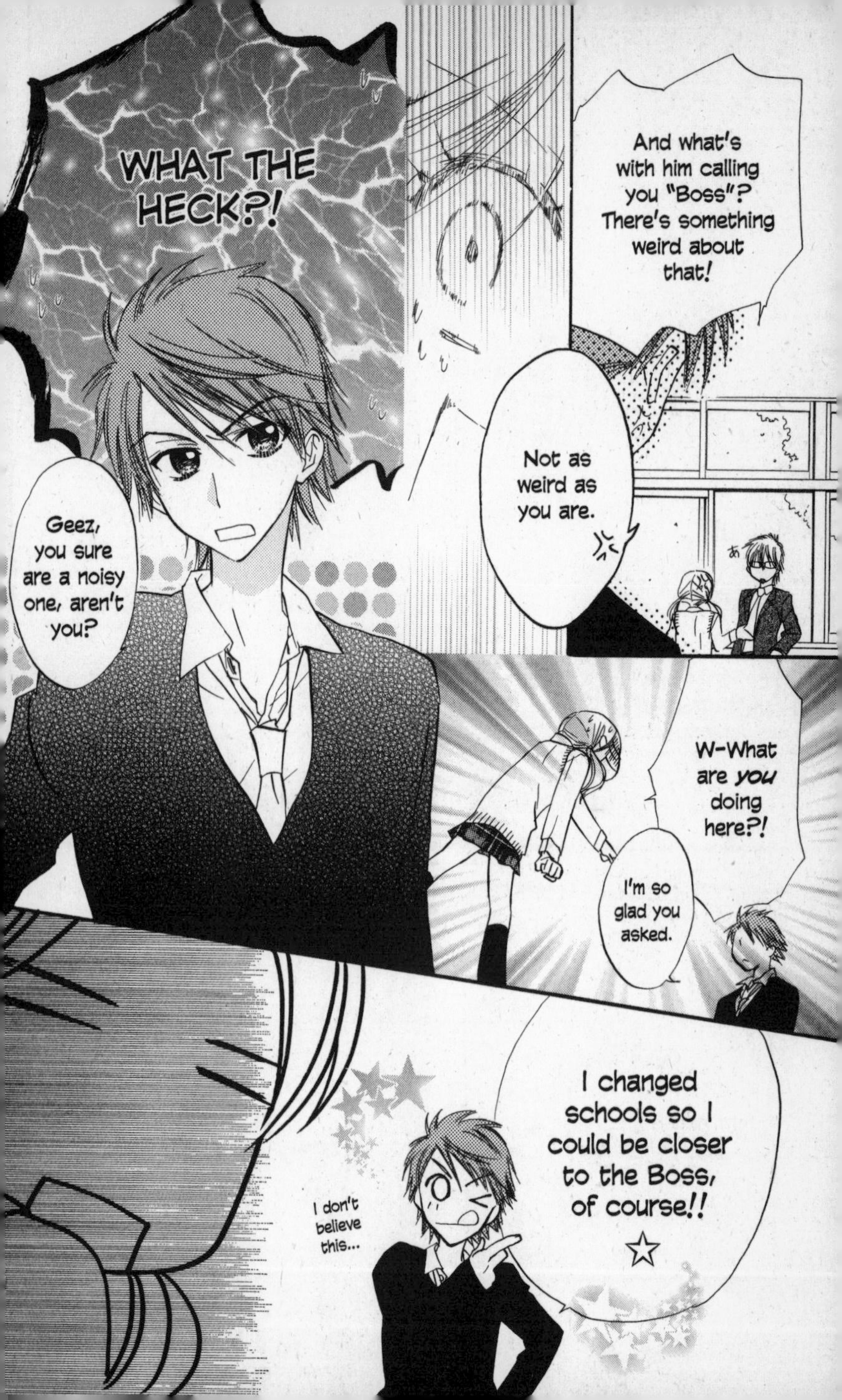
And what's with him calling you "Boss"? There's something weird about that!
Not as weird as you are.
WHAT THE HECK?!
Geez, you sure are a noisy one, aren't you?
W-What are *you* doing here?!
I'm so glad you asked.
I changed schools so I could be closer to the Boss, of course!! ☆
I don't believe this...

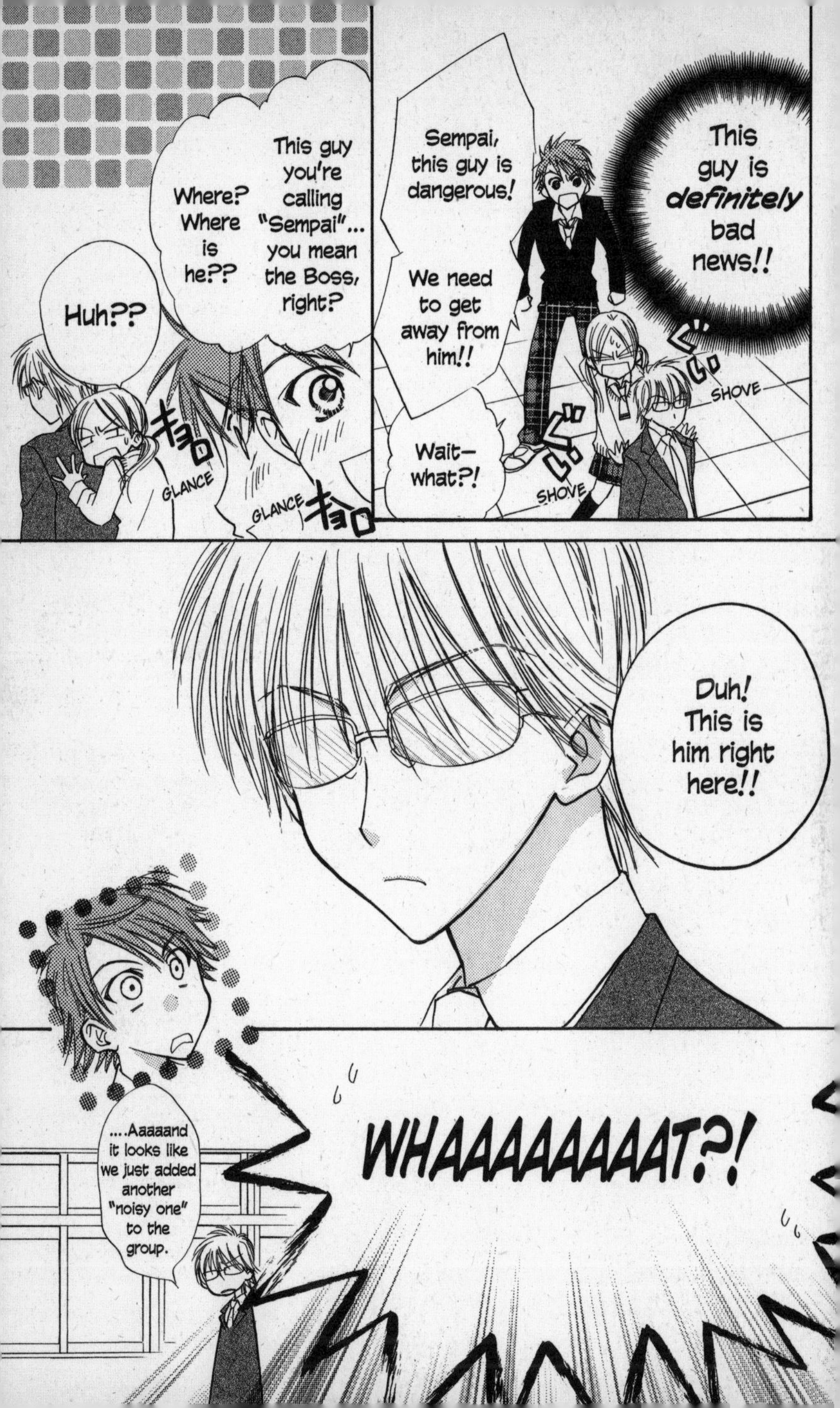
This guy is *definitely* bad news!!
Sempai, this guy is dangerous!
We need to get away from him!!
Wait—what?!
SHOVE
SHOVE
This guy you're calling "Sempai"... you mean the Boss, right?
Where? Where is he??
Huh??
GLANCE
GLANCE
Duh! This is him right here!!
WHAAAAAAAAT?!
....Aaaaand it looks like we just added another "noisy one" to the group.

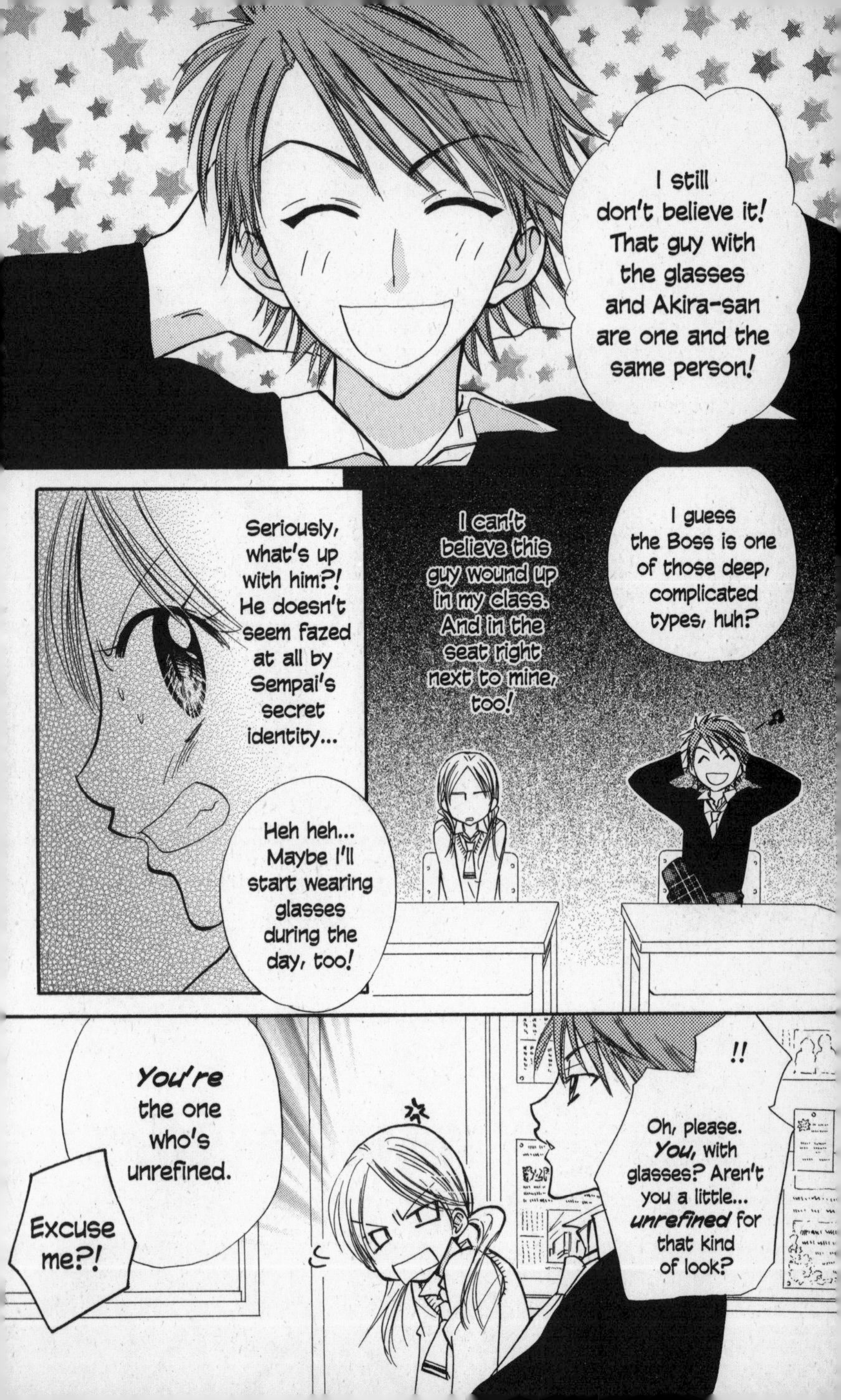

I still don't believe it! That guy with the glasses and Akira-san are one and the same person!
I guess the Boss is one of those deep, complicated types, huh?
I can't believe this guy wound up in my class. And in the seat right next to mine, too!
Heh heh... Maybe I'll start wearing glasses during the day, too!
Seriously, what's up with him?! He doesn't seem fazed at all by Sempai's secret identity...
!!
Oh, please. *You,* with glasses? Aren't you a little... *unrefined* for that kind of look?
You're the one who's unrefined.
Excuse me?!

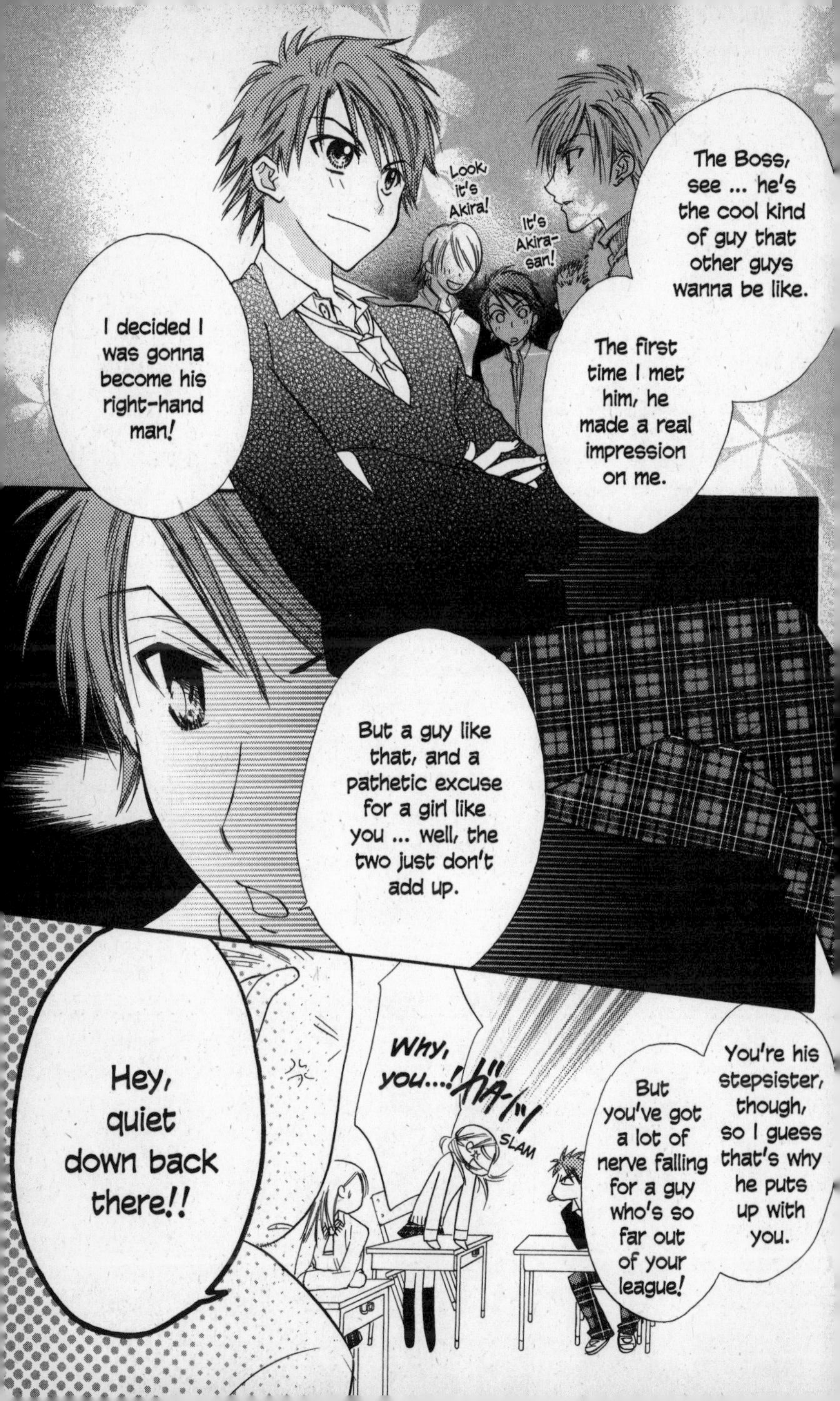

The Boss, see ... he's the cool kind of guy that other guys wanna be like.
Look, it's Akira!
It's Akira-san!
The first time I met him, he made a real impression on me.
I decided I was gonna become his right-hand man!
But a guy like that, and a pathetic excuse for a girl like you ... well, the two just don't add up.
You're his stepsister, though, so I guess that's why he puts up with you.
But you've got a lot of nerve falling for a guy who's so far out of your league!
Why, you...!
SLAM
Hey, quiet down back there!!

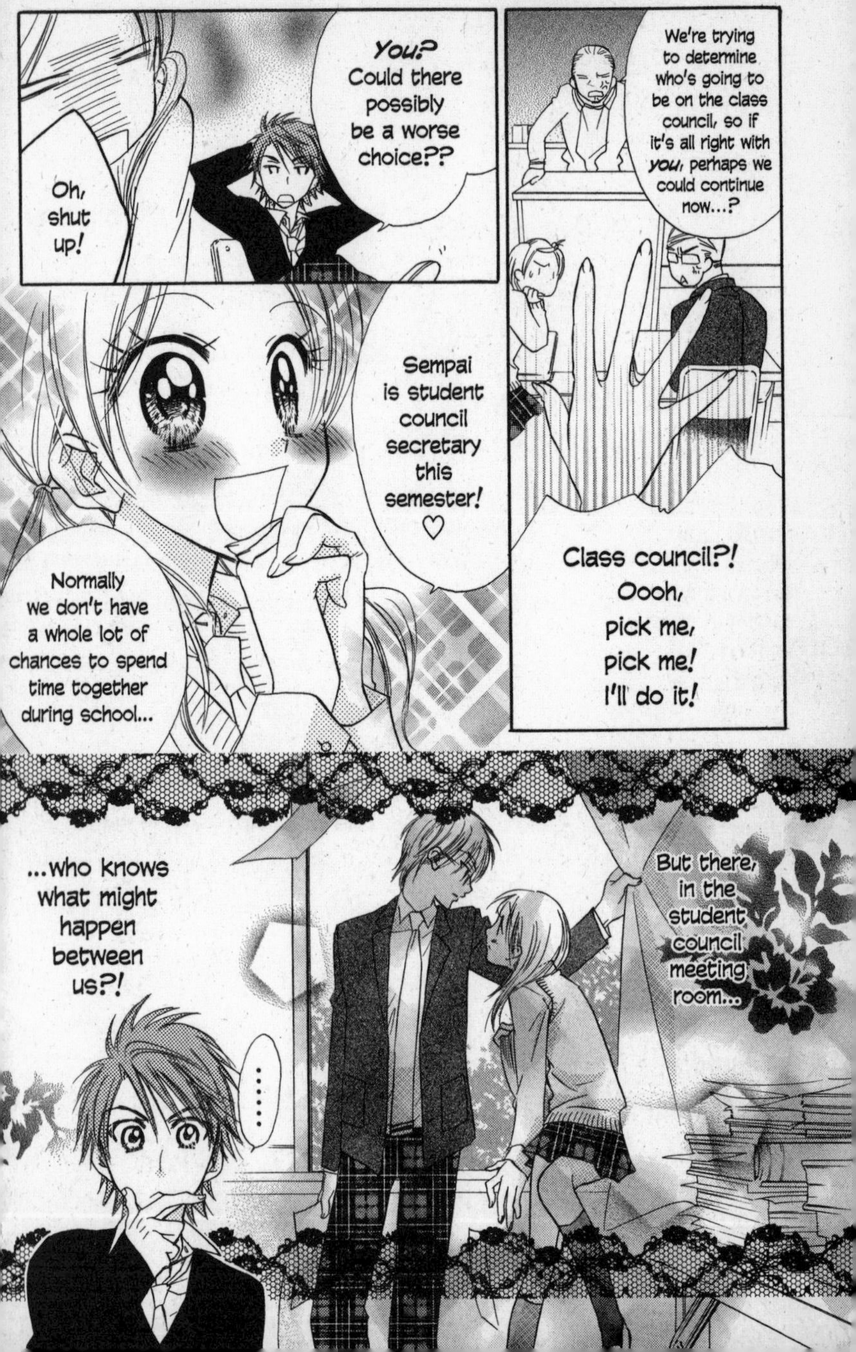
We're trying to determine who's going to be on the class council, so if it's all right with *you*, perhaps we could continue now...?
Class council?! Oooh, pick me, pick me! I'll do it!
You? Could there possibly be a worse choice??
Oh, shut up!
Sempai is student council secretary this semester! ♡
Normally we don't have a whole lot of chances to spend time together during school...
But there, in the student council meeting room...
...who knows what might happen between us?!
......

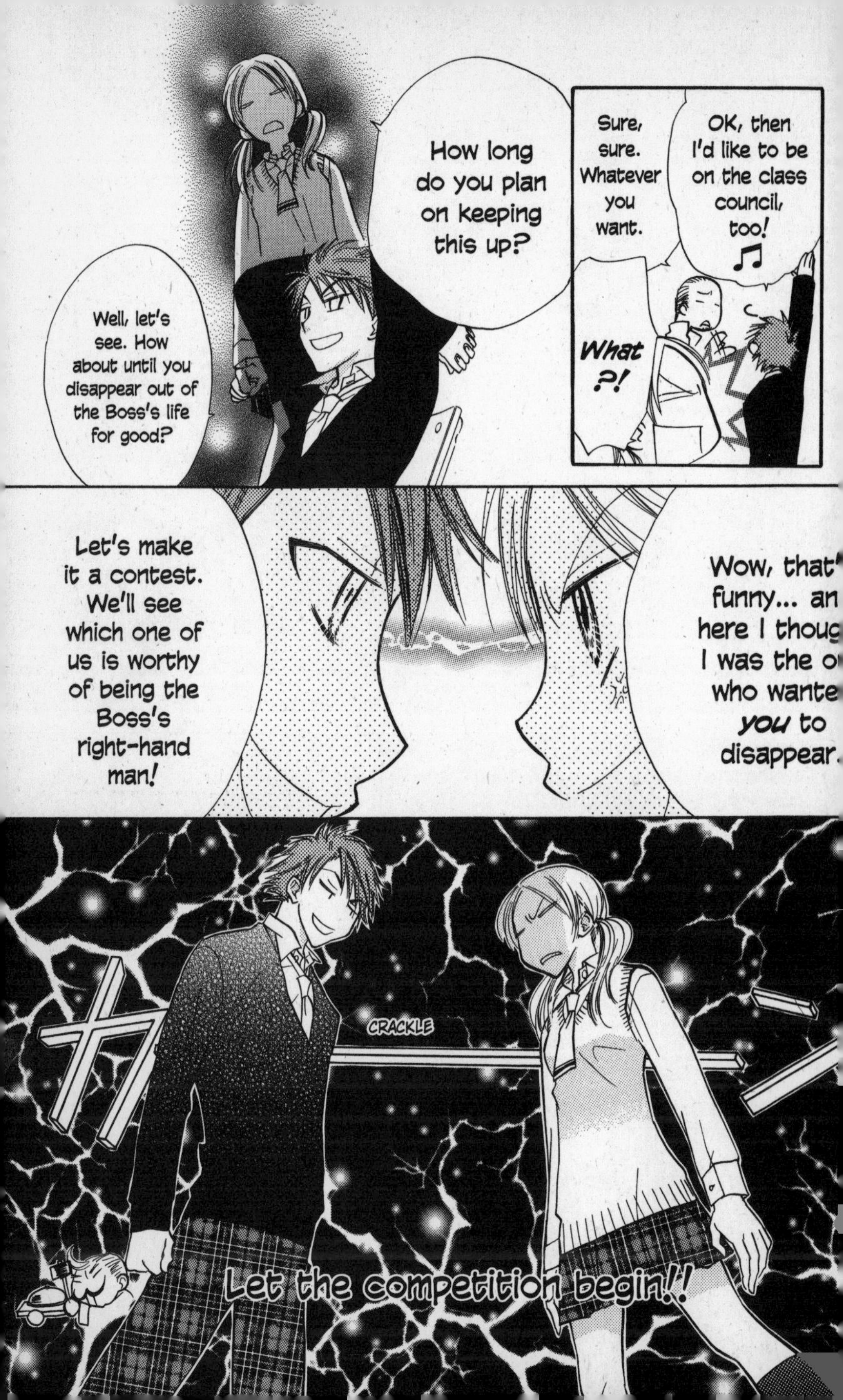

OK, then I'd like to be on the class council, too! ♫
Sure, sure. Whatever you want.
What?!
How long do you plan on keeping this up?
Well, let's see. How about until you disappear out of the Boss's life for good?
Wow, that' funny... an here I thoug I was the o who wante *you* to disappear.
Let's make it a contest. We'll see which one of us is worthy of being the Boss's right-hand man!
CRACKLE
Let the competition begin!!

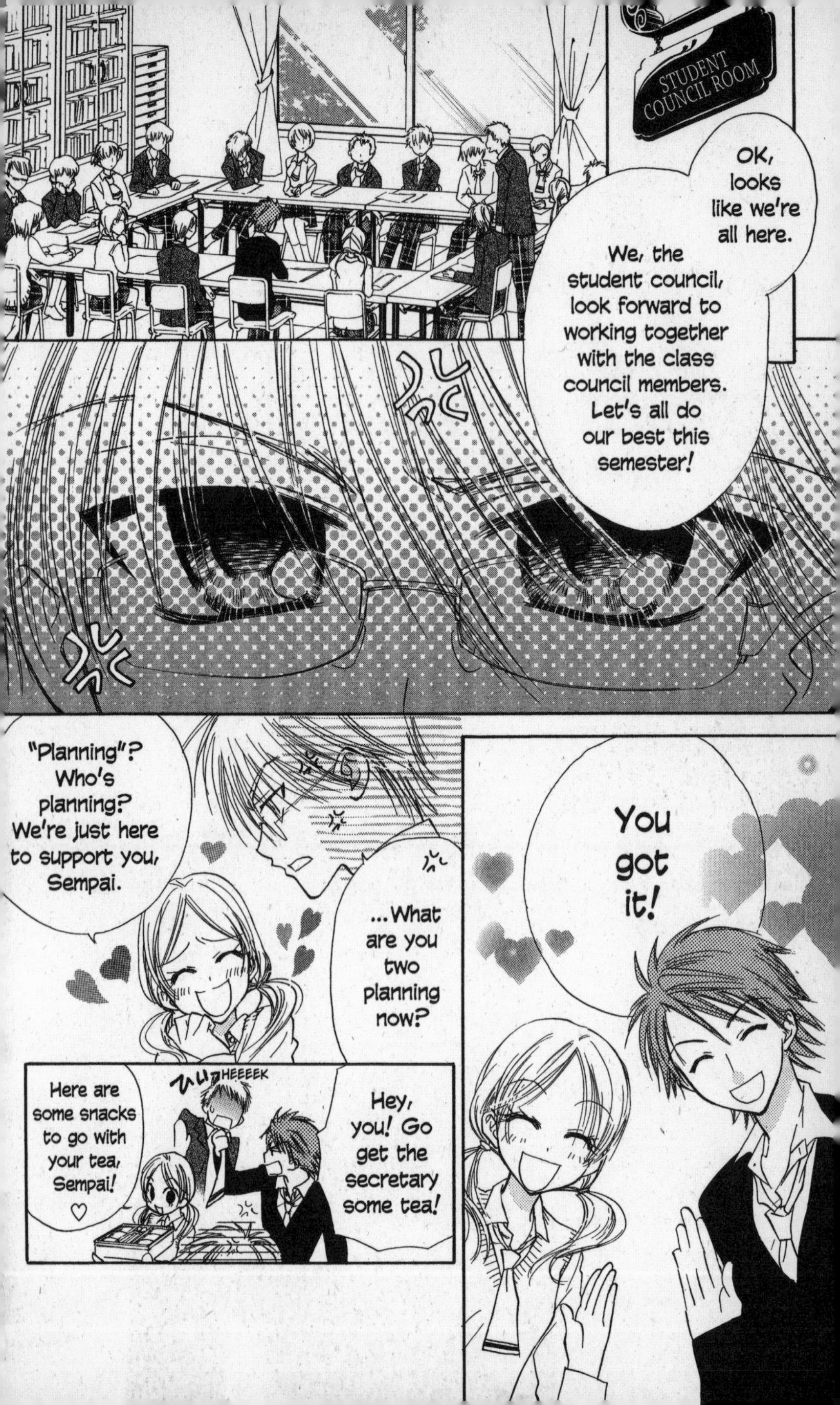

STUDENT COUNCIL ROOM
OK, looks like we're all here.
We, the student council, look forward to working together with the class council members. Let's all do our best this semester!
You got it!
...What are you two planning now?
"Planning"? Who's planning? We're just here to support you, Sempai.
Hey, you! Go get the secretary some tea!
HEEEEK
Here are some snacks to go with your tea, Sempai! ♡

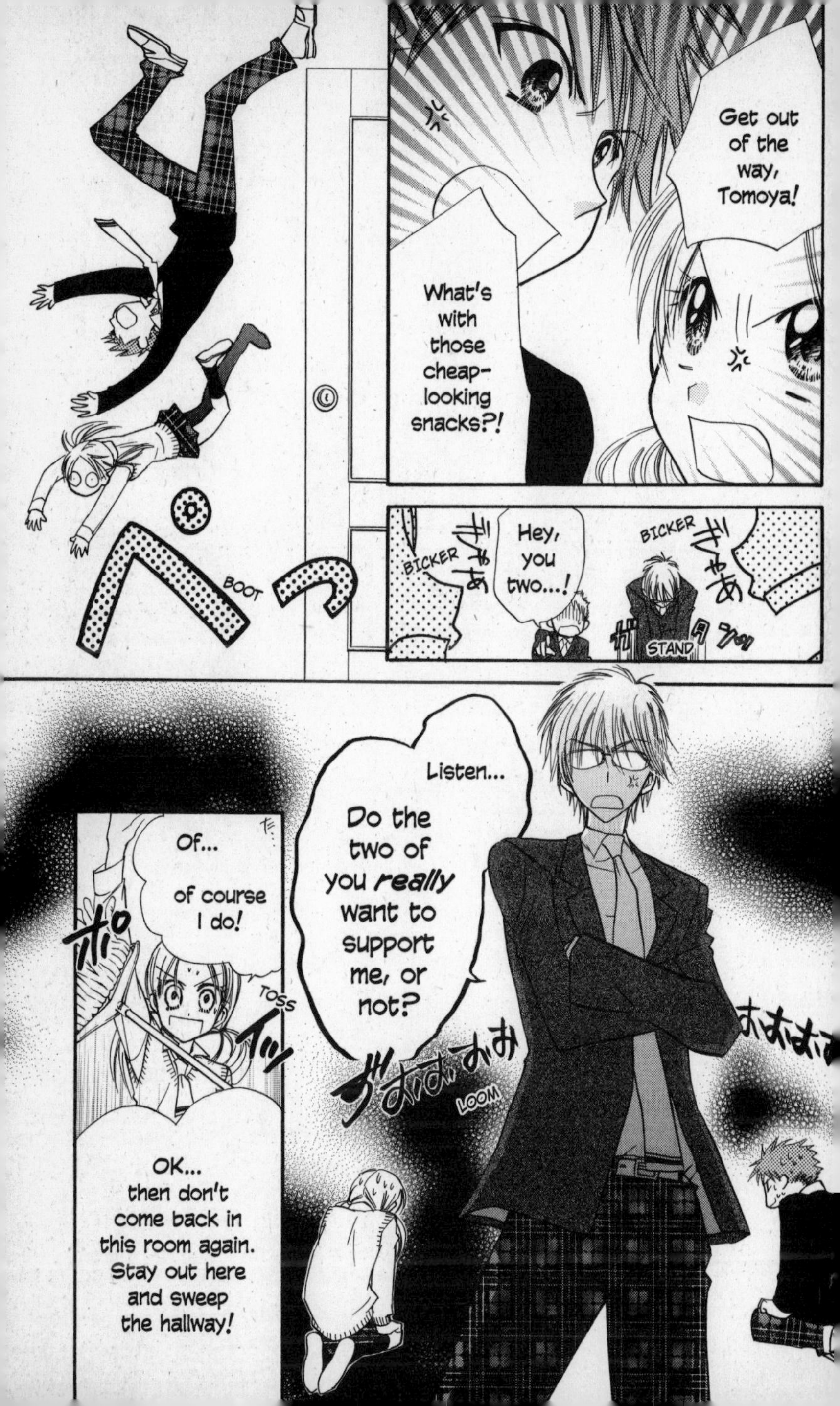

Get out of the way, Tomoya!
What's with those cheap-looking snacks?!
BICKER
STAND
Hey, you two...!
BICKER
BOOT
Listen...
Do the two of you *really* want to support me, or not?
LOOM
Of...
of course I do!
TOSS
OK... then don't come back in this room again. Stay out here and sweep the hallway!

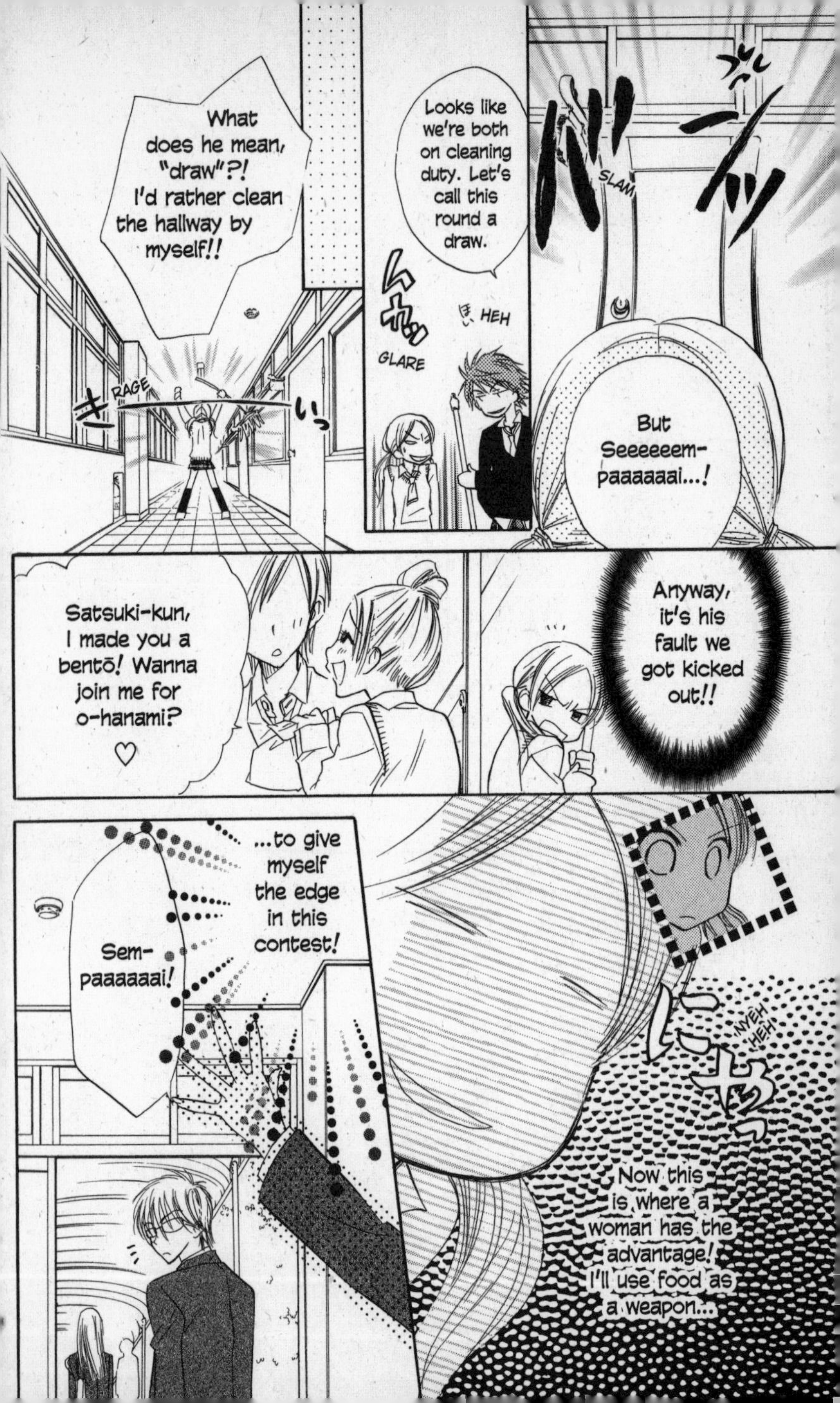
SLAM
But Seeeeeem-paaaaaai...!
Looks like we're both on cleaning duty. Let's call this round a draw.
HEH
GLARE
What does he mean, "draw"?! I'd rather clean the hallway by myself!!
RAGE
Anyway, it's his fault we got kicked out!!
Satsuki-kun, I made you a bentō! Wanna join me for o-hanami? ♡
NYEH HEH
Now this is where a woman has the advantage! I'll use food as a weapon...
...to give myself the edge in this contest!
Sem-paaaaaai!

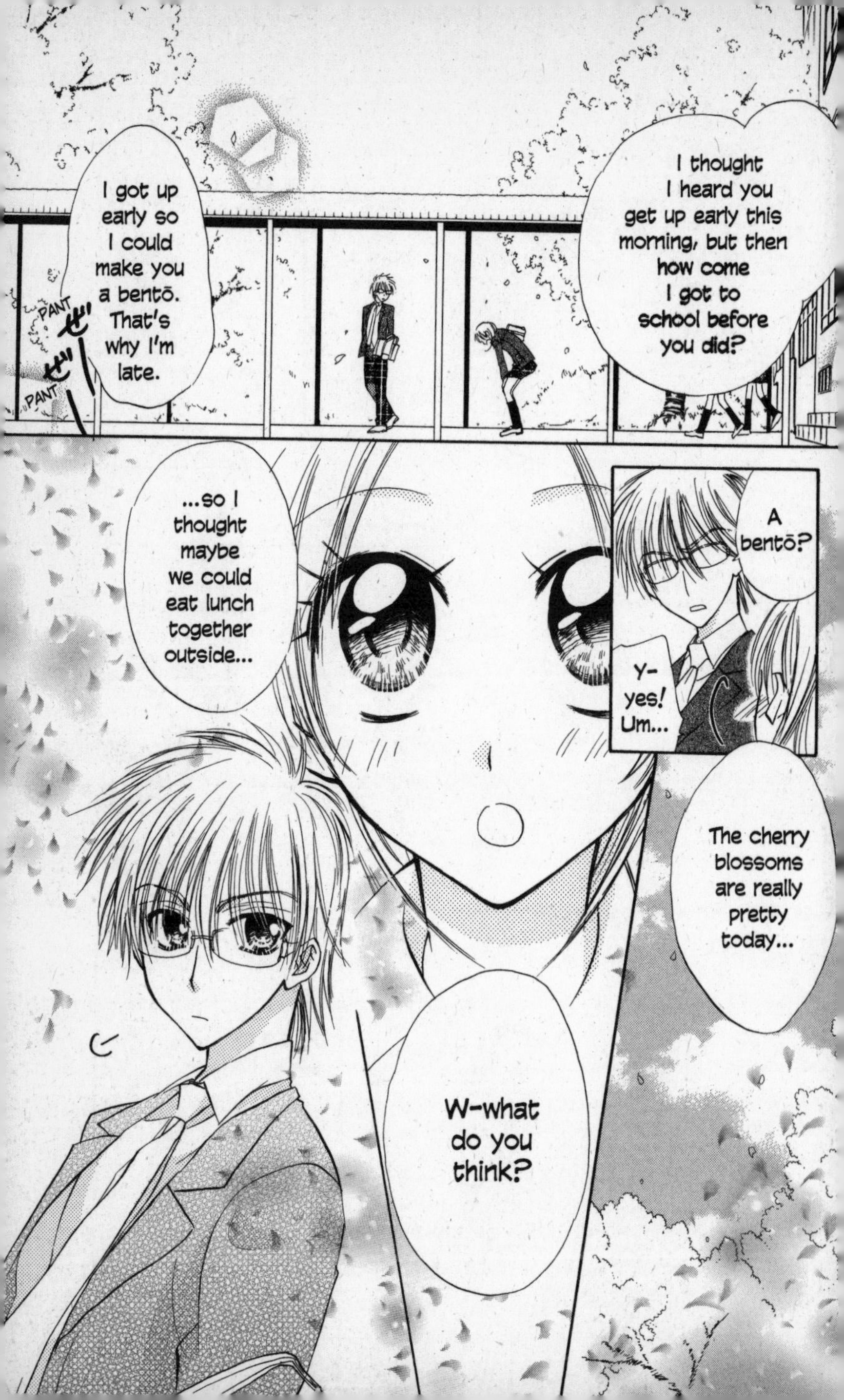
I thought I heard you get up early this morning, but then how come I got to school before you did?
I got up early so I could make you a bentō. That's why I'm late.
PANT ぜ
ぜ PANT
A bentō?
Y-yes! Um...
The cherry blossoms are really pretty today...
...so I thought maybe we could eat lunch together outside...
W-what do you think?

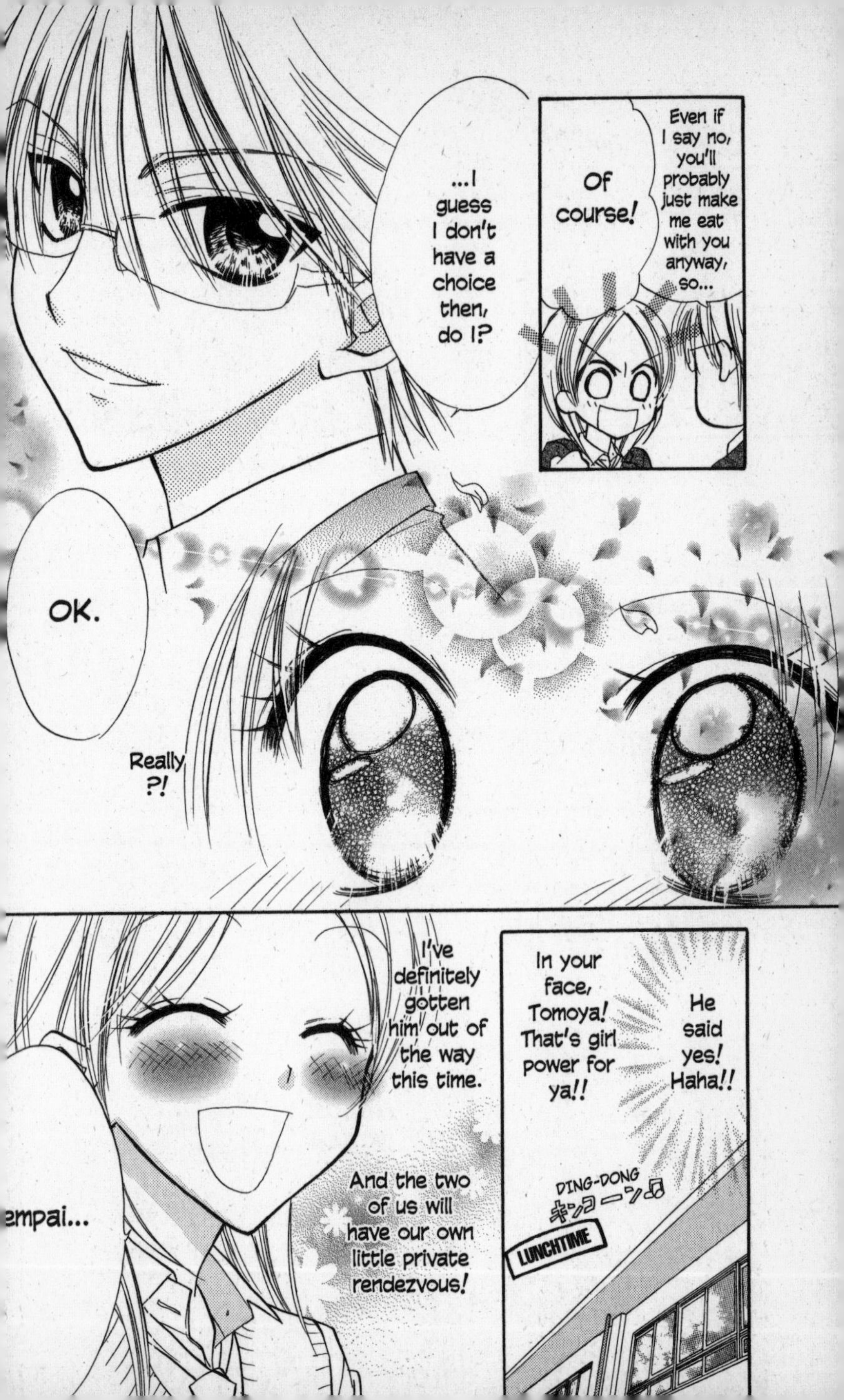
Even if I say no, you'll probably just make me eat with you anyway, so...
Of course!
...I guess I don't have a choice then, do I?
OK.
Really ?!
He said yes! Haha!!
In your face, Tomoya! That's girl power for ya!!
DING-DONG
LUNCHTIME
I've definitely gotten him out of the way this time.
And the two of us will have our own little private rendezvous!
empai...

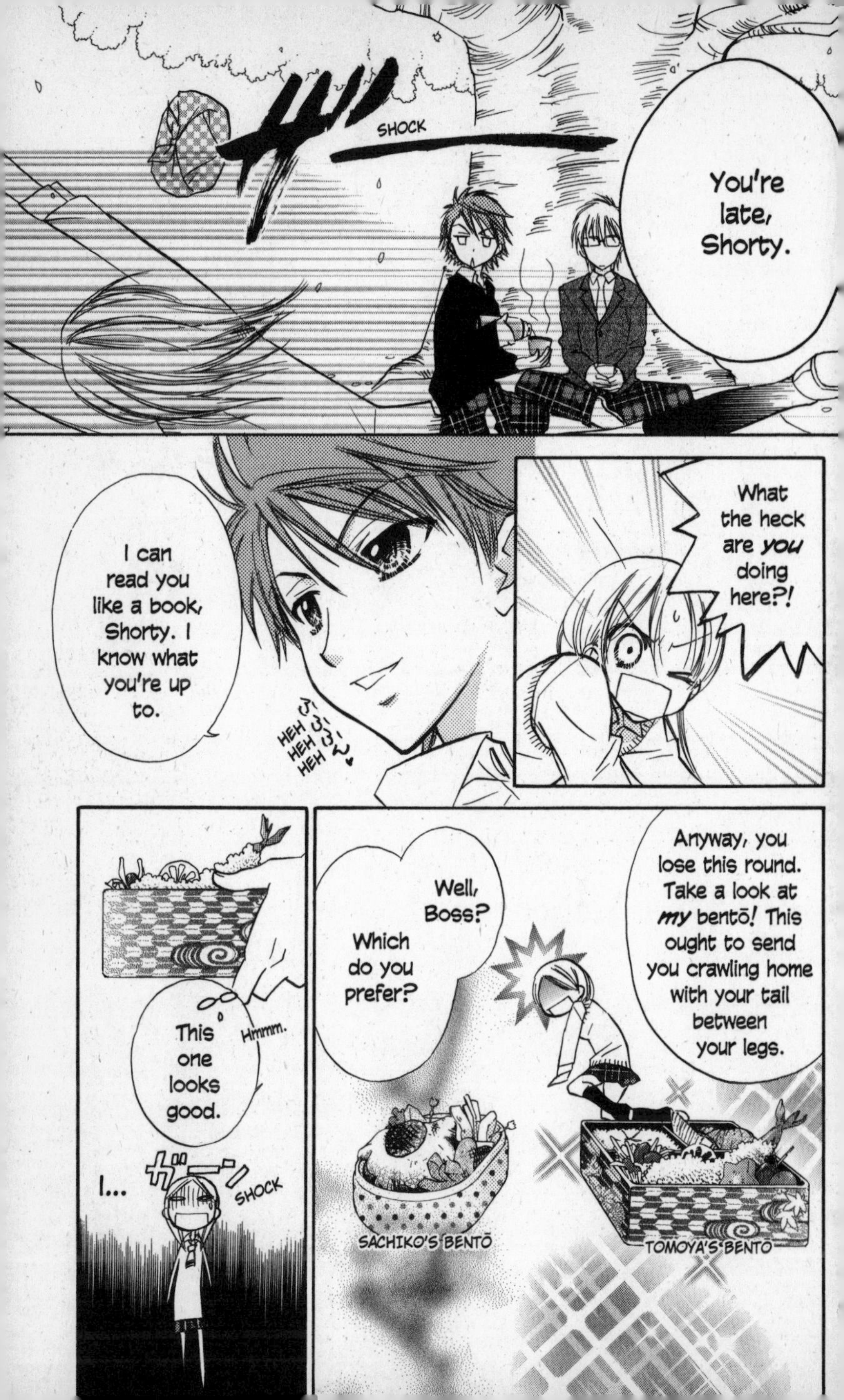
You're late, Shorty.
SHOCK
What the heck are *you* doing here?!
I can read you like a book, Shorty. I know what you're up to.
HEH HEH HEH
Anyway, you lose this round. Take a look at *my* bentō! This ought to send you crawling home with your tail between your legs.
Well, Boss? Which do you prefer?
TOMOYA'S BENTO
SACHIKO'S BENTŌ
Hmmm.
This one looks good.
I...
SHOCK

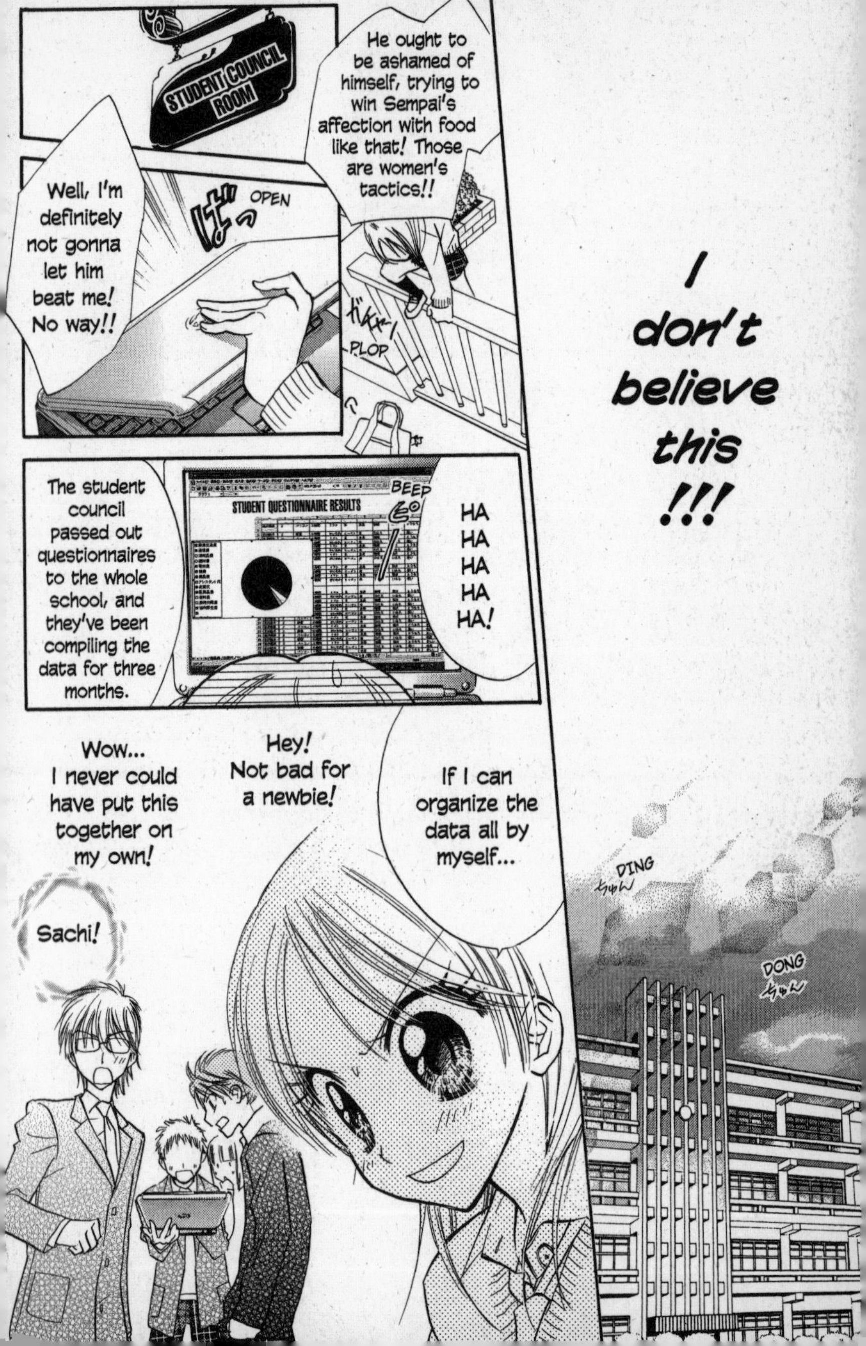
I don't believe this!!!
DING
DONG
He ought to be ashamed of himself, trying to win Sempai's affection with food like that! Those are women's tactics!!
PLOP
STUDENT COUNCIL ROOM
OPEN
Well, I'm definitely not gonna let him beat me! No way!!
HA HA HA HA HA!
BEEP
STUDENT QUESTIONNAIRE RESULTS
The student council passed out questionnaires to the whole school, and they've been compiling the data for three months.
If I can organize the data all by myself...
Hey! Not bad for a newbie!
Wow... I never could have put this together on my own!
Sachi!

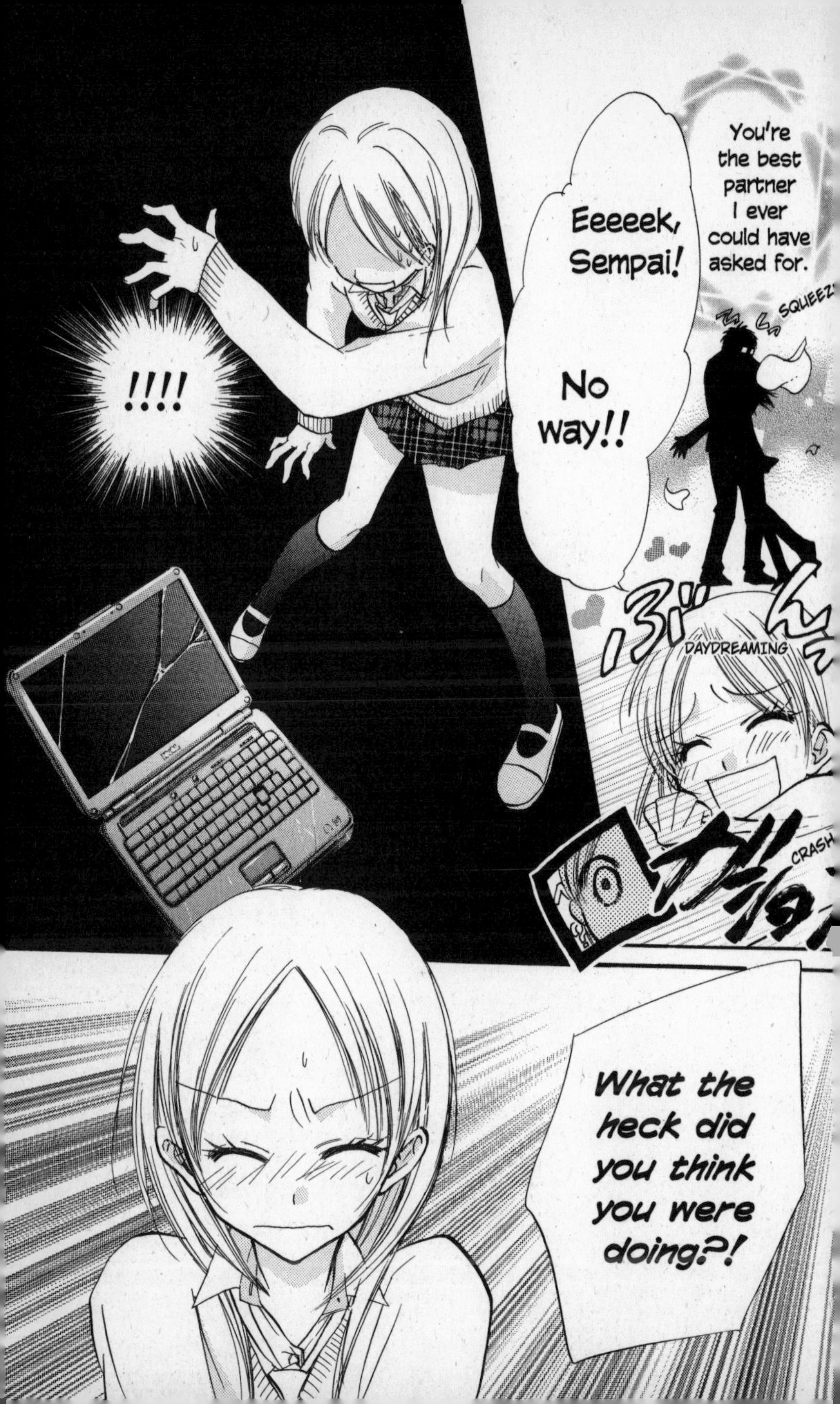
You're the best partner I ever could have asked for.
SQUEEZ
Eeeeek, Sempai!
No way!!
DAYDREAMING
CRASH
!!!!
What the heck did you think you were doing?!

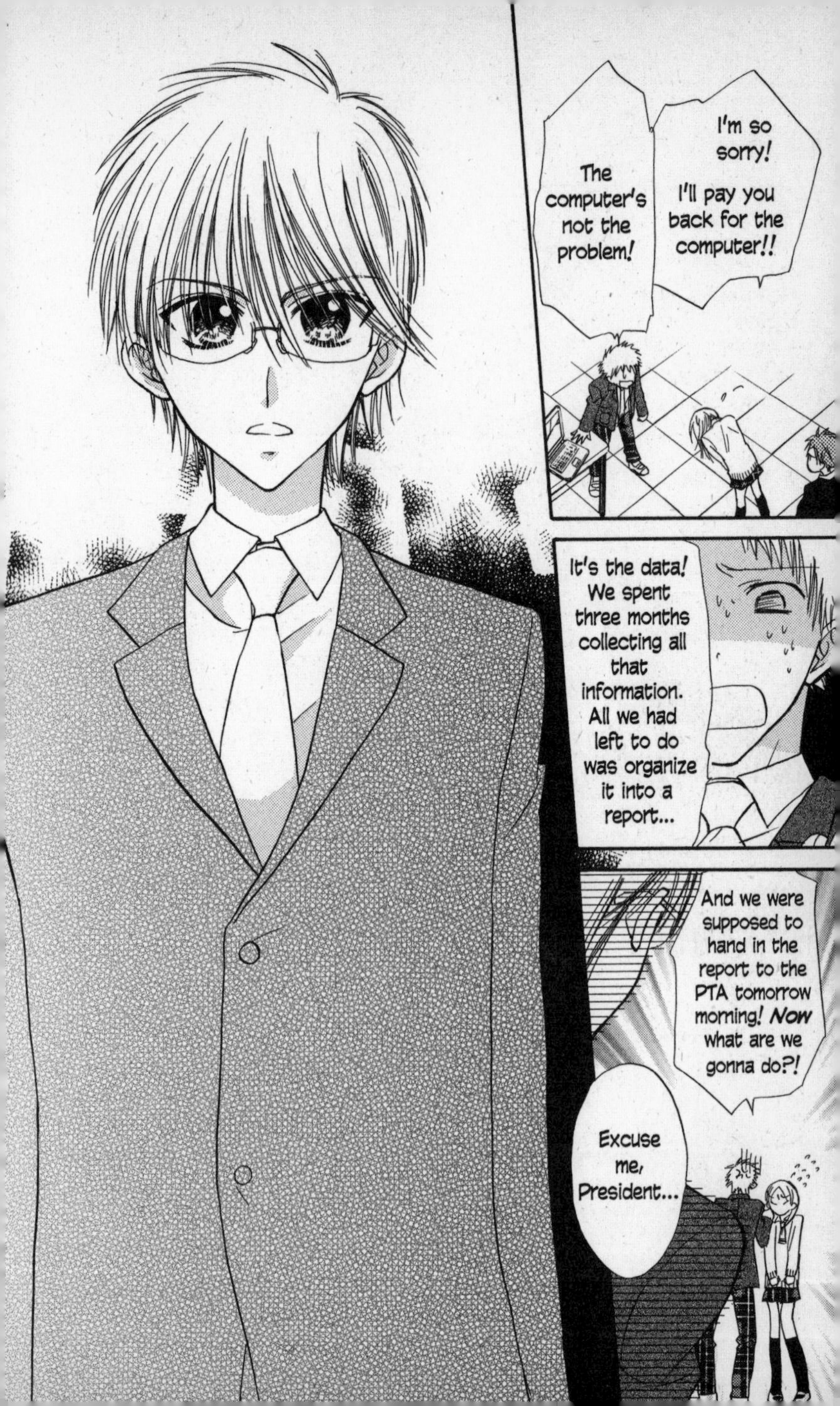
I'm so sorry! I'll pay you back for the computer!!
The computer's not the problem!
It's the data! We spent three months collecting all that information. All we had left to do was organize it into a report...
And we were supposed to hand in the report to the PTA tomorrow morning! *Now* what are we gonna do?!
Excuse me, President...

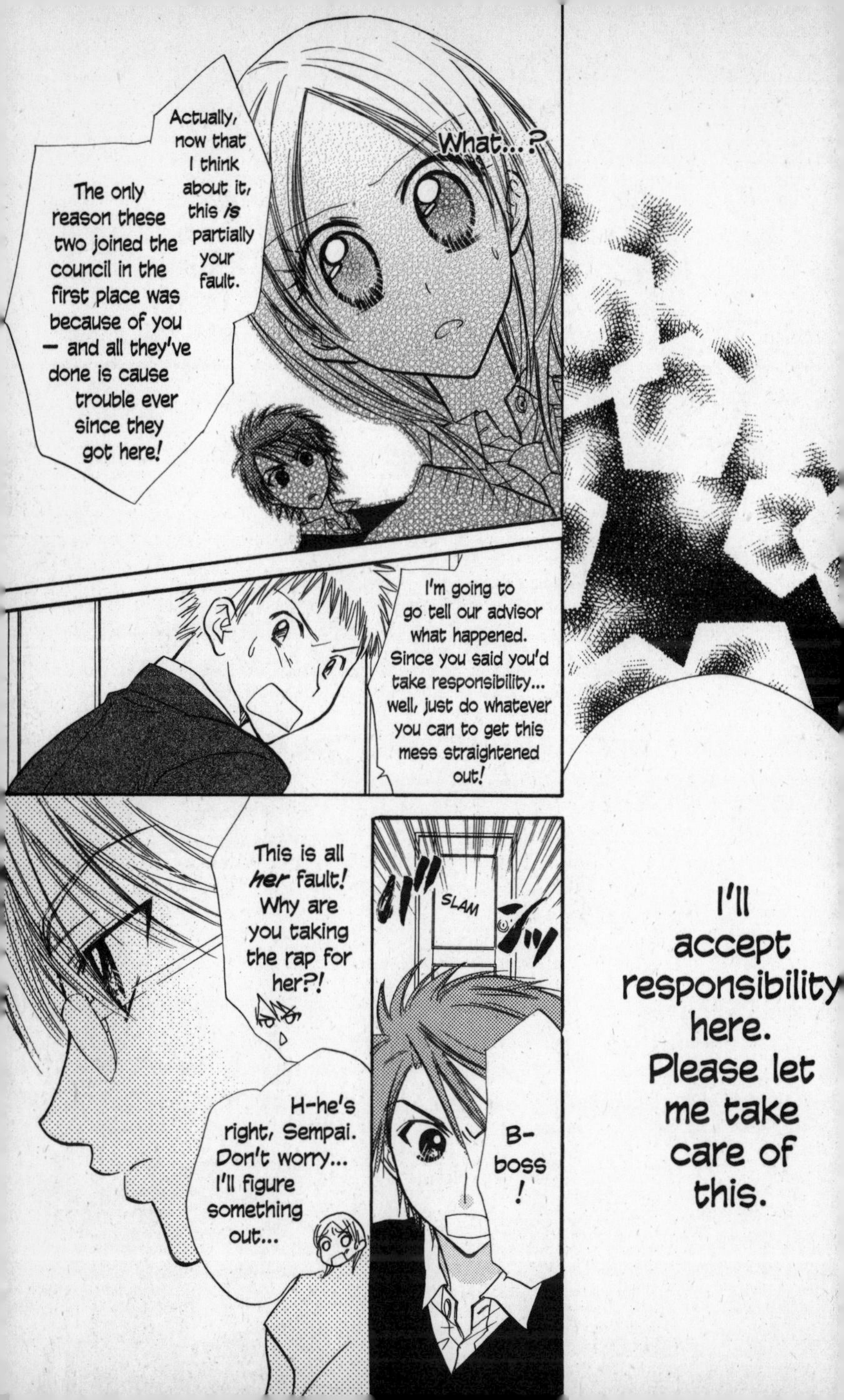
I'll accept responsibility here. Please let me take care of this.
What...?
Actually, now that I think about it, this *is* partially your fault.
The only reason these two joined the council in the first place was because of you — and all they've done is cause trouble ever since they got here!
I'm going to go tell our advisor what happened. Since you said you'd take responsibility... well, just do whatever you can to get this mess straightened out!
SLAM
B-boss!
This is all ***her*** fault! Why are you taking the rap for her?!
H-he's right, Sempai. Don't worry... I'll figure something out...

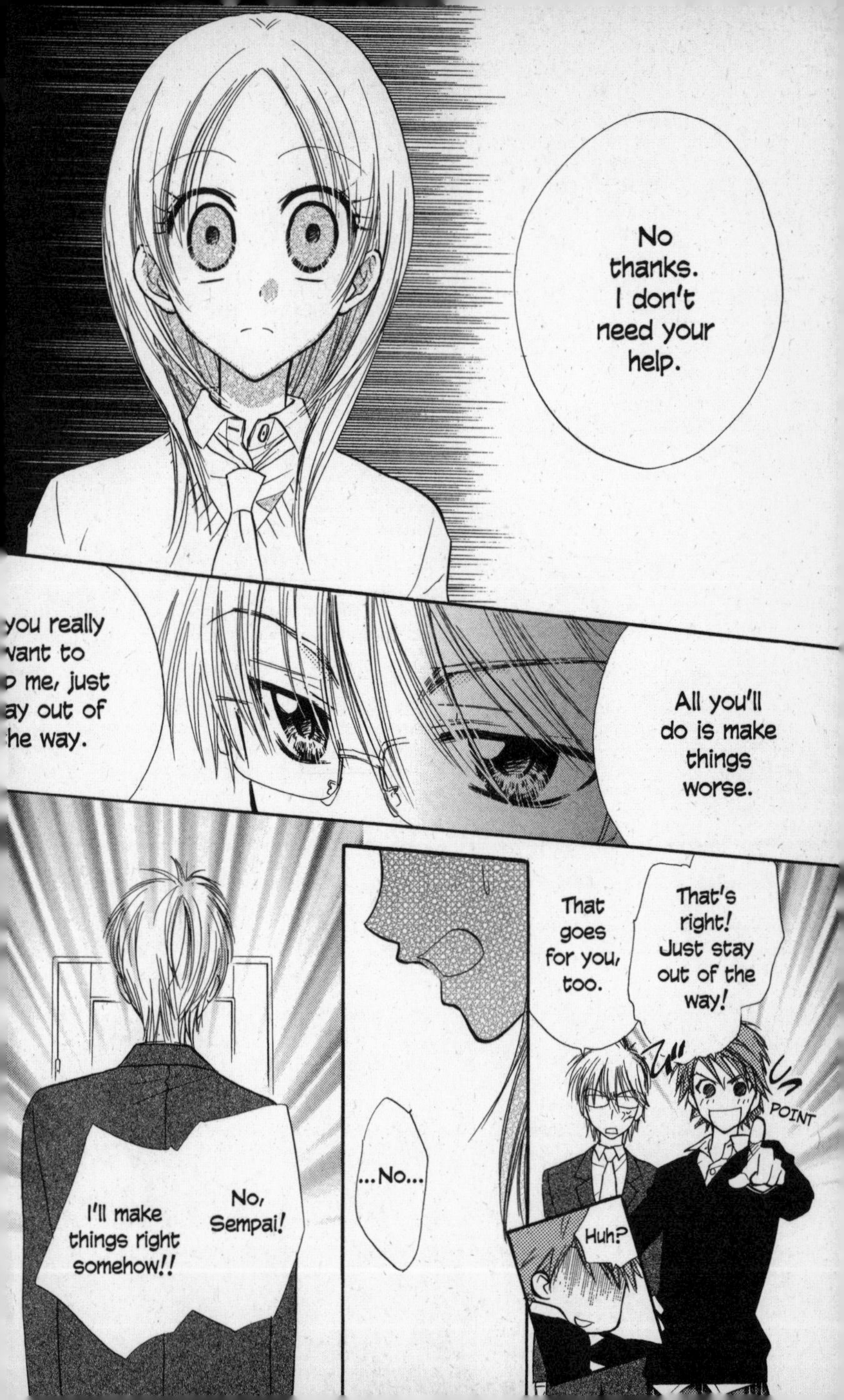
No thanks. I don't need your help.
All you'll do is make things worse.
you really vant to o me, just ay out of he way.
That's right! Just stay out of the way!
That goes for you, too.
POINT
Huh?
...No...
No, Sempai!
I'll make things right somehow!!

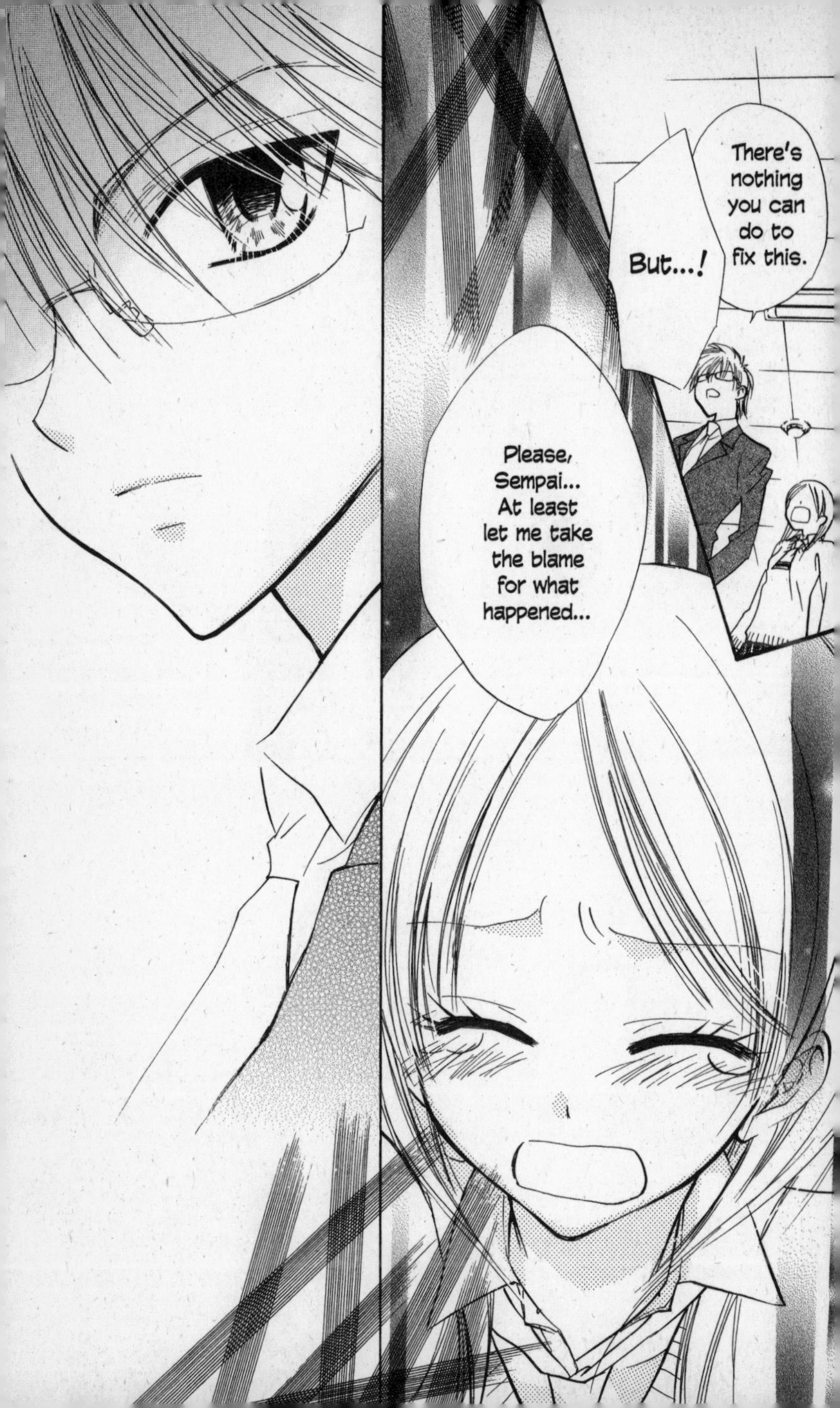
There's nothing you can do to fix this.
But...!
Please, Sempai... At least let me take the blame for what happened...

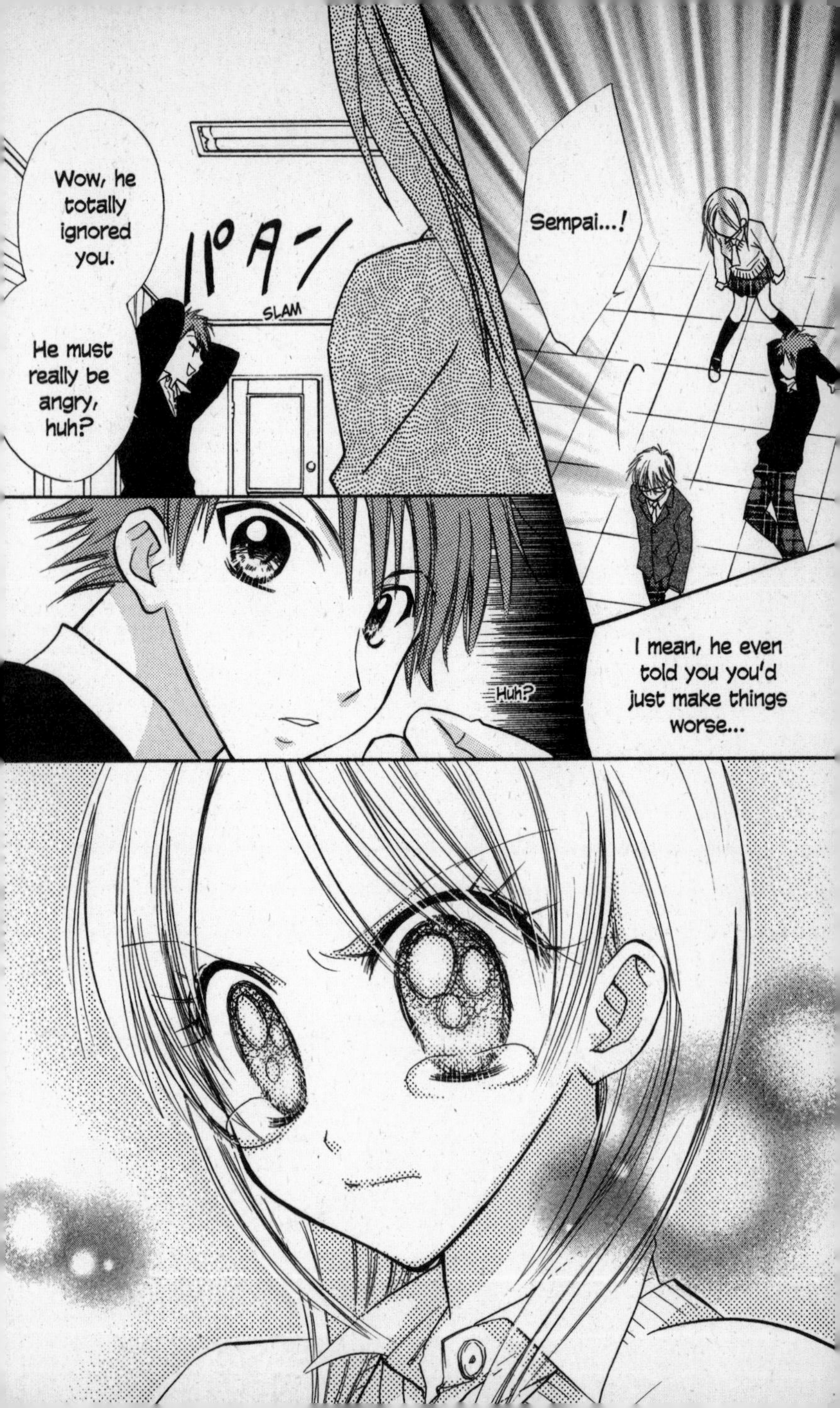
Sempai...!
Wow, he totally ignored you.
パタン
SLAM
He must really be angry, huh?
I mean, he even told you you'd just make things worse...
Huh?

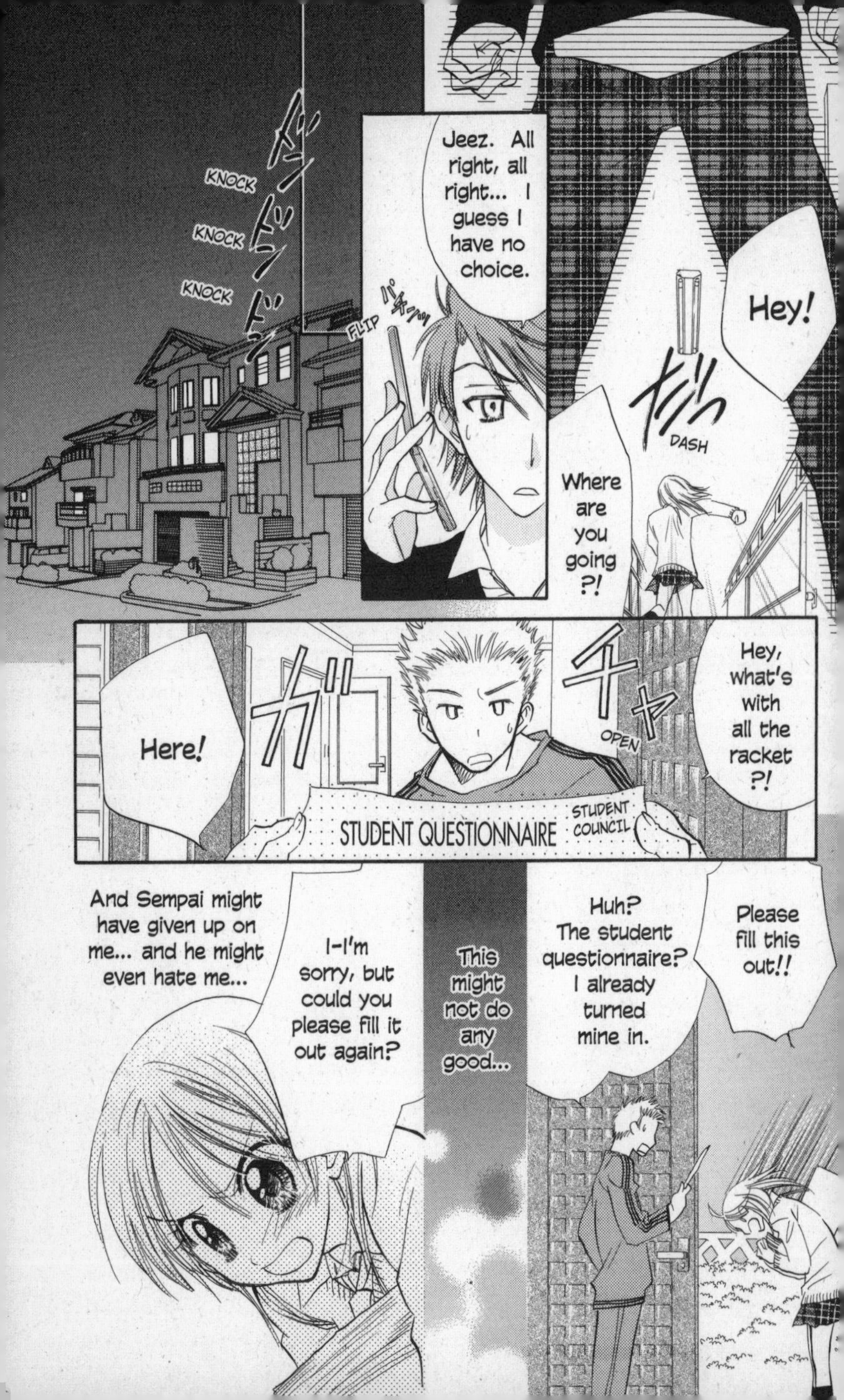
Hey!
DASH
Where are you going ?!
Jeez. All right, all right... I guess I have no choice.
FLIP
KNOCK
KNOCK
KNOCK
Hey, what's with all the racket ?!
OPEN
STUDENT COUNCIL
STUDENT QUESTIONNAIRE
Here!
Please fill this out!!
Huh? The student questionnaire? I already turned mine in.
This might not do any good...
I-I'm sorry, but could you please fill it out again?
And Sempai might have given up on me... and he might even hate me...

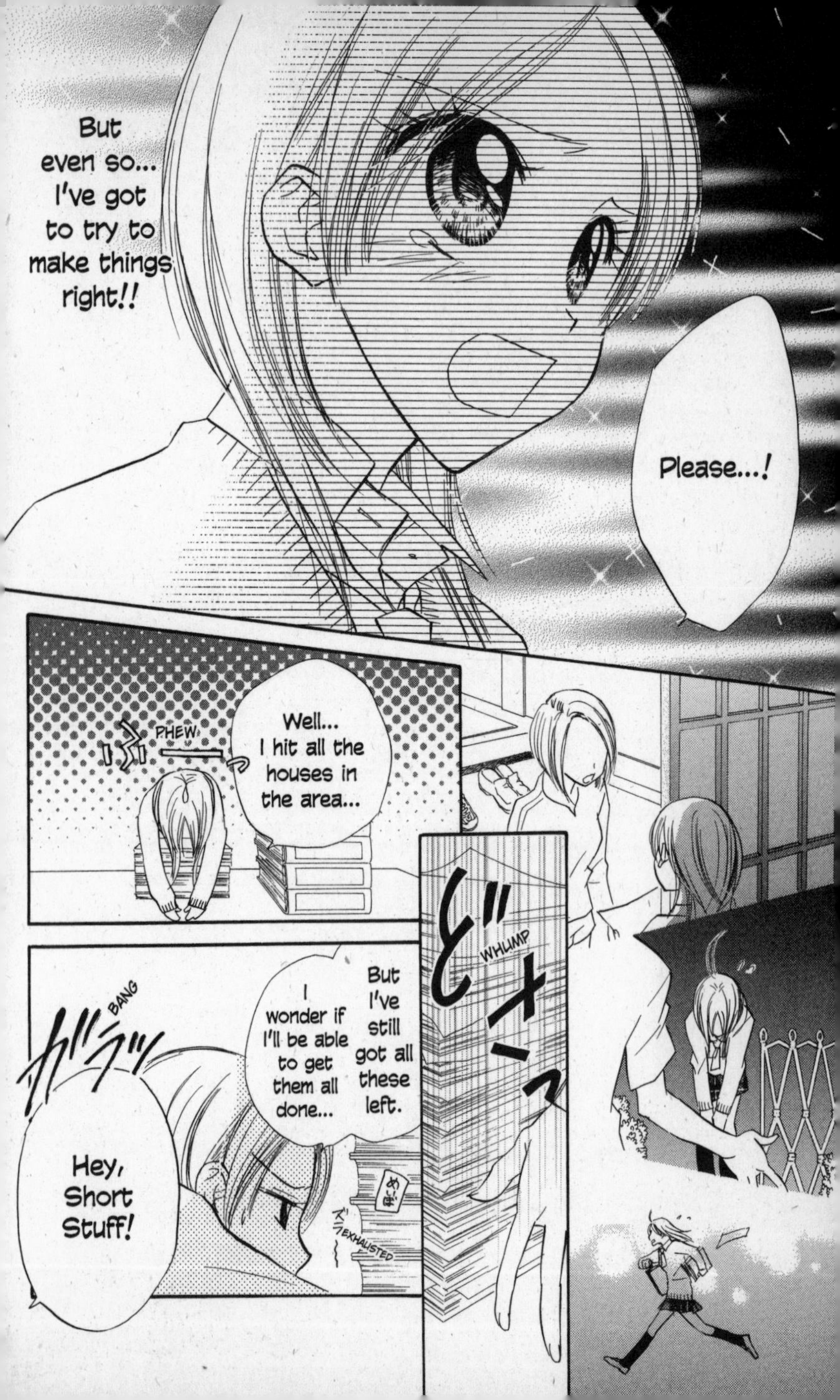
But even so... I've got to try to make things right!!
Please...!
PHEW
Well... I hit all the houses in the area...
WHUMP
But I've still got all these left.
I wonder if I'll be able to get them all done...
EXHAUSTED
BANG
Hey, Short Stuff!

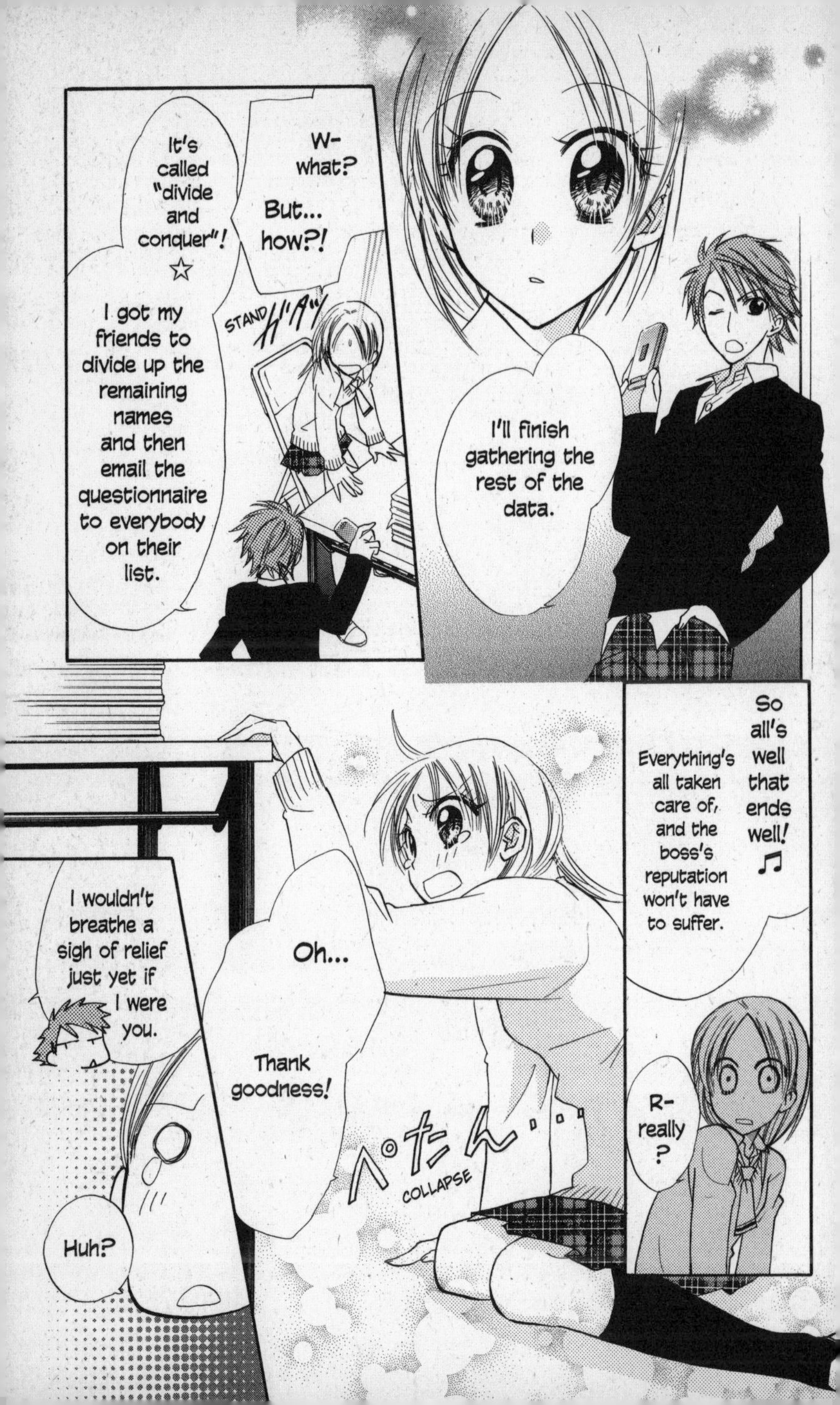
I'll finish gathering the rest of the data.
W- what?
But... how?!
STAND ガタッ
It's called "divide and conquer"! ☆
I got my friends to divide up the remaining names and then email the questionnaire to everybody on their list.
So all's well that ends well! ♫
Everything's all taken care of, and the boss's reputation won't have to suffer.
R- really?
Oh...
Thank goodness!
へたん...
COLLAPSE
I wouldn't breathe a sigh of relief just yet if I were you.
Huh?

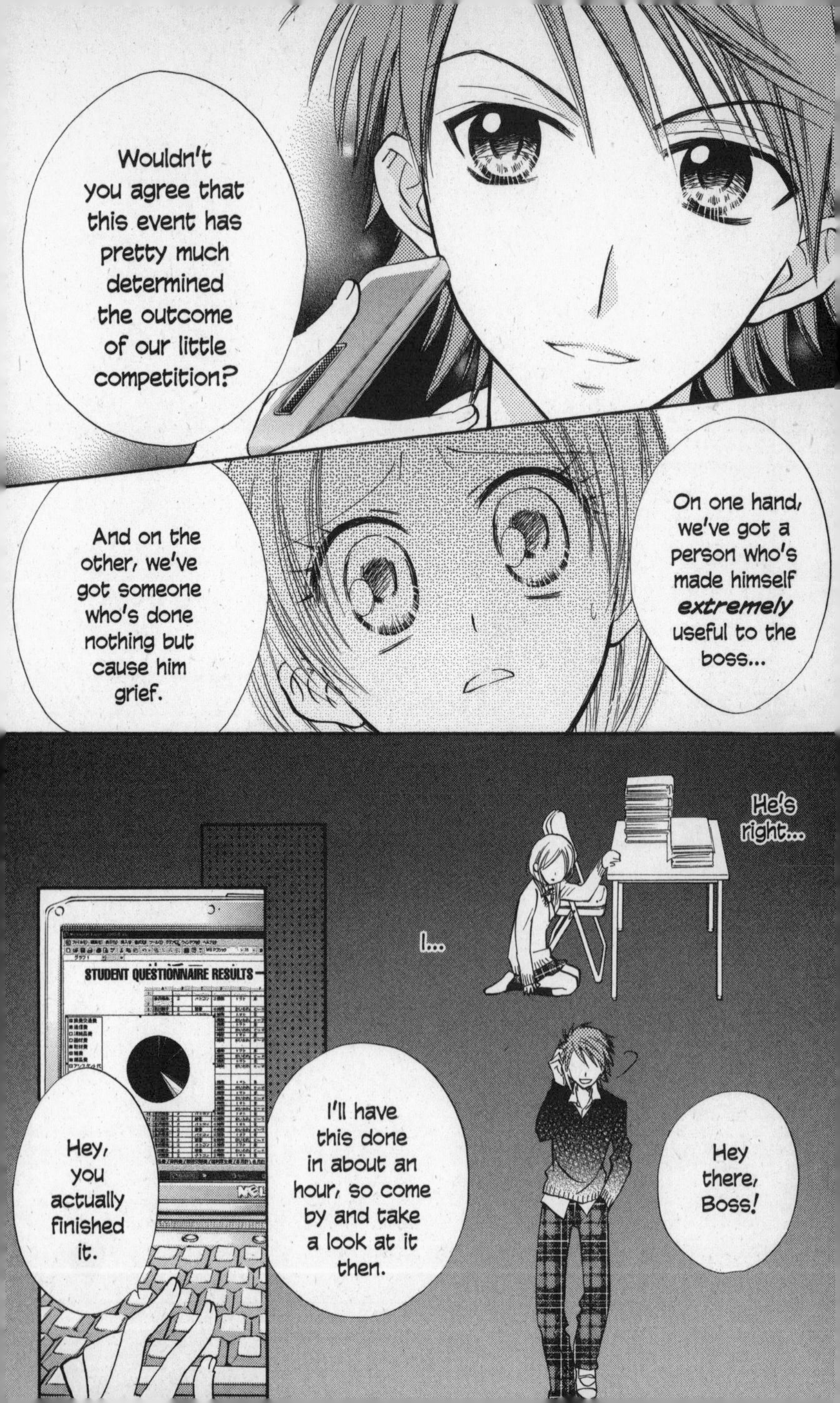
Wouldn't you agree that this event has pretty much determined the outcome of our little competition?
On one hand, we've got a person who's made himself *extremely* useful to the boss...
And on the other, we've got someone who's done nothing but cause him grief.
He's right...
I...
STUDENT QUESTIONNAIRE RESULTS
Hey there, Boss!
I'll have this done in about an hour, so come by and take a look at it then.
Hey, you actually finished it.

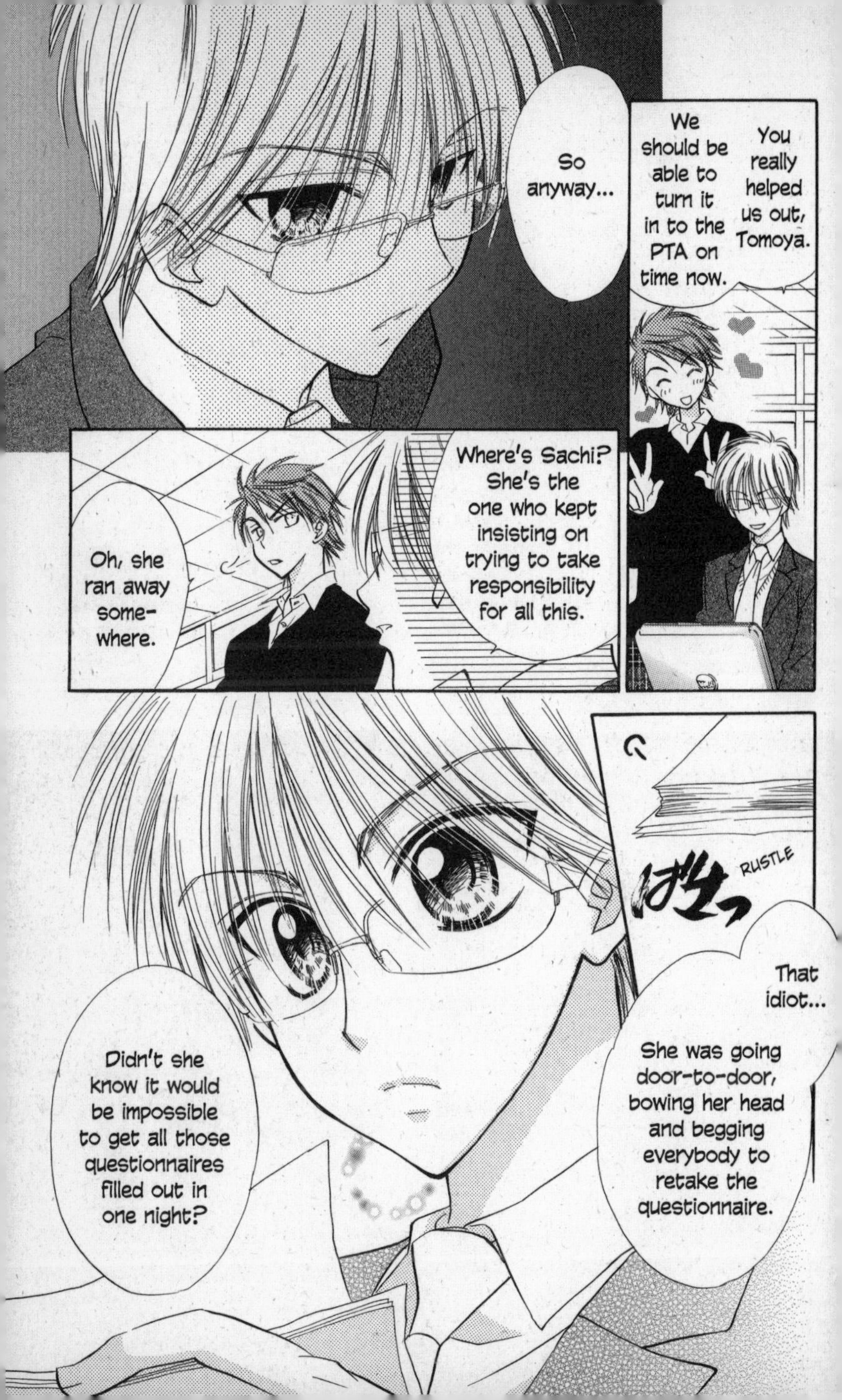
You really helped us out, Tomoya.
We should be able to turn it in to the PTA on time now.
So anyway...
Where's Sachi? She's the one who kept insisting on trying to take responsibility for all this.
Oh, she ran away somewhere.
RUSTLE
That idiot...
She was going door-to-door, bowing her head and begging everybody to retake the questionnaire.
Didn't she know it would be impossible to get all those questionnaires filled out in one night?

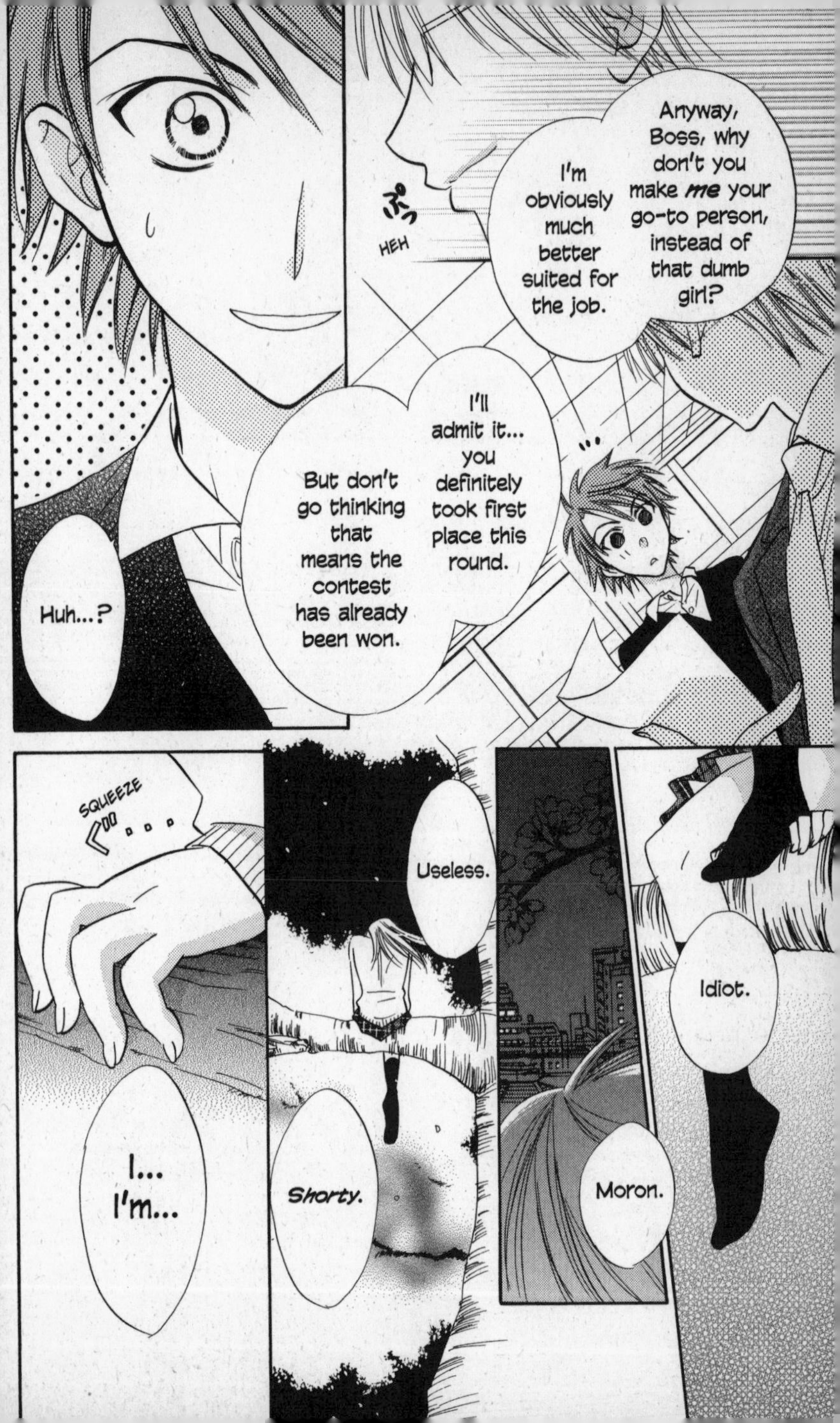
Anyway, Boss, why don't you make *me* your go-to person, instead of that dumb girl?
I'm obviously much better suited for the job.
ぷっ
HEH
I'll admit it... you definitely took first place this round.
...
But don't go thinking that means the contest has already been won.
Huh...?
Idiot.
Moron.
Useless.
Shorty.
SQUEEZE
I... I'm...

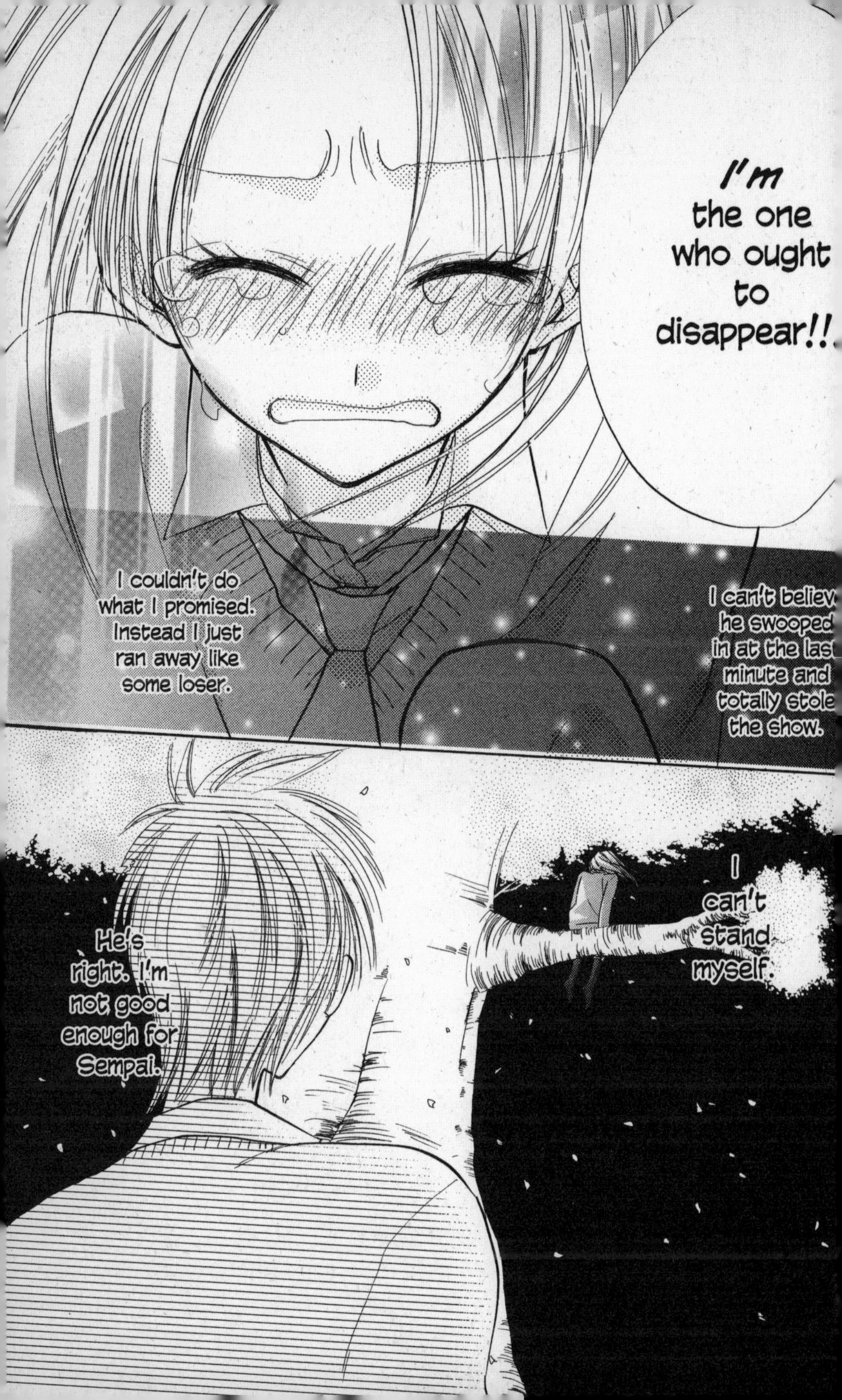
I'm the one who ought to disappear!!
I can't believ he swooped in at the las minute and totally stole the show.
I couldn't do what I promised. Instead I just ran away like some loser.
I can't stand myself.
He's right. I'm not good enough for Sempai.

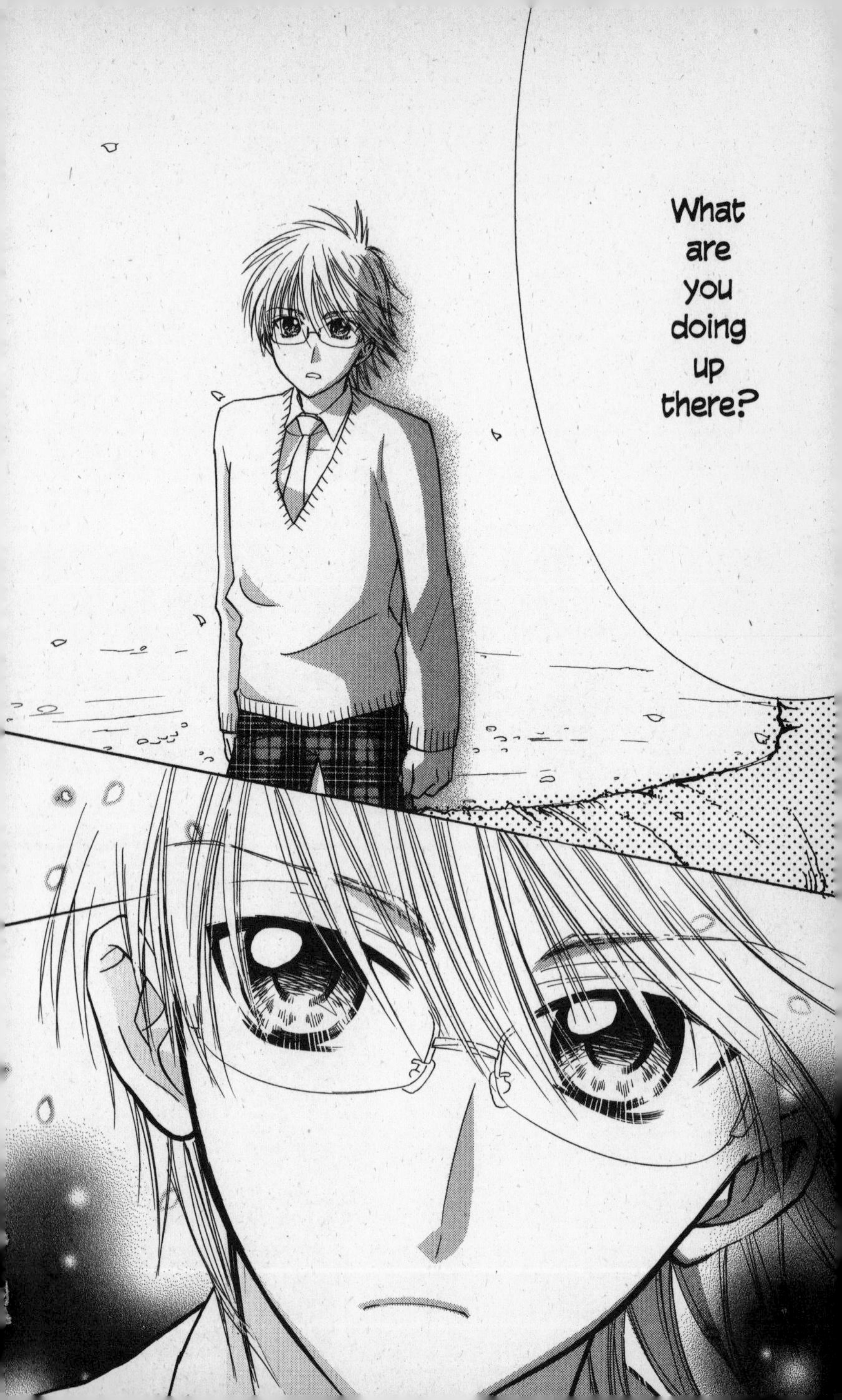
What are you doing up there?

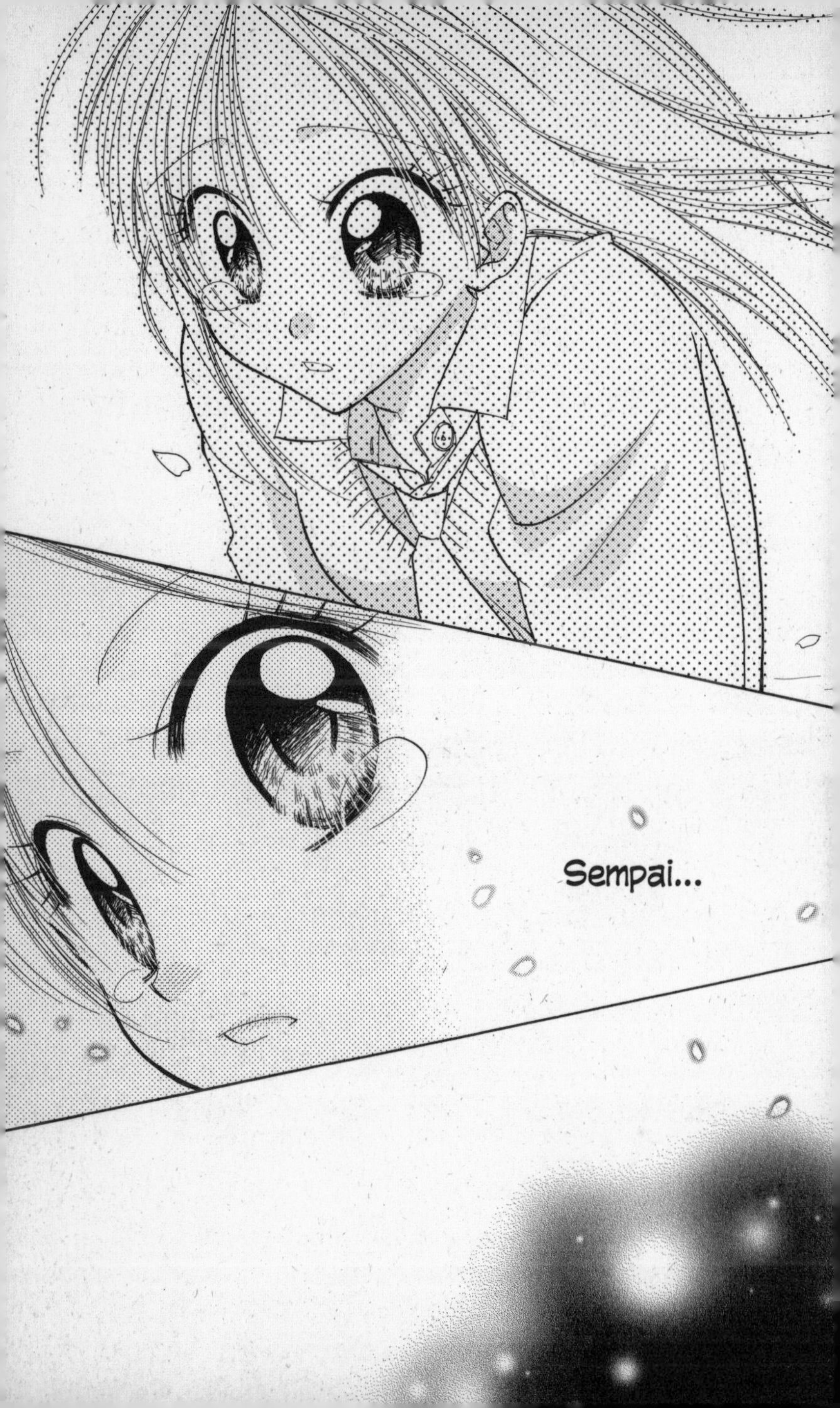
Sempai...

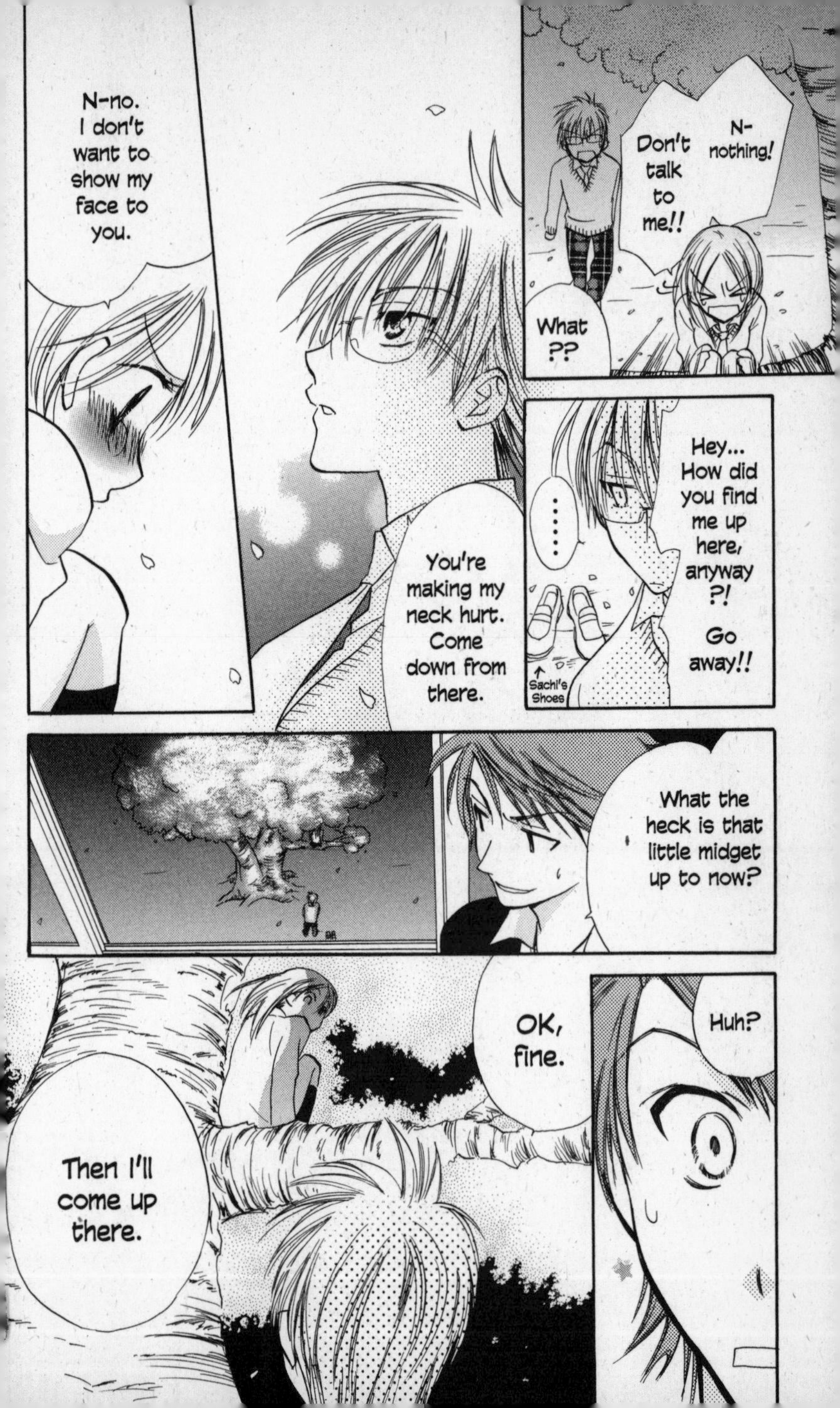

N-nothing!
Don't talk to me!!
What ??
Hey... How did you find me up here, anyway ?!
Go away!!
......
Sachi's Shoes
You're making my neck hurt. Come down from there.
N-no. I don't want to show my face to you.
What the heck is that little midget up to now?
Huh?
OK, fine.
Then I'll come up there.

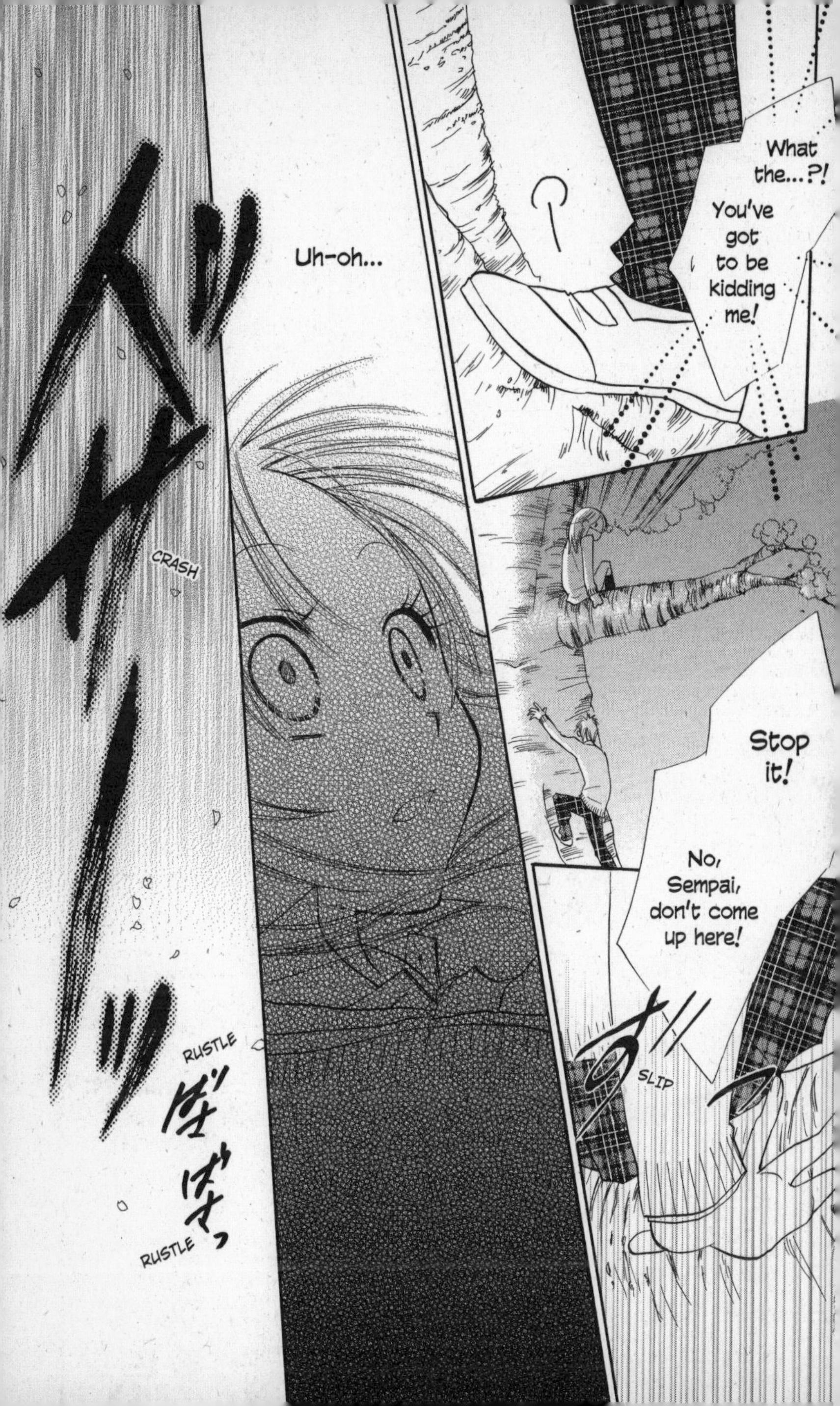
What the...?!
You've got to be kidding me!
Stop it!
No, Sempai, don't come up here!
SLIP
Uh-oh...
CRASH
RUSTLE
RUSTLE

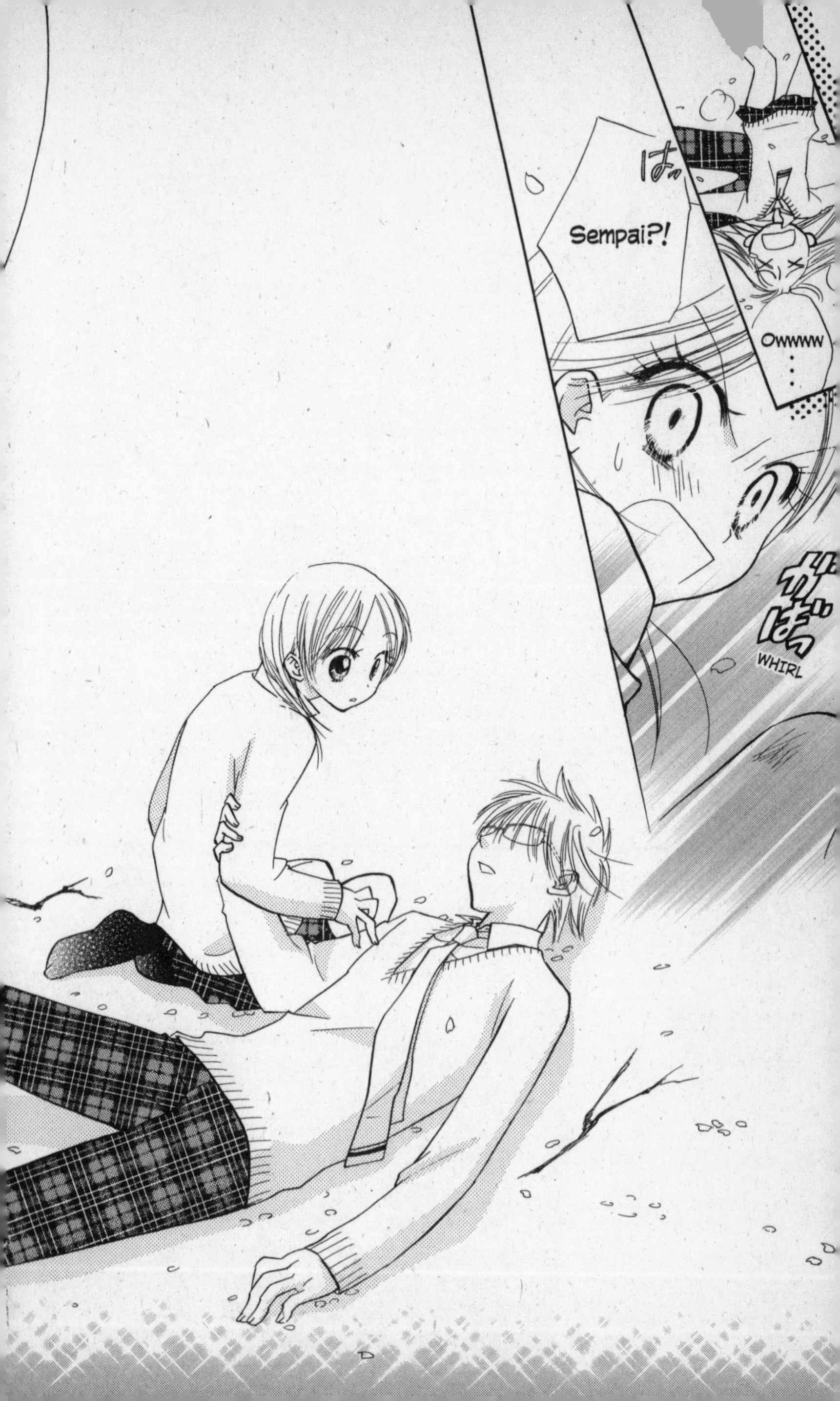
Owwww . . .
はっ
Sempai?!
がばっ
WHIRL

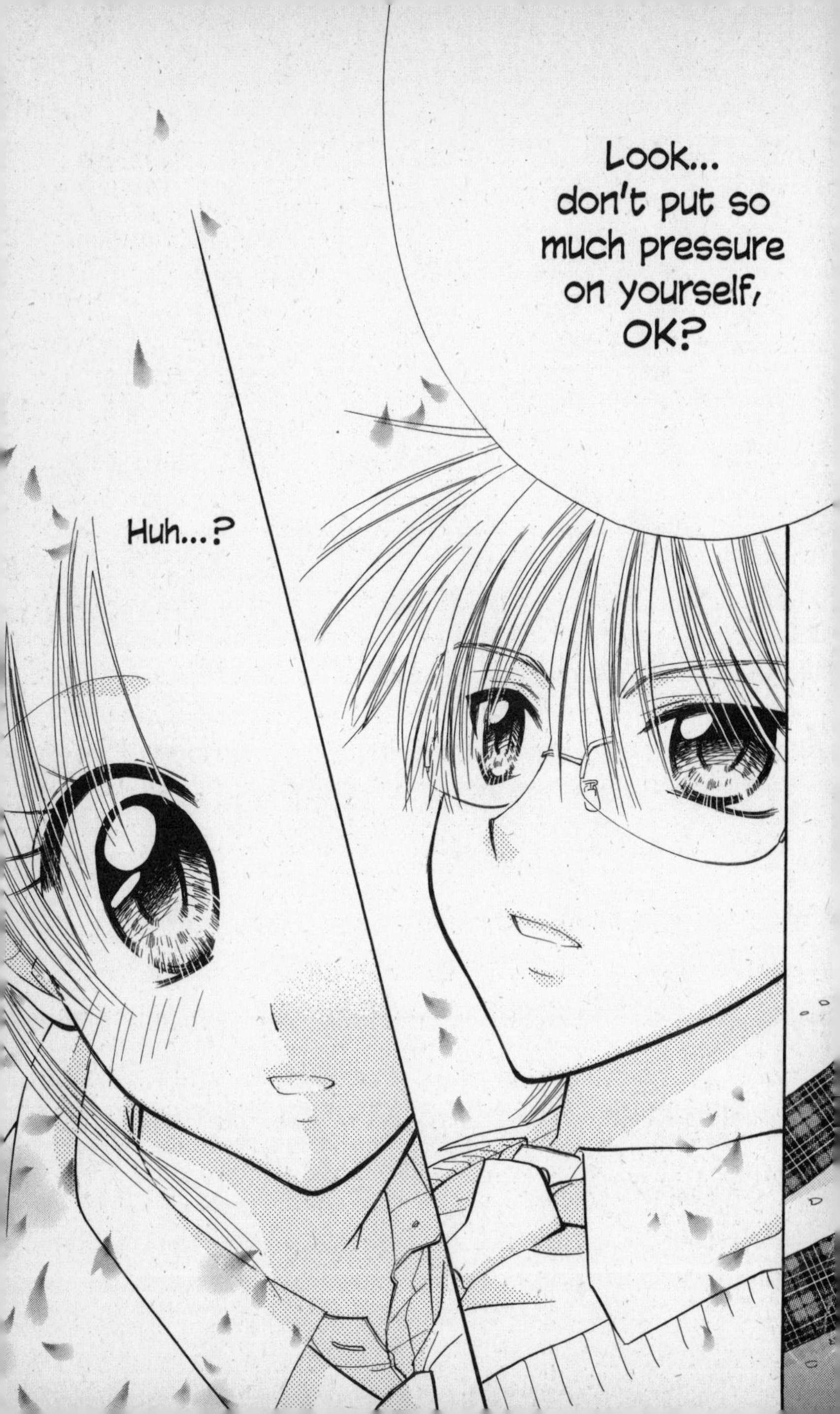
Look... don't put so much pressure on yourself, OK?
Huh...?

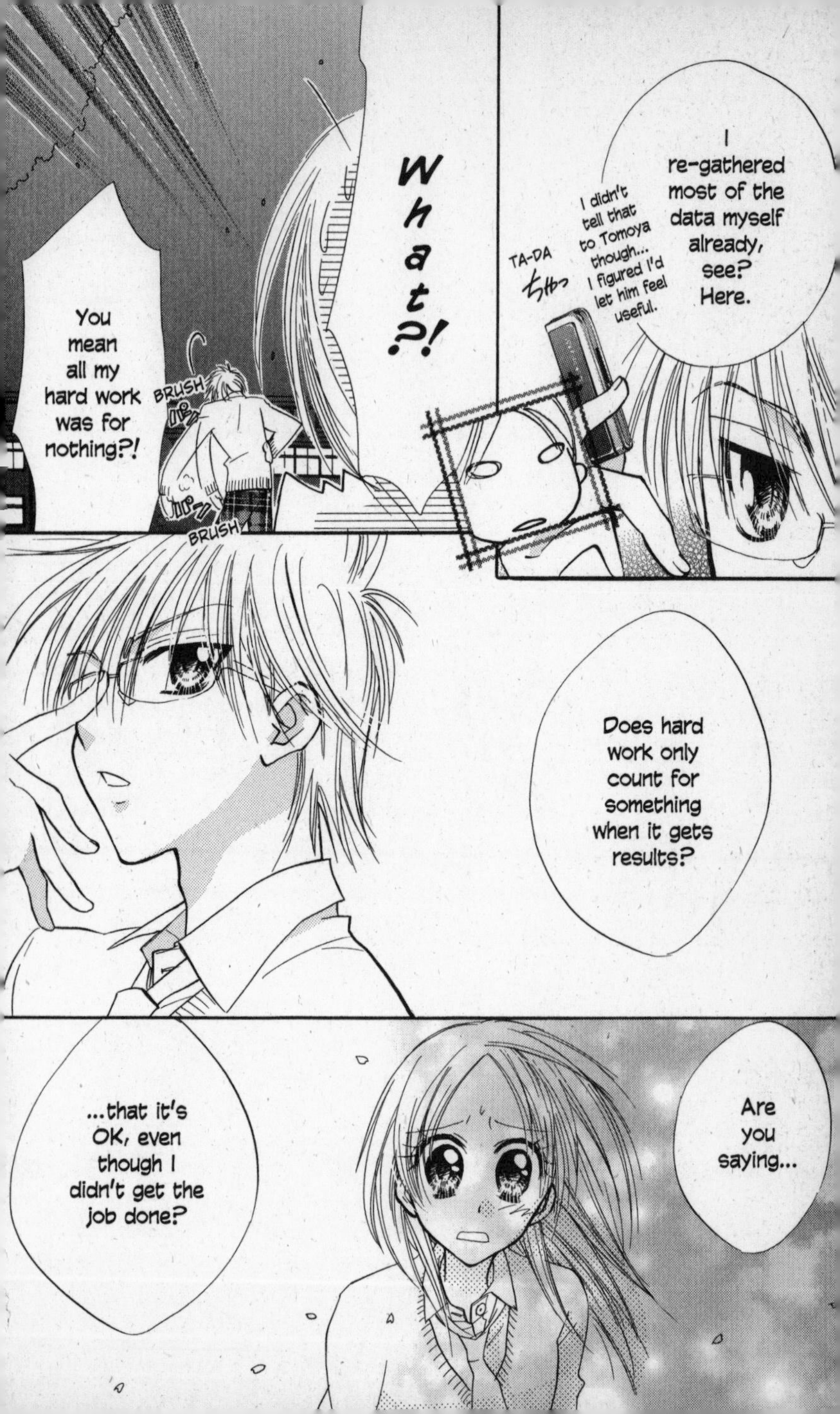
I re-gathered most of the data myself already, see? Here.
I didn't tell that to Tomoya though... I figured I'd let him feel useful.
TA-DA
What?!
You mean all my hard work was for nothing?!
BRUSH
BRUSH
Does hard work only count for something when it gets results?
Are you saying...
...that it's OK, even though I didn't get the job done?

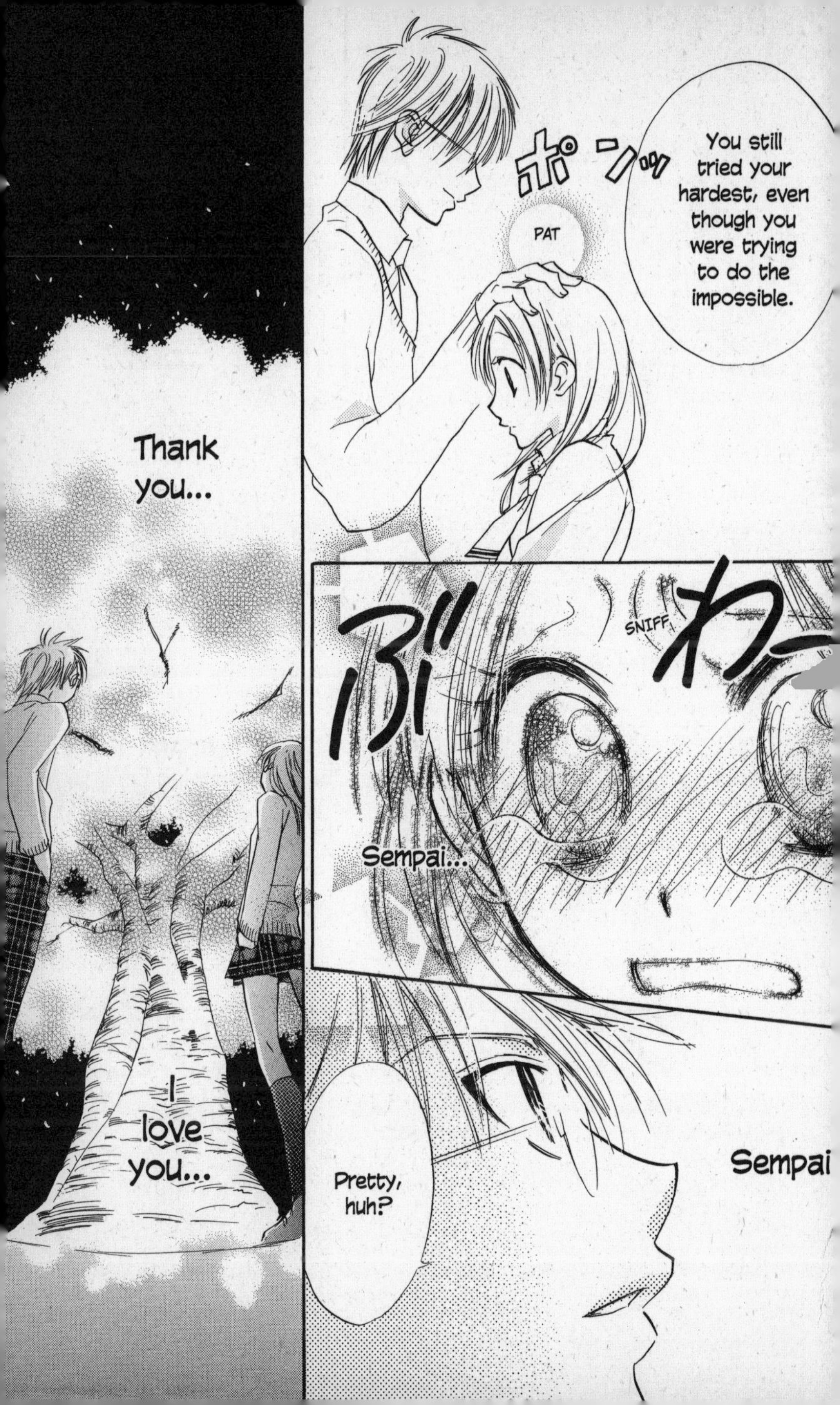
You still tried your hardest, even though you were trying to do the impossible.
PAT
SNIFF
Sempai...
Sempai
Pretty, huh?
Thank you...
I love you...

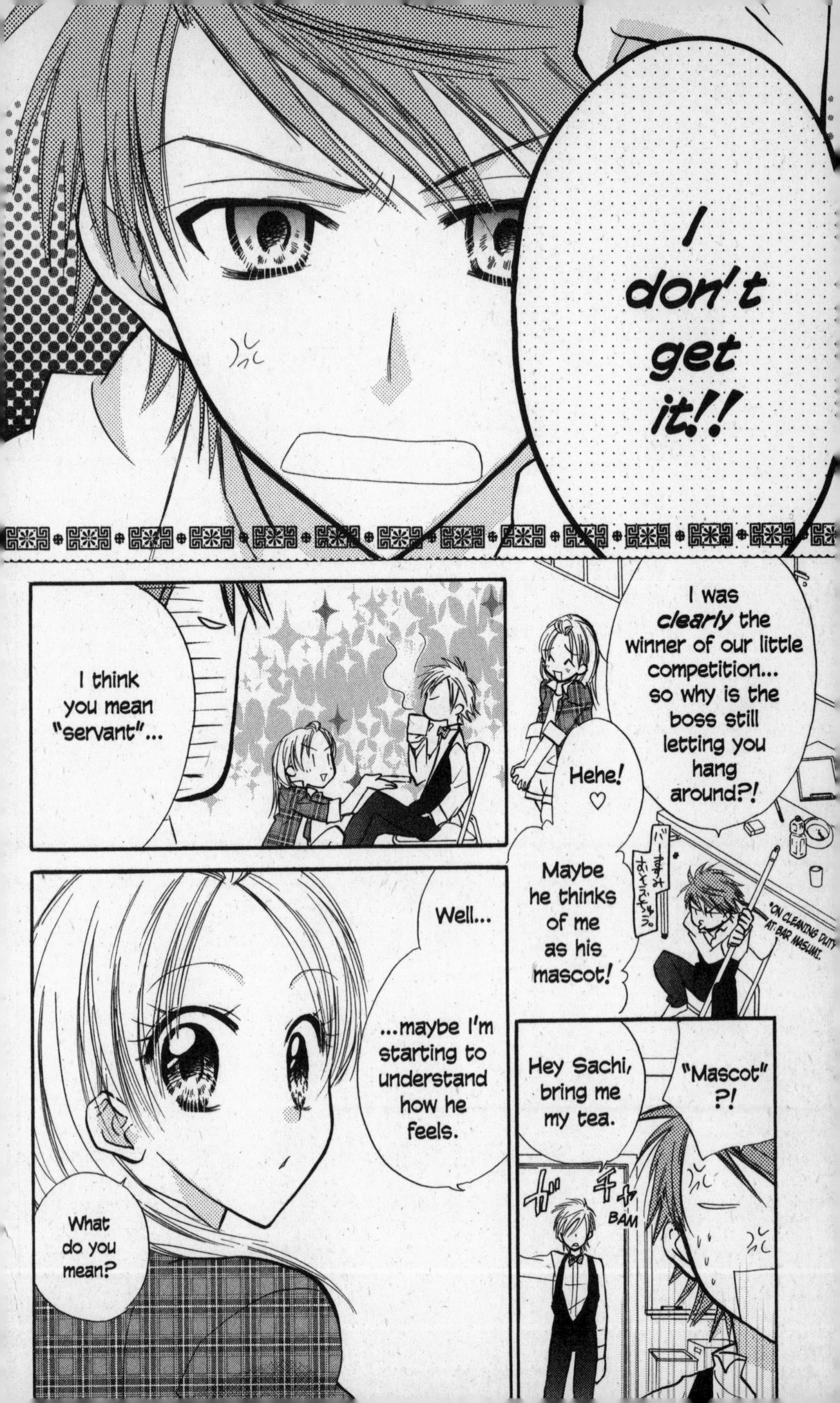
I don't get it!!
I was *clearly* the winner of our little competition... so why is the boss still letting you hang around?!
Hehe! ♡
Maybe he thinks of me as his mascot!
バーますみ おそうじがかり
*ON CLEANING DUTY AT BAR MASUMI.
I think you mean "servant"...
"Mascot" ?!
Hey Sachi, bring me my tea.
BAM
Well...
...maybe I'm starting to understand how he feels.
What do you mean?

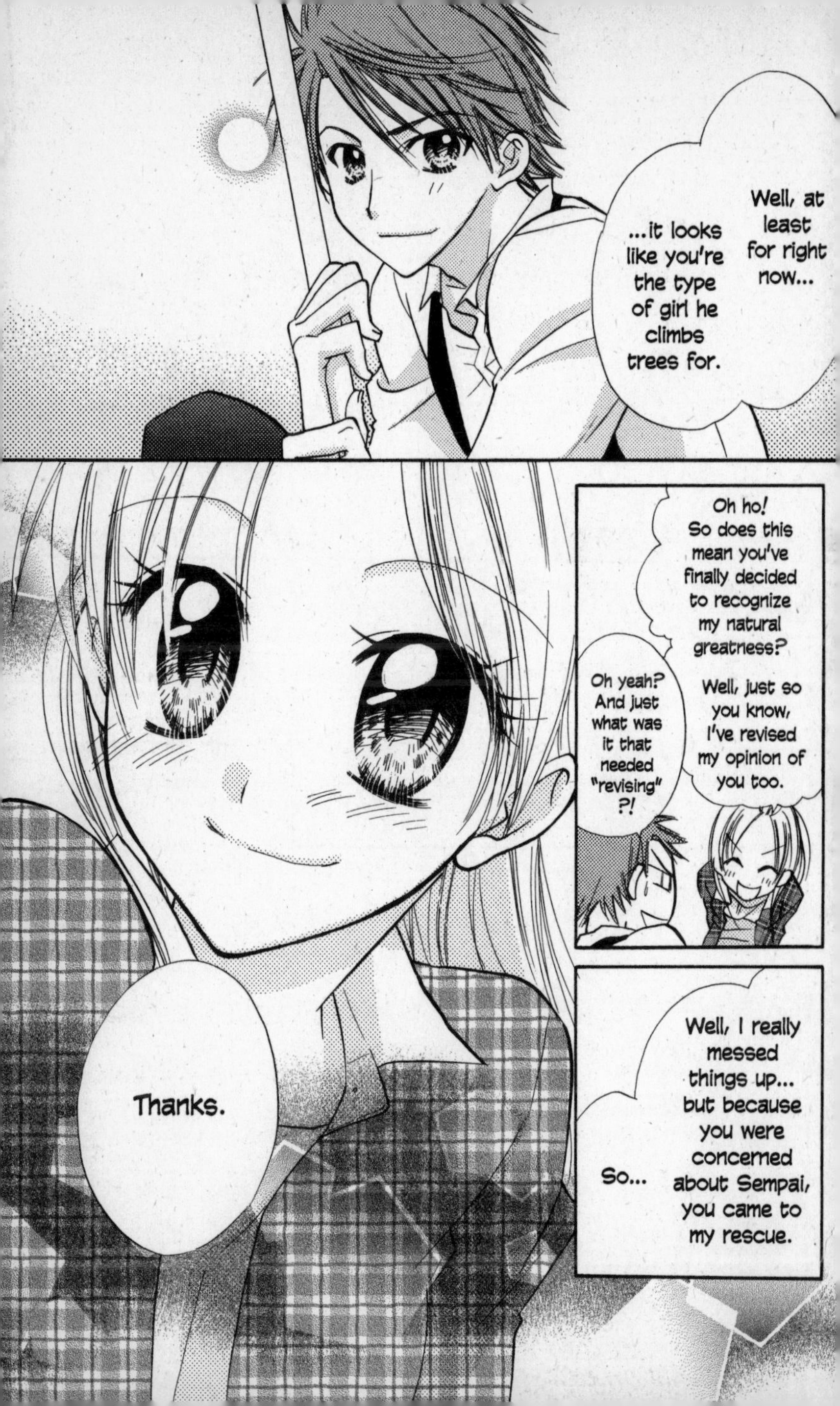
Well, at least for right now...
...it looks like you're the type of girl he climbs trees for.
Oh ho! So does this mean you've finally decided to recognize my natural greatness?
Well, just so you know, I've revised my opinion of you too.
Oh yeah? And just what was it that needed "revising"?!
Well, I really messed things up... but because you were concerned about Sempai, you came to my rescue.
So...
Thanks.

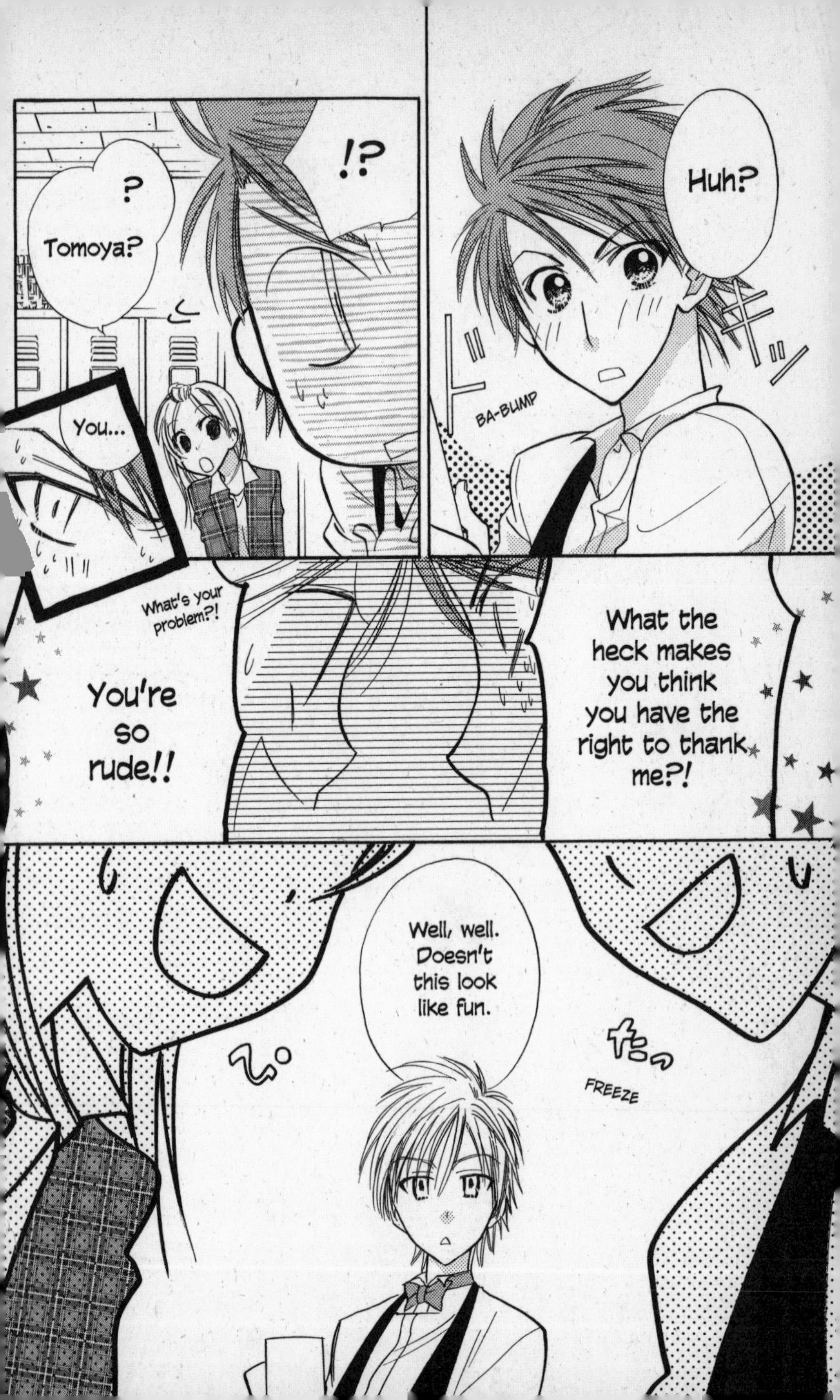
Huh?
BA-BUMP
!?
? Tomoya?
You...
What the heck makes you think you have the right to thank me?!
What's your problem?!
You're so rude!!
Well, well. Doesn't this look like fun.
FREEZE

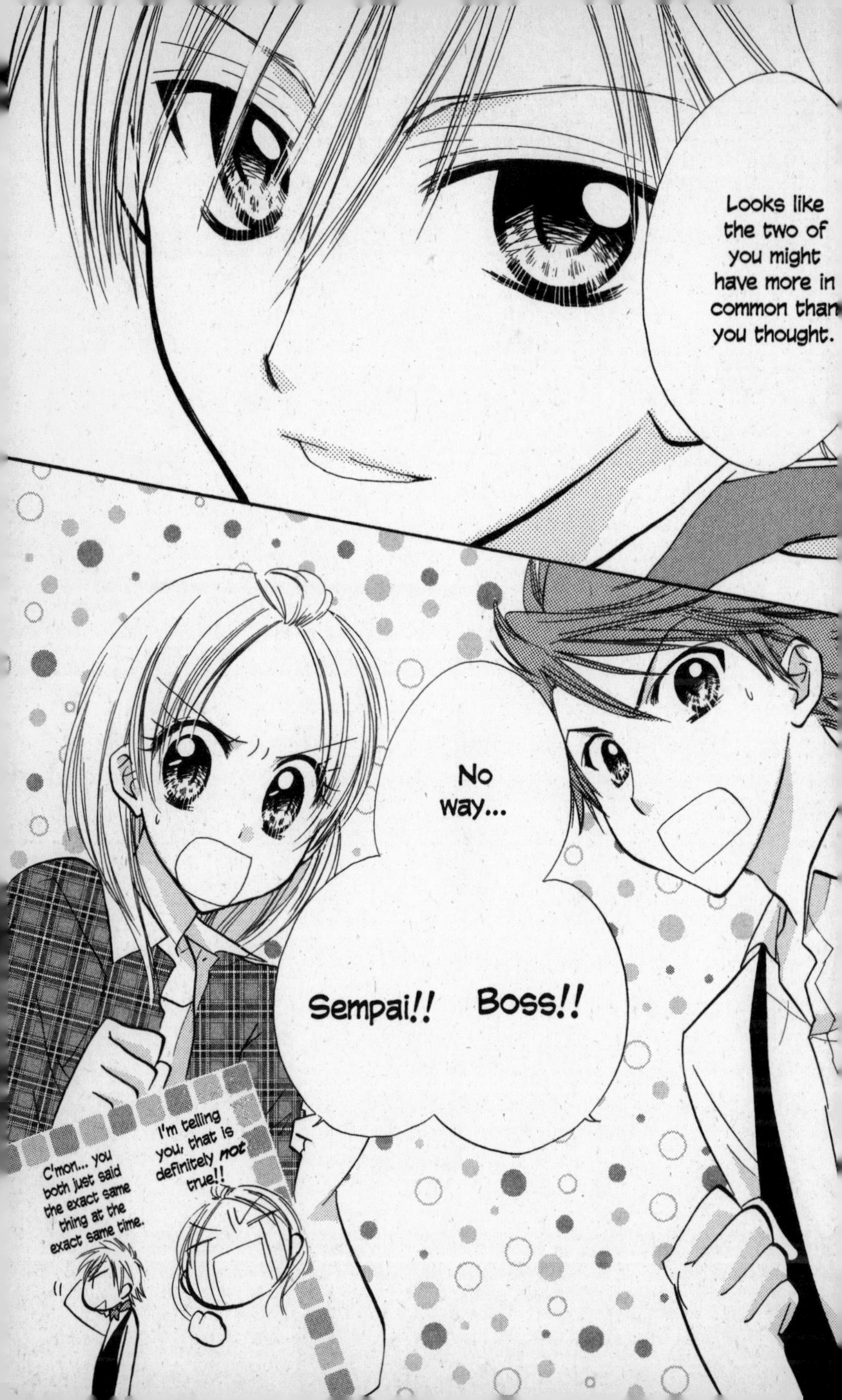
Looks like the two of you might have more in common than you thought.
No way...
Sempai!! Boss!!
I'm telling you, that is definitely *not* true!!
C'mon... you both just said the exact same thing at the exact same time.

Greetings!

Hi! This is Mizukami.
Seems like this has happened kinda fast, but here we are at Vol. 3!
It's all thanks to the readers who have cheered me on, and of course,
to Prince S (?) as well!

In Vol. 3 we get to meet a new
character. Tomoya's going to be a
regular from now on. He's stubborn
and outspoken, which makes
him a good contrast for the hard-to-
read Four-Eyed Prince. I think
those characteristics also make him
easy to draw...

Here's my ranking of which
characters are easiest to draw.

DUMMY

1 Sachiko

2 Tomoya

DUMMY #2

3 Akira

PLAYER

Last Place

Akihiko

MYSTERIOUS

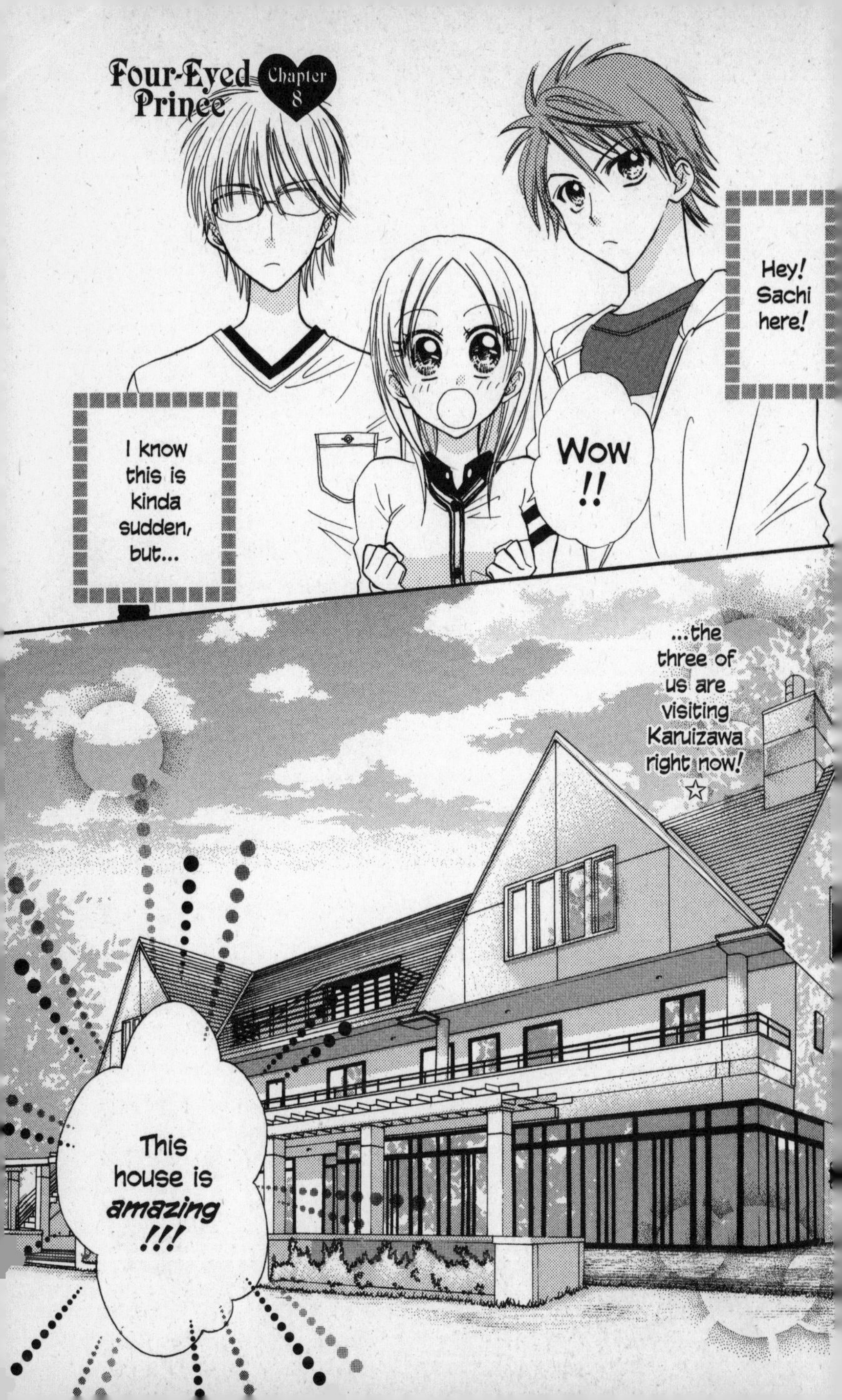
Four-Eyed Prince
Chapter 8
Hey! Sachi here!
Wow!!
I know this is kinda sudden, but...
...the three of us are visiting Karuizawa right now! ☆
This house is amazing!!!

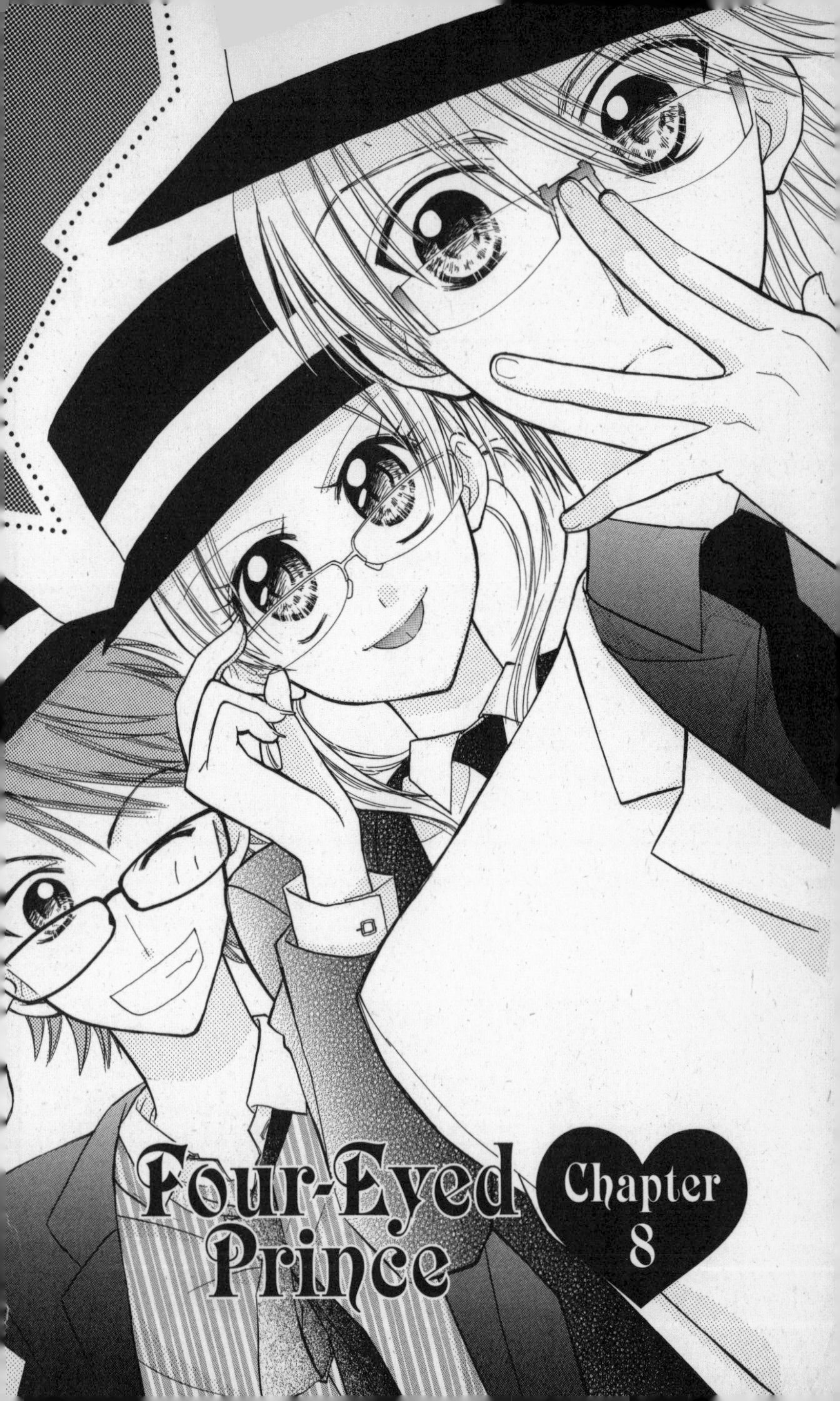
Four-Eyed Prince
Chapter 8

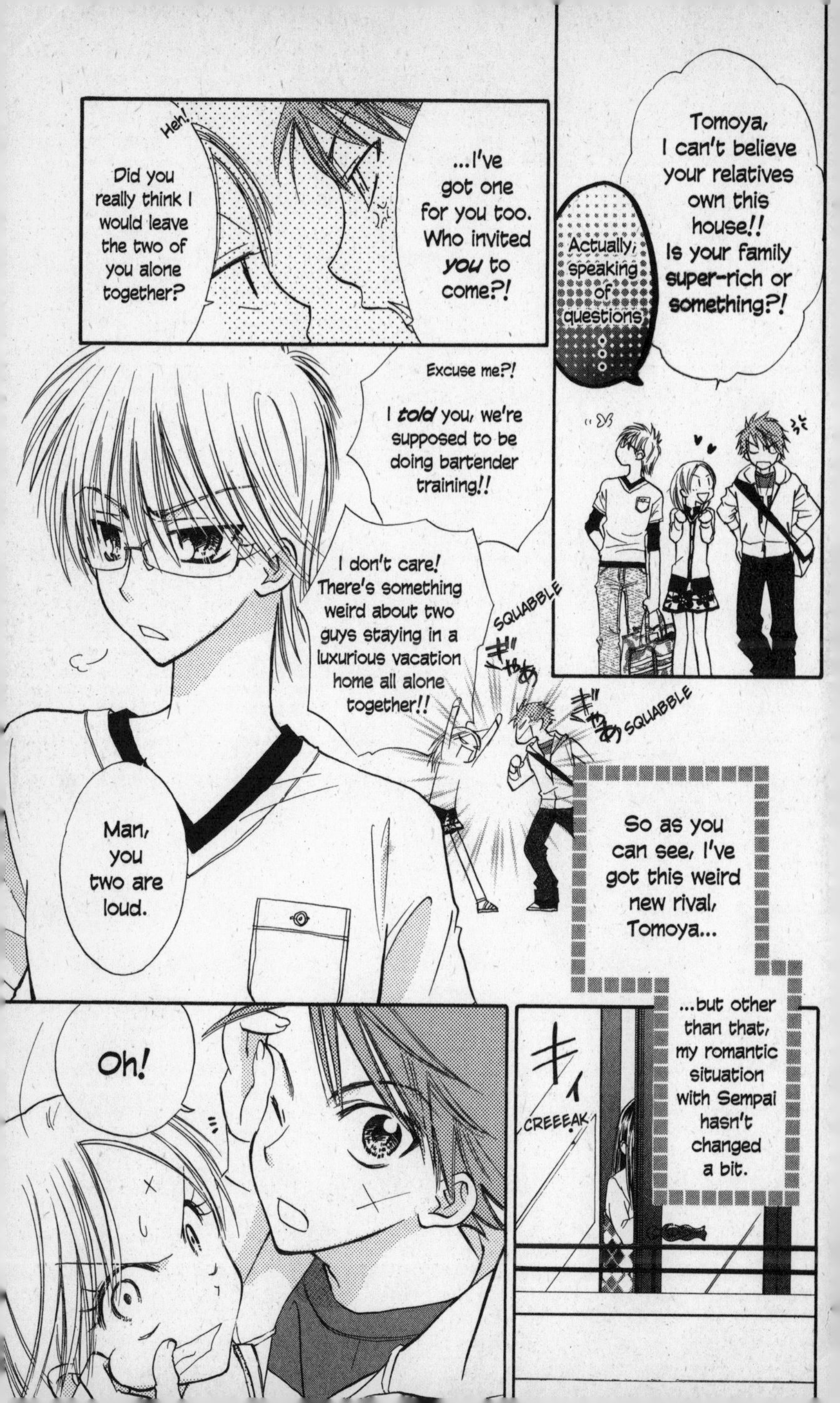

Tomoya, I can't believe your relatives own this house!! Is your family super-rich or something?!
Actually, speaking of questions...
...I've got one for you too. Who invited *you* to come?!
Heh!
Did you really think I would leave the two of you alone together?
Excuse me?!
I *told* you, we're supposed to be doing bartender training!!
I don't care! There's something weird about two guys staying in a luxurious vacation home all alone together!!
SQUABBLE
SQUABBLE
Man, you two are loud.
So as you can see, I've got this weird new rival, Tomoya...
...but other than that, my romantic situation with Sempai hasn't changed a bit.
CREEEAK
Oh!

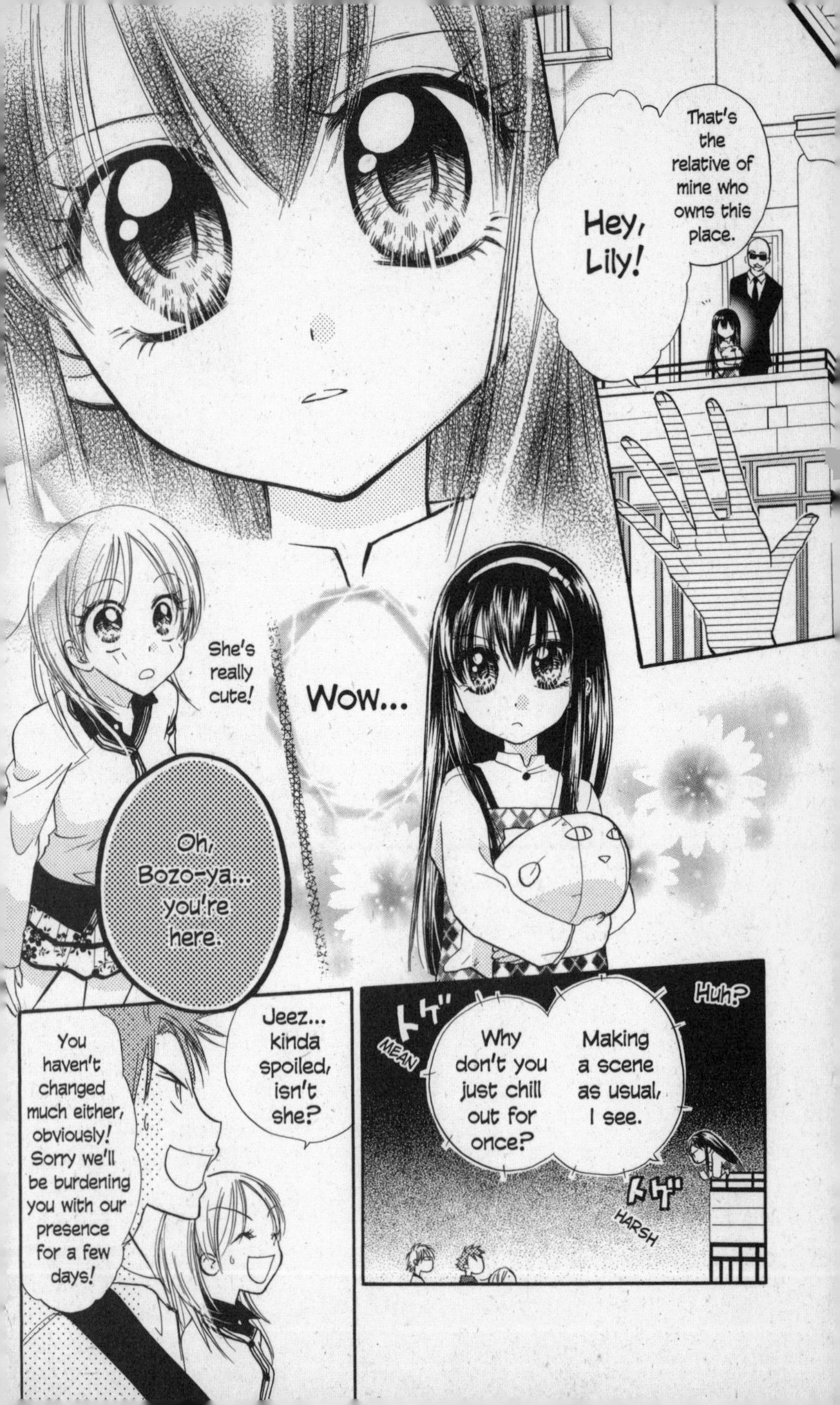
That's the relative of mine who owns this place.
Hey, Lily!
Wow...
She's really cute!
Oh, Bozo-ya... you're here.
Huh?
Making a scene as usual, I see.
Why don't you just chill out for once?
MEAN
HARSH
Jeez... kinda spoiled, isn't she?
You haven't changed much either, obviously! Sorry we'll be burdening you with our presence for a few days!

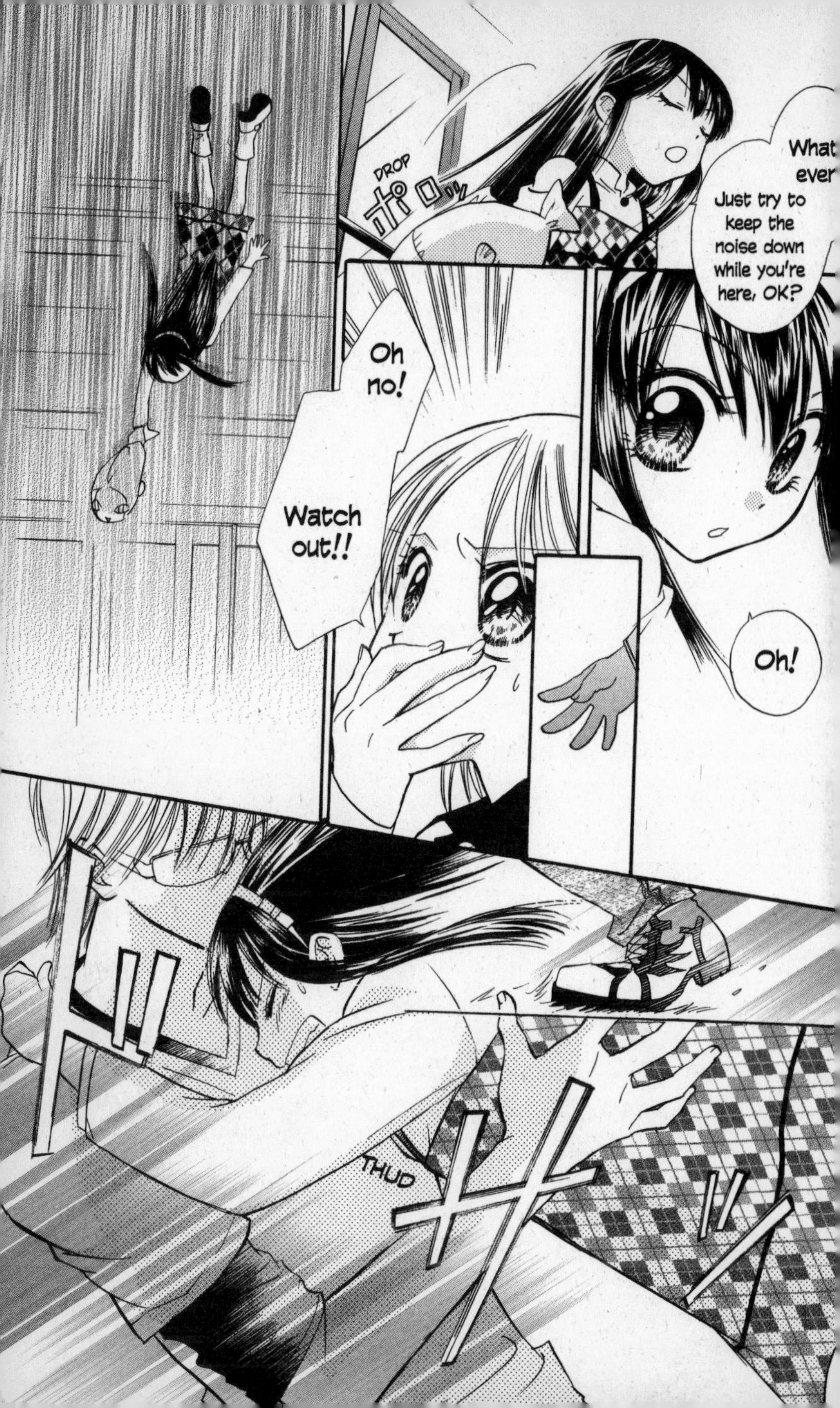
DROP
What ever
Just try to keep the noise down while you're here, OK?
Oh!
Oh no!
Watch out!!
THUD

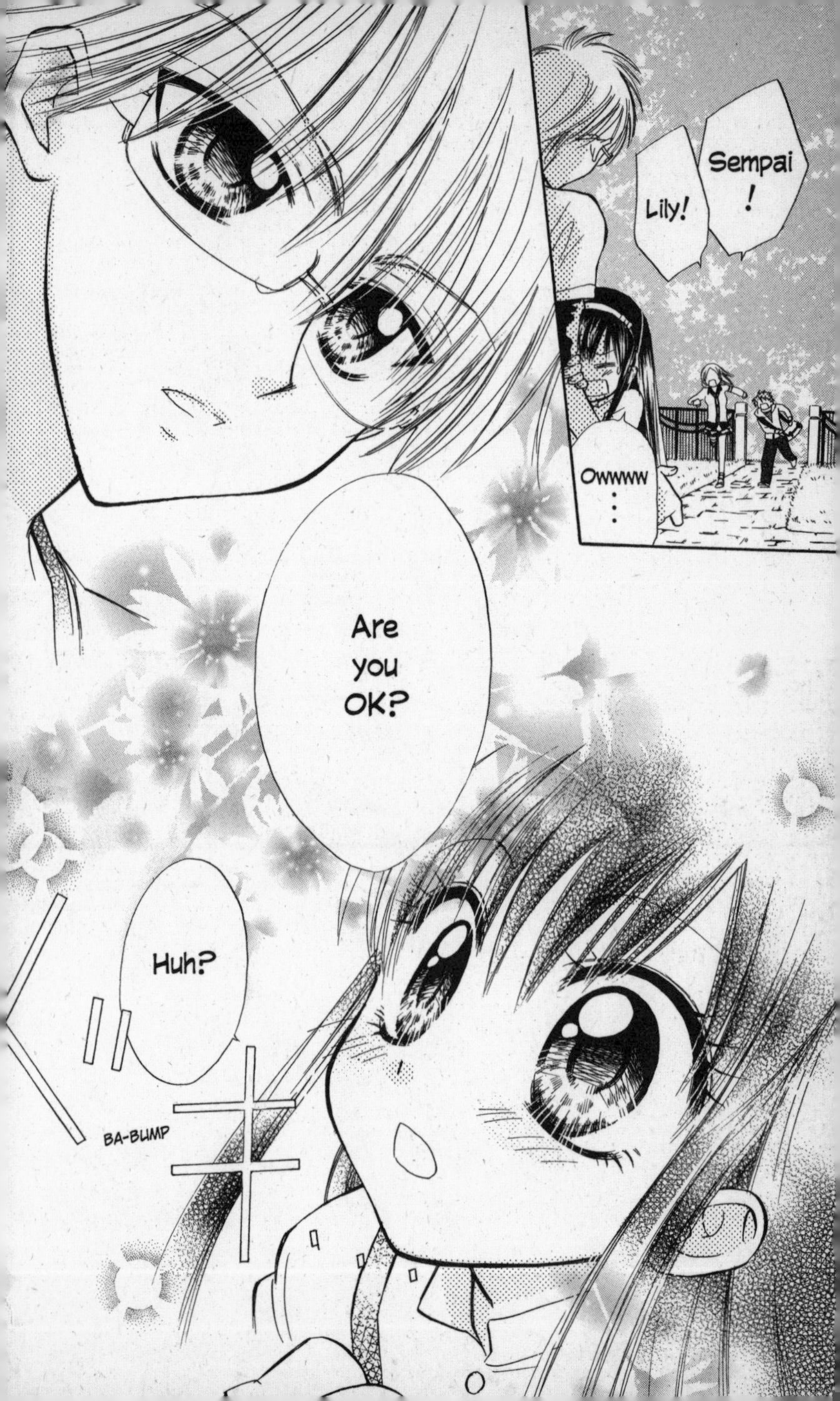
Sempai!
Lily!
Owwww...
Are you OK?
Huh?
BA-BUMP

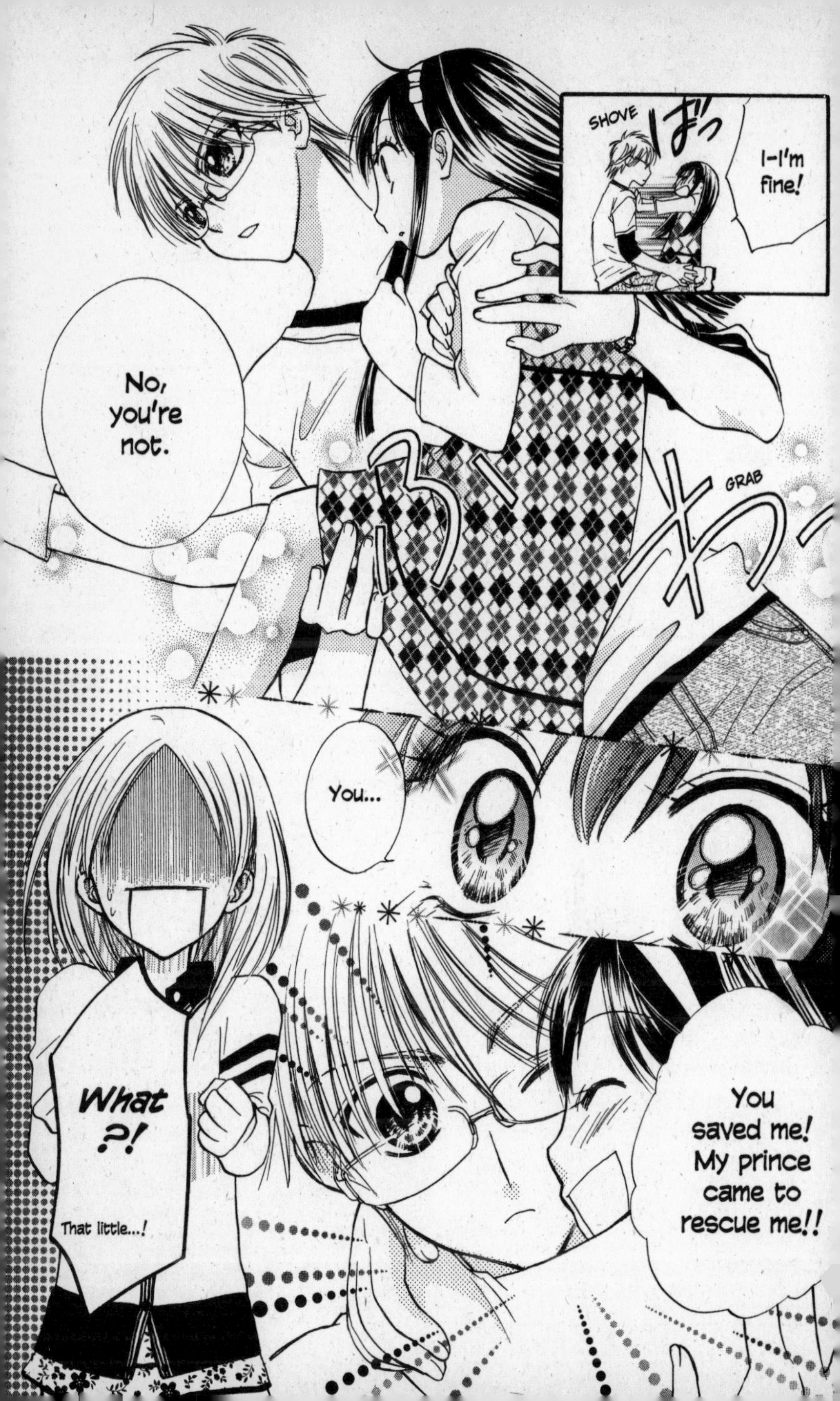

SHOVE
ばっ
I-I'm fine!
No, you're not.
GRAB
You...
You saved me! My prince came to rescue me!!
What?!
That little...!

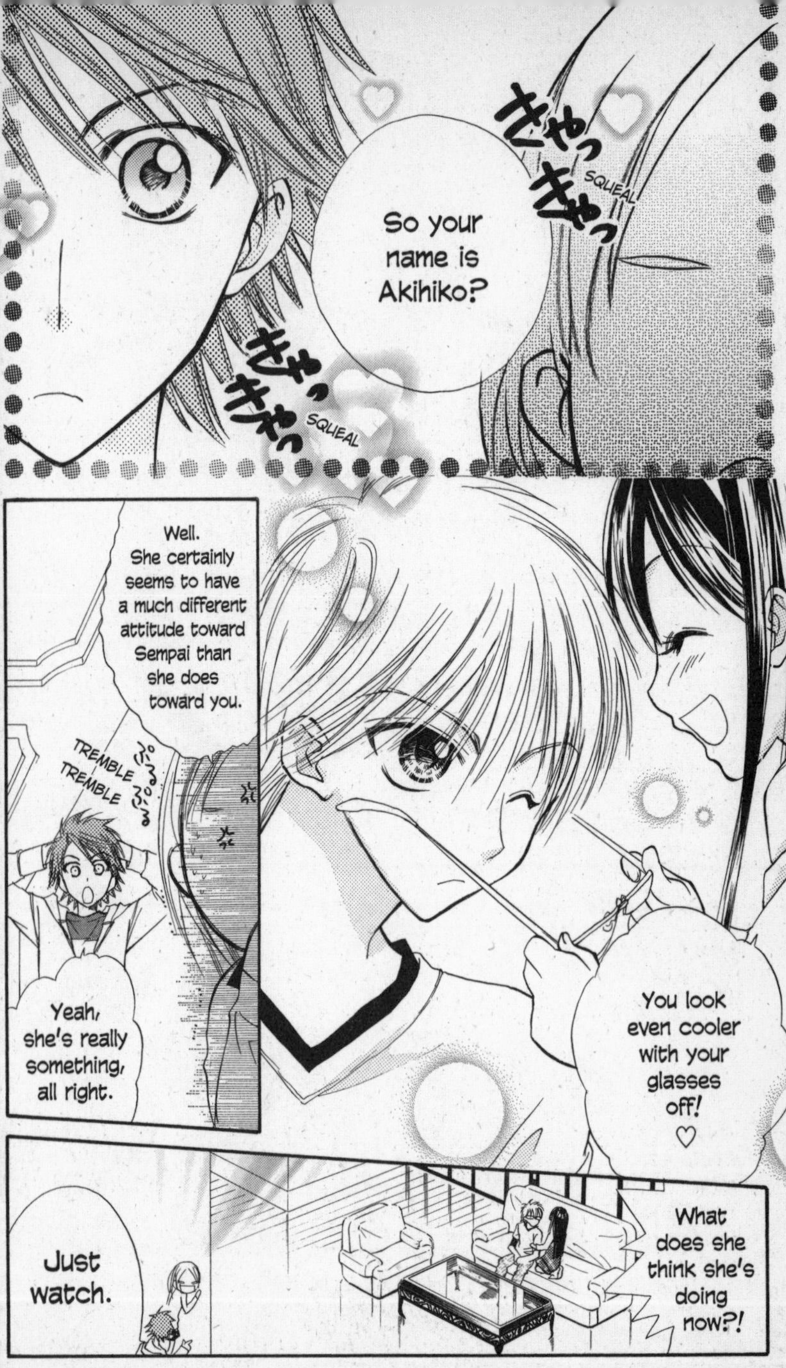
きゃっきゃっ
SQUEAL
So your name is Akihiko?
きゃっきゃっ
SQUEAL
You look even cooler with your glasses off! ♡
Well. She certainly seems to have a much different attitude toward Sempai than she does toward you.
ぷるぷる
TREMBLE TREMBLE
Yeah, she's really something, all right.
What does she think she's doing now?!
Just watch.

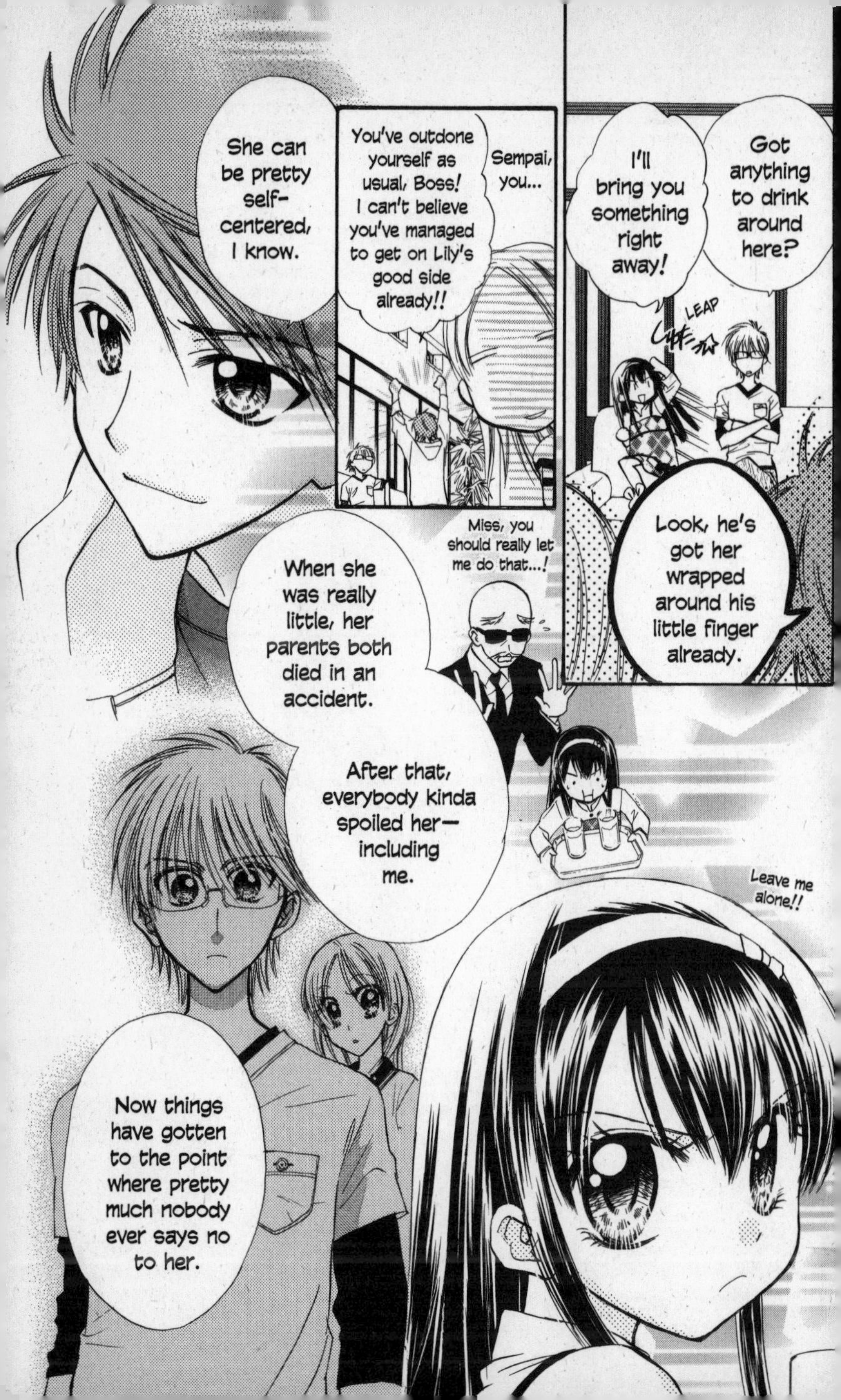

Got anything to drink around here?
I'll bring you something right away!
LEAP
Look, he's got her wrapped around his little finger already.
Sempai, you...
You've outdone yourself as usual, Boss! I can't believe you've managed to get on Lily's good side already!!
She can be pretty self-centered, I know.
When she was really little, her parents both died in an accident.
Miss, you should really let me do that...!
After that, everybody kinda spoiled her—including me.
Leave me alone!!
Now things have gotten to the point where pretty much nobody ever says no to her.

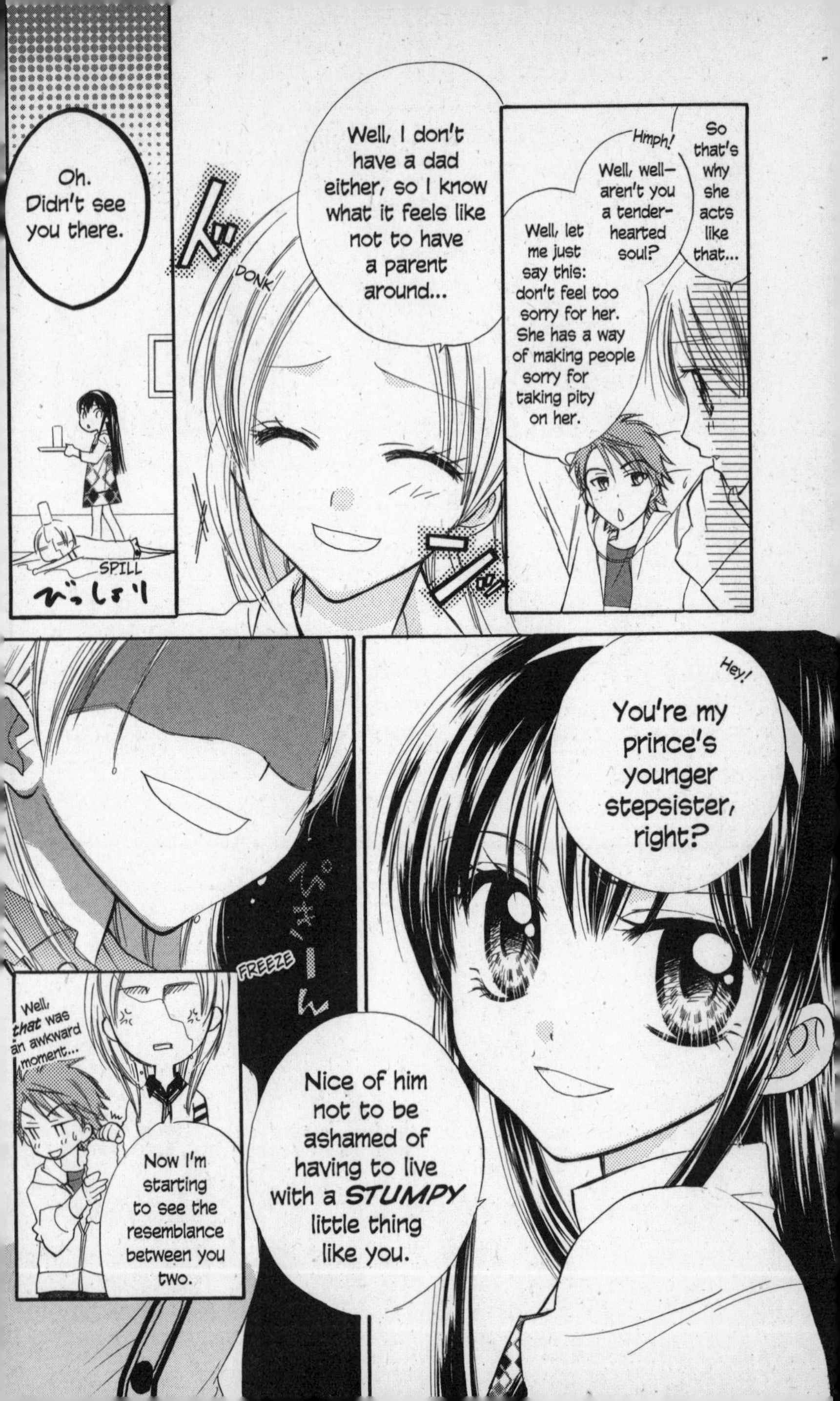
So that's why she acts like that...
Hmph!
Well, well— aren't you a tender-hearted soul?
Well, let me just say this: don't feel too sorry for her. She has a way of making people sorry for taking pity on her.
Well, I don't have a dad either, so I know what it feels like not to have a parent around...
ド
DONK
Oh. Didn't see you there.
SPILL
びっしょり
Hey!
You're my prince's younger stepsister, right?
Nice of him not to be ashamed of having to live with a *STUMPY* little thing like you.
ぴきーん
FREEZE
Well, *that* was an awkward moment...
Now I'm starting to see the resemblance between you two.

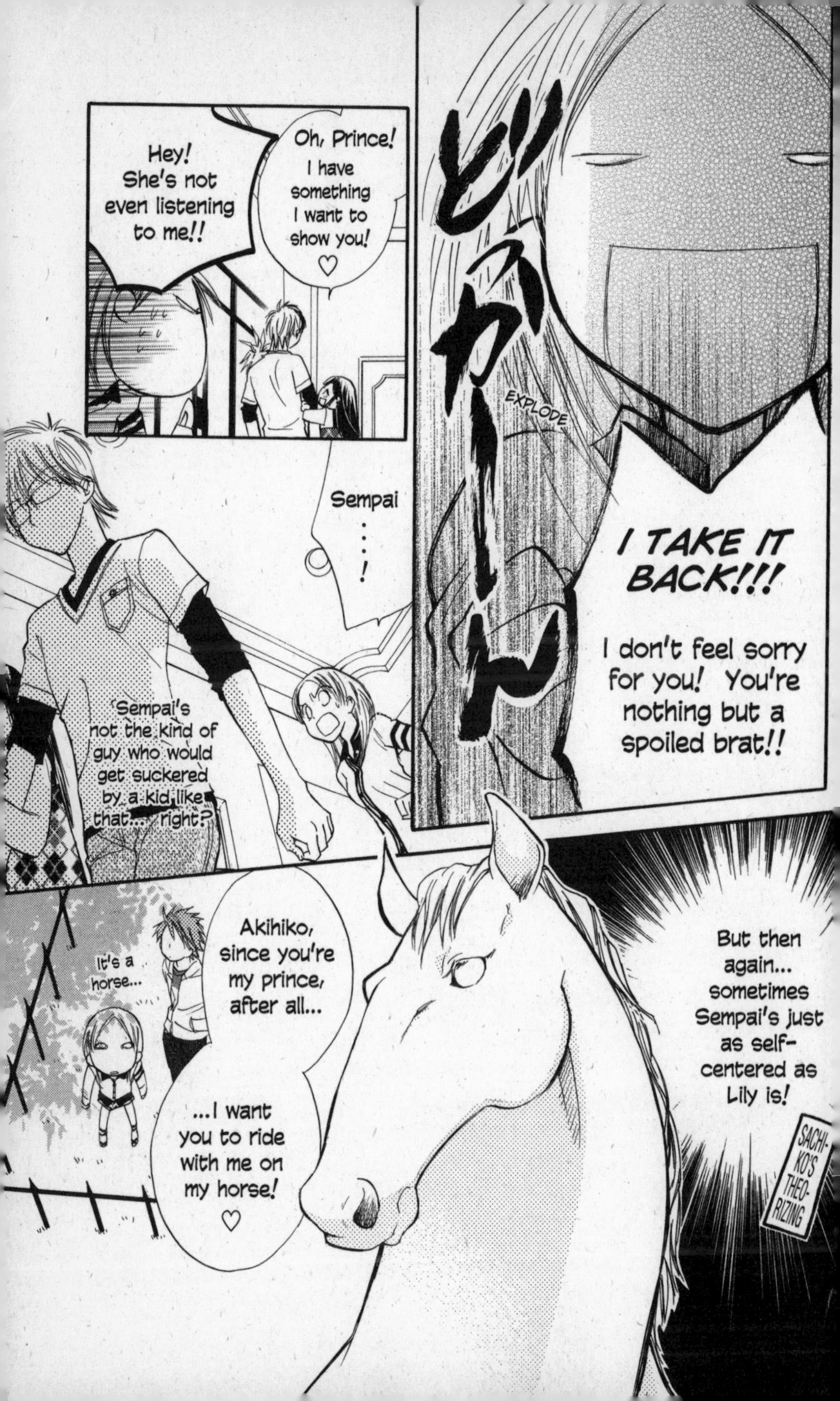

EXPLODE
I TAKE IT BACK!!!
I don't feel sorry for you! You're nothing but a spoiled brat!!
Oh, Prince! I have something I want to show you! ♡
Hey! She's not even listening to me!!
Sempai...!
Sempai's not the kind of guy who would get suckered by a kid like that... right?
But then again... sometimes Sempai's just as self-centered as Lily is!
SACHIKO'S THEORIZING
Akihiko, since you're my prince, after all...
...I want you to ride with me on my horse! ♡
It's a horse...

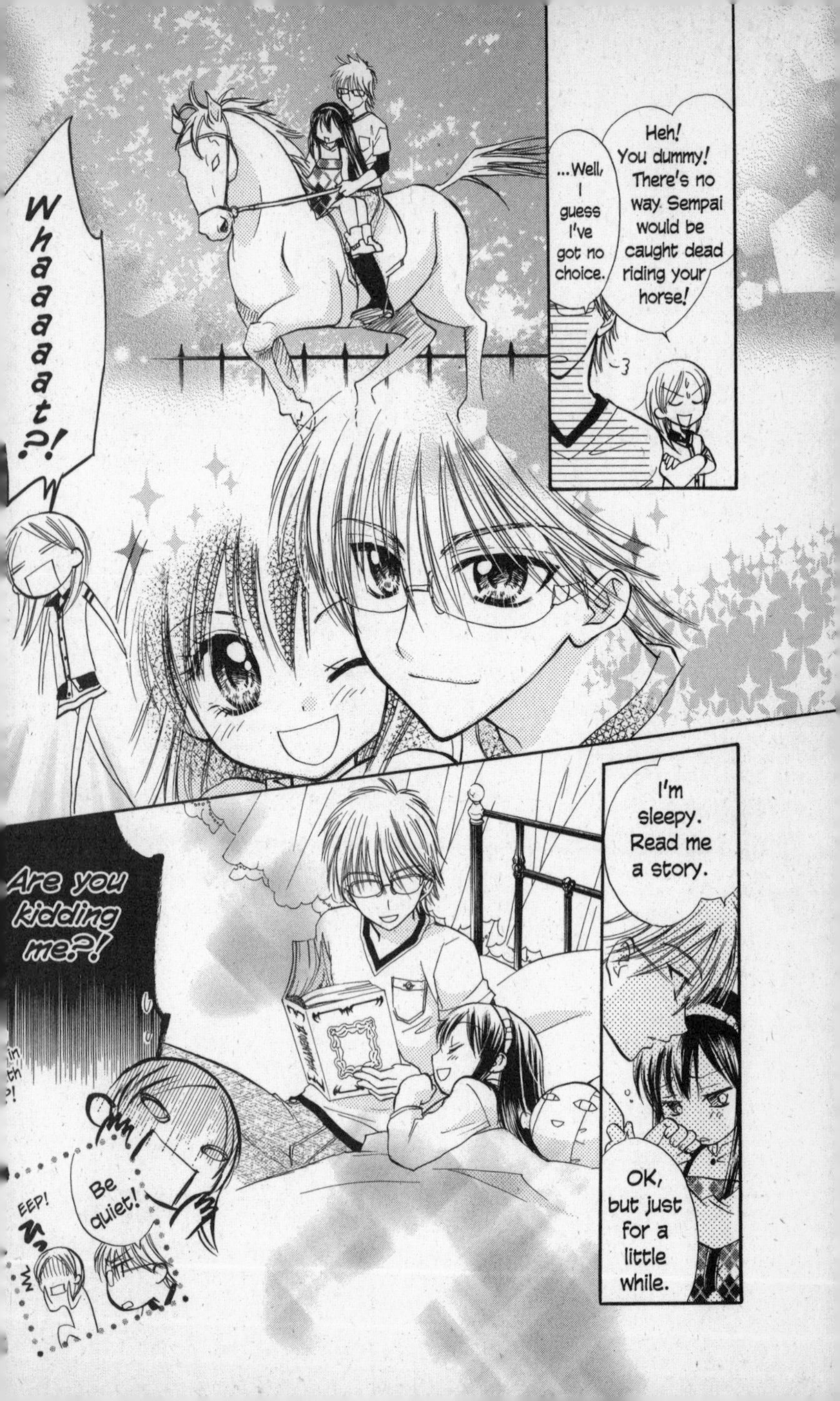

Heh! You dummy! There's no way Sempai would be caught dead riding your horse!
...Well, I guess I've got no choice.
Whaaaaaat?!
I'm sleepy. Read me a story.
OK, but just for a little while.
Are you kidding me?!
Be quiet!
EEP!

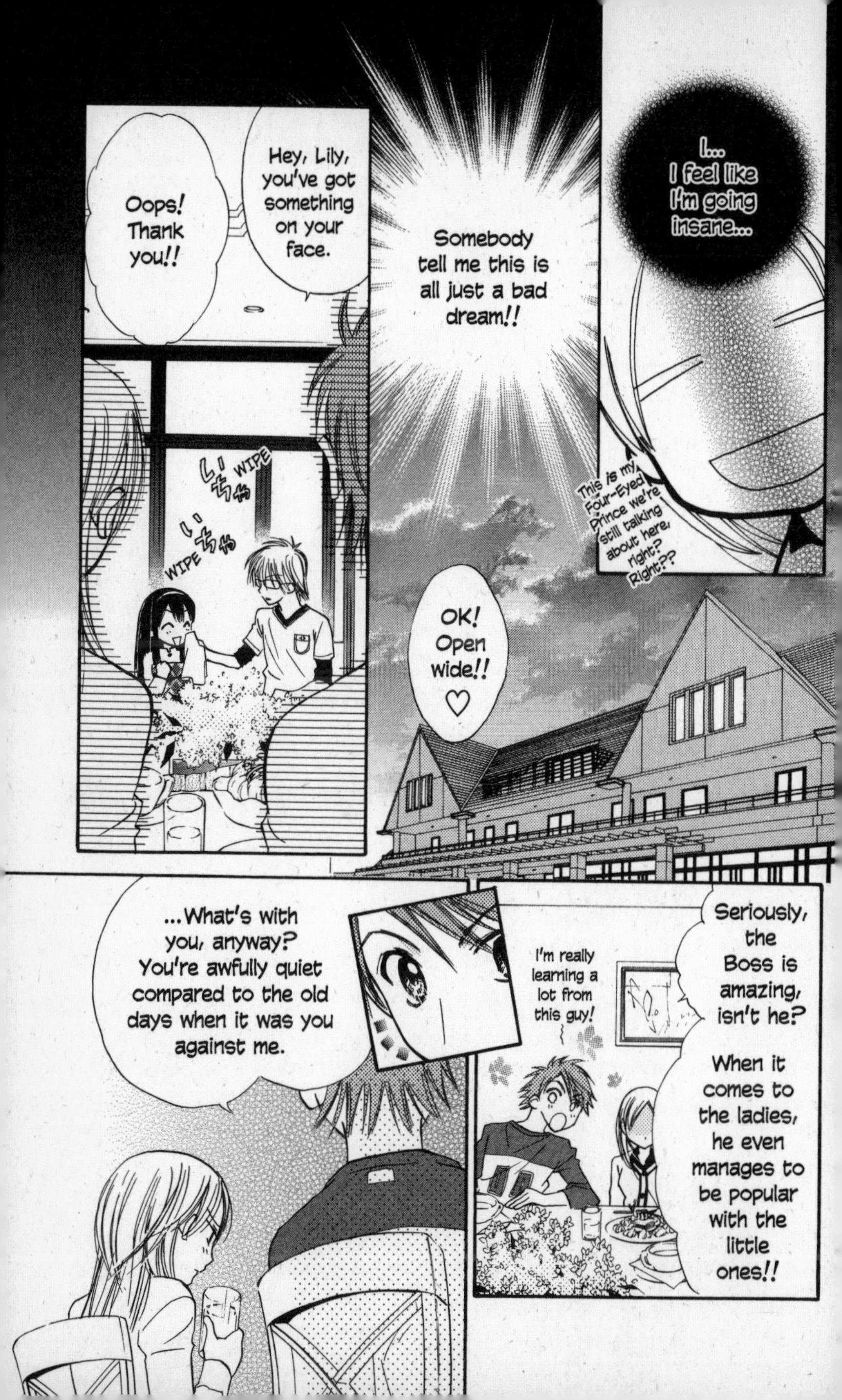

I... I feel like I'm going insane...
This is my Four-Eyed Prince we're still talking about here, right? Right??
Somebody tell me this is all just a bad dream!!
Hey, Lily, you've got something on your face.
Oops! Thank you!!
WIPE
WIPE
OK! Open wide!! ♡
Seriously, the Boss is amazing, isn't he?
When it comes to the ladies, he even manages to be popular with the little ones!!
I'm really learning a lot from this guy!
...What's with you, anyway? You're awfully quiet compared to the old days when it was you against me.

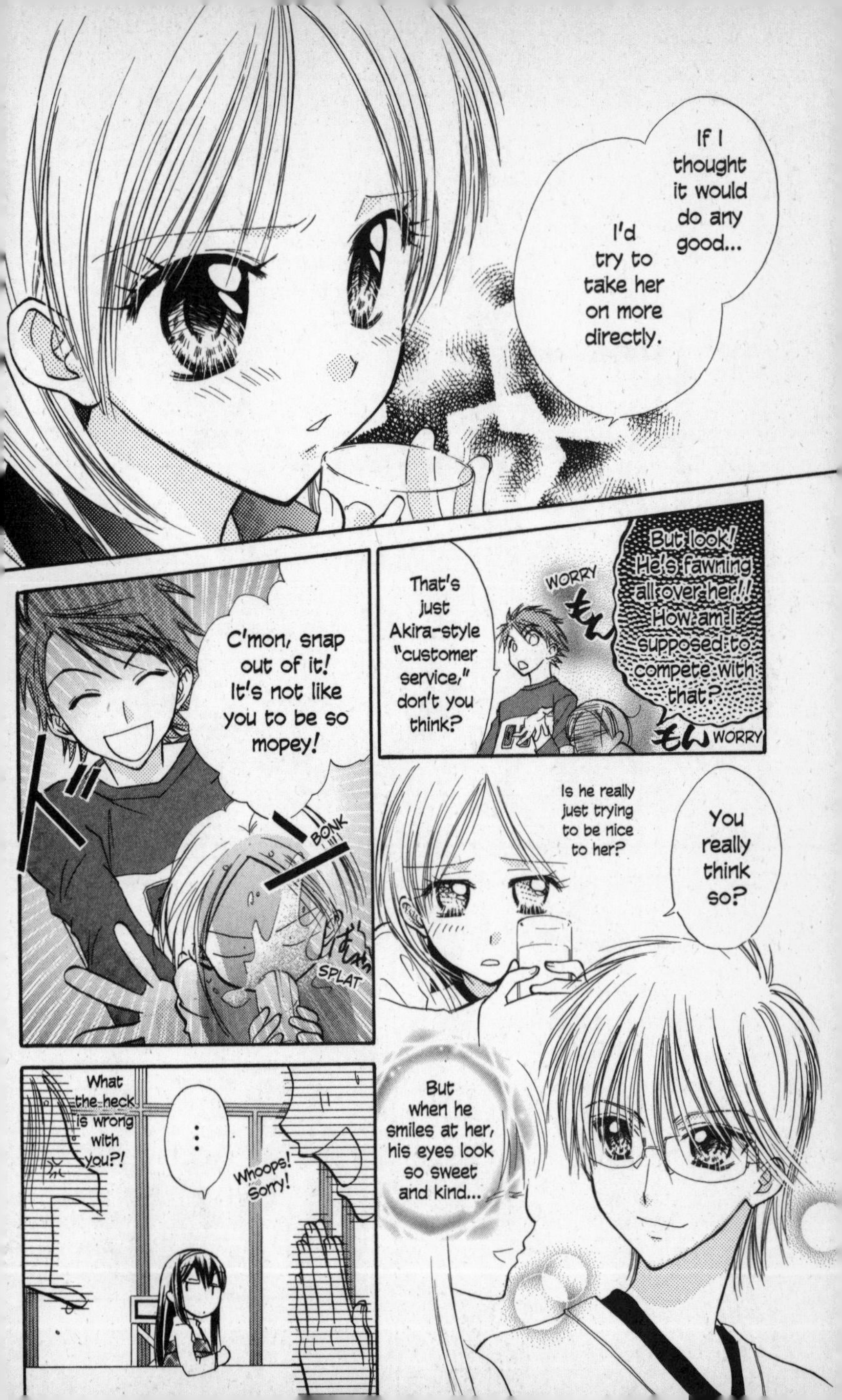
If I thought it would do any good...
I'd try to take her on more directly.
But look! He's fawning all over her!! How am I supposed to compete with that?
WORRY
もん
もん
WORRY
That's just Akira-style "customer service," don't you think?
C'mon, snap out of it! It's not like you to be so mopey!
BONK
SPLAT
You really think so?
Is he really just trying to be nice to her?
But when he smiles at her, his eyes look so sweet and kind...
...
Whoops! Sorry!
What the heck is wrong with you?!

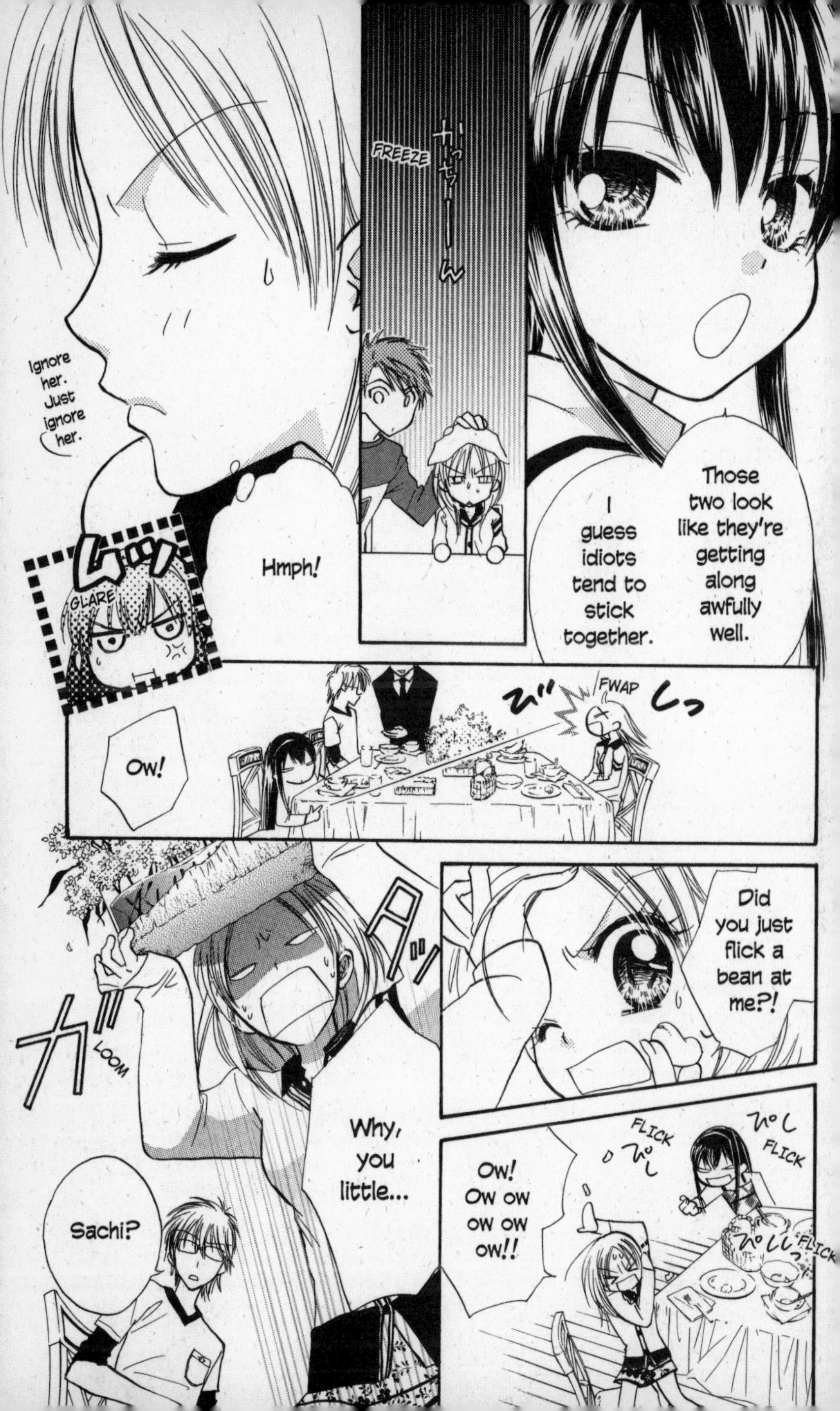

Those two look like they're getting along awfully well.
I guess idiots tend to stick together.
FREEZE
Ignore her. Just ignore her.
Hmph!
GLARE
FWAP
Ow!
Did you just flick a bean at me?!
FLICK
FLICK
FLICK
Ow! Ow ow ow ow ow!!
Why, you little...
LOOM
Sachi?

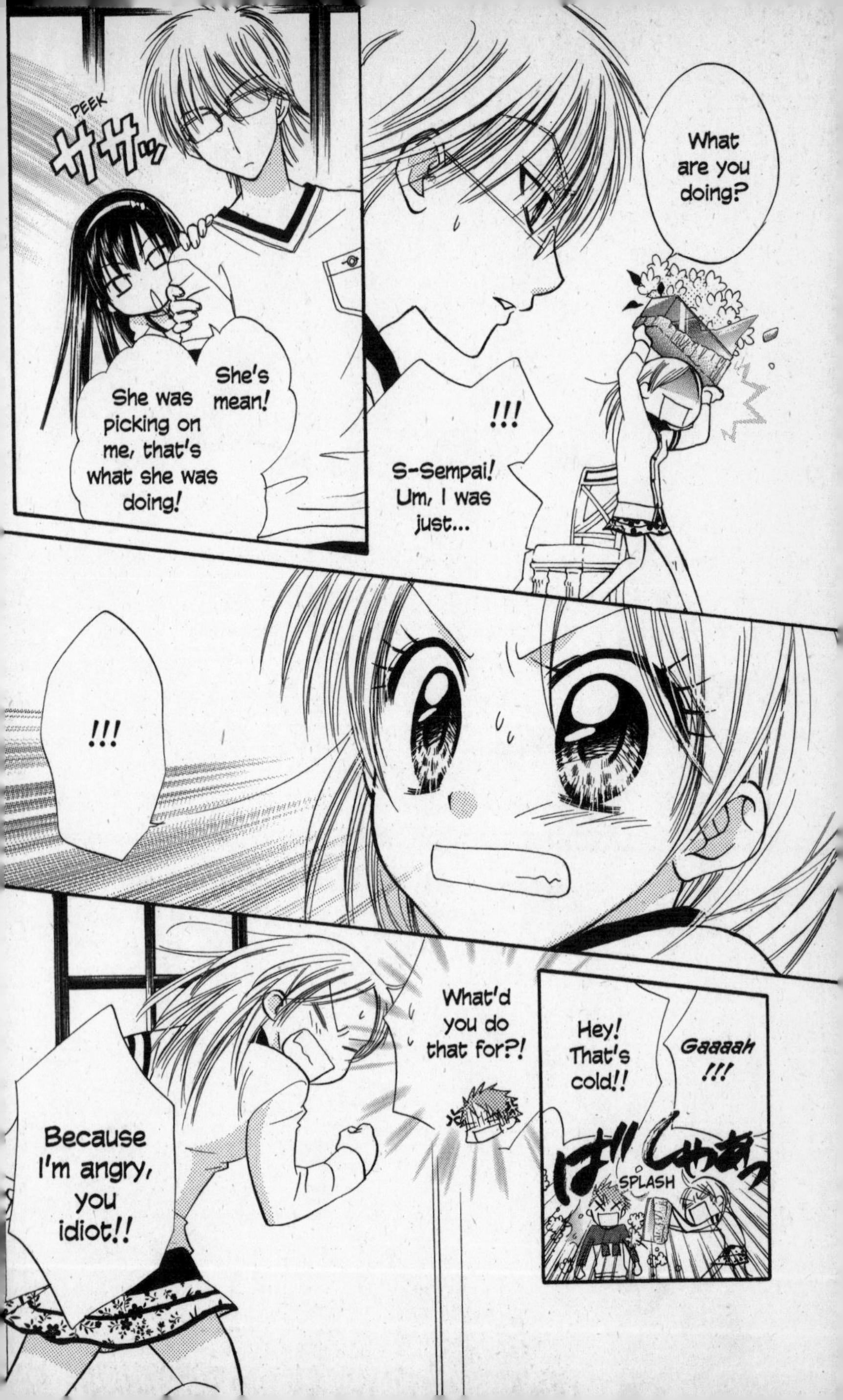
What are you doing?
!!!
S-Sempai! Um, I was just...
PEEK
She's mean!
She was picking on me, that's what she was doing!
!!!
Gaaaah!!!
Hey! That's cold!!
SPLASH
What'd you do that for?!
Because I'm angry, you idiot!!

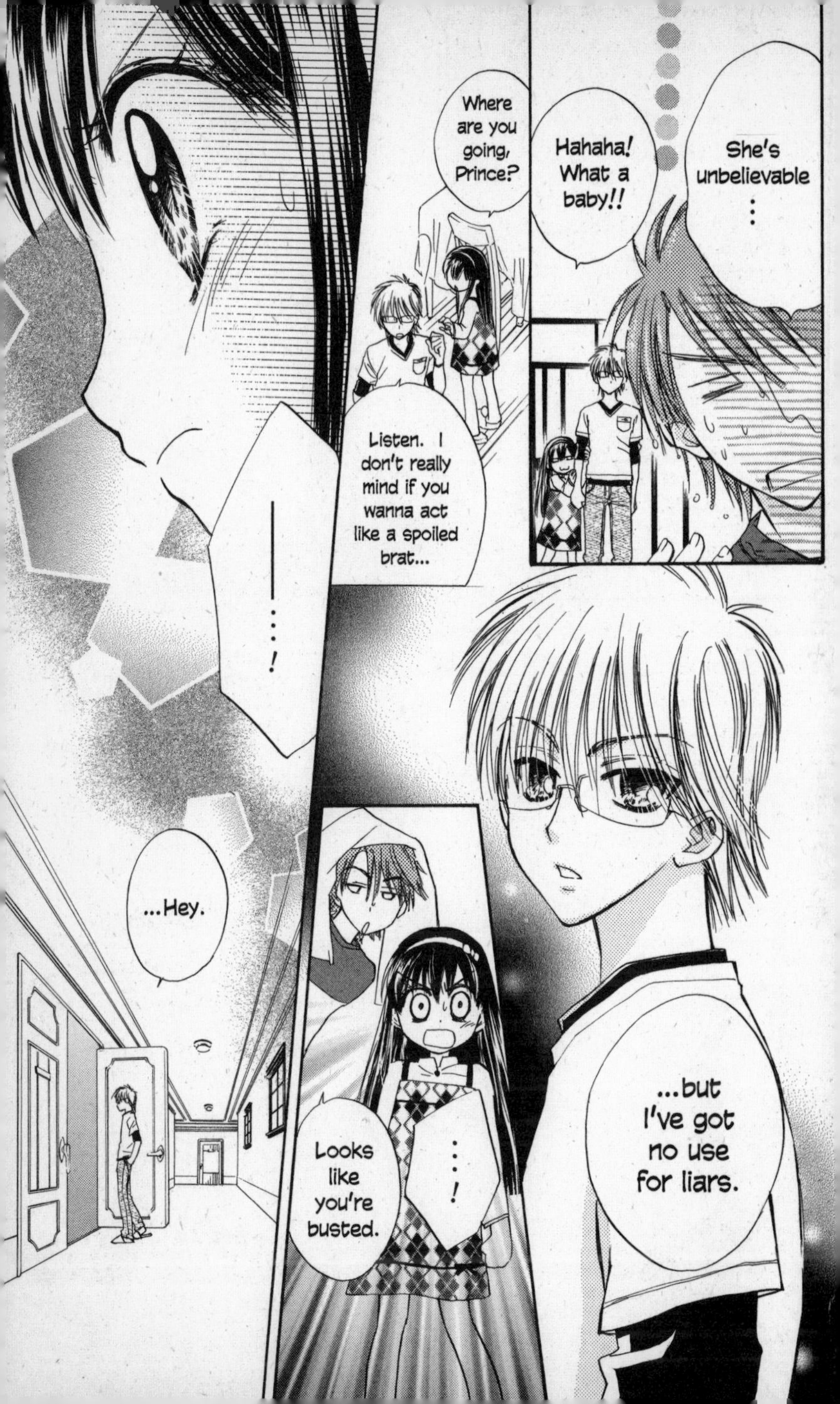

She's unbelievable...
Hahaha! What a baby!!
Where are you going, Prince?
Listen. I don't really mind if you wanna act like a spoiled brat...
—...!
...but I've got no use for liars.
...!
Looks like you're busted.
...Hey.

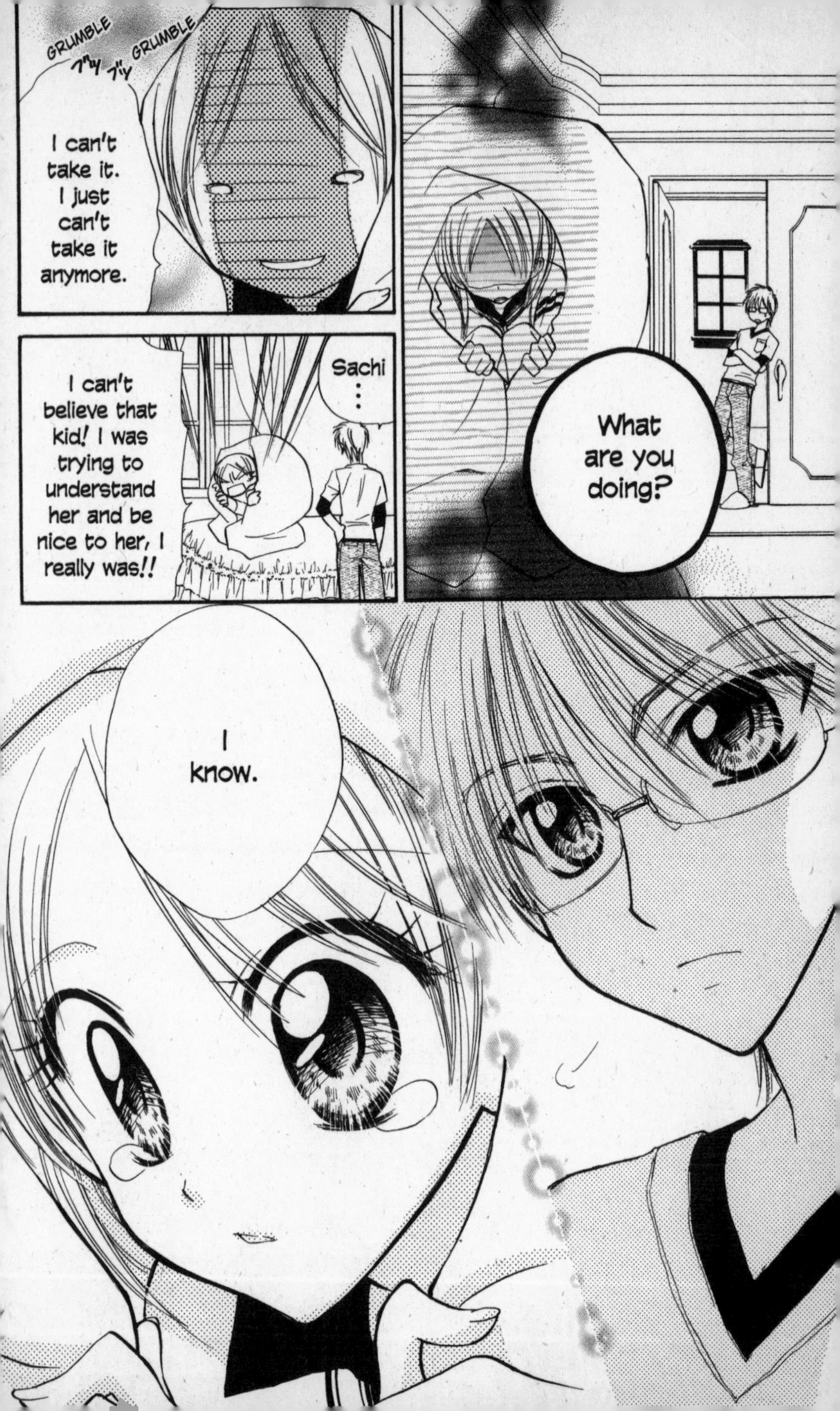
What are you doing?
GRUMBLE
ブツ
ブツ
GRUMBLE
I can't take it. I just can't take it anymore.
Sachi...
I can't believe that kid! I was trying to understand her and be nice to her, I really was!!
I know.

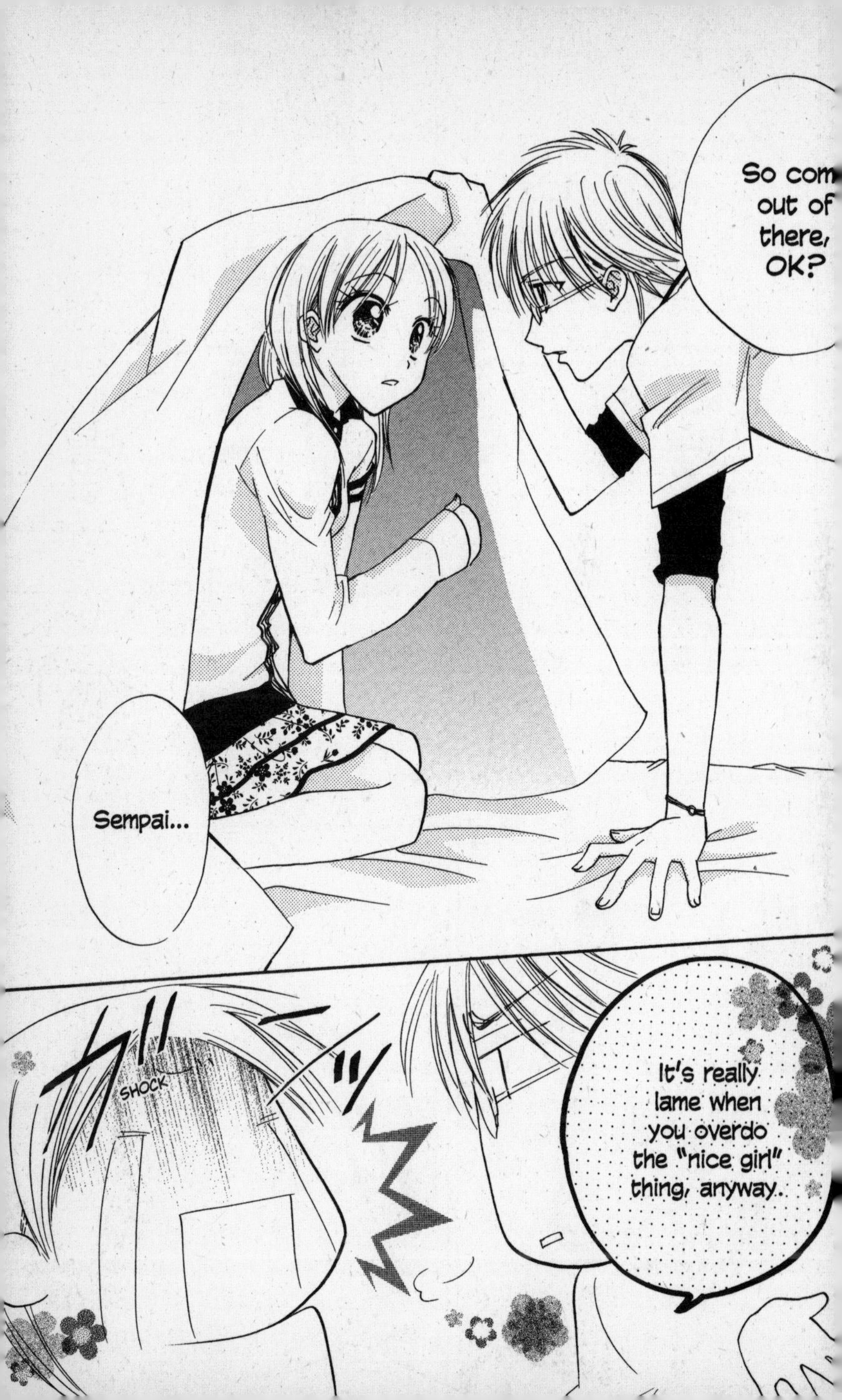
So com
out of
there,
OK?
Sempai...
It's really
lame when
you overdo
the "nice girl"
thing, anyway..
SHOCK

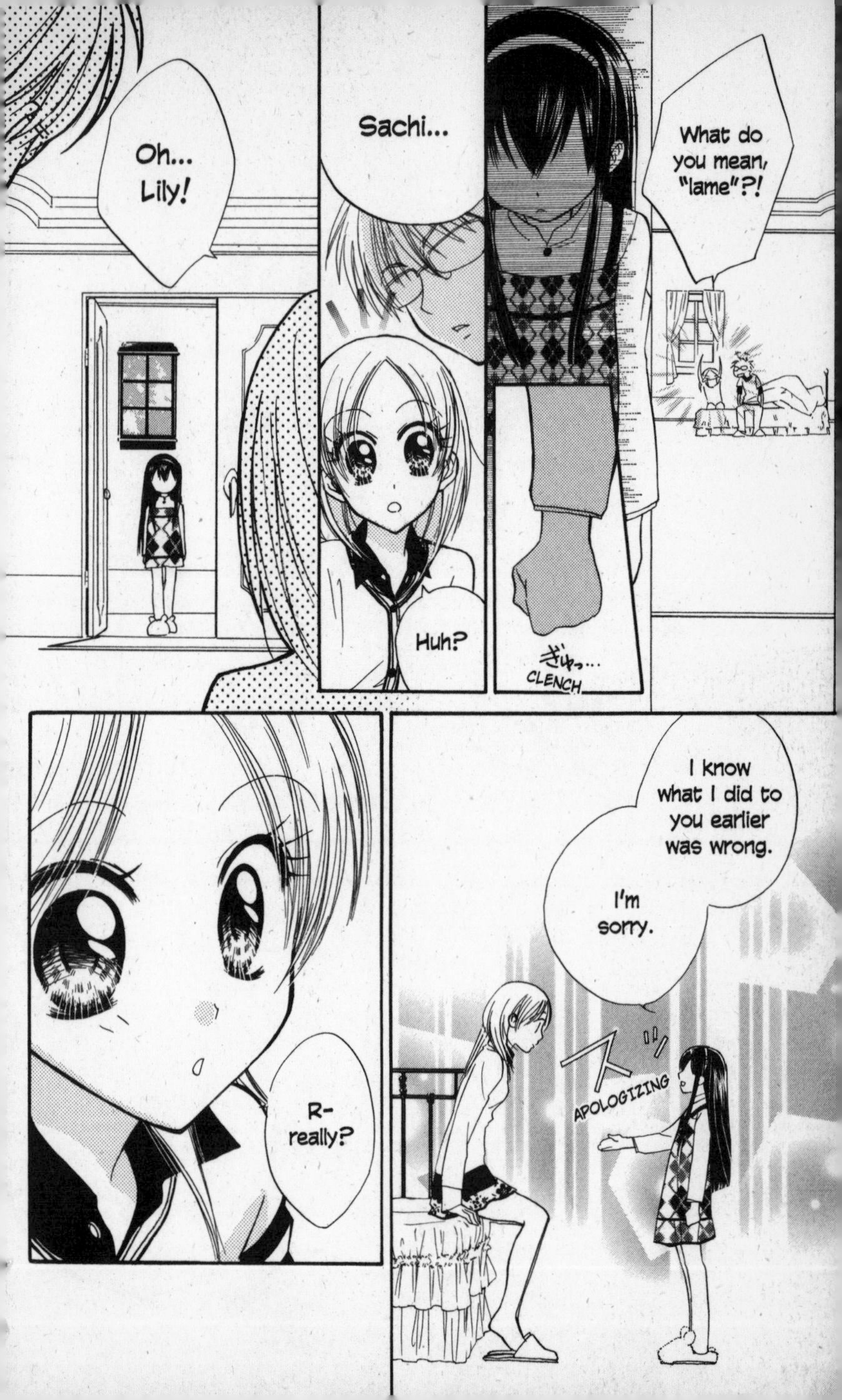

What do you mean, "lame"?!
ぎゅっ…
CLENCH
Sachi...
Huh?
Oh... Lily!
I know what I did to you earlier was wrong.
I'm sorry.
APOLOGIZING
R-really?

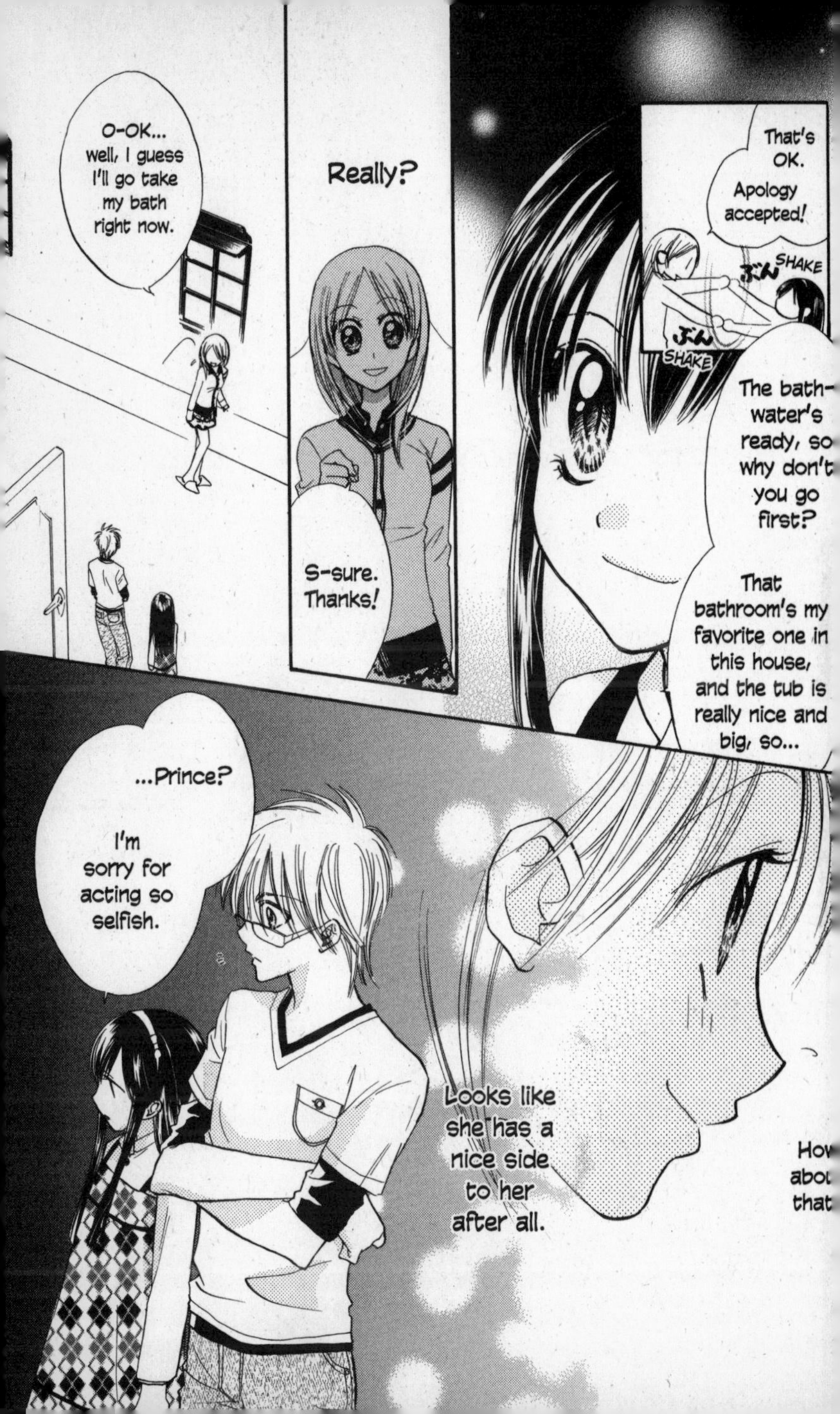
That's OK. Apology accepted!
ぶん SHAKE
ぶん SHAKE
The bath-water's ready, so why don't you go first?
That bathroom's my favorite one in this house, and the tub is really nice and big, so...
Really?
S-sure. Thanks!
O-OK... well, I guess I'll go take my bath right now.
How abou that
Looks like she has a nice side to her after all.
...Prince?
I'm sorry for acting so selfish.

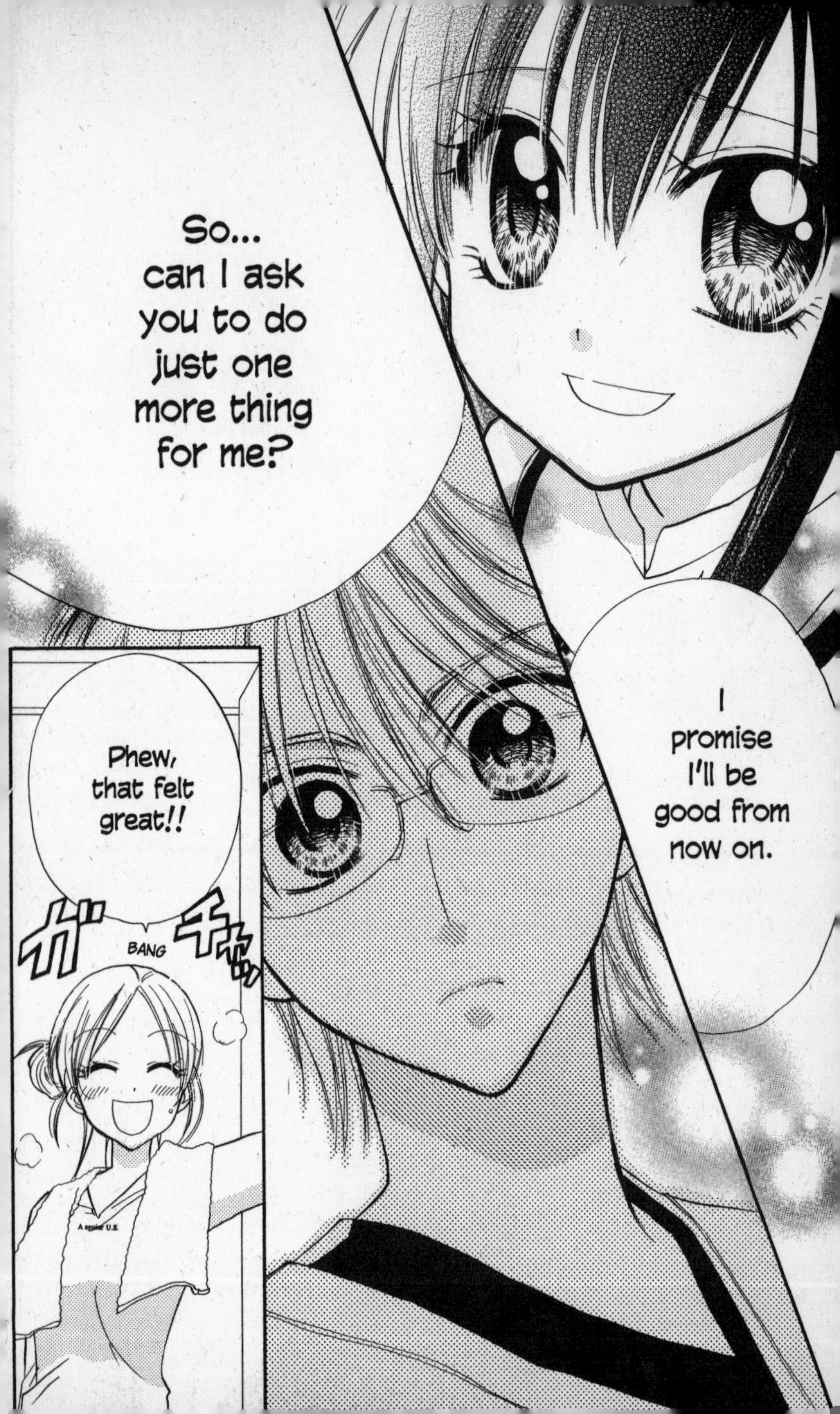
I promise I'll be good from now on.
So... can I ask you to do just one more thing for me?
BANG
Phew, that felt great!!

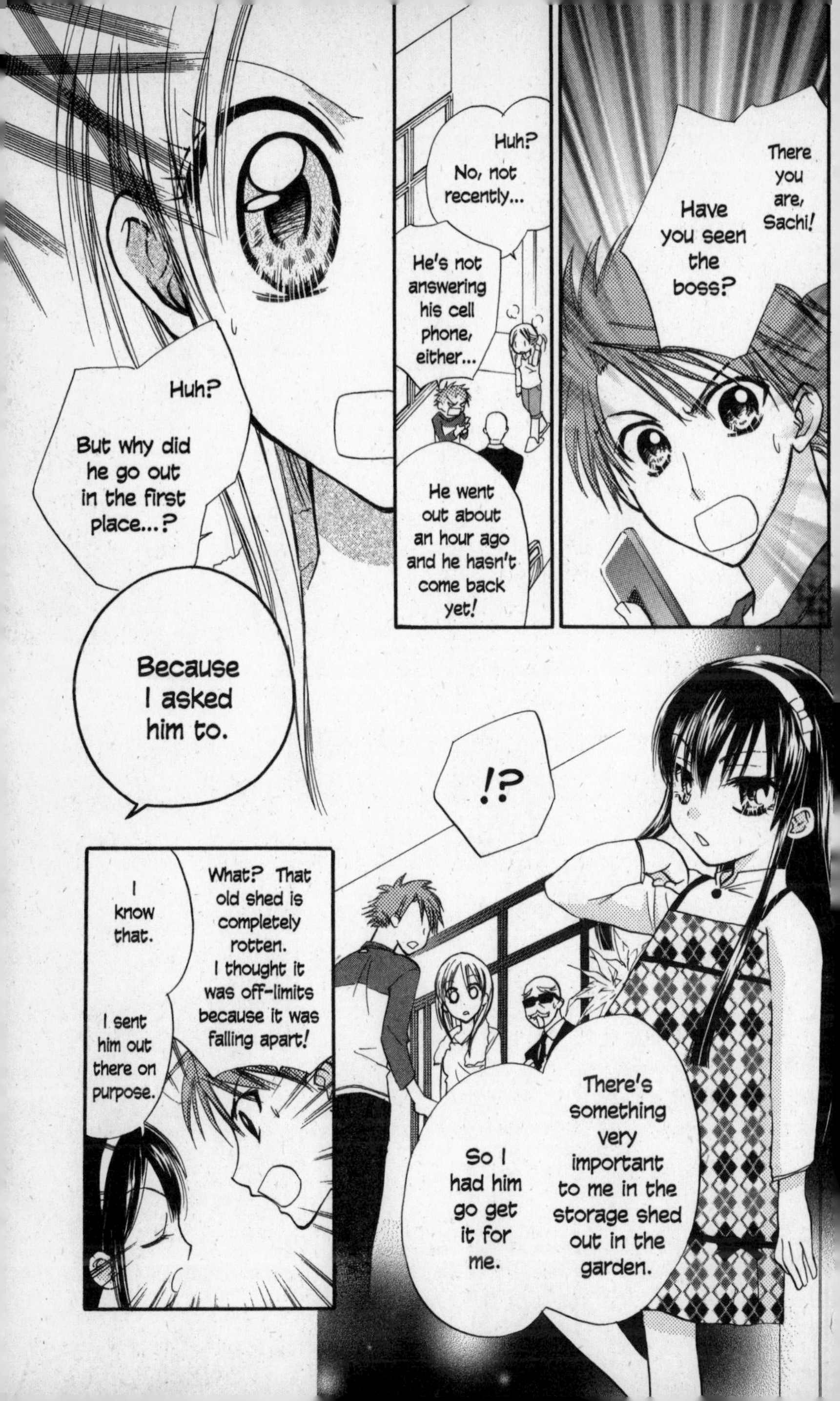
There you are, Sachi!
Have you seen the boss?
Huh? No, not recently...
He's not answering his cell phone, either...
He went out about an hour ago and he hasn't come back yet!
Huh?
But why did he go out in the first place...?
Because I asked him to.
!?
There's something very important to me in the storage shed out in the garden.
So I had him go get it for me.
What? That old shed is completely rotten. I thought it was off-limits because it was falling apart!
I know that.
I sent him out there on purpose.

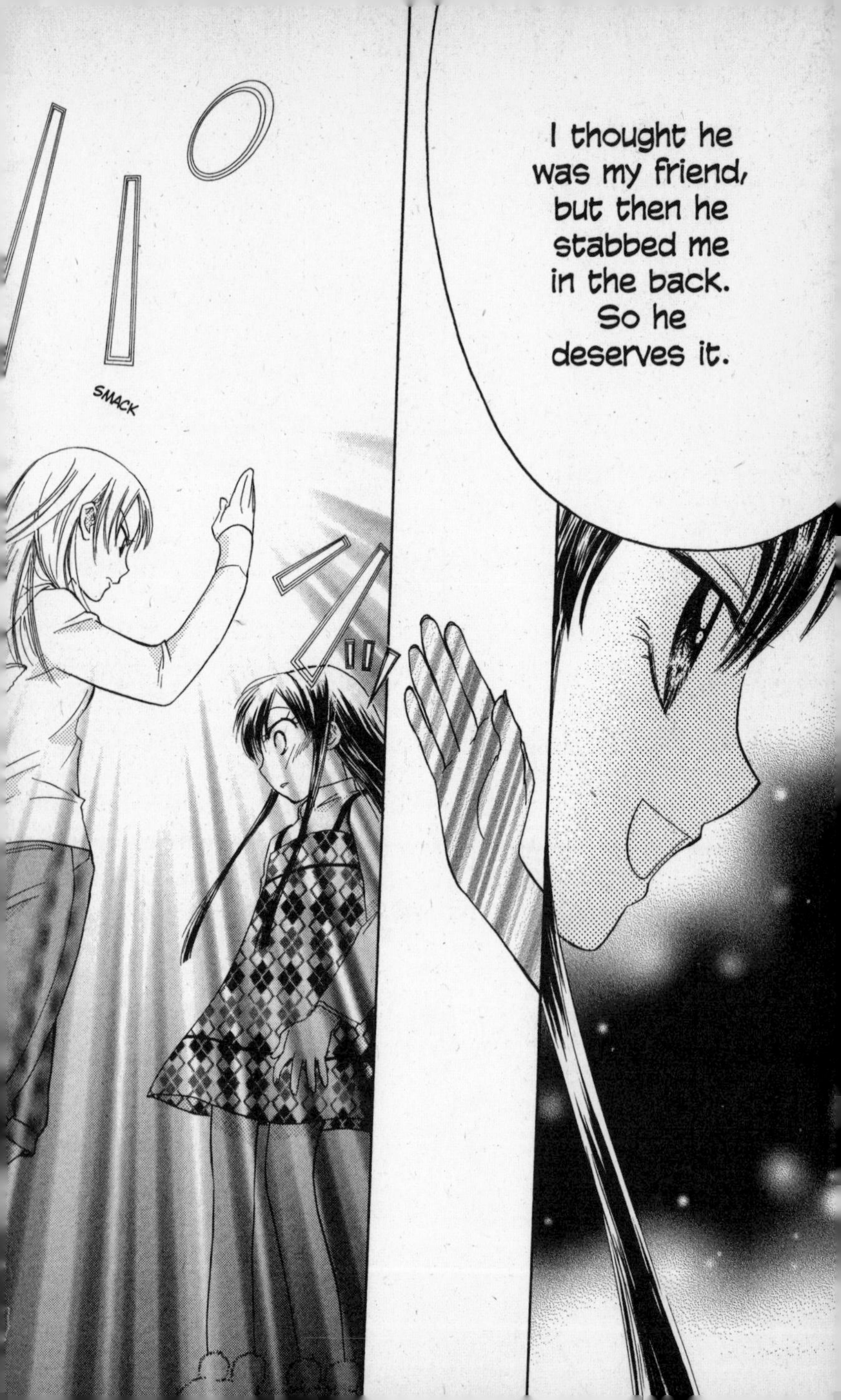
I thought he was my friend, but then he stabbed me in the back. So he deserves it.
SMACK

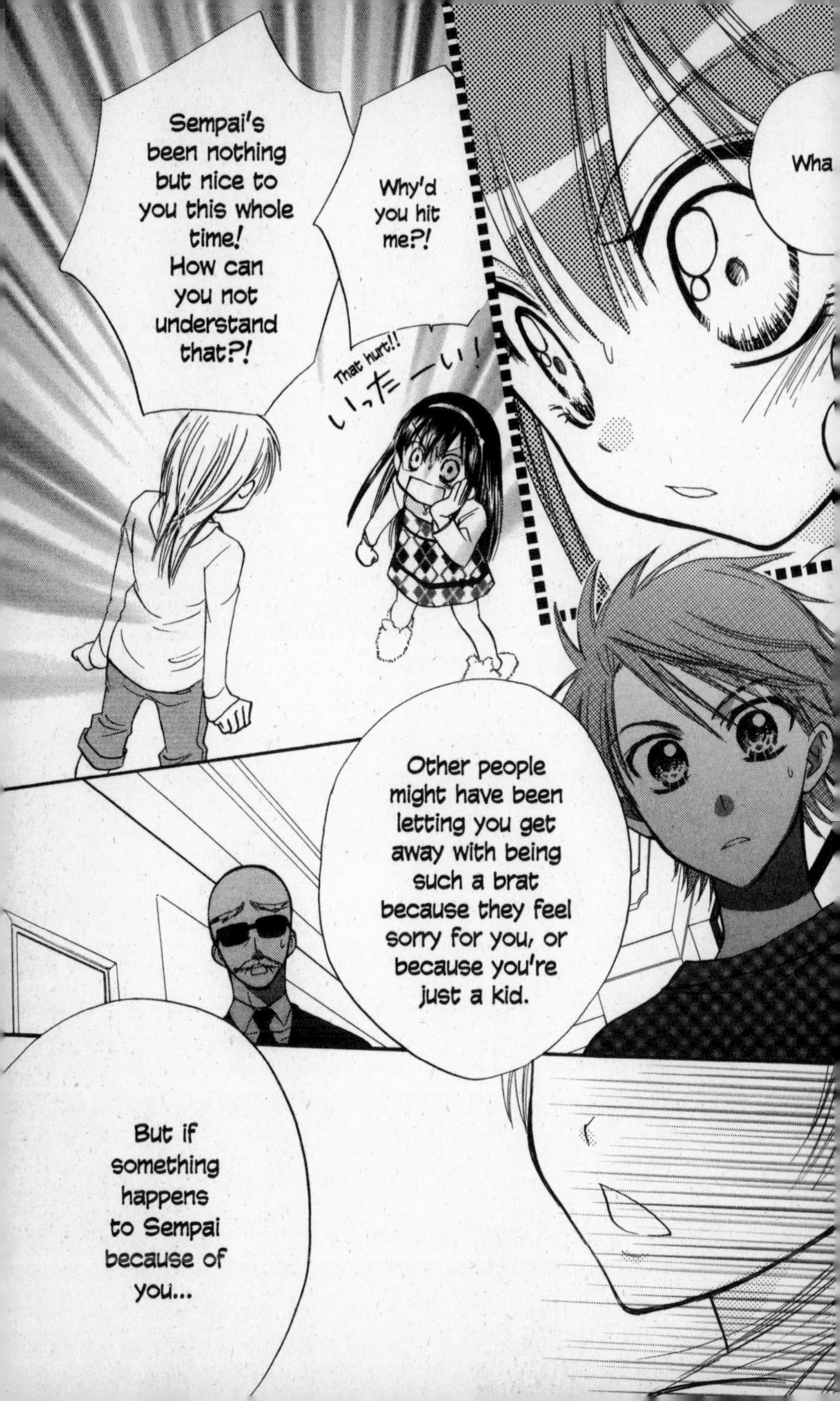
That hurt!!
いったーい!
Why'd you hit me?!
Sempai's been nothing but nice to you this whole time! How can you not understand that?!
Wha
Other people might have been letting you get away with being such a brat because they feel sorry for you, or because you're just a kid.
But if something happens to Sempai because of you...

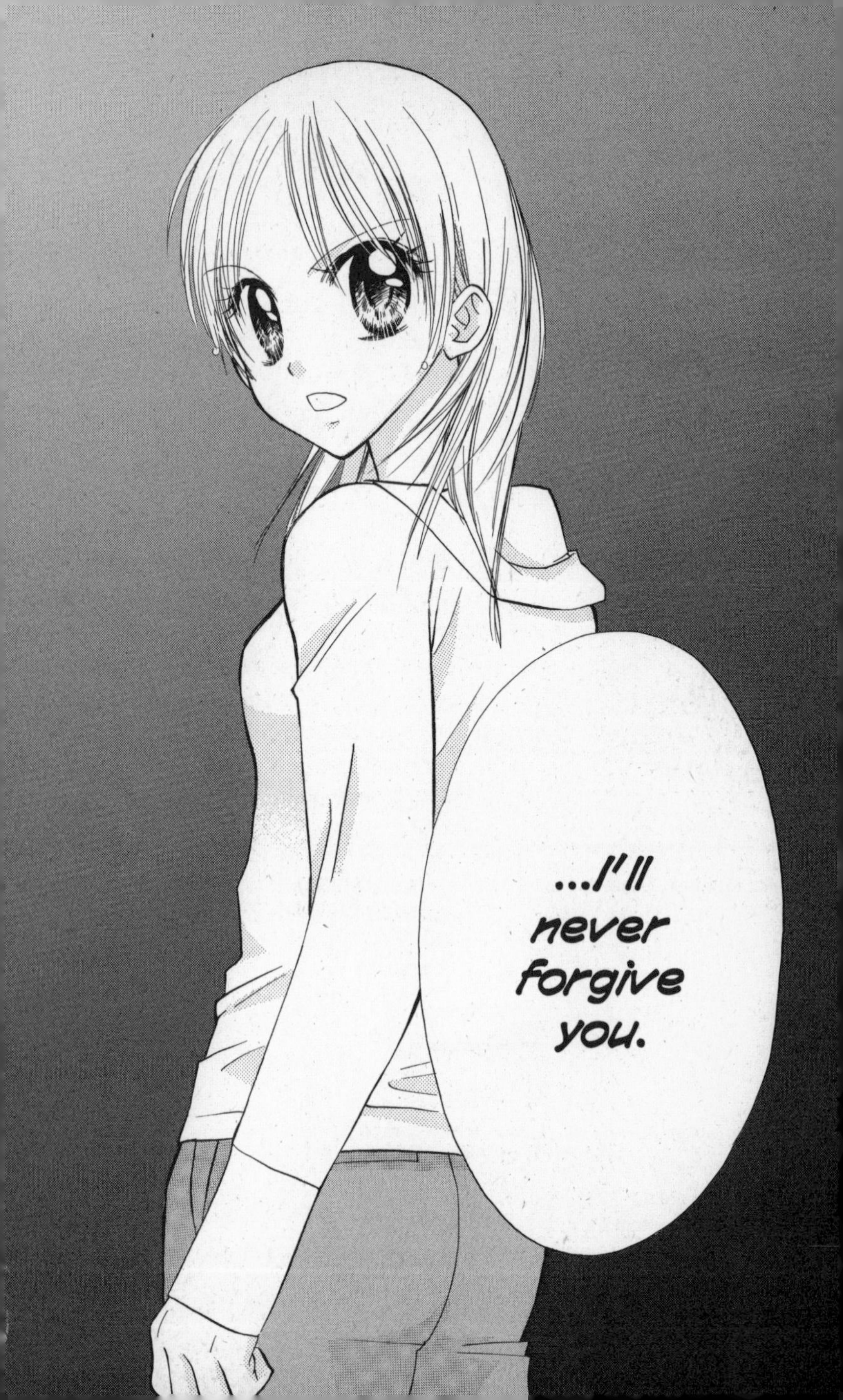
...I'll never forgive you.

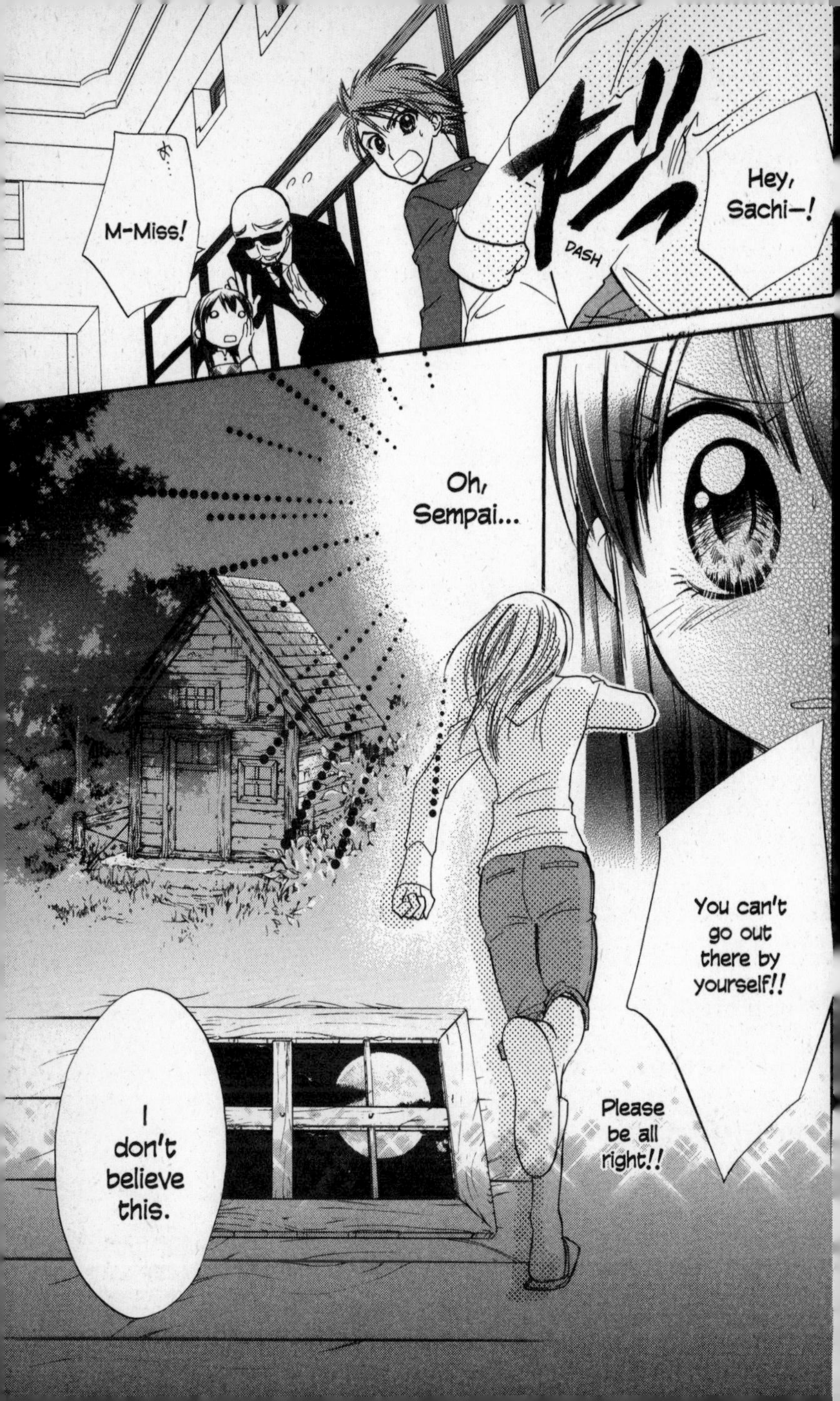
Hey, Sachi—!
DASH
M-Miss!
You can't go out there by yourself!!
Oh, Sempai...
Please be all right!!
I don't believe this.

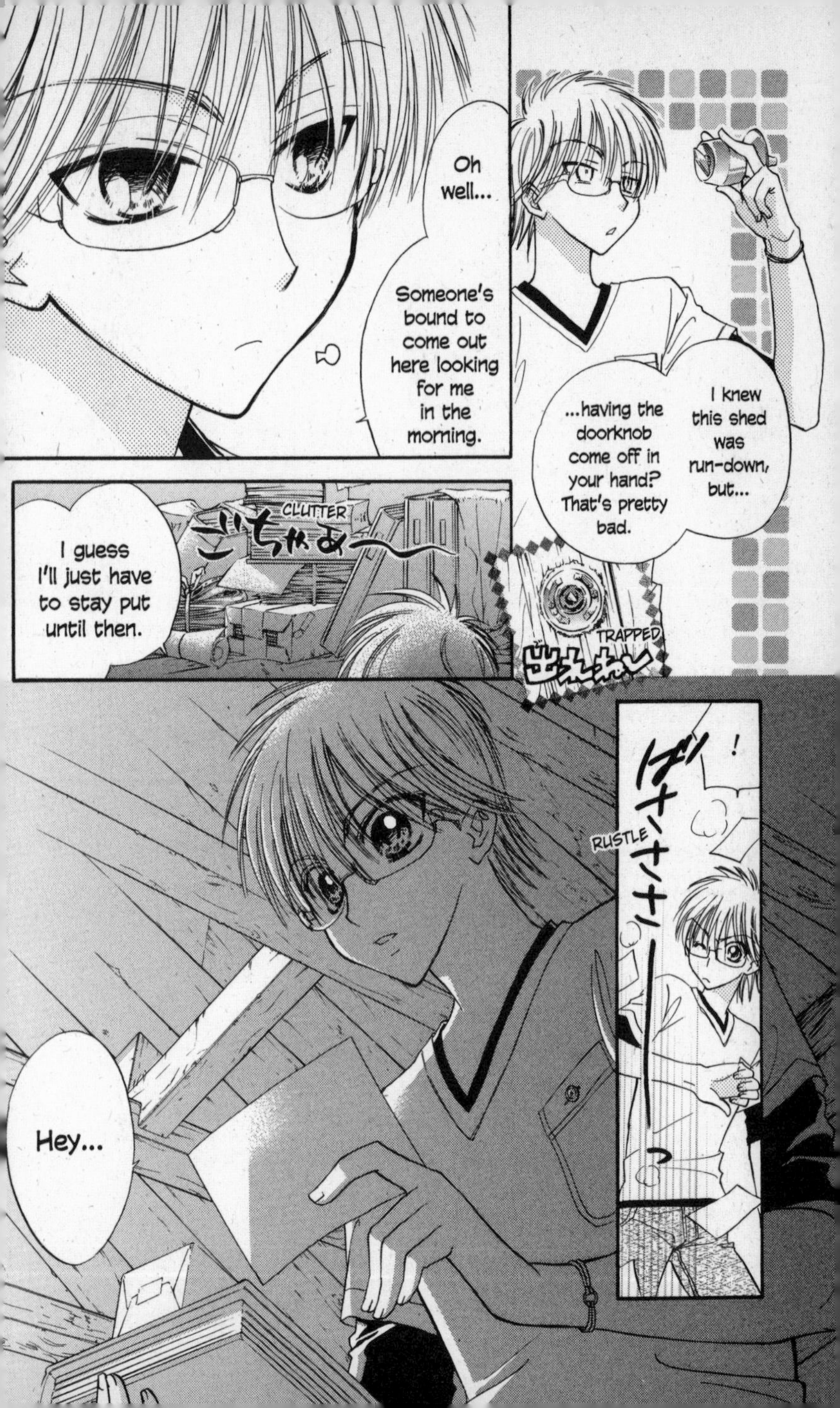
I knew this shed was run-down, but...
...having the doorknob come off in your hand? That's pretty bad.
TRAPPED
Oh well...
Someone's bound to come out here looking for me in the morning.
CLUTTER
I guess I'll just have to stay put until then.
!
RUSTLE
Hey...

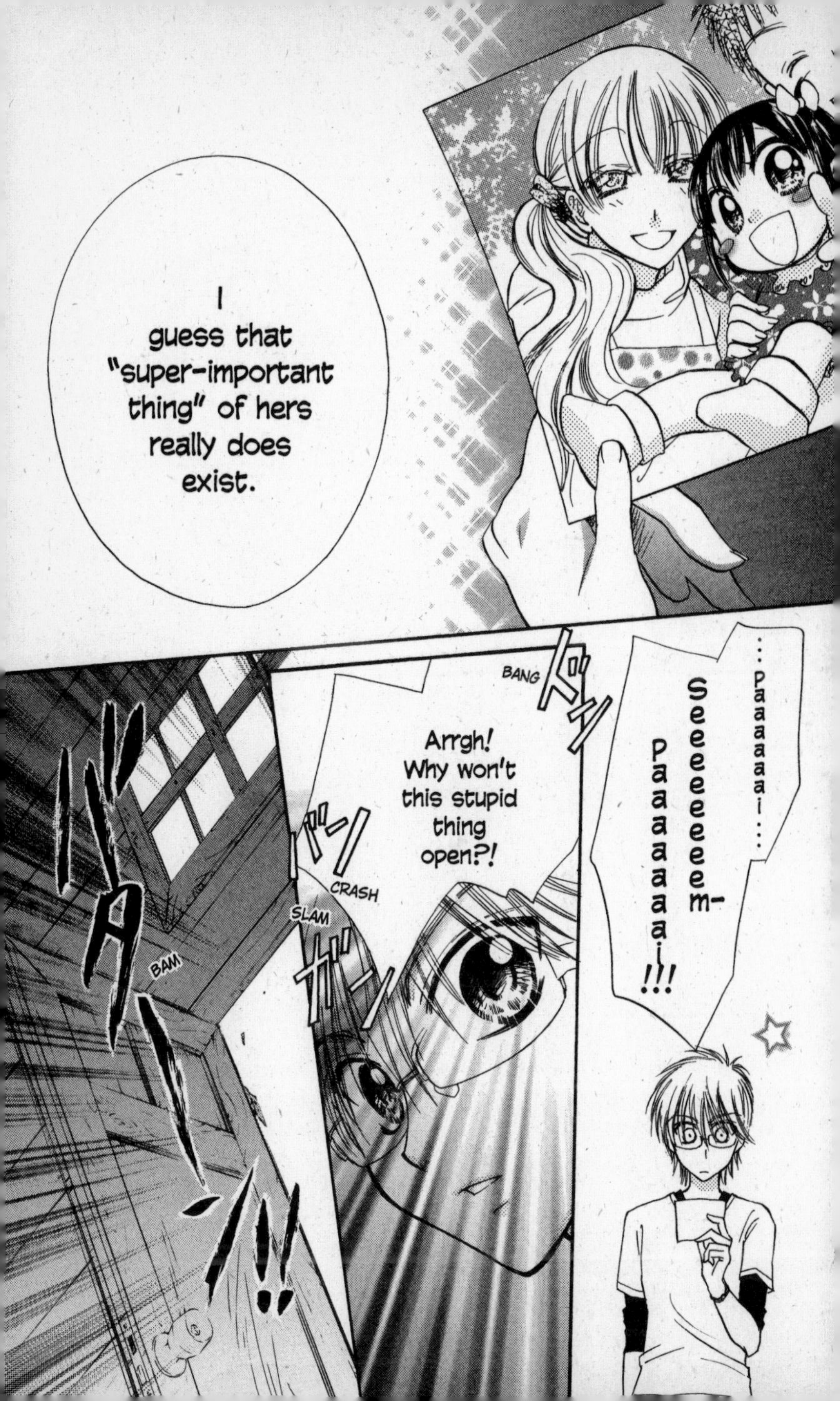
I guess that "super-important thing" of hers really does exist.
...Paaaaaai...
Seeeeeeem-Paaaaaaai!!!
BANG
Arrgh! Why won't this stupid thing open?!
CRASH
SLAM
BAM

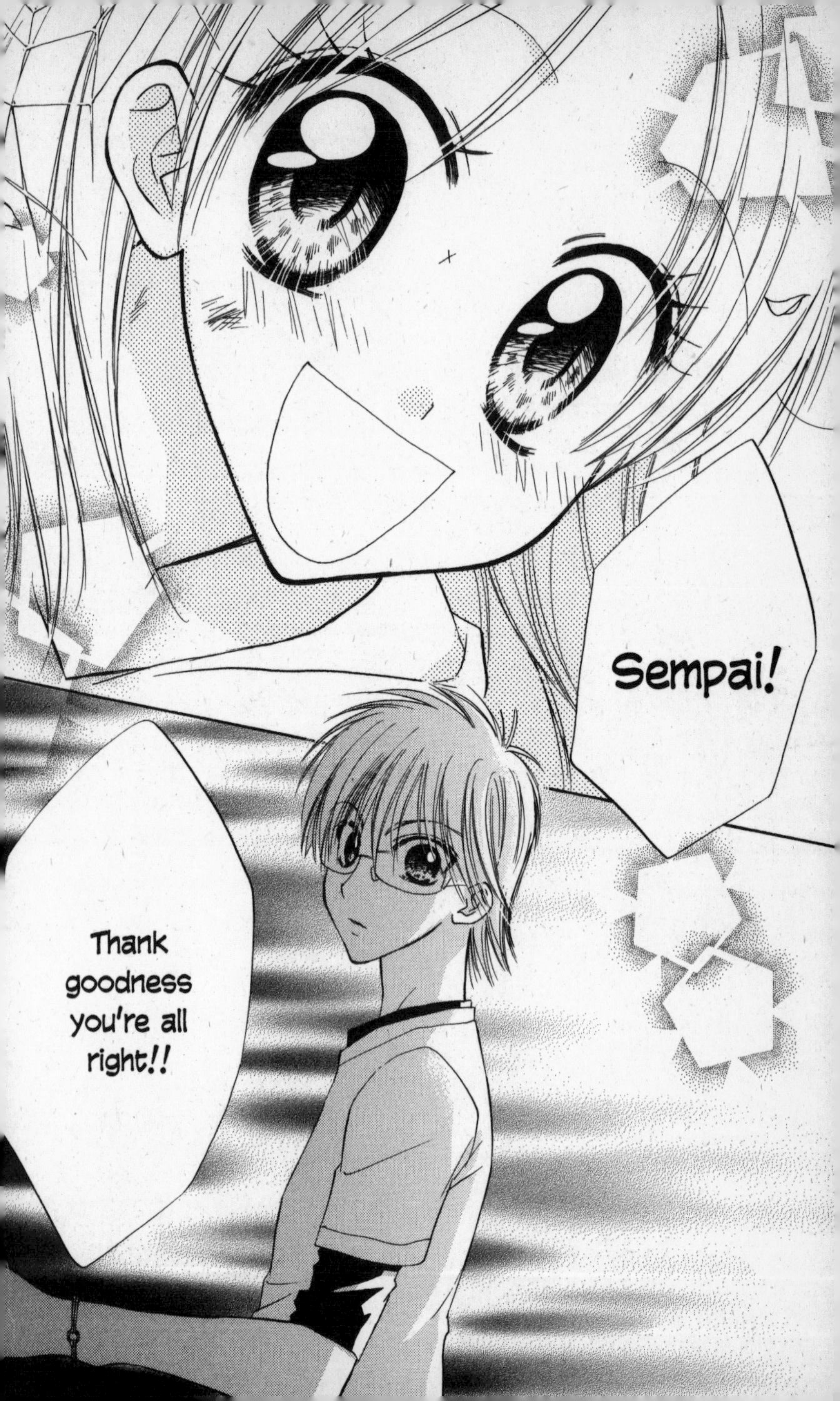
Sempai!
Thank goodness you're all right!!

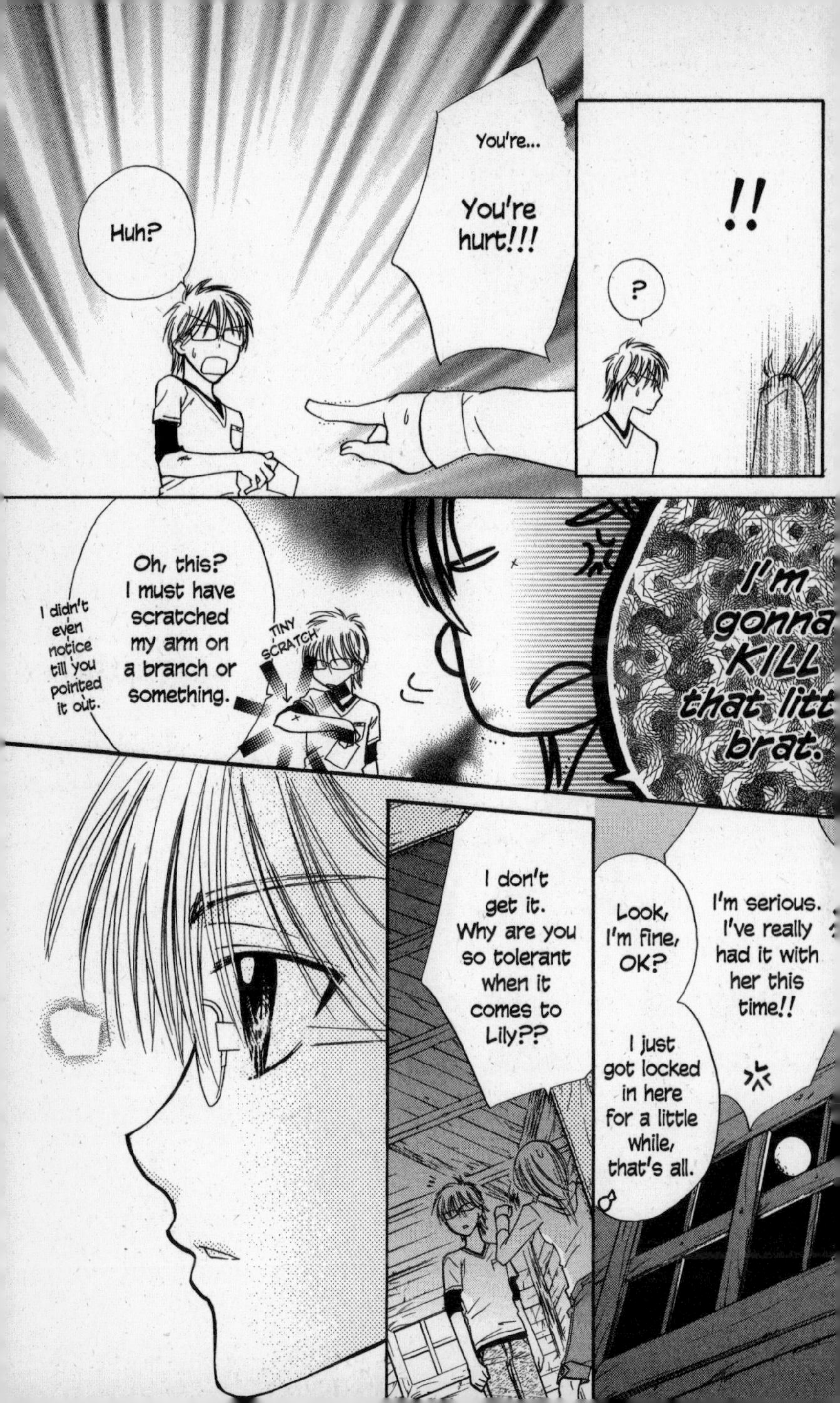
!!
?
You're...
You're hurt!!!
Huh?
I'm gonna KILL that litt brat.
Oh, this? I must have scratched my arm on a branch or something.
TINY SCRATCH
I didn't even notice till you pointed it out.
I'm serious. I've really had it with her this time!!
Look, I'm fine, OK?
I just got locked in here for a little while, that's all.
I don't get it. Why are you so tolerant when it comes to Lily??

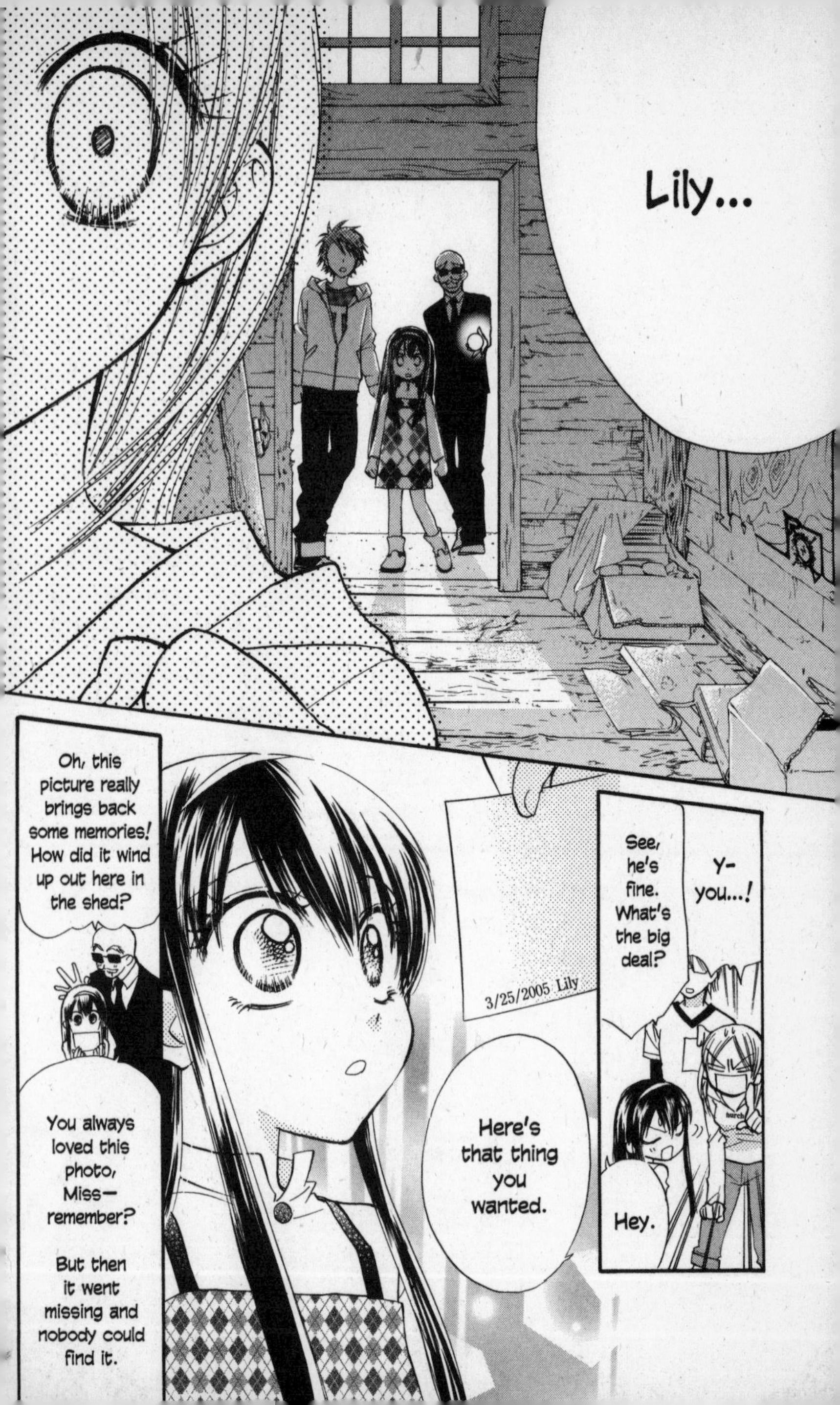
Lily...
Y-
you...!
See, he's fine. What's the big deal?
Hey.
3/25/2005 Lily
Here's that thing you wanted.
Oh, this picture really brings back some memories! How did it wind up out here in the shed?
You always loved this photo, Miss—remember?
But then it went missing and nobody could find it.

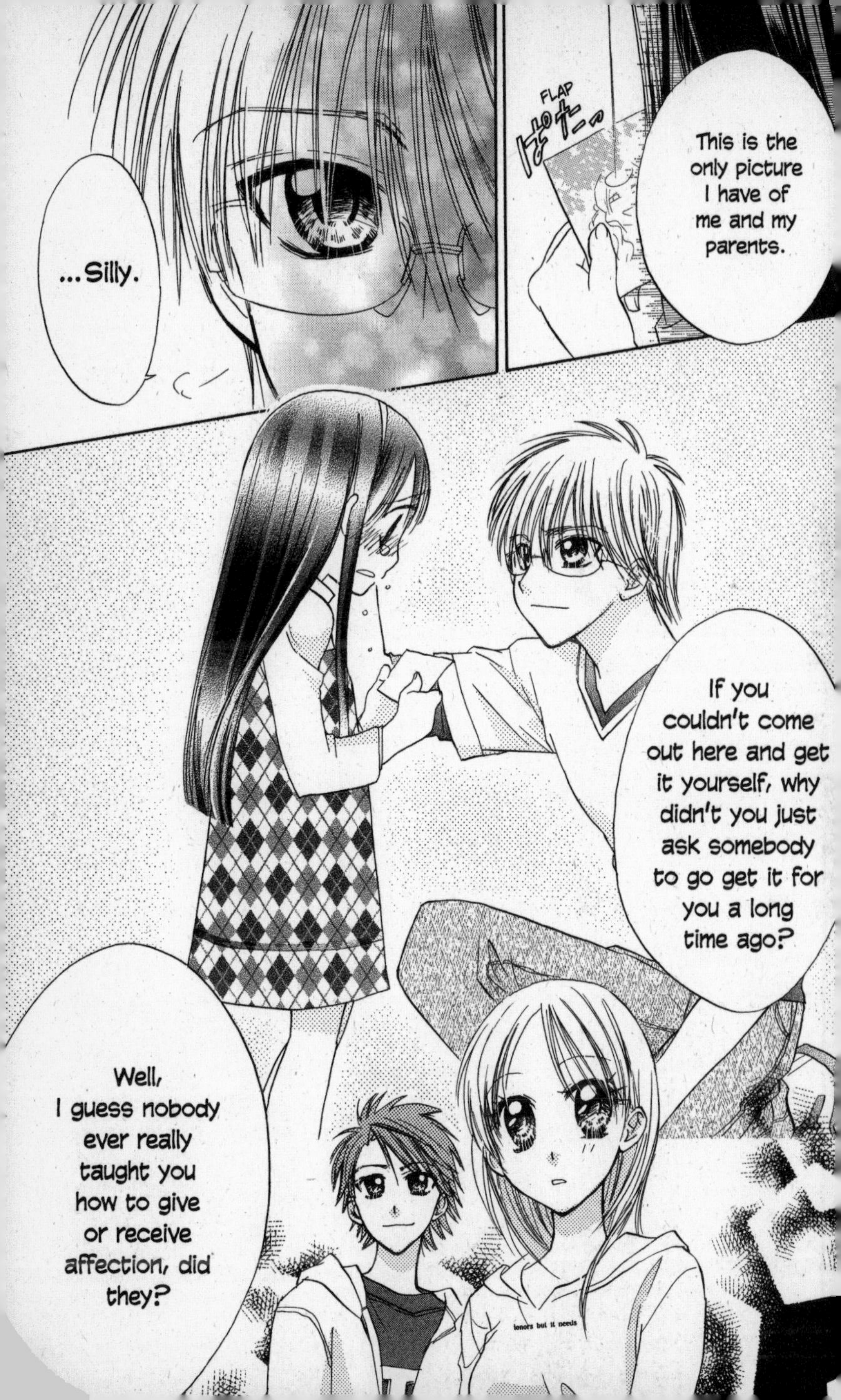
FLAP
This is the only picture I have of me and my parents.
...Silly.
If you couldn't come out here and get it yourself, why didn't you just ask somebody to go get it for you a long time ago?
Well, I guess nobody ever really taught you how to give or receive affection, did they?

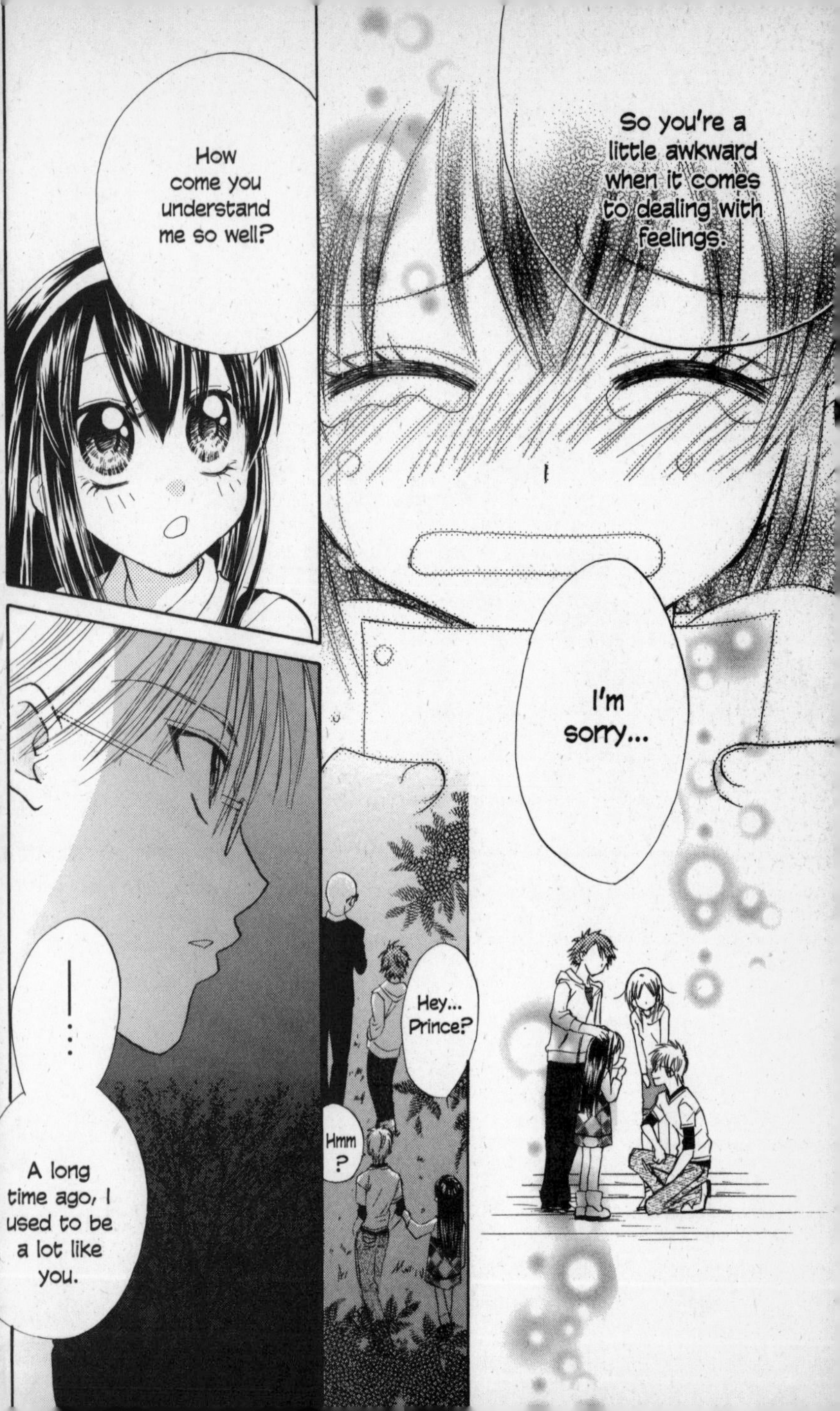

So you're a little awkward when it comes to dealing with feelings.
I'm sorry...
Hey... Prince?
Hmm ?
How come you understand me so well?
—...
A long time ago, I used to be a lot like you.

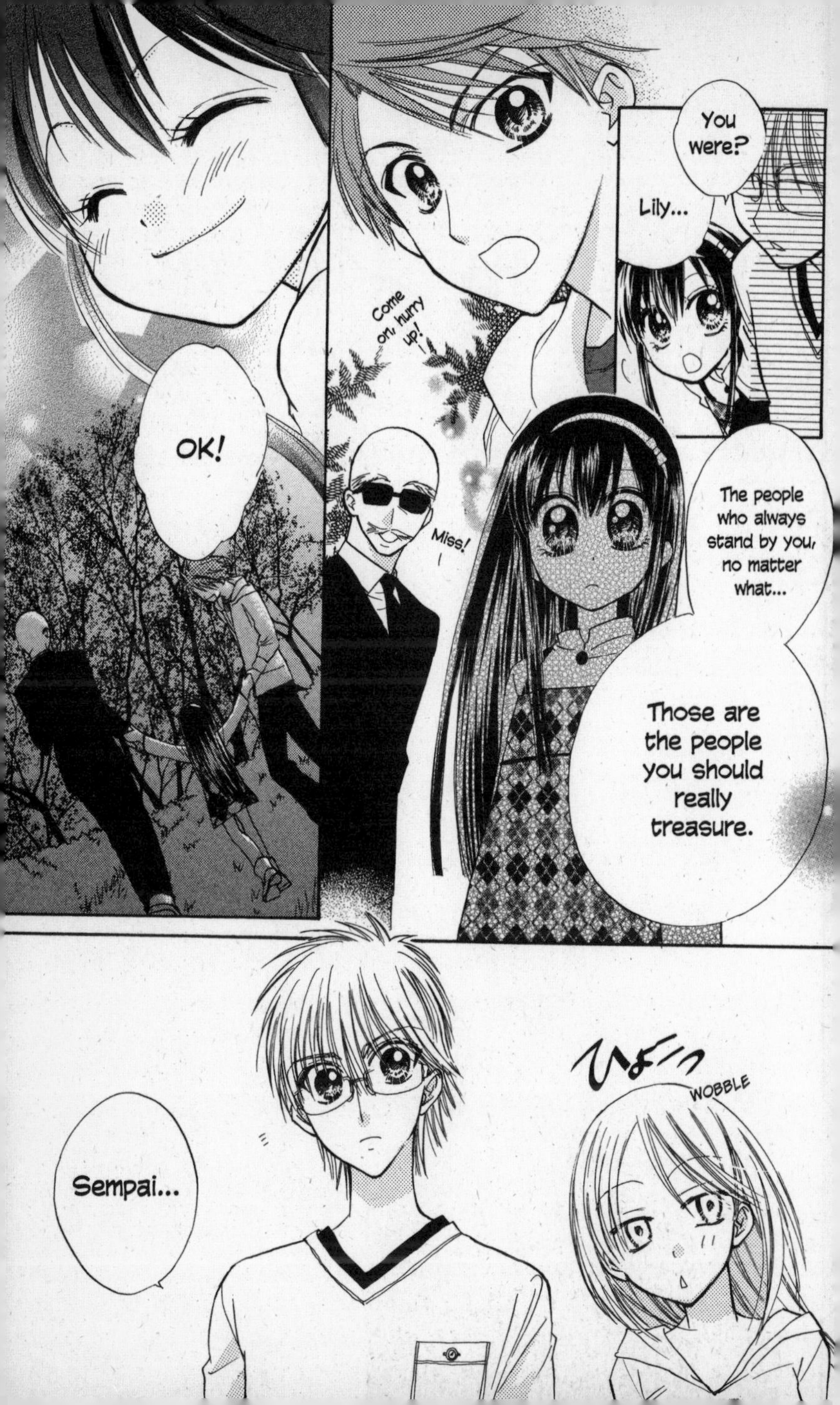
You were?
Lily...
The people who always stand by you, no matter what...
Those are the people you should really treasure.
Come on, hurry up!
Miss!
OK!
ひょーっ
WOBBLE
Sempai...

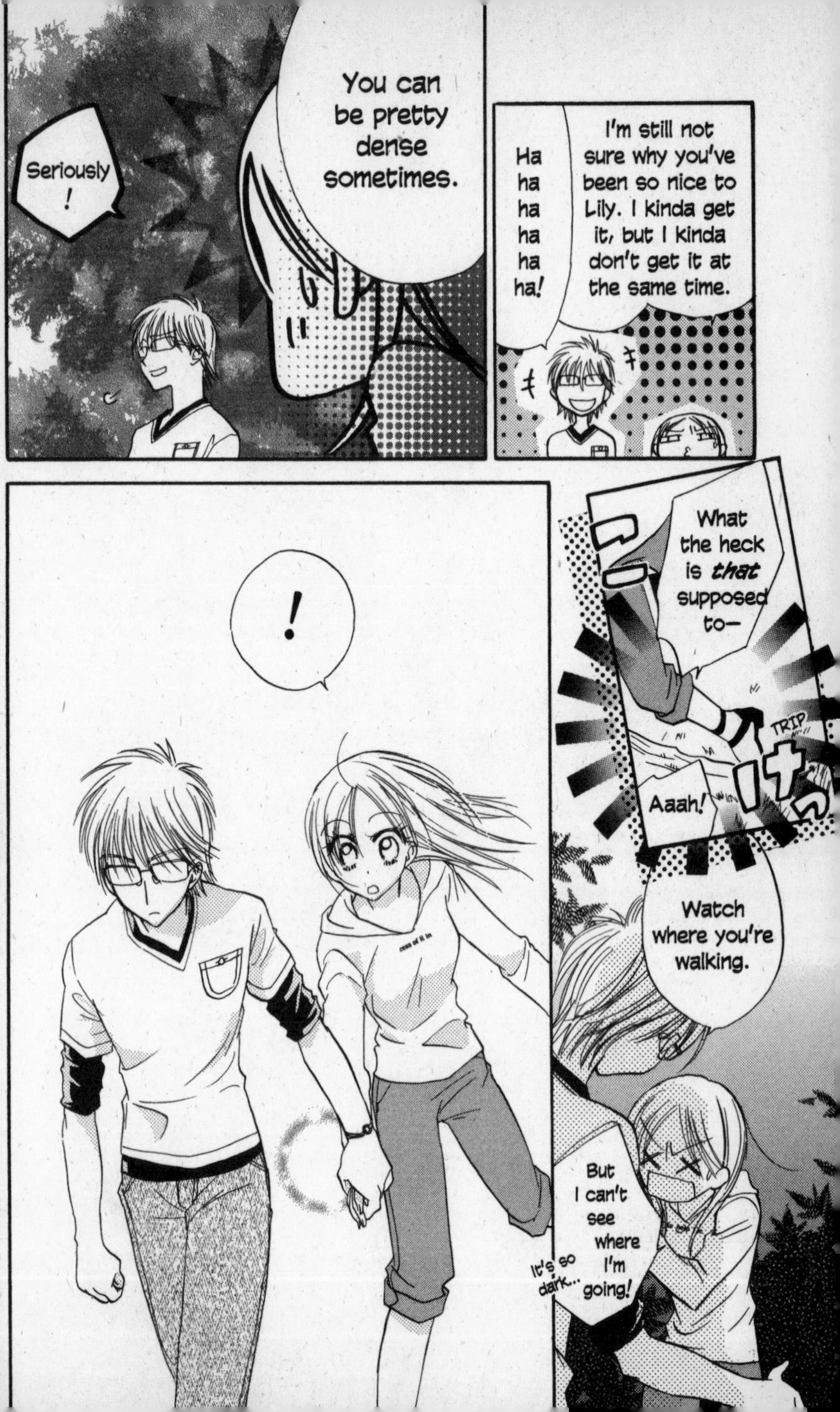

I'm still not sure why you've been so nice to Lily. I kinda get it, but I kinda don't get it at the same time.
Ha ha ha ha ha ha!
You can be pretty dense sometimes.
Seriously!
What the heck is *that* supposed to—
TRIP
Aaah!
Watch where you're walking.
But I can't see where I'm going!
It's so dark...
!

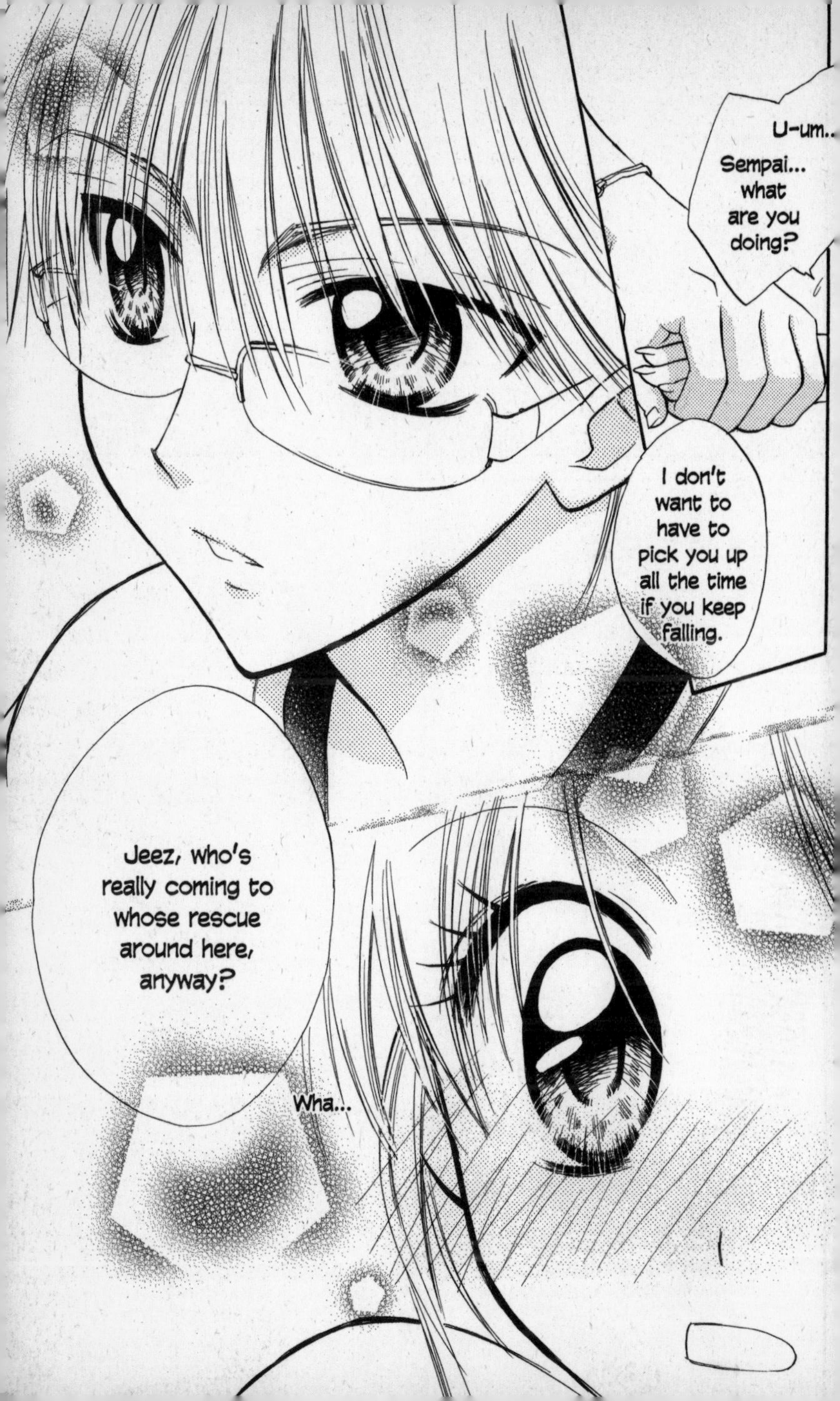
U-um..
Sempai... what are you doing?
I don't want to have to pick you up all the time if you keep falling.
Jeez, who's really coming to whose rescue around here, anyway?
Wha...

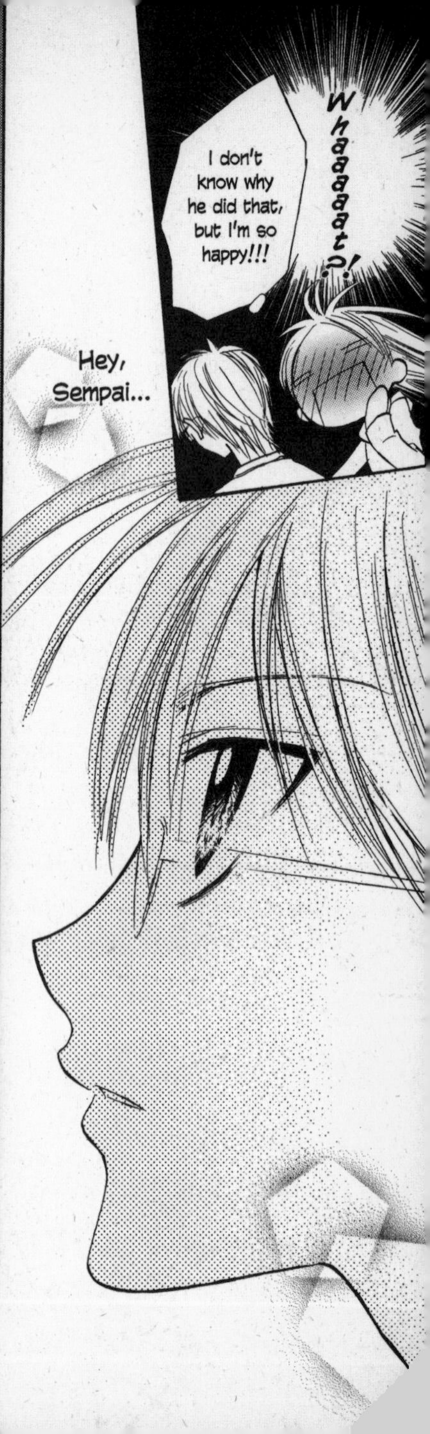
Whaaaaat?!
I don't know why he did that, but I'm so happy!!!
Hey, Sempai...
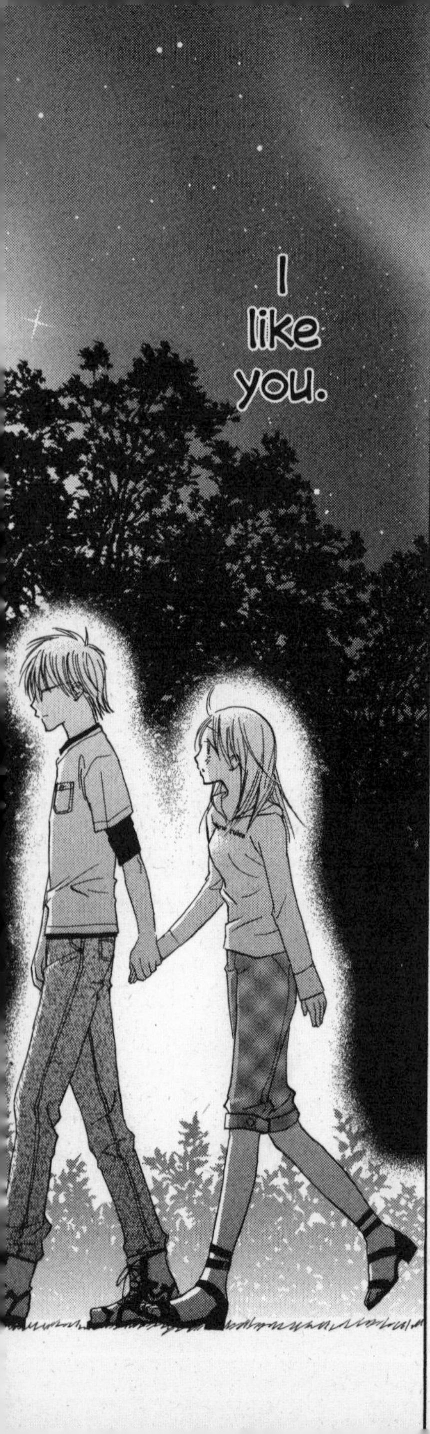
I like you.

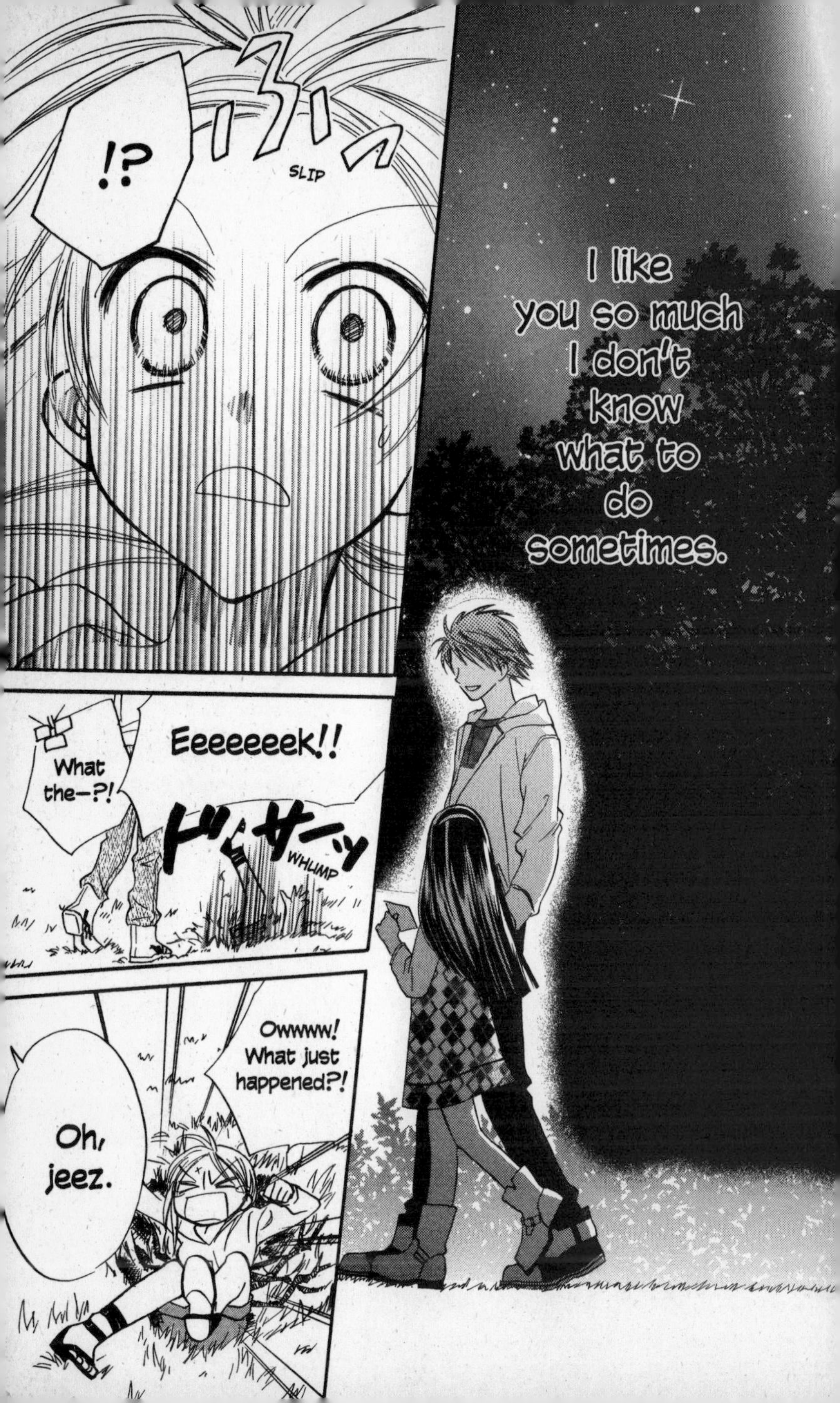
I like you so much I don't know what to do sometimes.
!?
SLIP
Eeeeeeek!!
What the–?!
WHUMP
Owwww! What just happened?!
Oh, jeez.

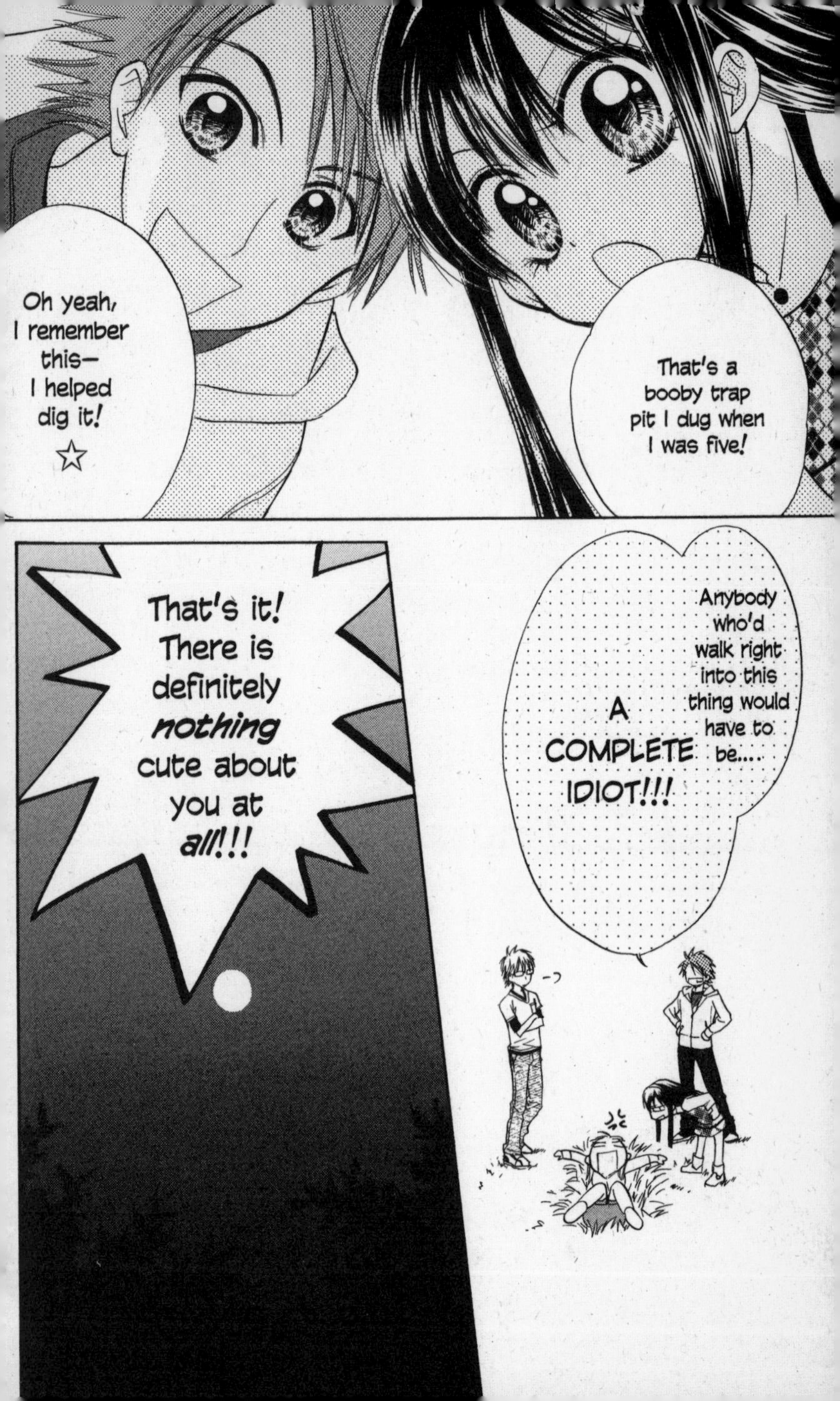
That's a booby trap pit I dug when I was five!
Oh yeah, I remember this— I helped dig it! ☆
Anybody who'd walk right into this thing would have to be....
A COMPLETE IDIOT!!!
That's it! There is definitely *nothing* cute about you at *all*!!!

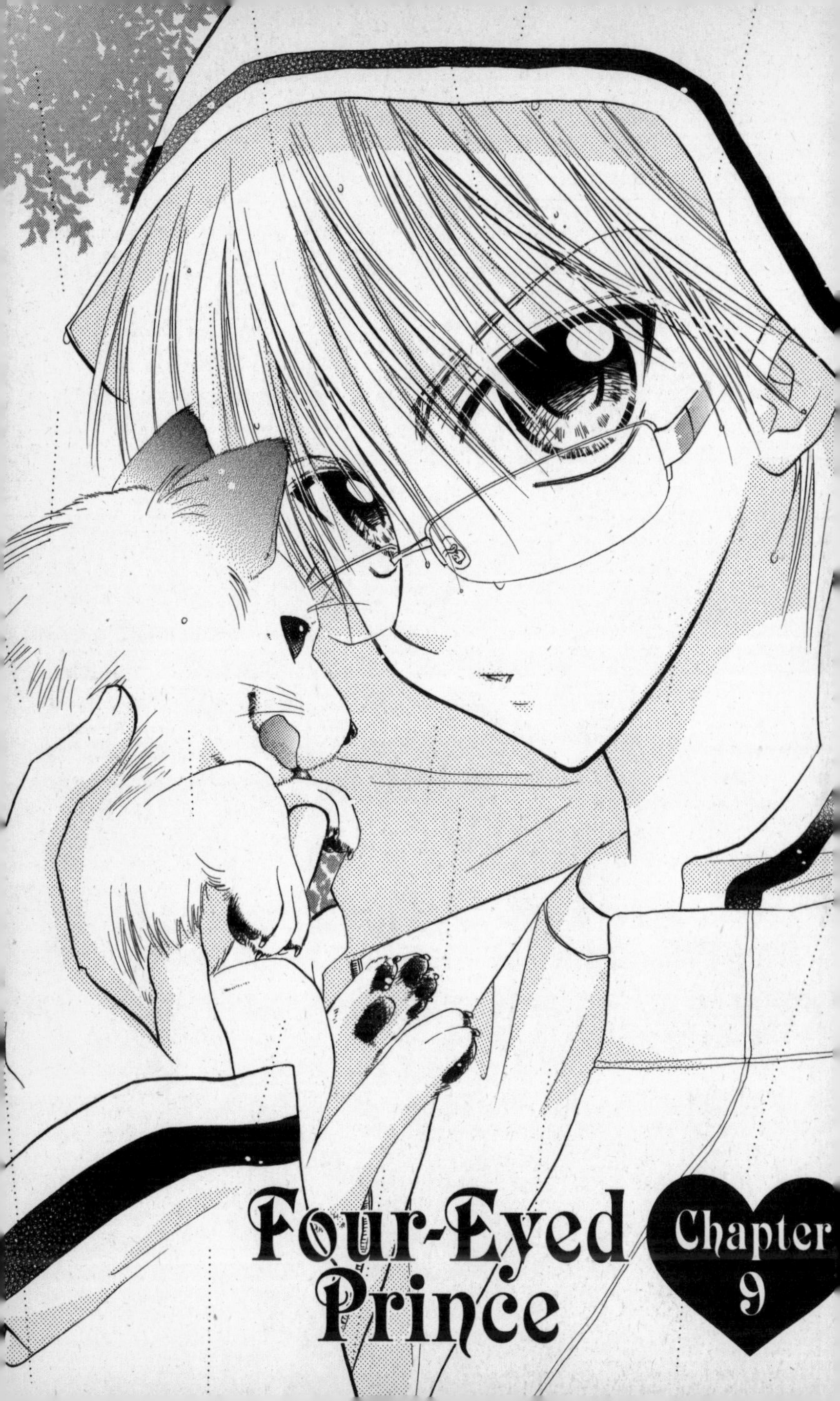
Four-Eyed Prince
Chapter 9

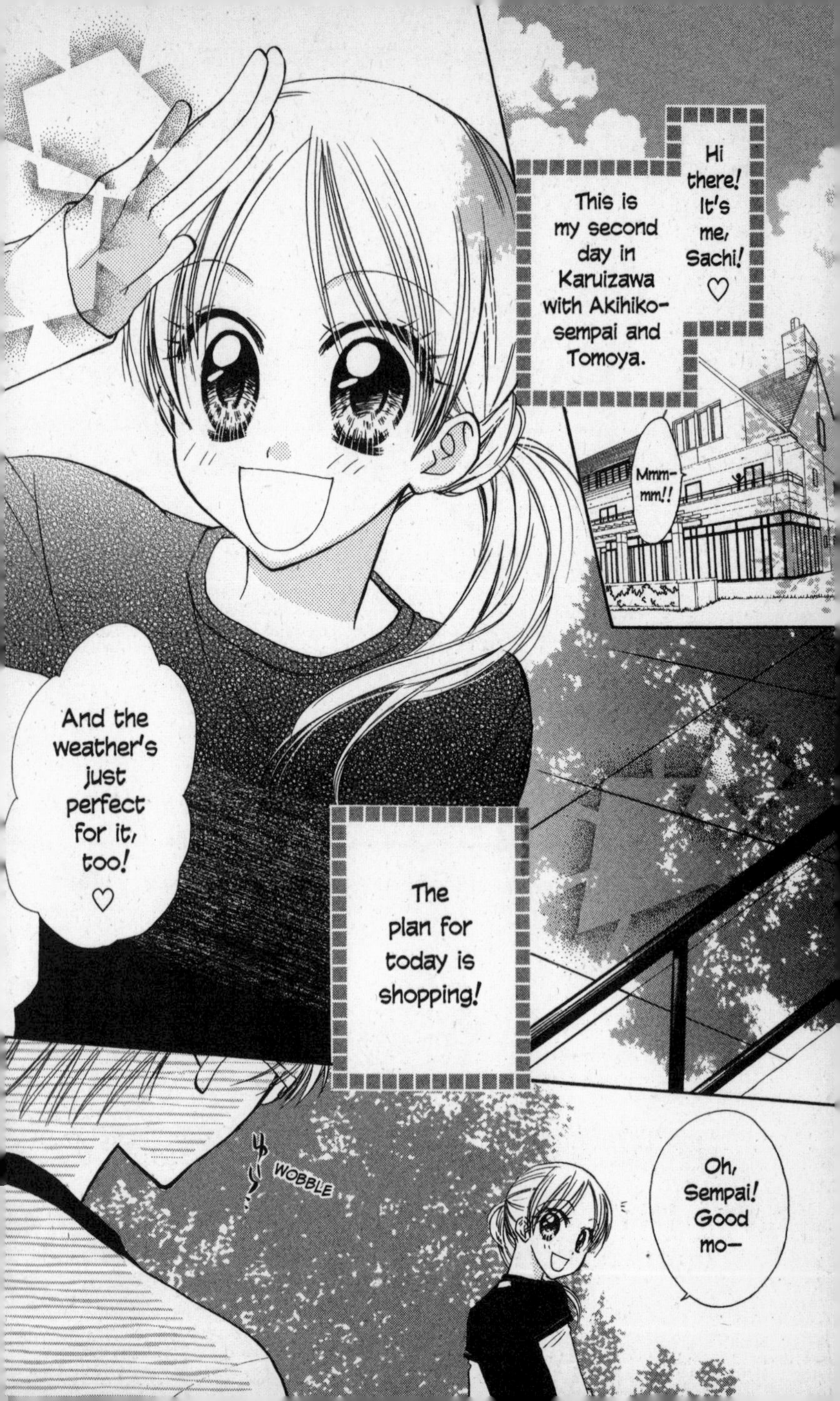

Hi there! It's me, Sachi! ♡
This is my second day in Karuizawa with Akihiko-sempai and Tomoya.
Mmm-mm!!
And the weather's just perfect for it, too! ♡
The plan for today is shopping!
Oh, Sempai! Good mo—
WOBBLE

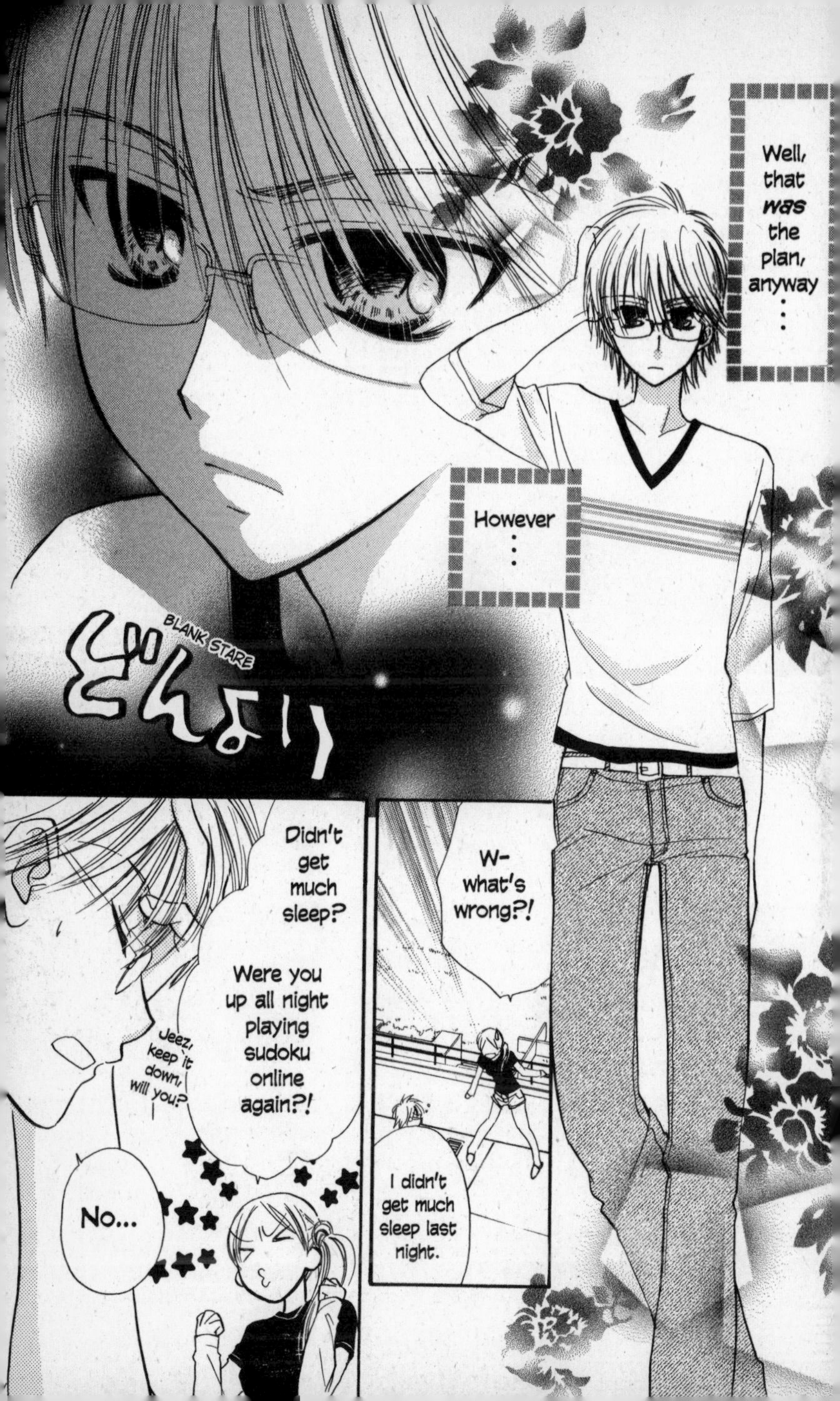

Well, that *was* the plan, anyway...
However...
BLANK STARE
どんより
W-what's wrong?!
I didn't get much sleep last night.
Didn't get much sleep?
Were you up all night playing sudoku online again?!
Jeez, keep it down, will you?
No...

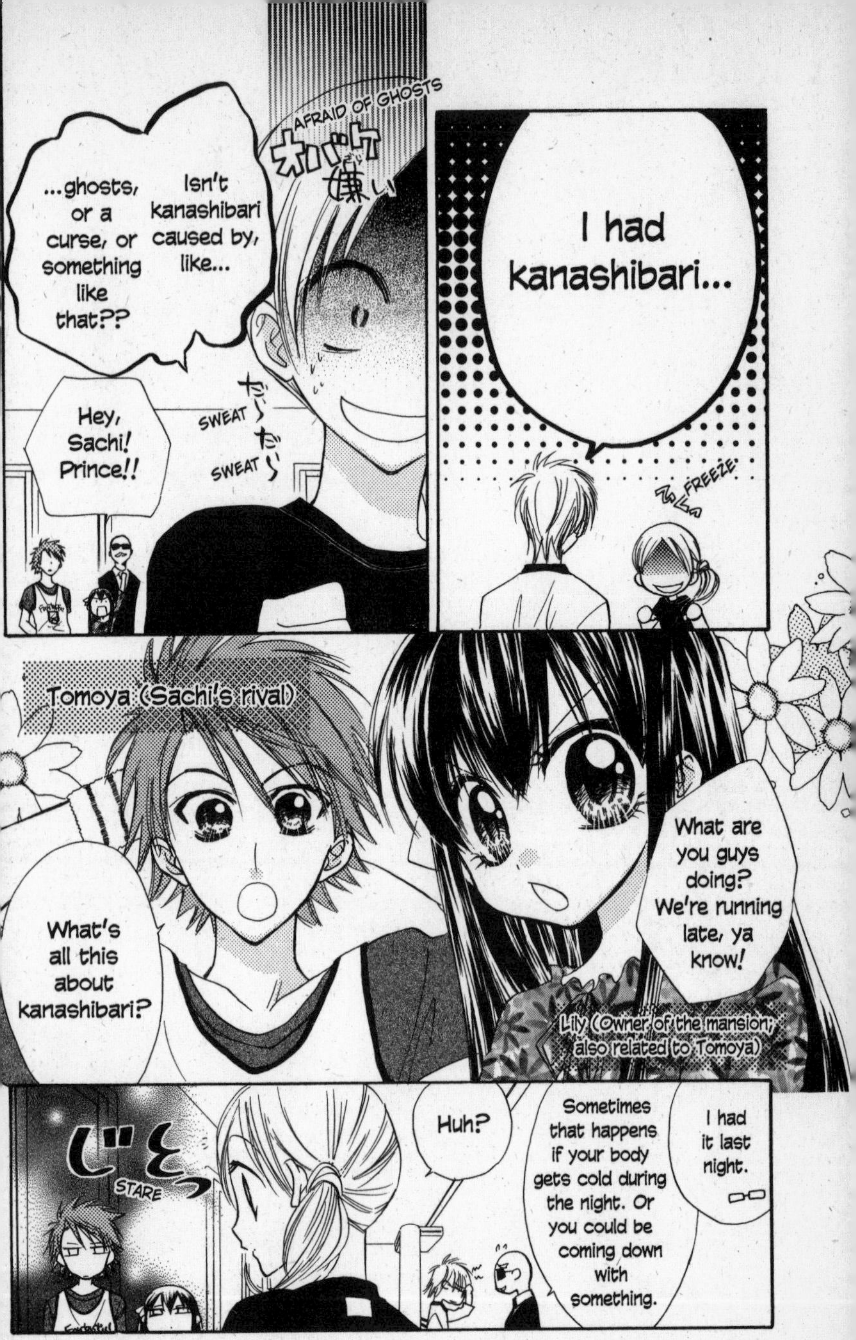
I had kanashibari...
FREEZE
AFRAID OF GHOSTS
Isn't kanashibari caused by, like...
...ghosts, or a curse, or something like that??
SWEAT
SWEAT
Hey, Sachi! Prince!!
What are you guys doing? We're running late, ya know!
Lily (Owner of the mansion; also related to Tomoya)
Tomoya (Sachi's rival)
What's all this about kanashibari?
I had it last night.
Sometimes that happens if your body gets cold during the night. Or you could be coming down with something.
Huh?
STARE

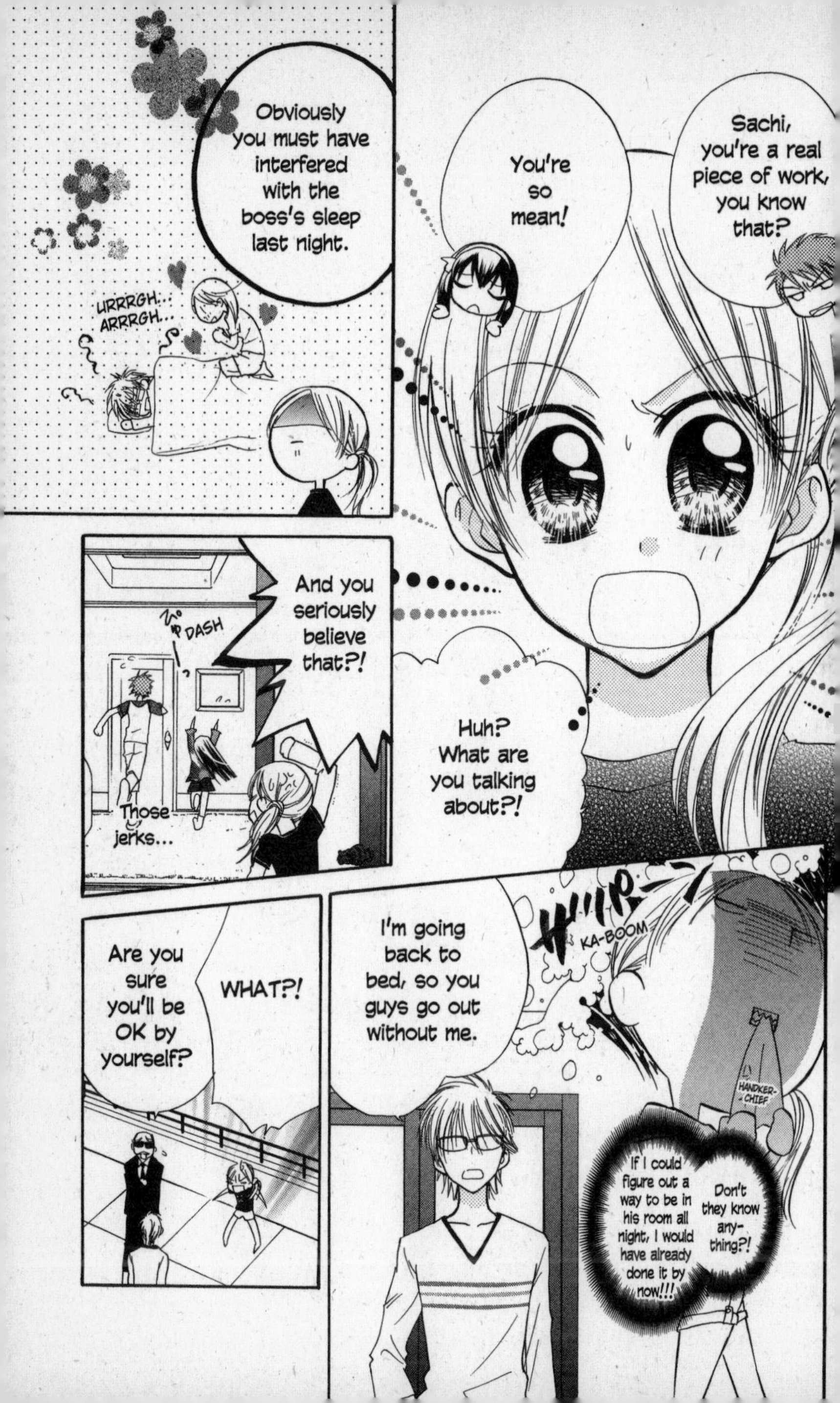
Sachi, you're a real piece of work, you know that?
You're so mean!
Huh? What are you talking about?!
Obviously you must have interfered with the boss's sleep last night.
URRRGH... ARRRGH...
And you seriously believe that?!
DASH
Those jerks...
HWIP
KA-BOOM
HANDKER-CHIEF
Don't they know any-thing?!
If I could figure out a way to be in his room all night, I would have already done it by now!!!
I'm going back to bed, so you guys go out without me.
WHAT?!
Are you sure you'll be OK by yourself?

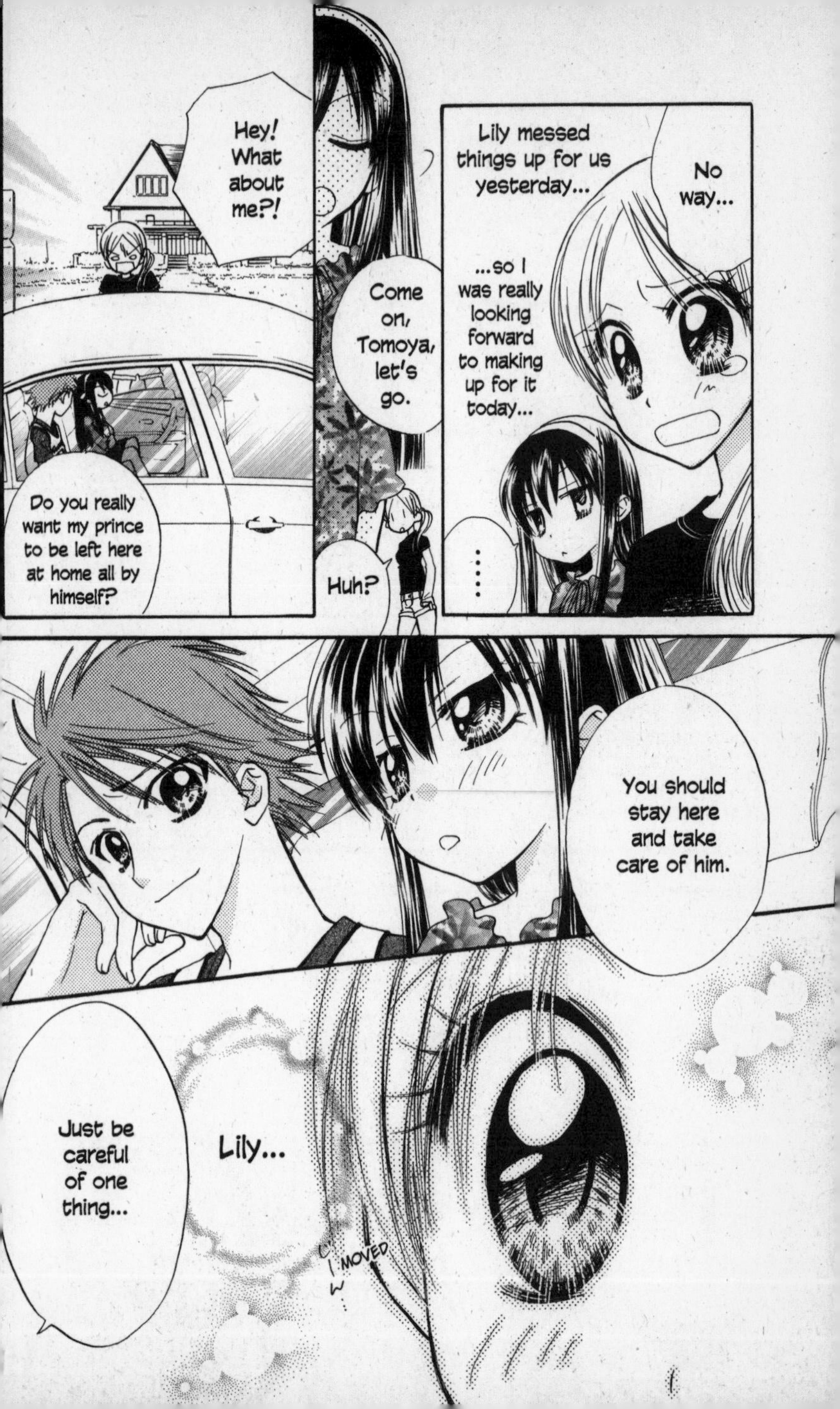
No way...
Lily messed things up for us yesterday...
...so I was really looking forward to making up for it today...
.....
Come on, Tomoya, let's go.
Huh?
Hey! What about me?!
Do you really want my prince to be left here at home all by himself?
You should stay here and take care of him.
Lily...
Just be careful of one thing...
MOVED

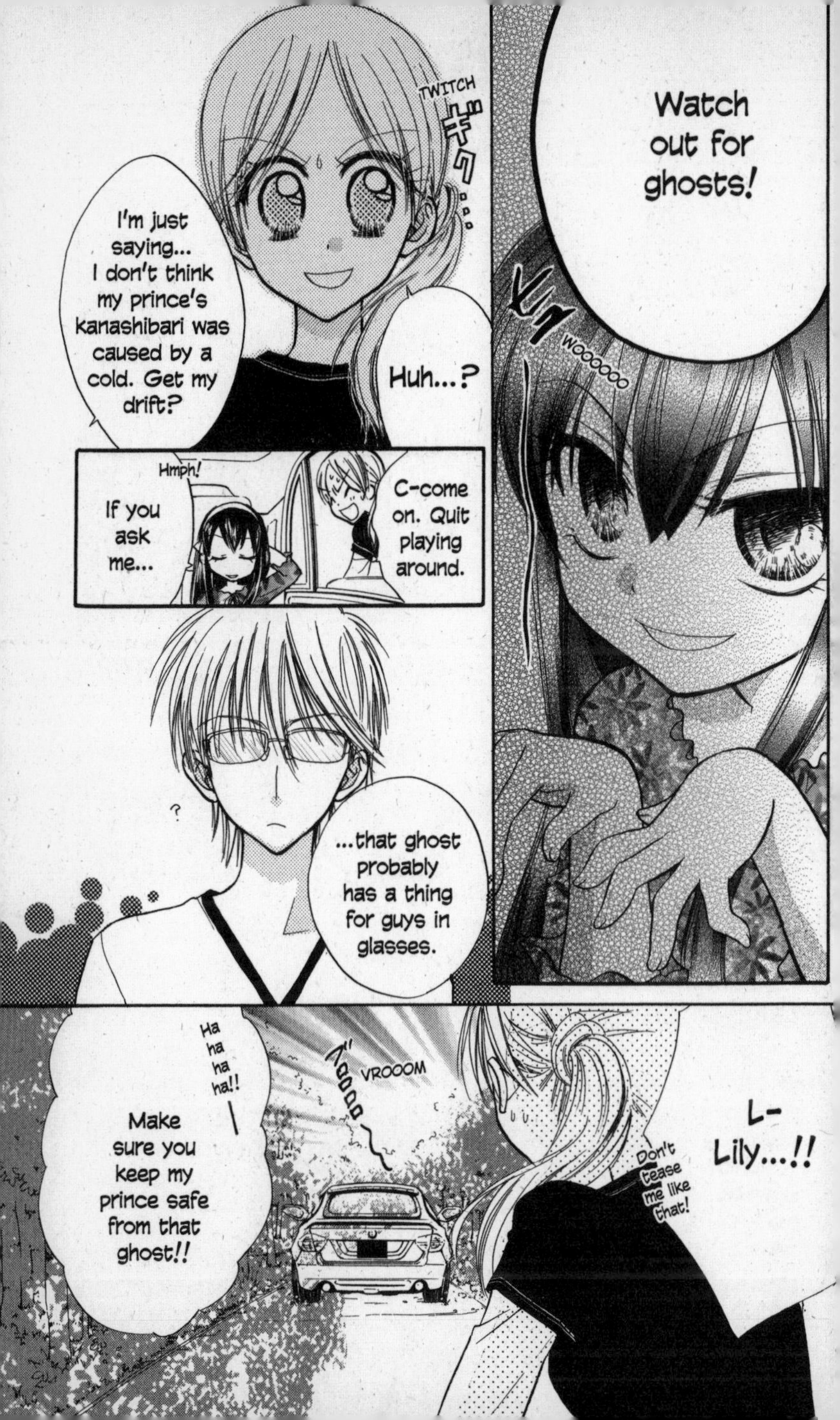
Watch out for ghosts!
WOOOOOO
TWITCH
I'm just saying... I don't think my prince's kanashibari was caused by a cold. Get my drift?
Huh...?
C-come on. Quit playing around.
Hmph!
If you ask me...
...that ghost probably has a thing for guys in glasses.
L- Lily...!!
Don't tease me like that!
VROOOM
Ha ha ha ha!!
Make sure you keep my prince safe from that ghost!!

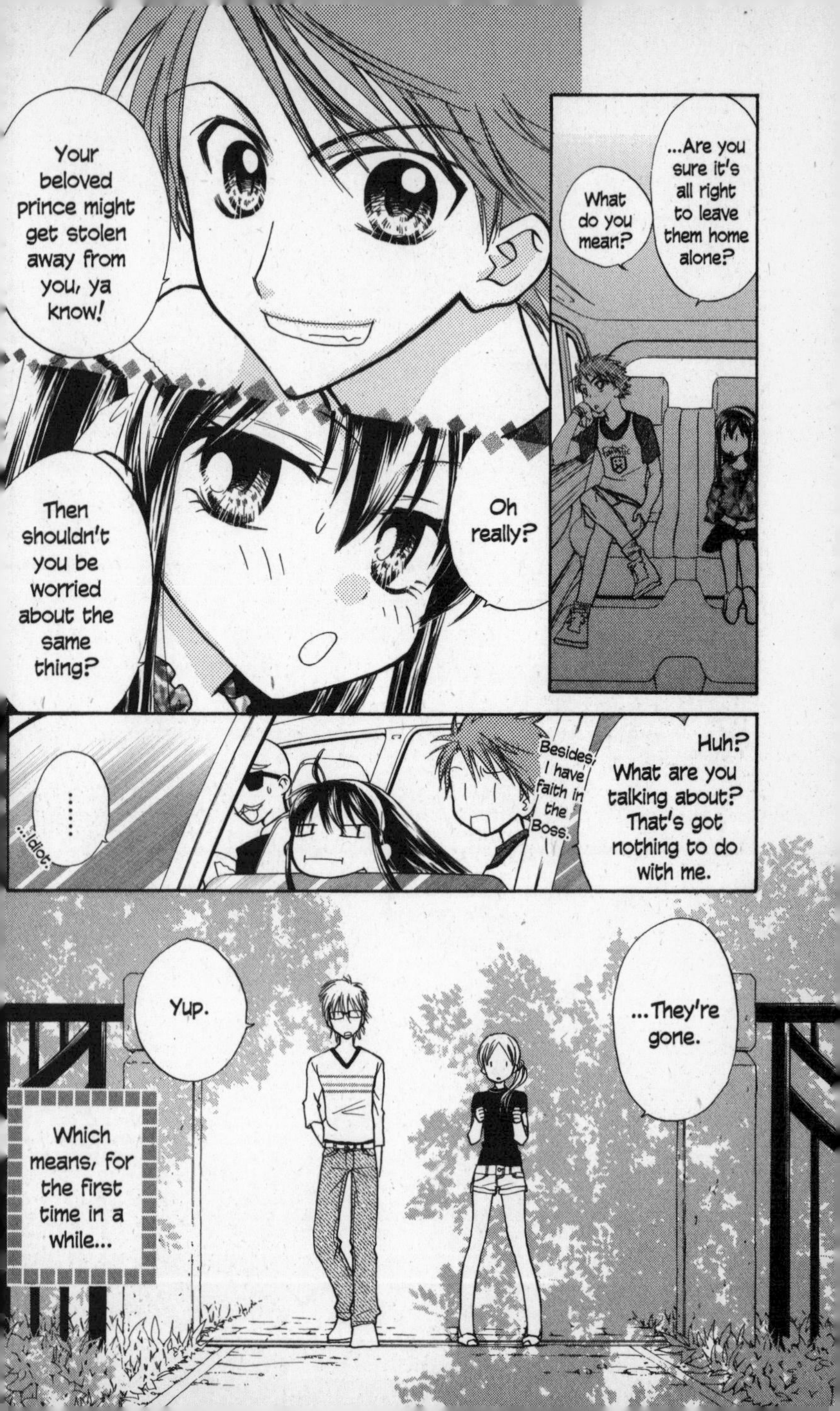
...Are you sure it's all right to leave them home alone?
What do you mean?
Your beloved prince might get stolen away from you, ya know!
Oh really?
Then shouldn't you be worried about the same thing?
Huh? What are you talking about? That's got nothing to do with me.
Besides, I have faith in the Boss.
......
...idiot.
...They're gone.
Yup.
Which means, for the first time in a while...

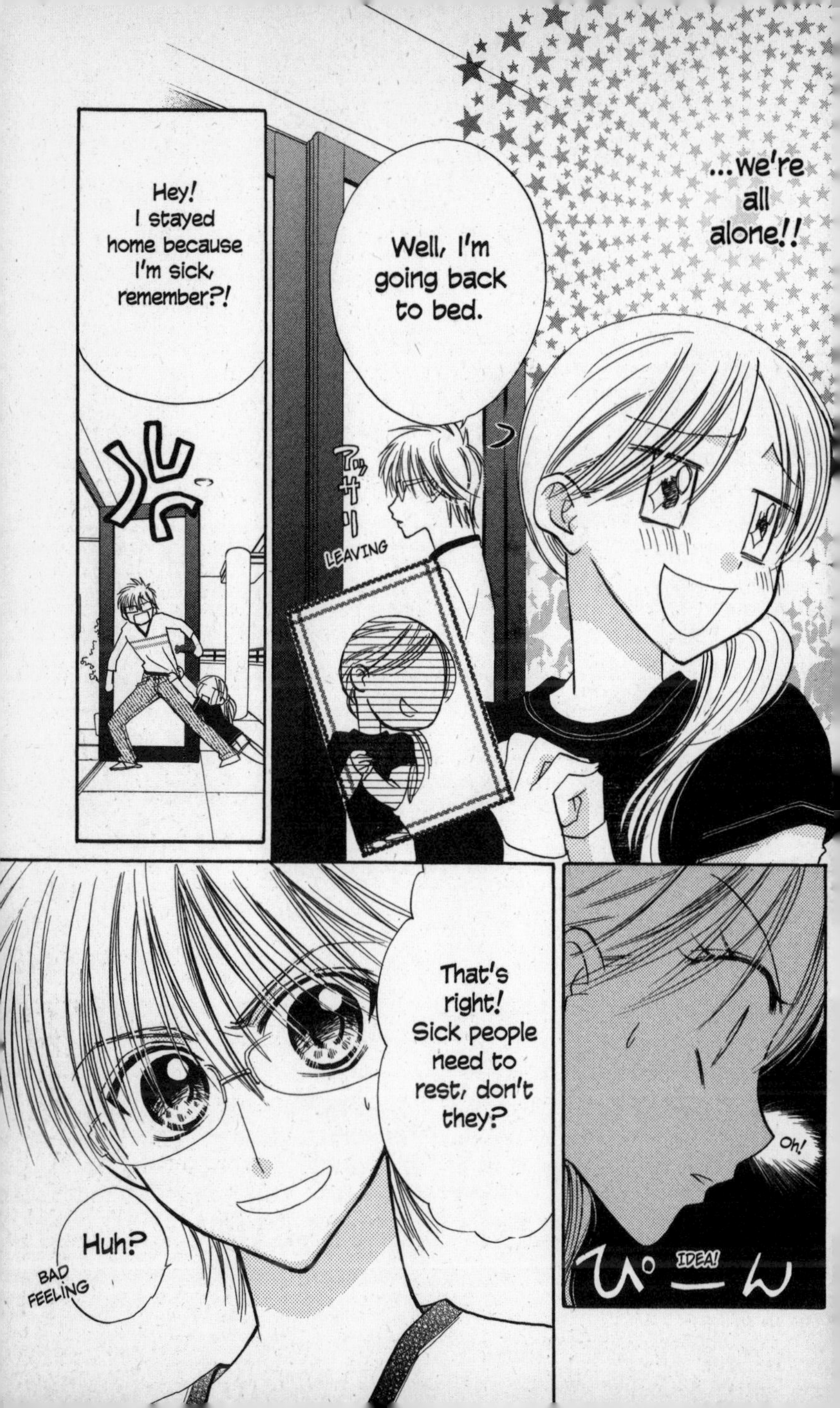
...we're all alone!!
Well, I'm going back to bed.
LEAVING
Hey! I stayed home because I'm sick, remember?!
Oh!
IDEA!
That's right! Sick people need to rest, don't they?
Huh?
BAD FEELING

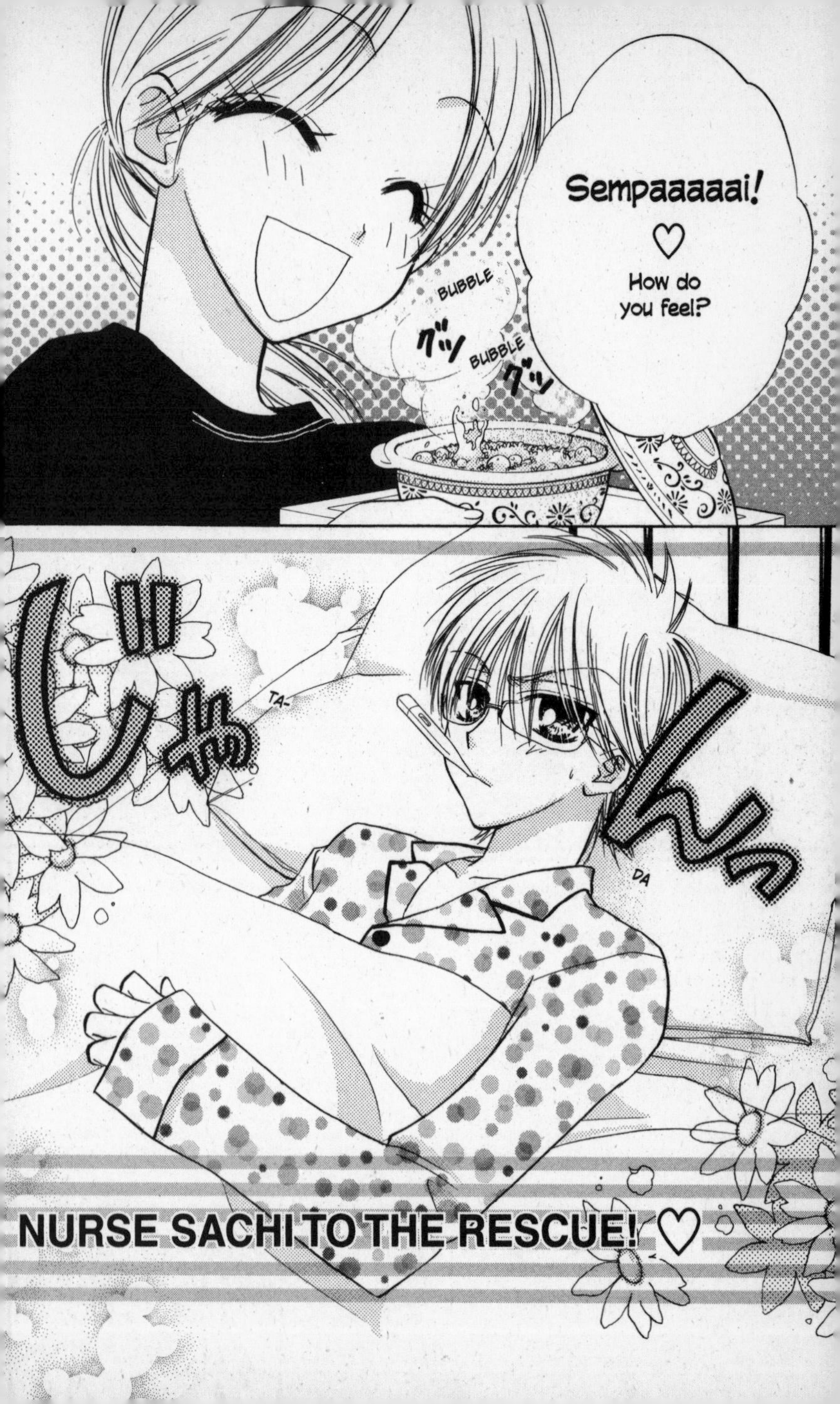
Sempaaaaaai!
♡
How do you feel?
BUBBLE
グツ
BUBBLE
グツ
じ
TA-
ん
DA
NURSE SACHI TO THE RESCUE! ♡

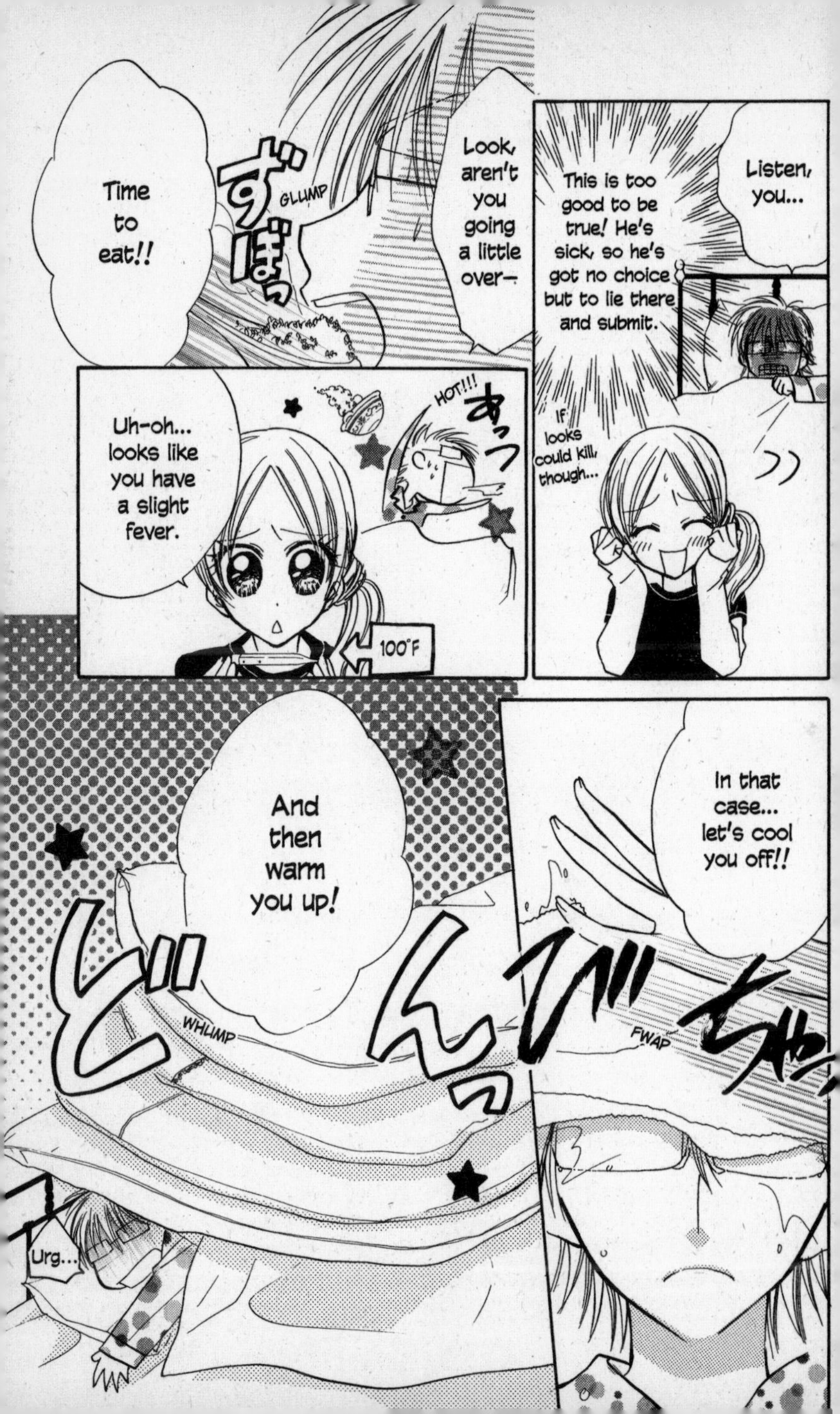

Listen, you...
This is too good to be true! He's sick, so he's got no choice but to lie there and submit.
If looks could kill, though...
Time to eat!!
ずぼっ
GLUMP
Look, aren't you going a little over—
Uh-oh... looks like you have a slight fever.
あっつ
HOT!!!
100°F
In that case... let's cool you off!!
FWAP
And then warm you up!
どんっ
WHUMP
Urg...

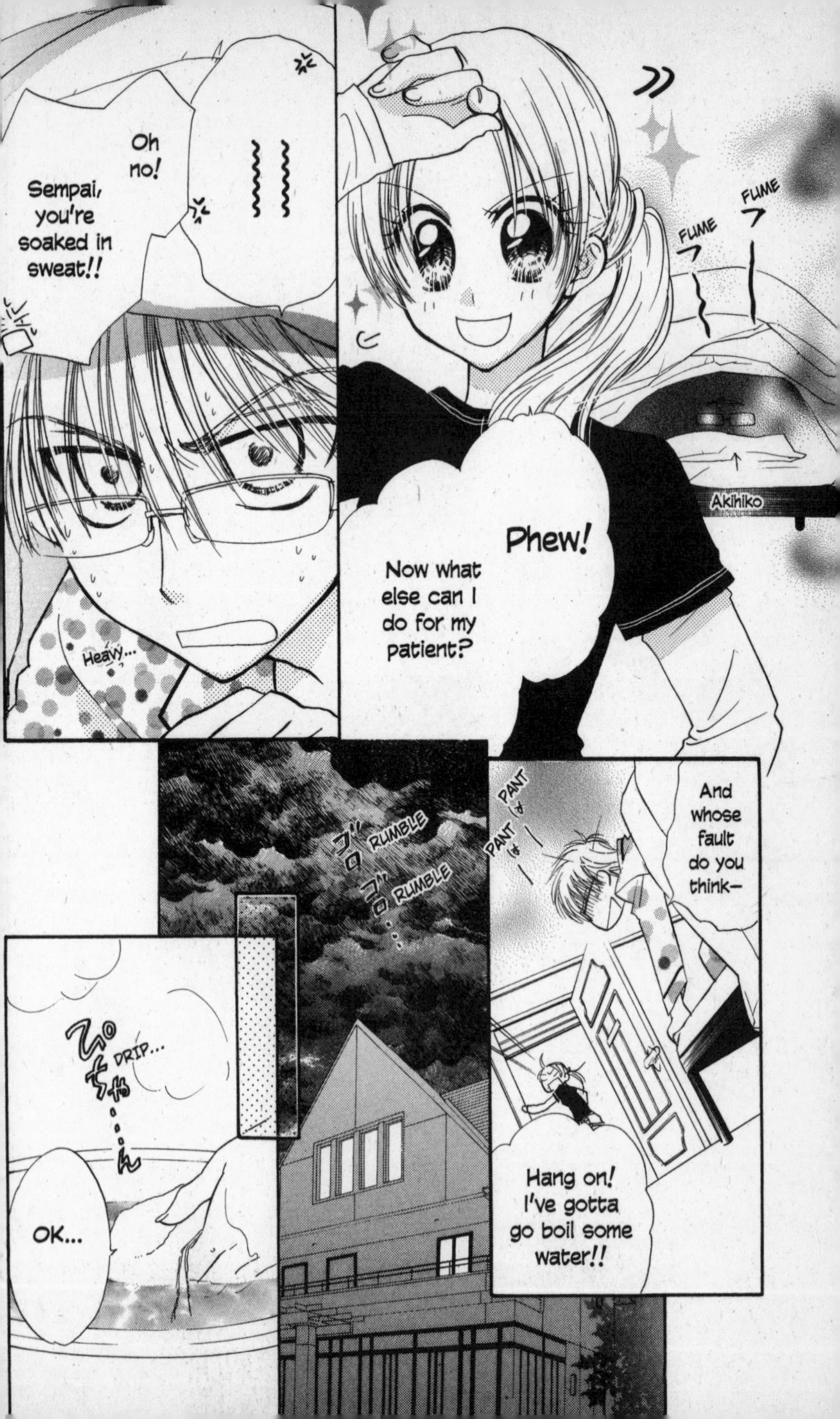
FUME
FUME
Akihiko
Phew!
Now what else can I do for my patient?
Oh no!
Sempai, you're soaked in sweat!!
Heavy...
PANT
PANT
And whose fault do you think—
Hang on! I've gotta go boil some water!!
RUMBLE
RUMBLE
DRIP...
OK...

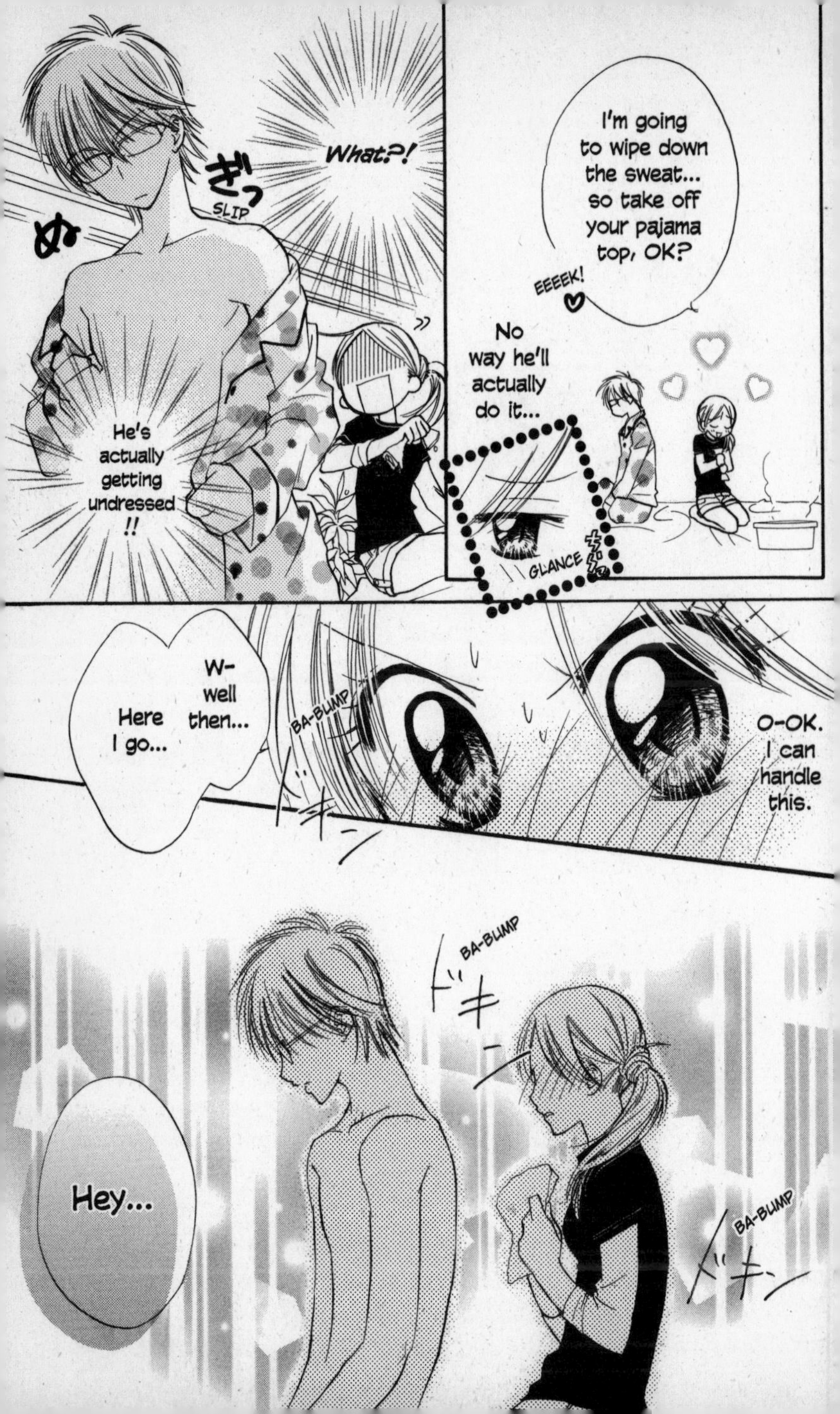
I'm going to wipe down the sweat... so take off your pajama top, OK?
EEEEK!
No way he'll actually do it...
GLANCE
What?!
ぎっ
SLIP
ぬ
He's actually getting undressed!!
O-OK. I can handle this.
BA-BUMP
W-well then... Here I go...
BA-BUMP
BA-BUMP
Hey...

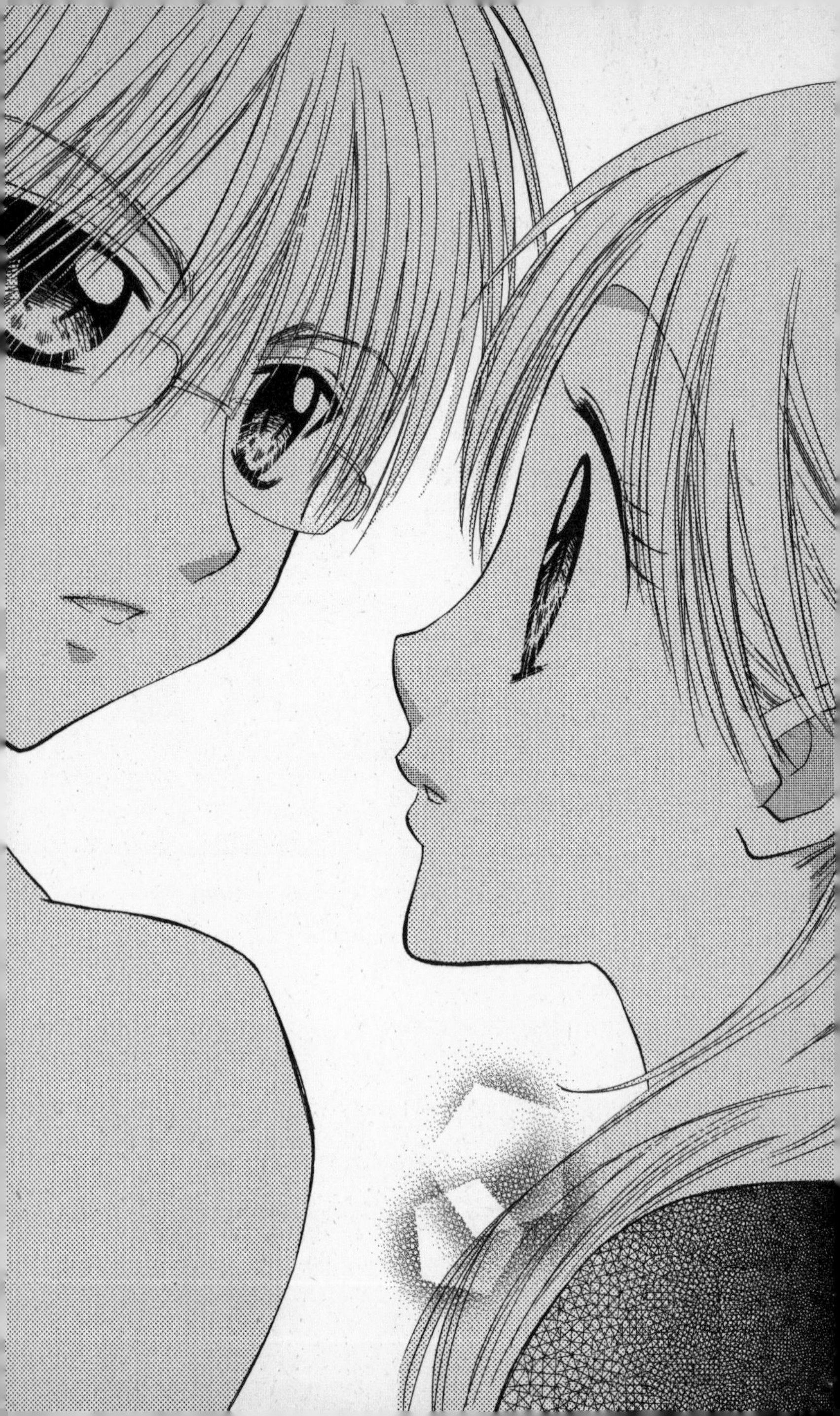

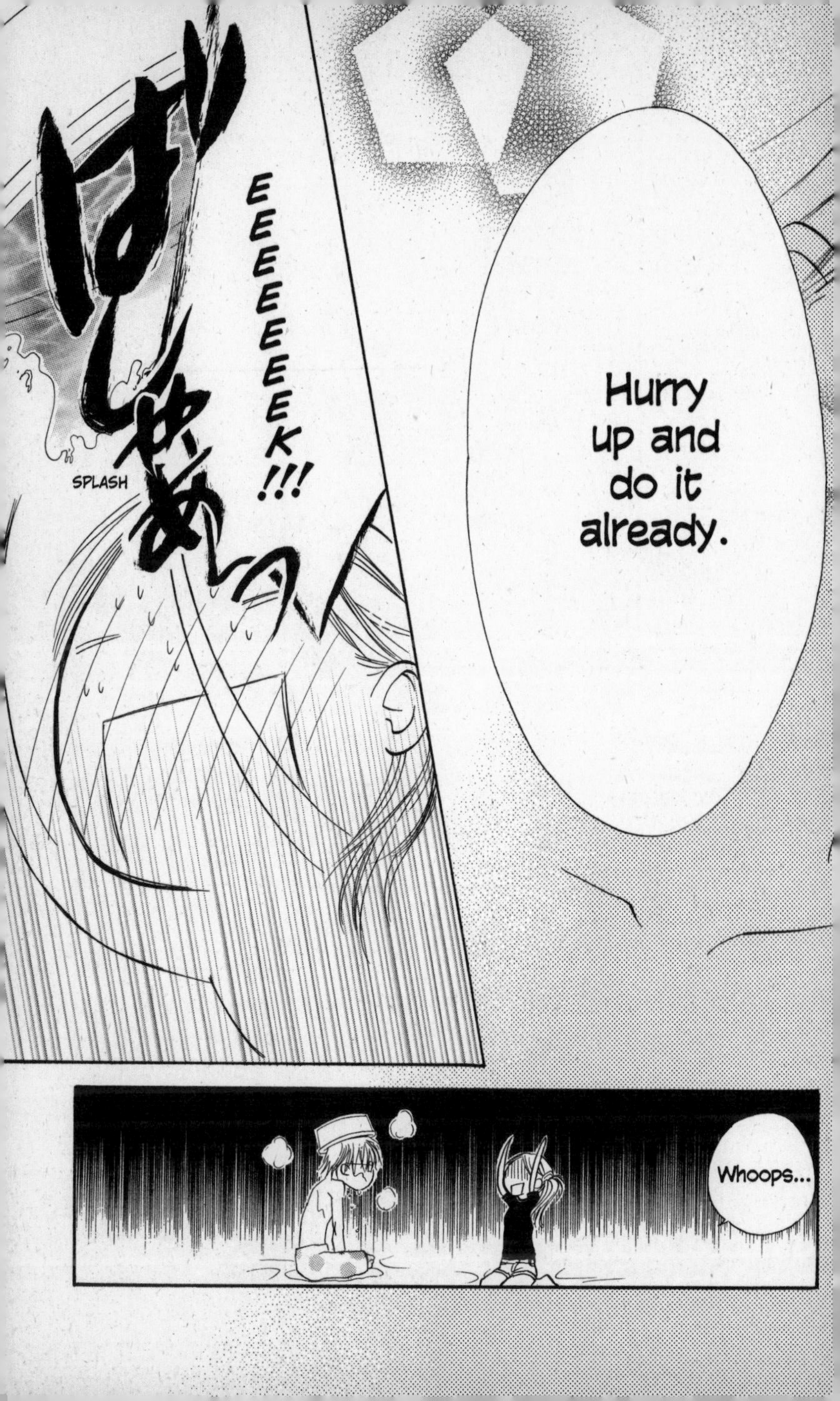
Hurry up and do it already.
EEEEEEEEK!!!
SPLASH
Whoops...

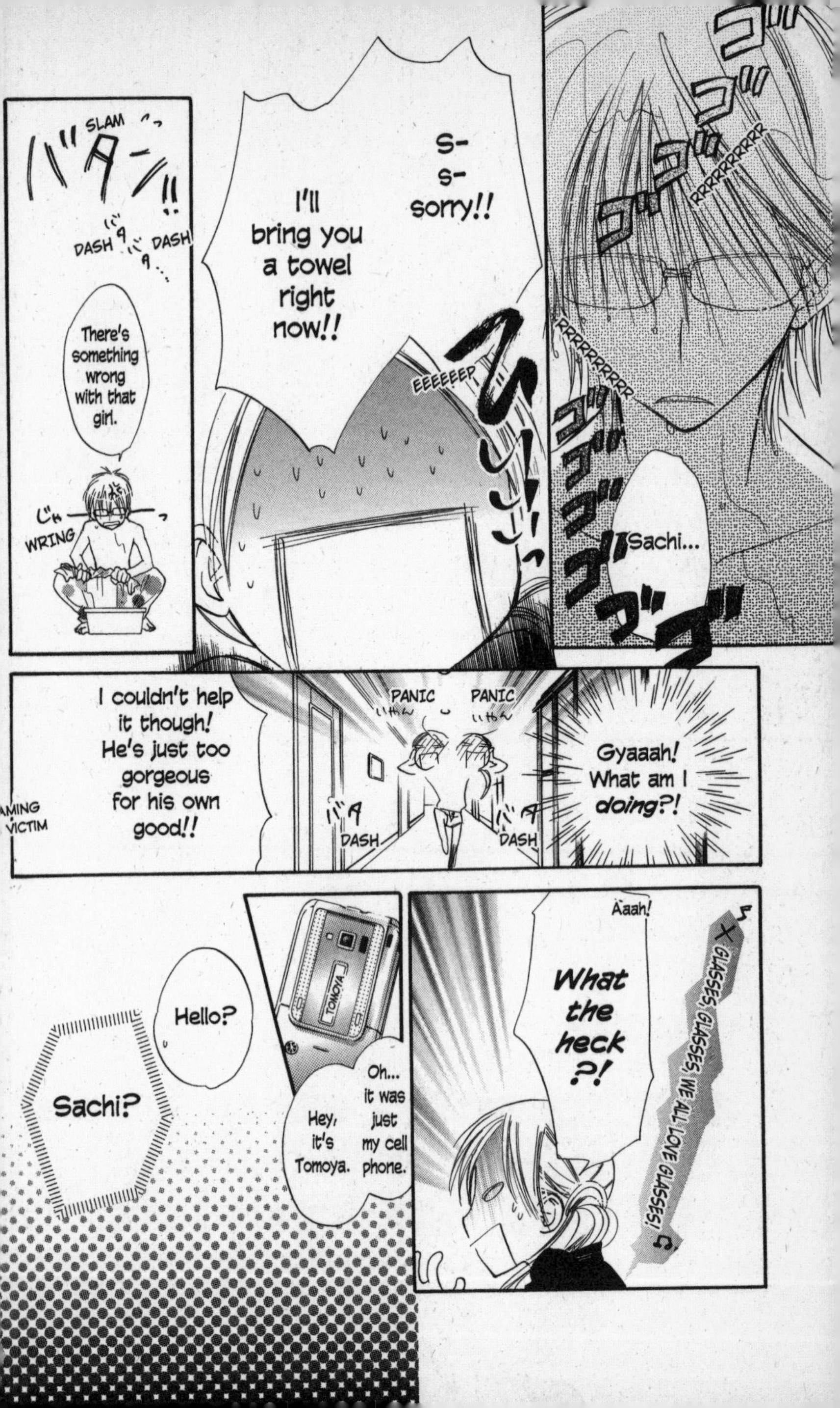
RRRRRRRRR
RRRRRRRRRR
Sachi...
S-s-sorry!!
I'll bring you a towel right now!!
EEEEEEP
SLAM
DASH
DASH
There's something wrong with that girl.
WRING
Gyaaah! What am I *doing*?!
PANIC
PANIC
DASH
DASH
I couldn't help it though! He's just too gorgeous for his own good!!
Aaah!
What the heck?!
GLASSES, GLASSES, WE ALL LOVE GLASSES!
TOMOYA
Oh... it was just my cell phone.
Hey, it's Tomoya.
Hello?
Sachi?

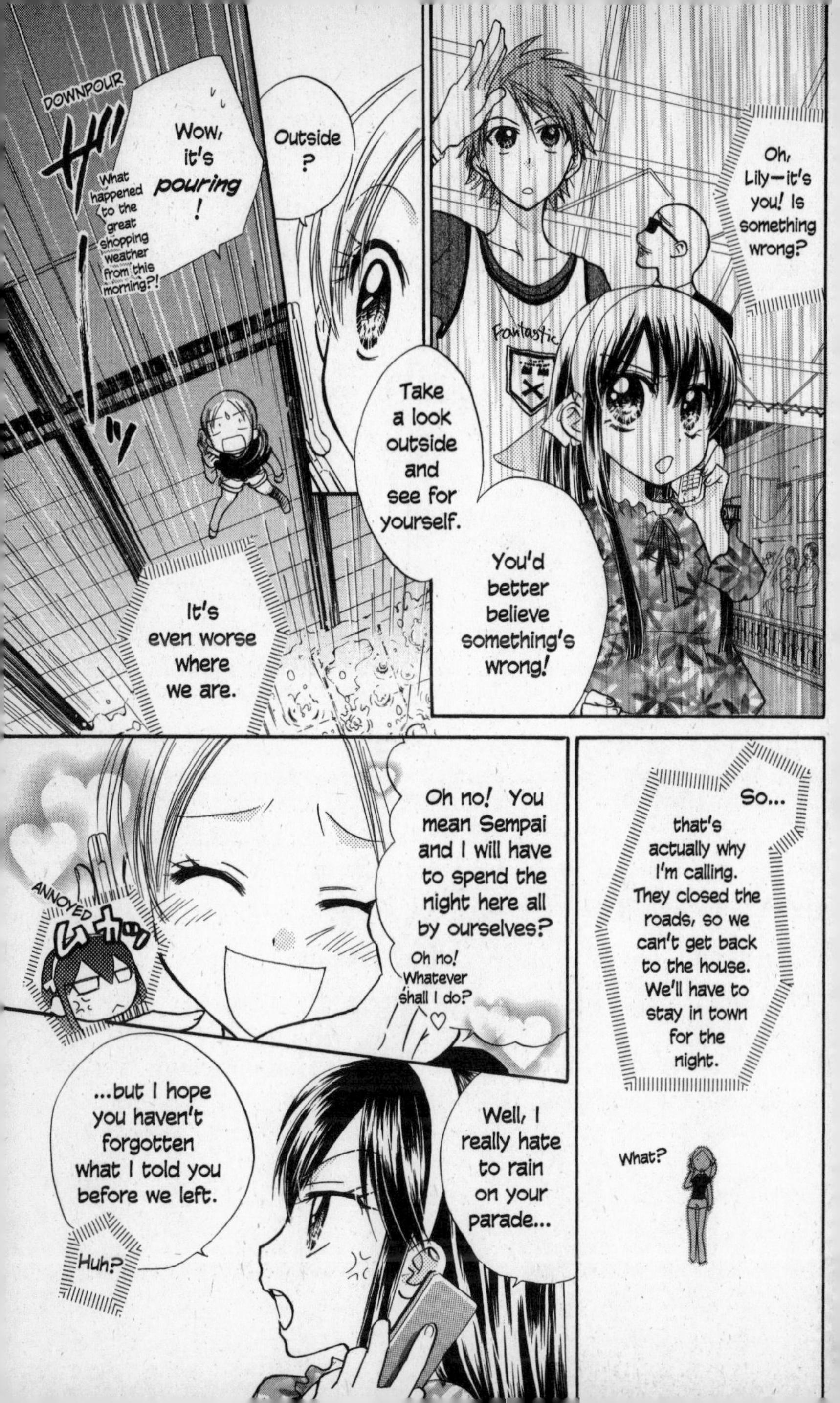

Oh, Lily—it's you! Is something wrong?
Take a look outside and see for yourself.
You'd better believe something's wrong!
Outside?
Wow, it's pouring!
DOWNPOUR
What happened to the great shopping weather from this morning?!
It's even worse where we are.
So... that's actually why I'm calling. They closed the roads, so we can't get back to the house. We'll have to stay in town for the night.
What?
Oh no! You mean Sempai and I will have to spend the night here all by ourselves?
Oh no! Whatever shall I do? ♡
ANNOYED
Well, I really hate to rain on your parade...
...but I hope you haven't forgotten what I told you before we left.
Huh?

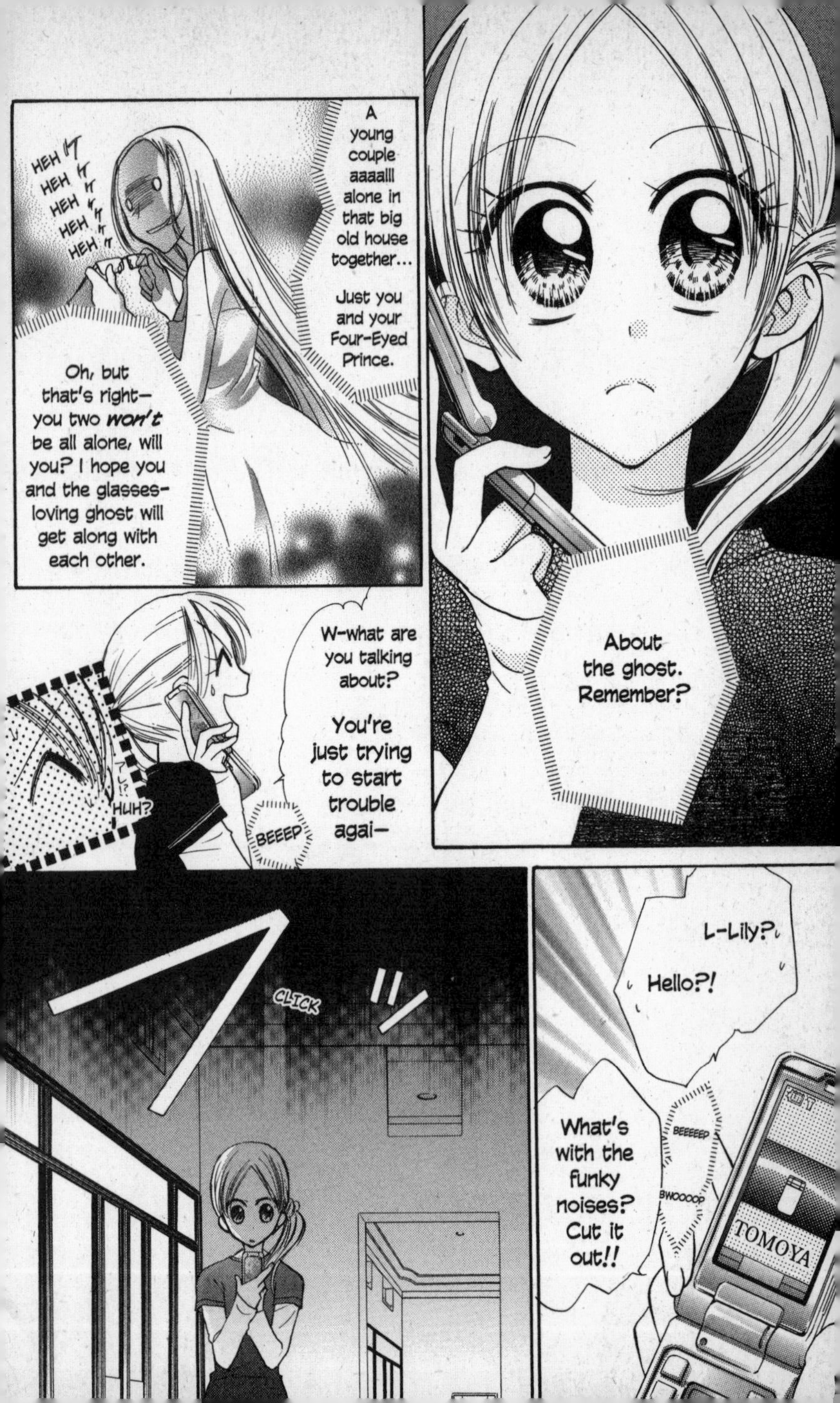
About the ghost. Remember?
HEH HEH HEH HEH HEH
A young couple aaaalll alone in that big old house together...
Just you and your Four-Eyed Prince.
Oh, but that's right—you two *won't* be all alone, will you? I hope you and the glasses-loving ghost will get along with each other.
W-what are you talking about?
You're just trying to start trouble agai—
BEEEP
HUH?
L-Lily?
Hello?!
What's with the funky noises? Cut it out!!
BEEEEEP
BWOOOOP
TOMOYA
CLICK

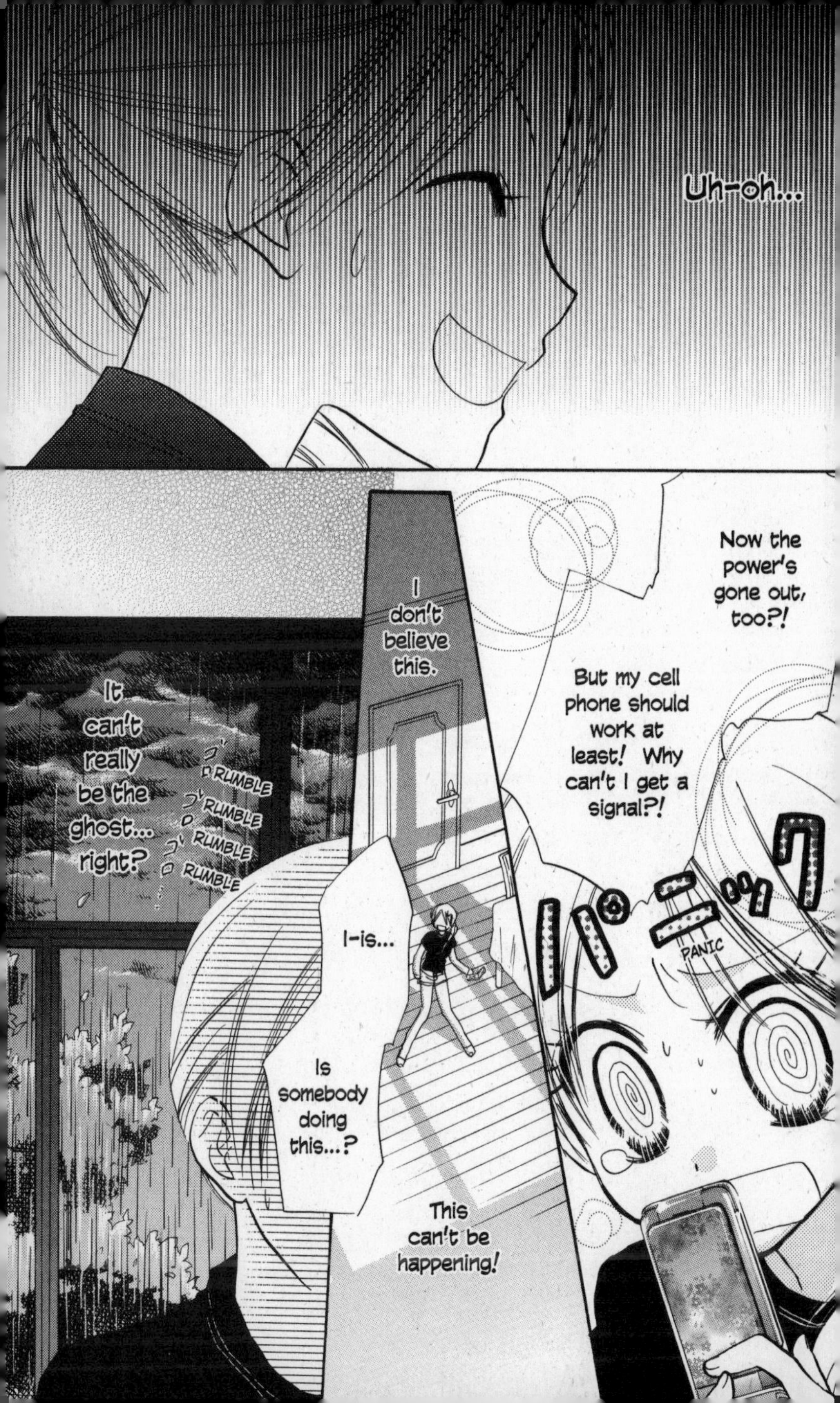
Uh-oh...
Now the power's gone out, too?!
But my cell phone should work at least! Why can't I get a signal?!
PANIC
I don't believe this.
I-is...
Is somebody doing this...?
This can't be happening!
It can't really be the ghost... right?
RUMBLE
RUMBLE
RUMBLE
RUMBLE

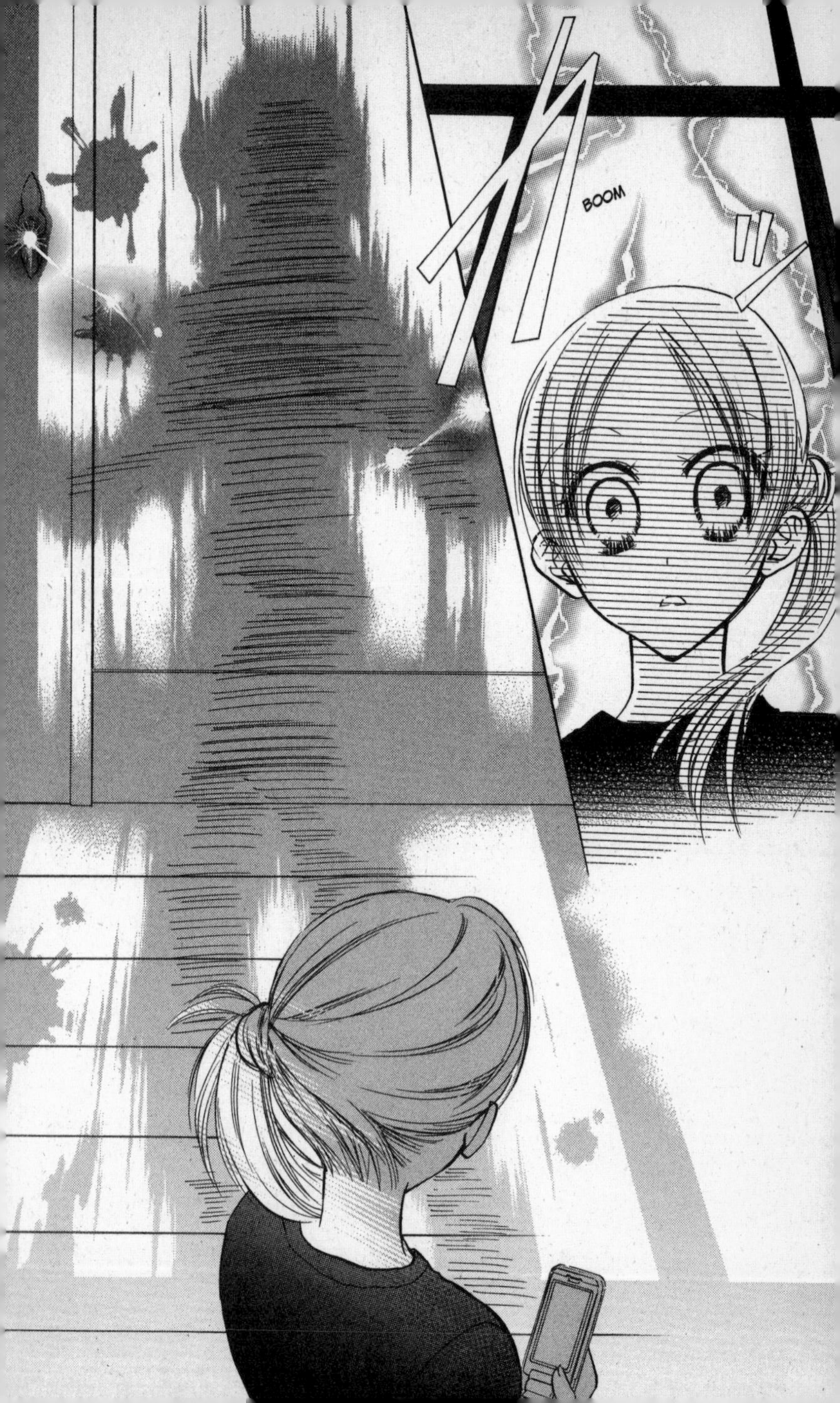
BOOM

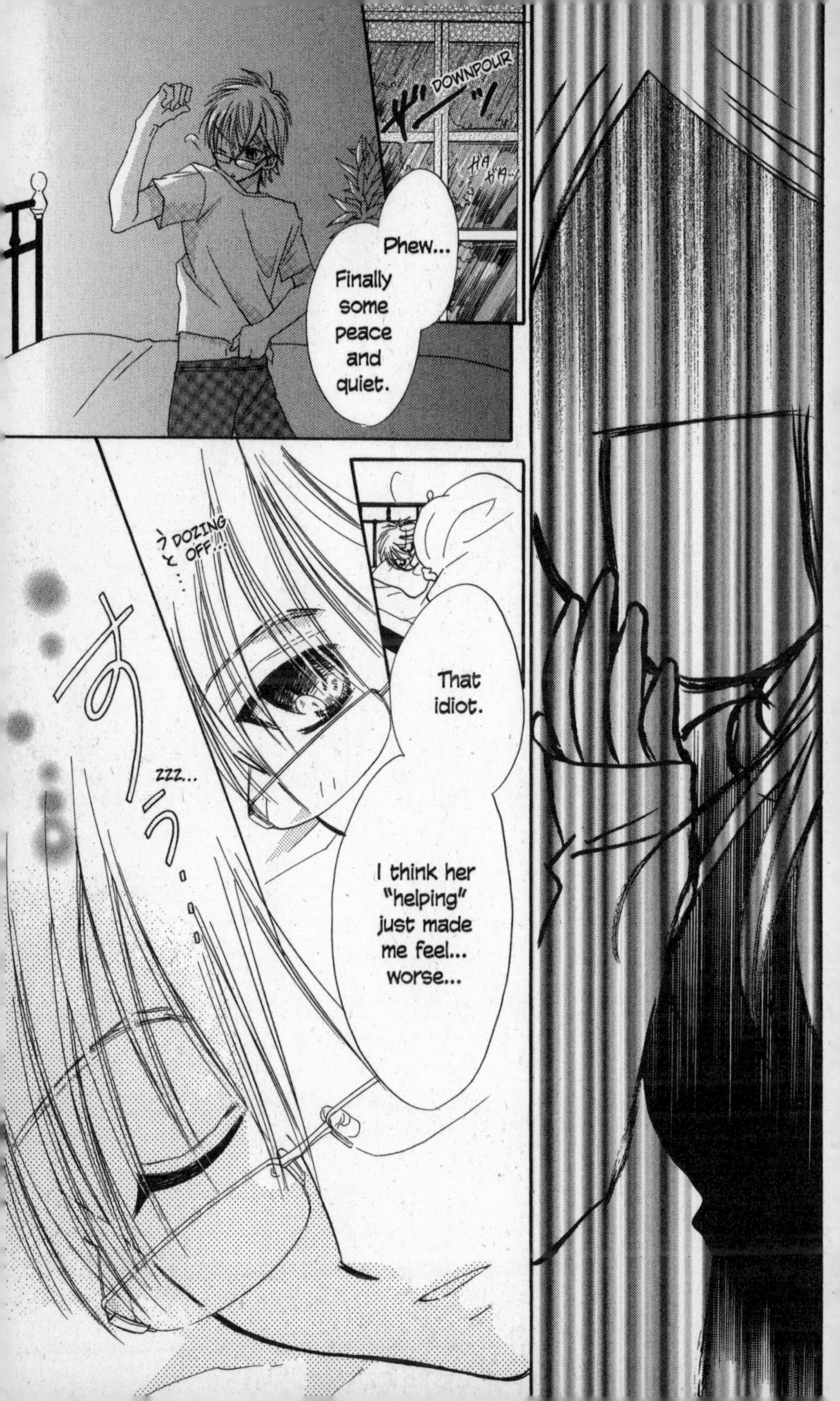
DOWNPOUR
HA
Phew... Finally some peace and quiet.
That idiot.
I think her "helping" just made me feel... worse...
DOZING OFF...
zzz...

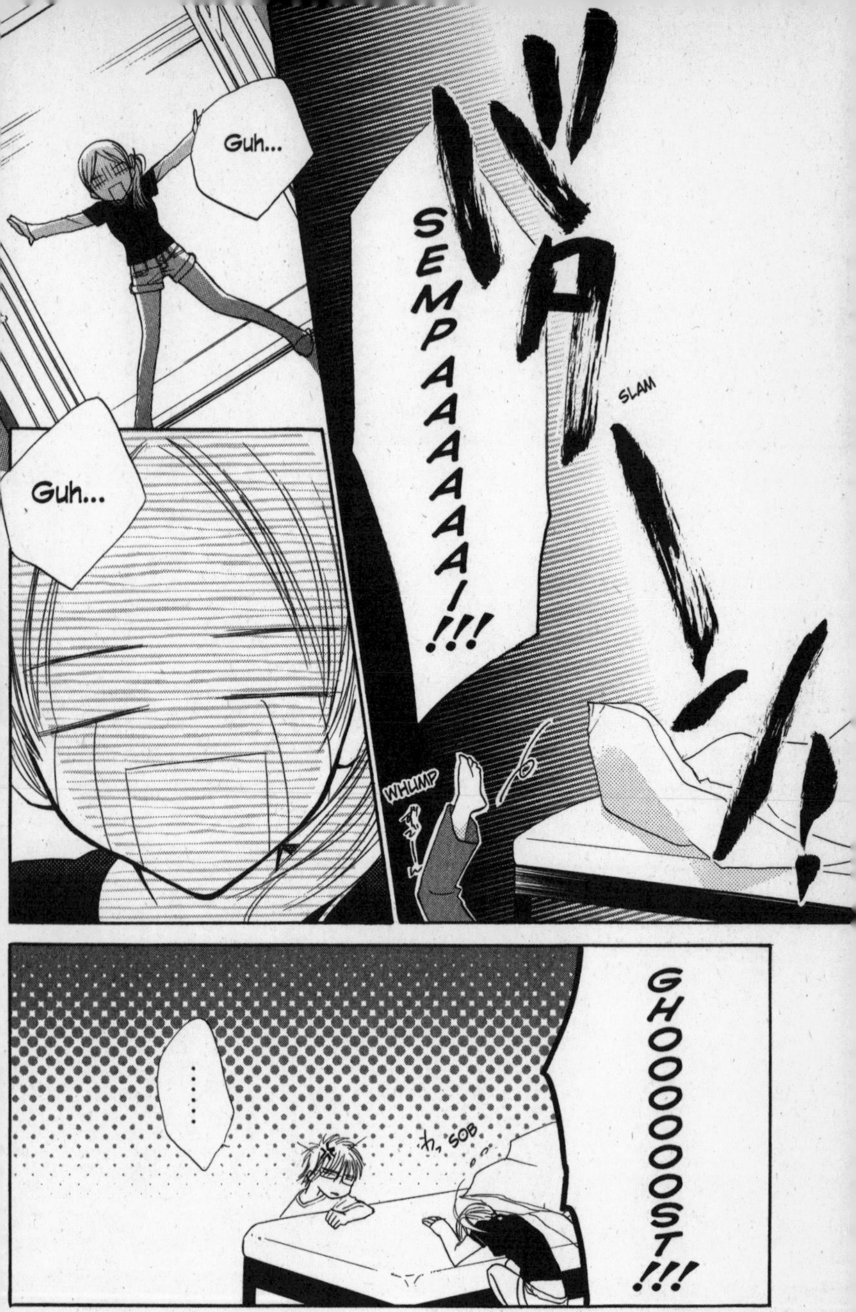
SEMPAAAAAAI!!!
SLAM
WHUMP
Guh...
Guh...
GHOOOOOOOST!!!
SOB
......

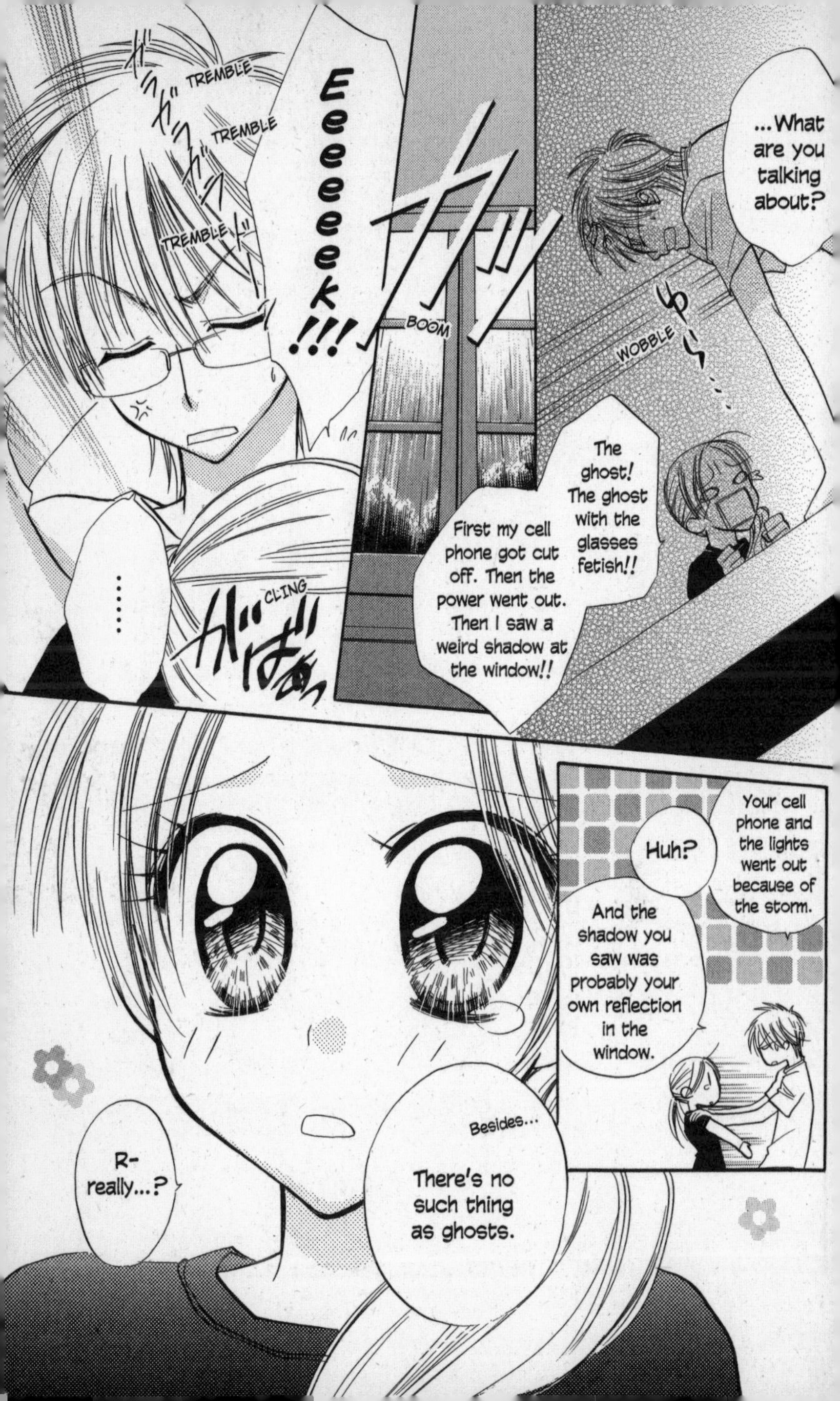
...What are you talking about?
WOBBLE
The ghost! The ghost with the glasses fetish!!
First my cell phone got cut off. Then the power went out. Then I saw a weird shadow at the window!!
BOOM
TREMBLE
TREMBLE
TREMBLE
Eeeeeeek!!!
CLING
......
Your cell phone and the lights went out because of the storm.
Huh?
And the shadow you saw was probably your own reflection in the window.
Besides...
There's no such thing as ghosts.
R-really...?

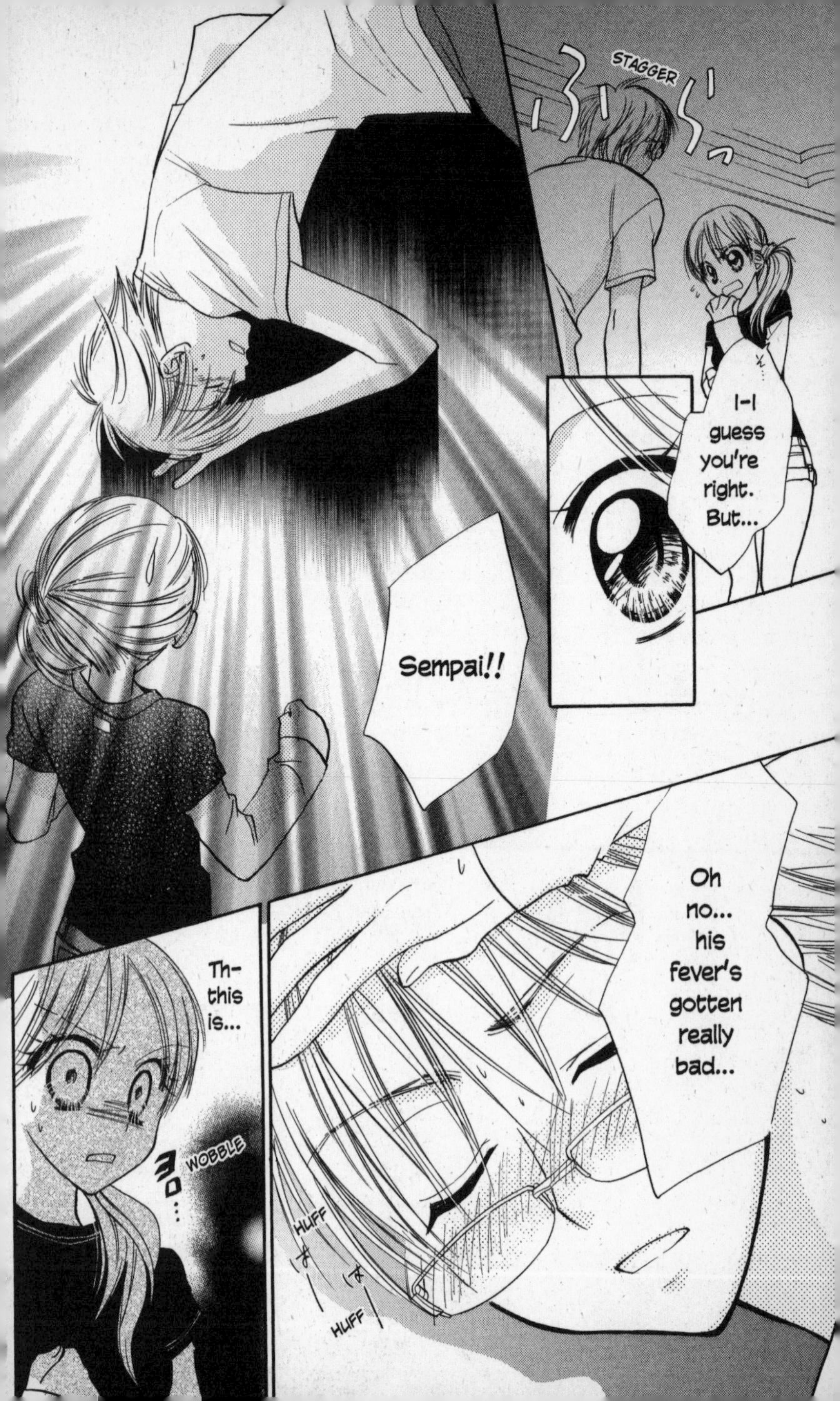
STAGGER
I-I guess you're right. But...
Sempai!!
Oh no... his fever's gotten really bad...
HUFF
HUFF
Th-this is...
WOBBLE

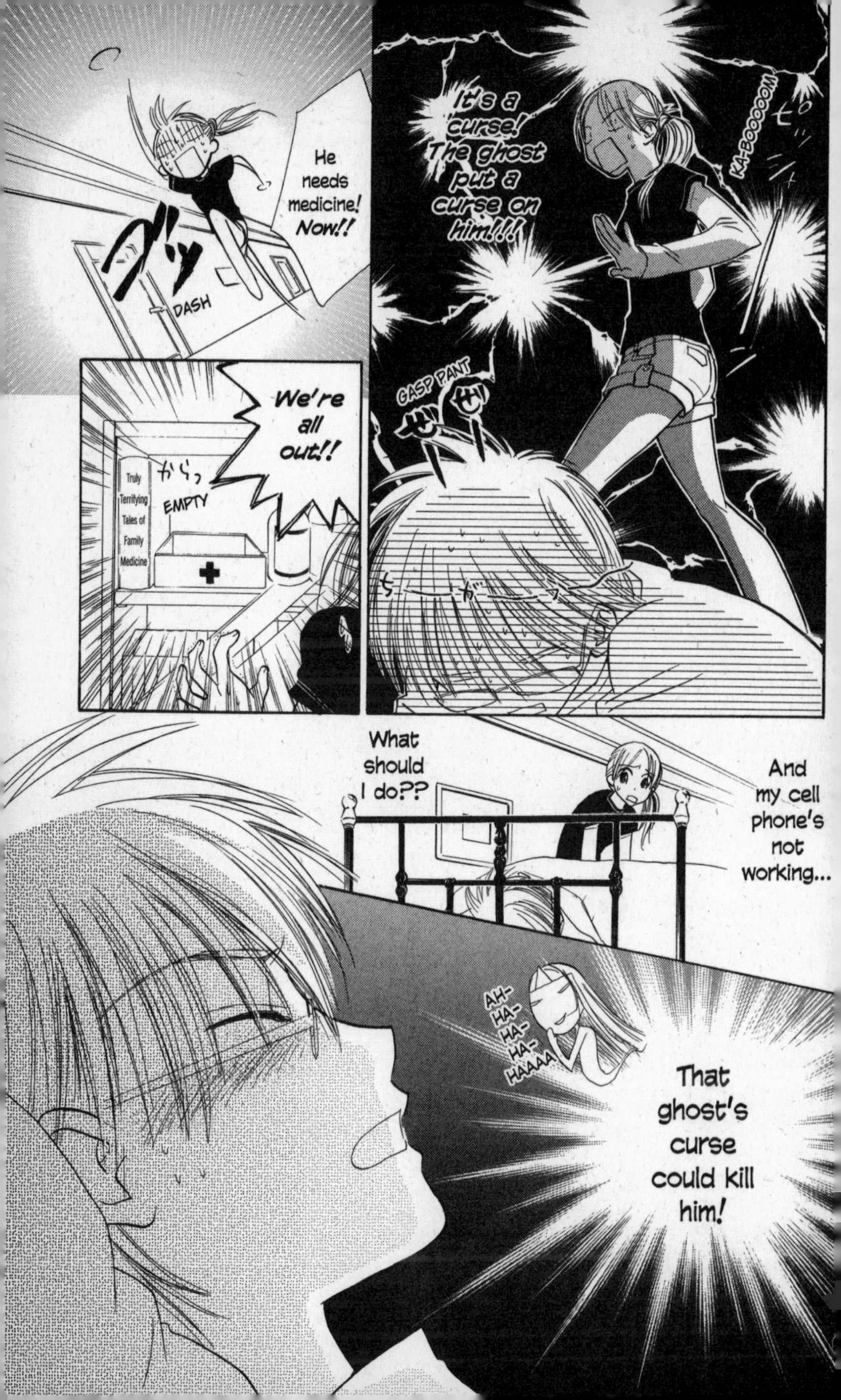
It's a curse! The ghost put a curse on him!!!
KA-BOOOOOM
GASP PANT
He needs medicine! Now!!
DASH
We're all out!!
Truly Terrifying Tales of Family Medicine
EMPTY
And my cell phone's not working...
What should I do??
AH-HA-HA-HA-HAAAA
That ghost's curse could kill him!

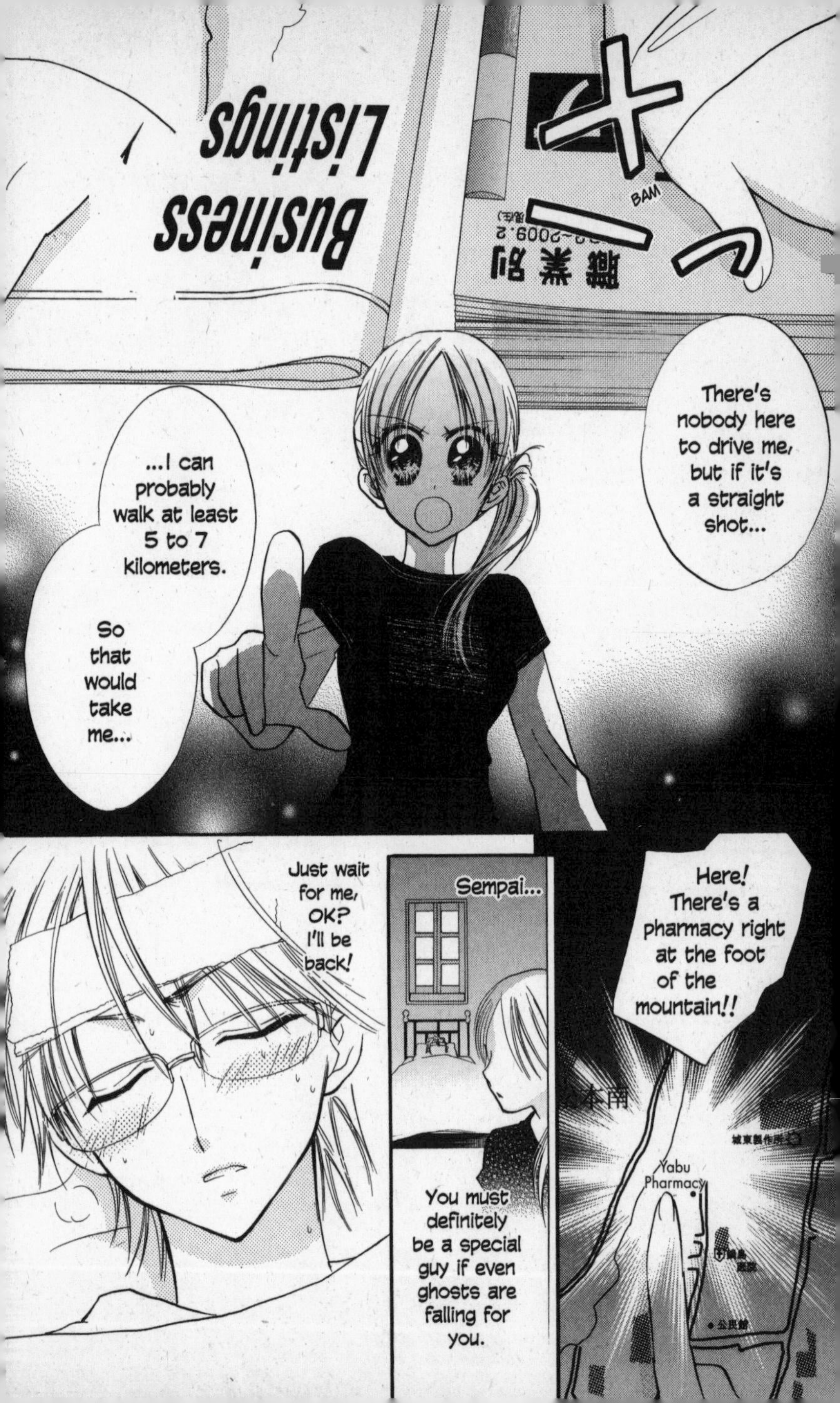
Business Listings
職業別
BAM
There's nobody here to drive me, but if it's a straight shot...
...I can probably walk at least 5 to 7 kilometers.
So that would take me...
Here! There's a pharmacy right at the foot of the mountain!!
Yabu Pharmacy
Sempai...
You must definitely be a special guy if even ghosts are falling for you.
Just wait for me, OK? I'll be back!

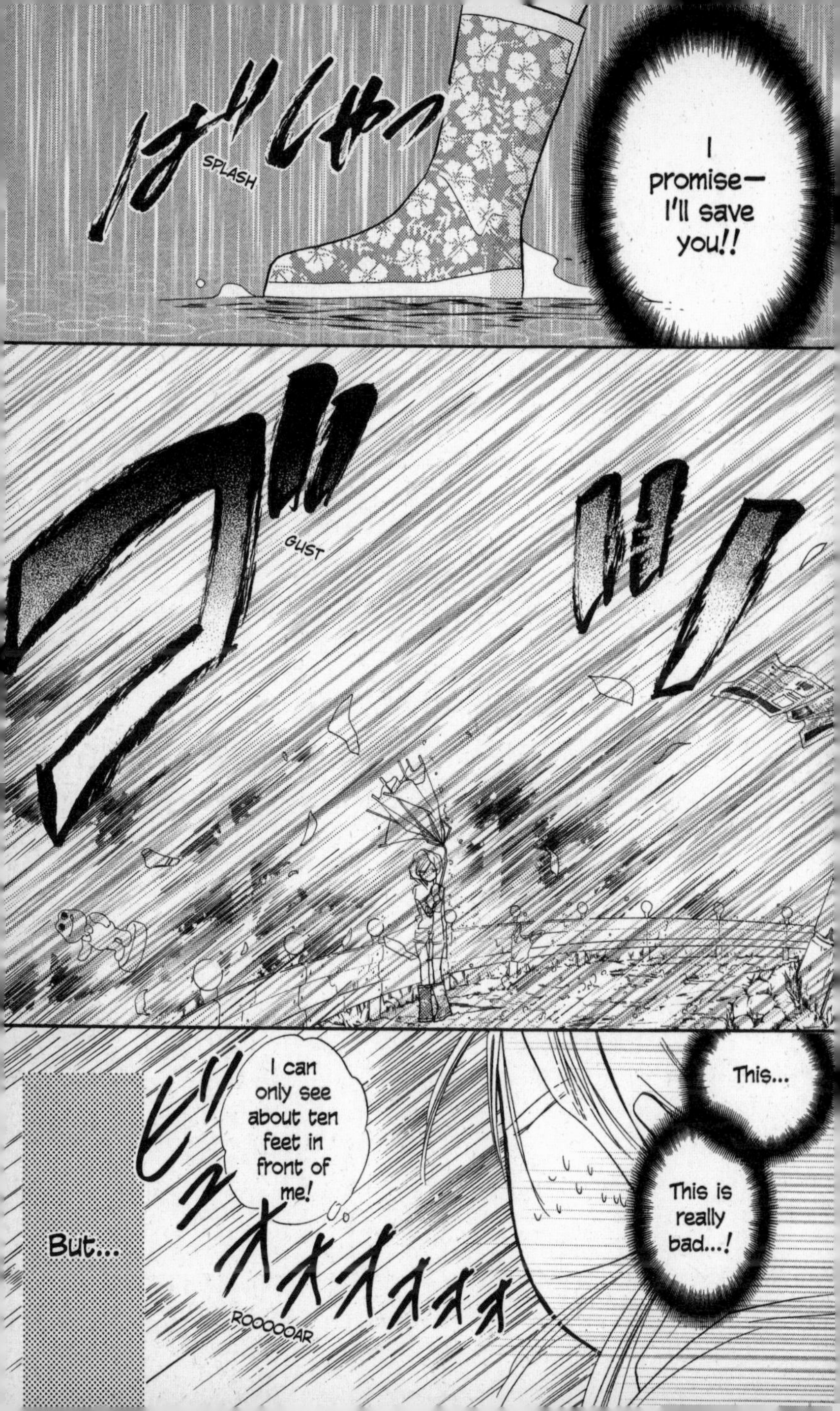
I promise— I'll save you!!
SPLASH
GUST
This...
This is really bad...!
I can only see about ten feet in front of me!
ROOOOOAR
But...

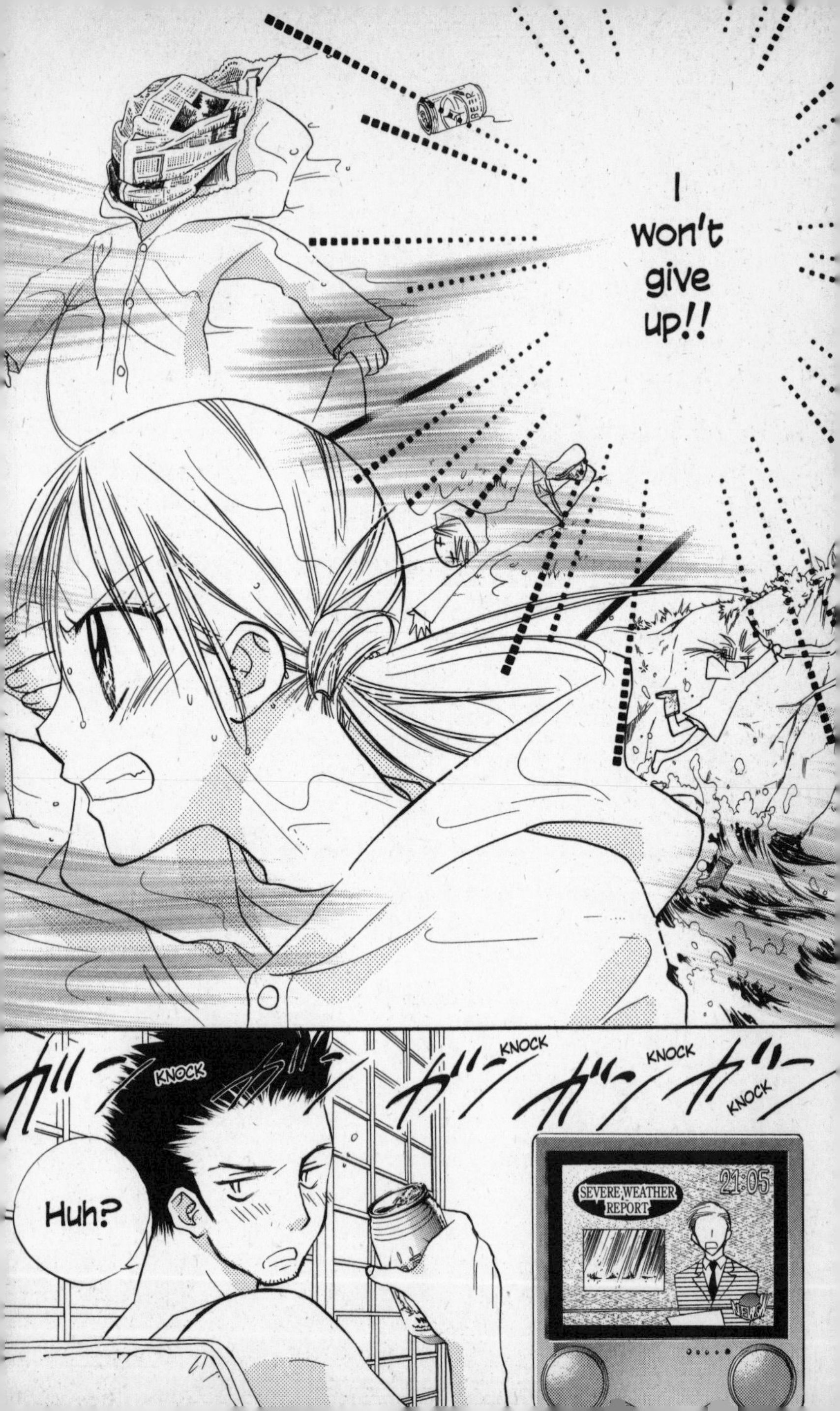

I won't give up!!
KNOCK
KNOCK
KNOCK
KNOCK
21:05
SEVERE WEATHER REPORT
Huh?

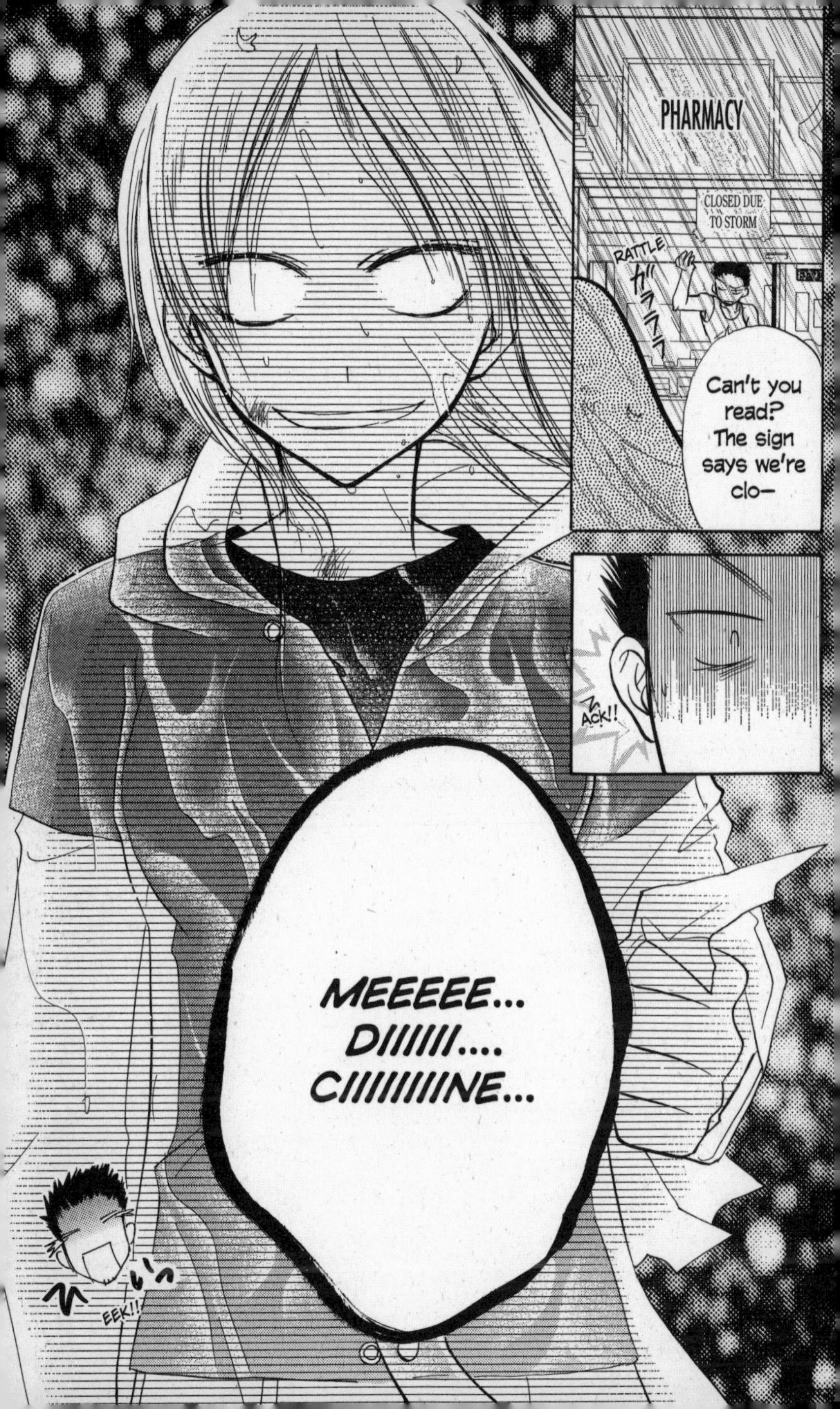
PHARMACY
CLOSED DUE TO STORM
RATTLE
ガラララ
Can't you read? The sign says we're clo—
ACK!!
MEEEEE... DIIIIII.... CIIIIIIIINE...
EEK!!

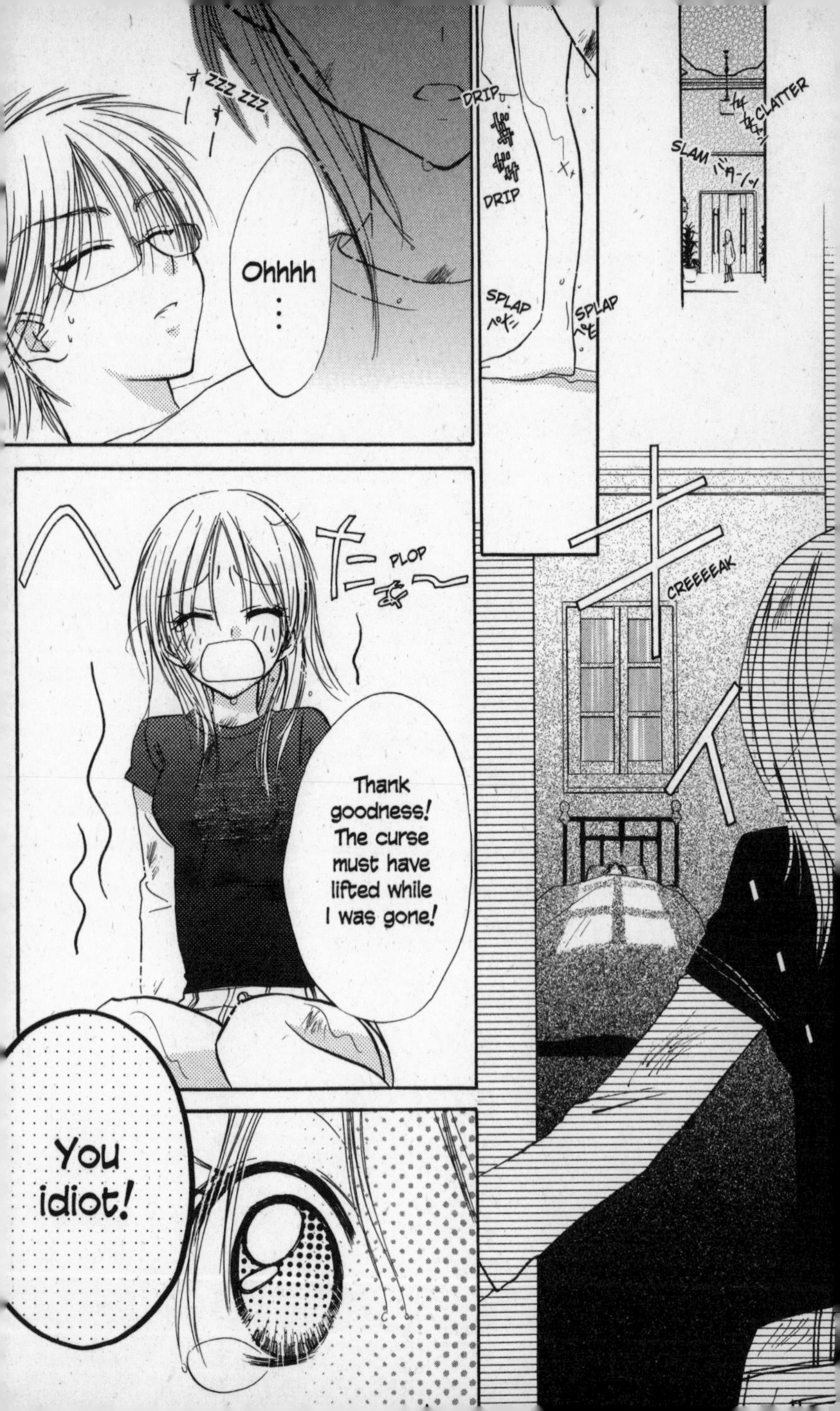
CLATTER
SLAM
DRIP
DRIP
SPLAP
SPLAP
ZZZ ZZZ
Ohhhh ...
CREEEEAK
PLOP
Thank goodness! The curse must have lifted while I was gone!
You idiot!

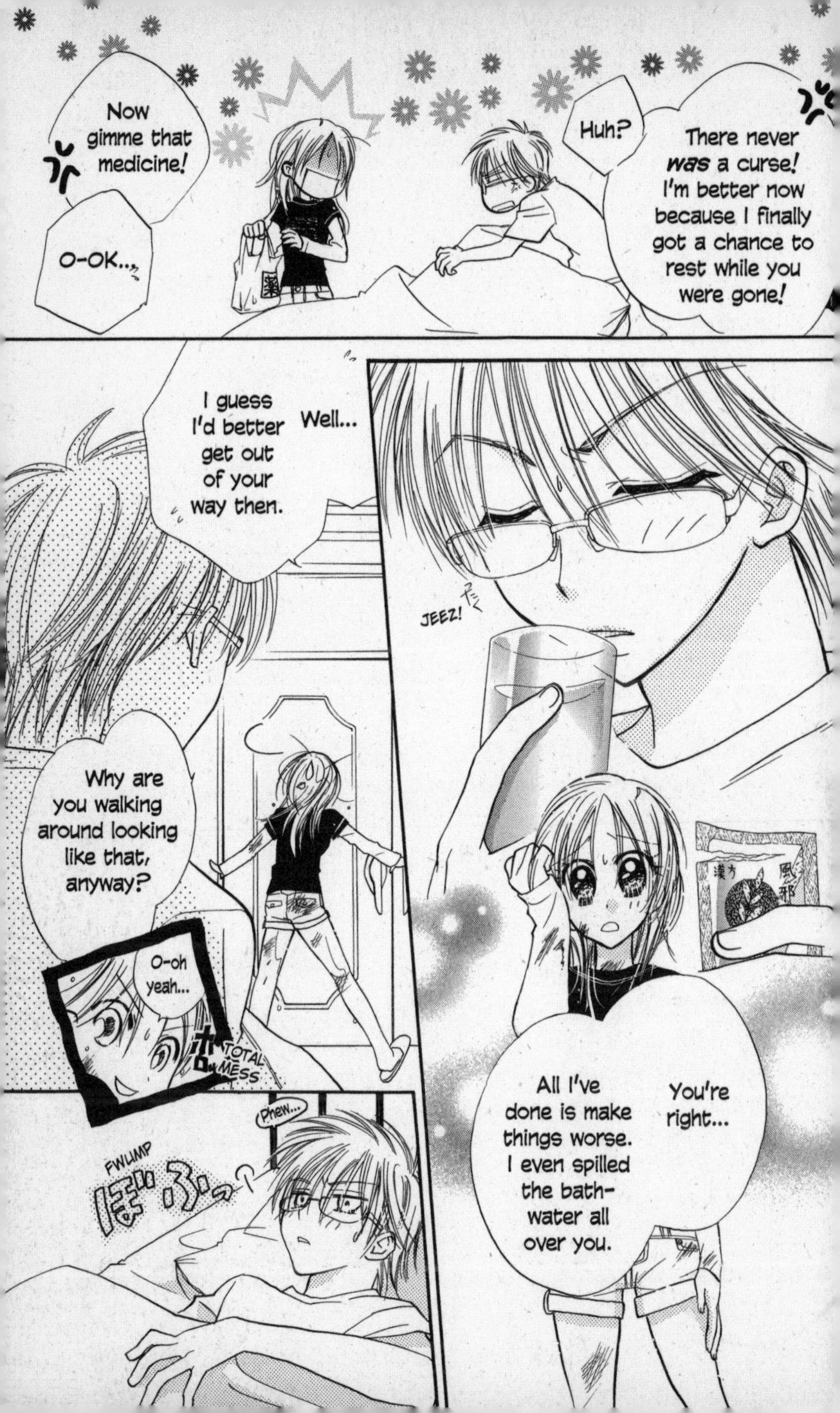
There never *was* a curse! I'm better now because I finally got a chance to rest while you were gone!
Huh?
Now gimme that medicine!
O-OK...
JEEZ!
You're right...
All I've done is make things worse. I even spilled the bath-water all over you.
Well...
I guess I'd better get out of your way then.
Why are you walking around looking like that, anyway?
O-oh yeah...
TOTAL MESS
Phew...
FWUMP

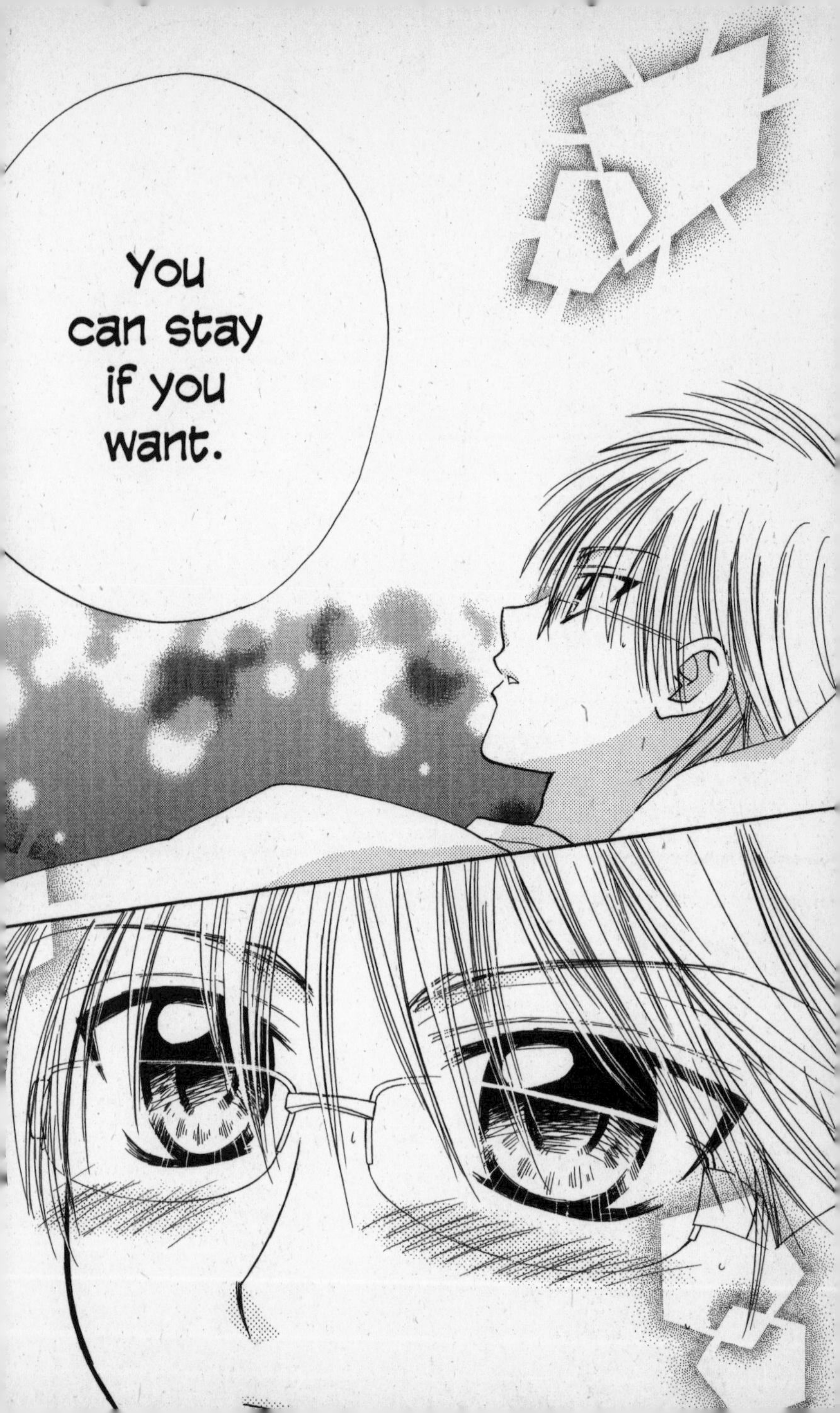
You can stay if you want.

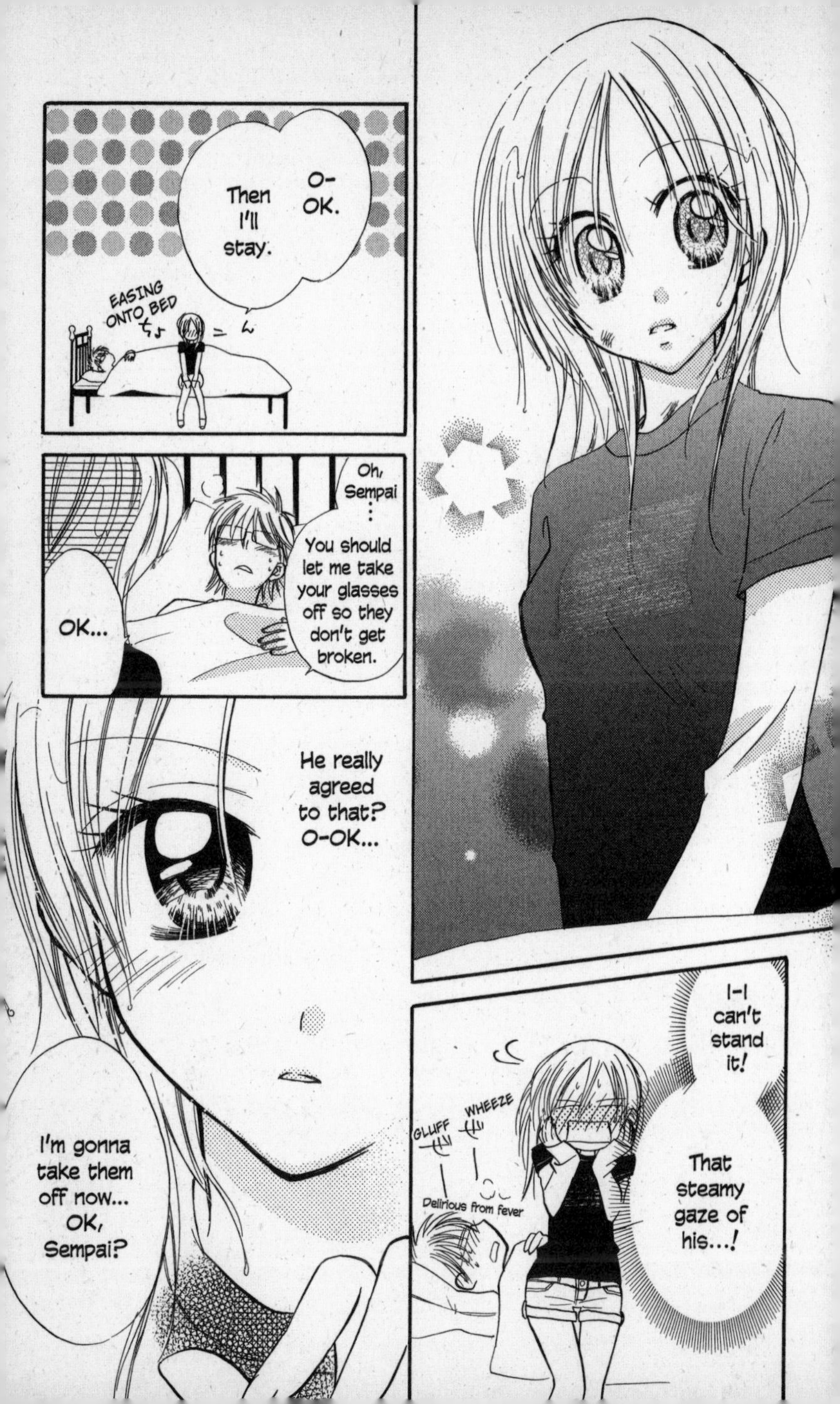
I-I can't stand it!
That steamy gaze of his...!
WHEEZE
GLUFF
Delirious from fever
O-OK.
Then I'll stay.
EASING ONTO BED
Oh, Sempai...
You should let me take your glasses off so they don't get broken.
OK...
He really agreed to that? O-OK...
I'm gonna take them off now... OK, Sempai?

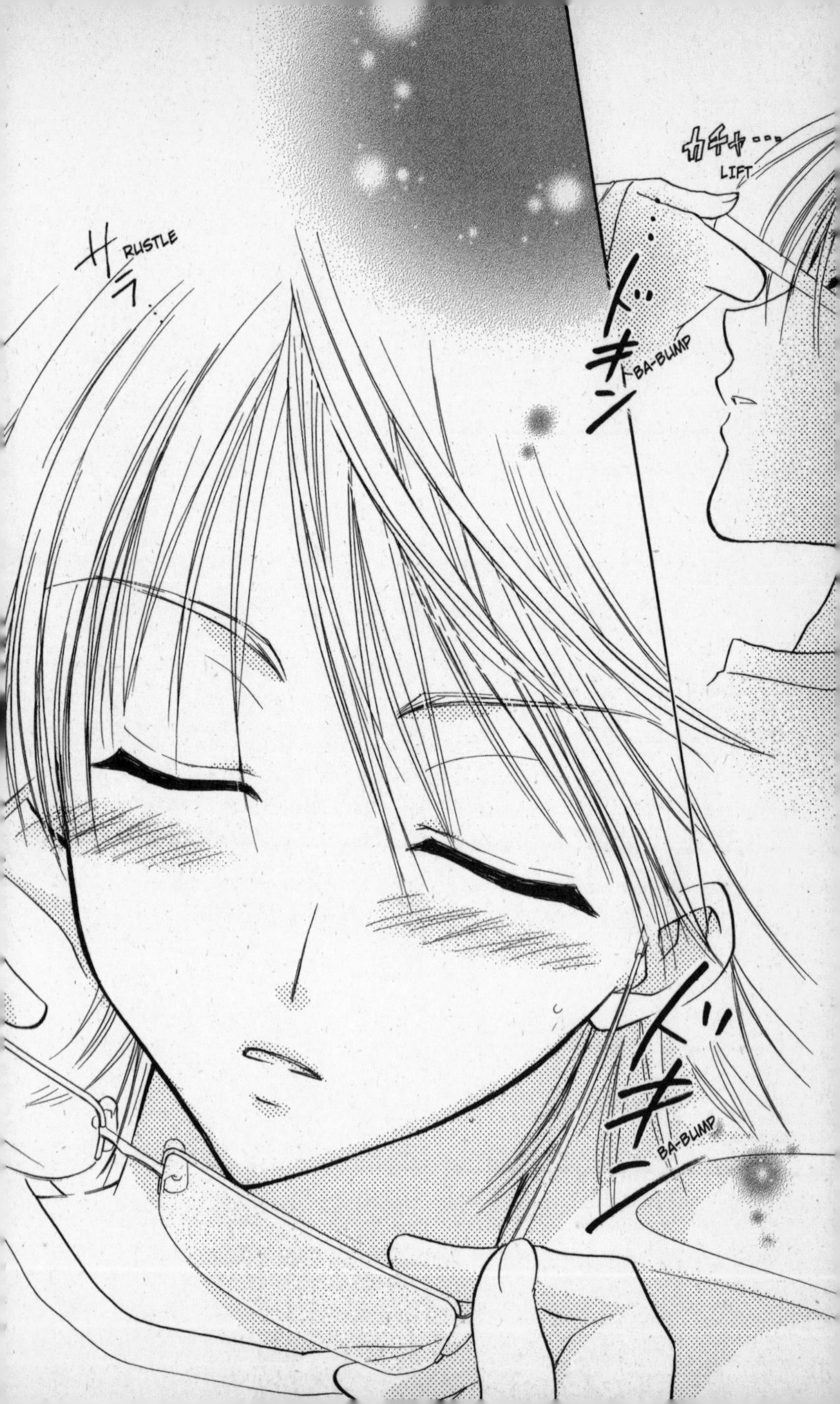

カチャ...
LIFT
ドキン
BA-BUMP
サラ
RUSTLE
ドキン
BA-BUMP

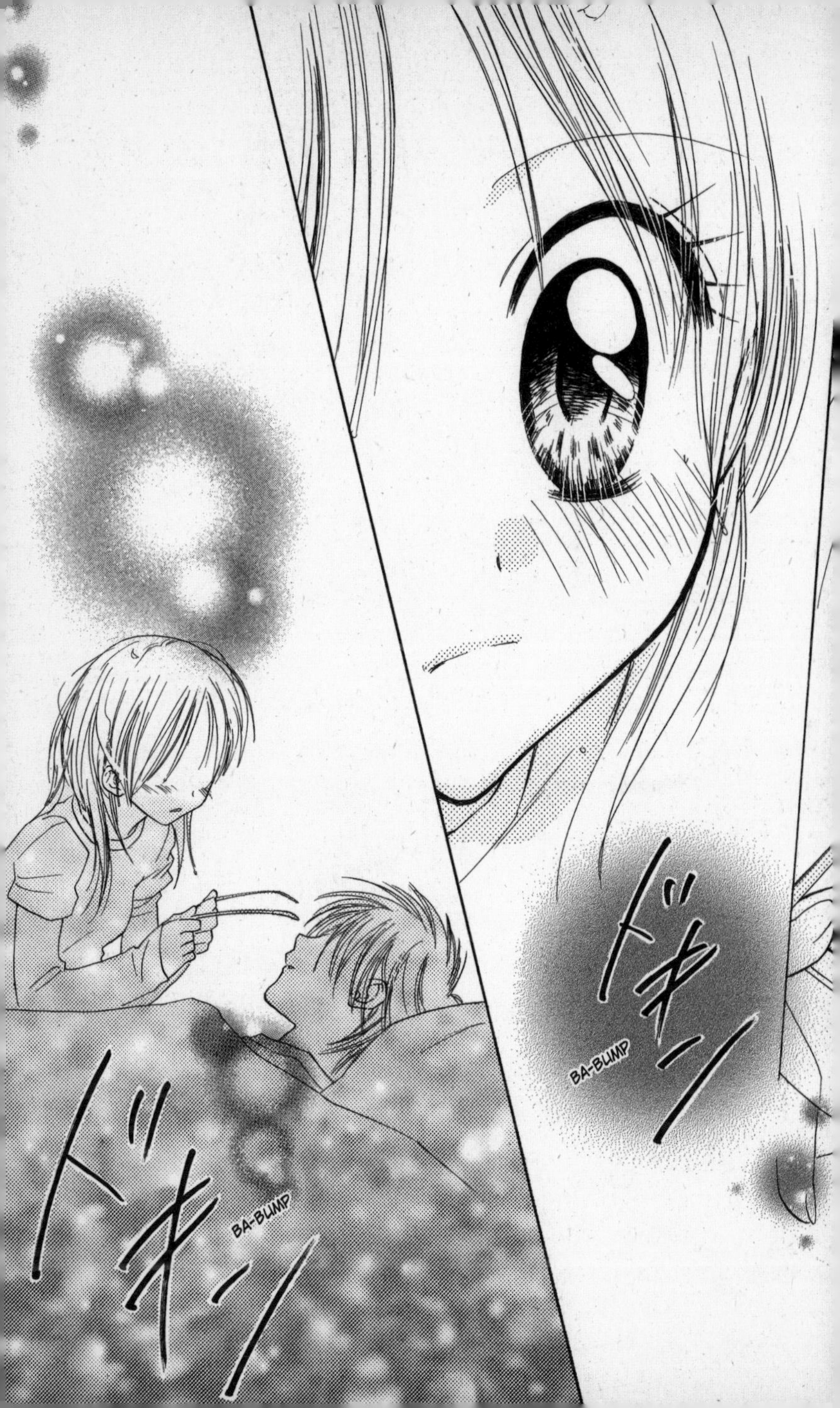
ドキン
BA-BUMP
ドキン
BA-BUMP

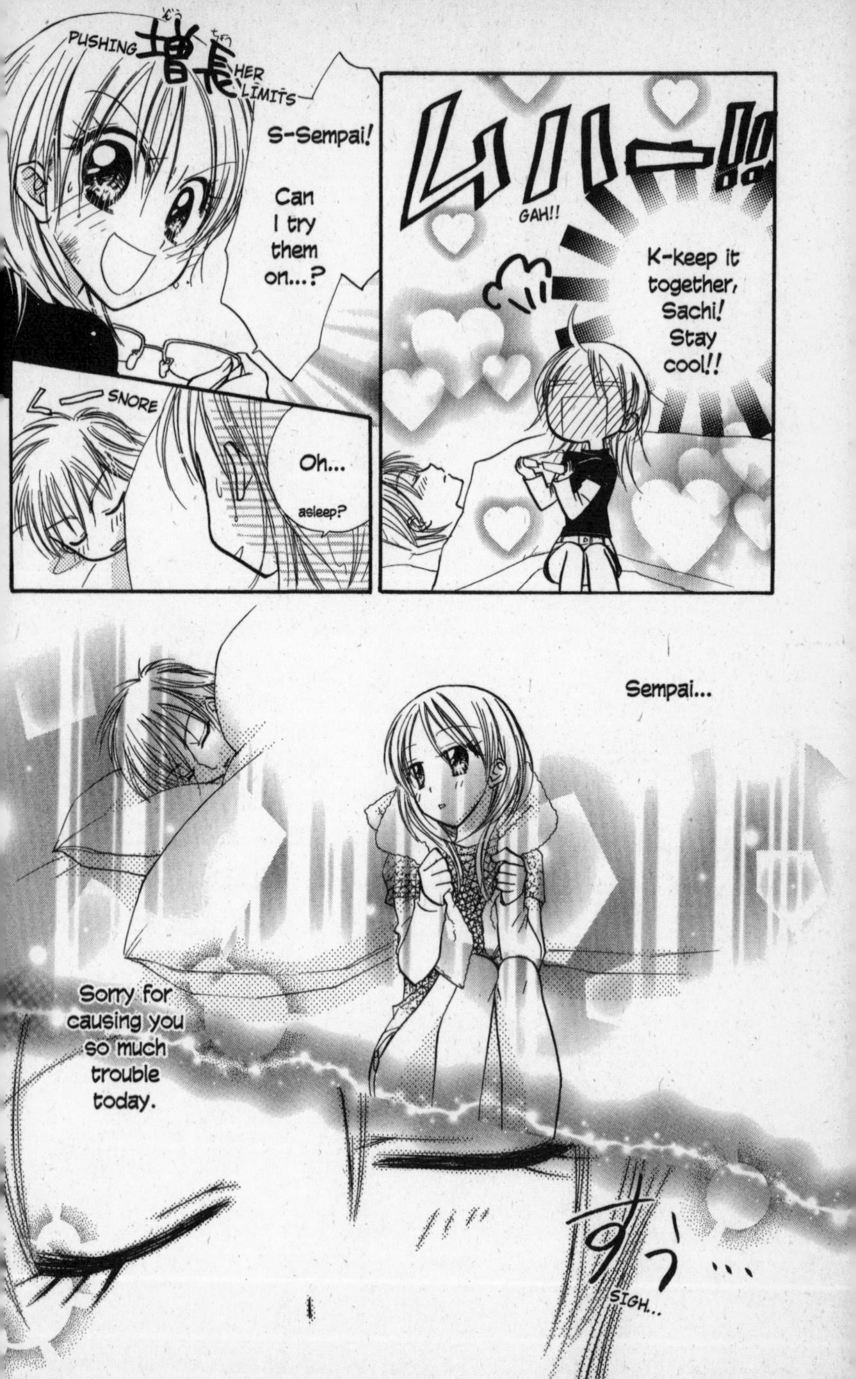

GAH!!
K-keep it together, Sachi! Stay cool!!
増長
PUSHING HER LIMITS
S-Sempai!
Can I try them on...?
SNORE
Oh...
asleep?
Sempai...
Sorry for causing you so much trouble today.
SIGH...

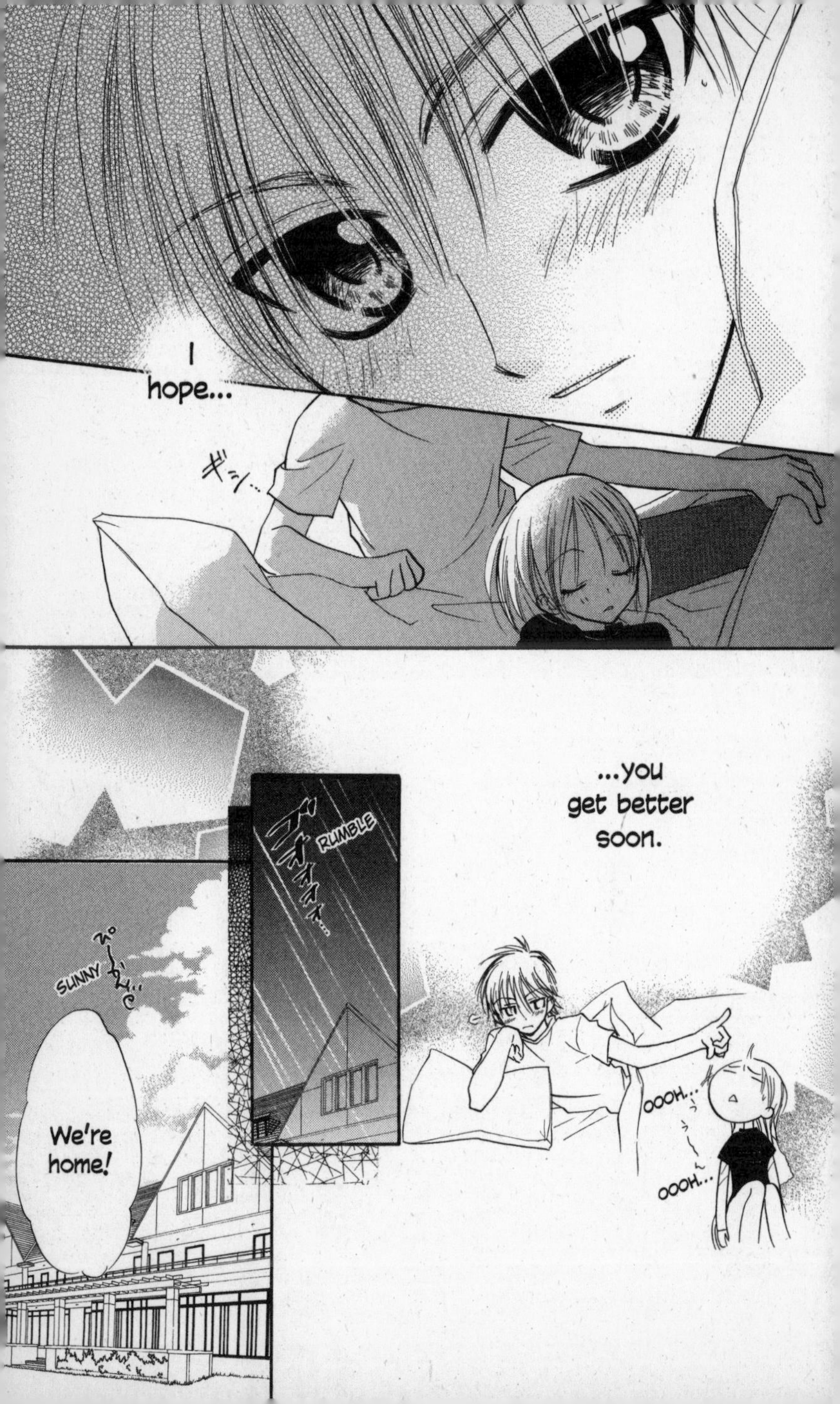
I hope...
...you get better soon.
OOOH...
OOOH...
RUMBLE
SUNNY
We're home!

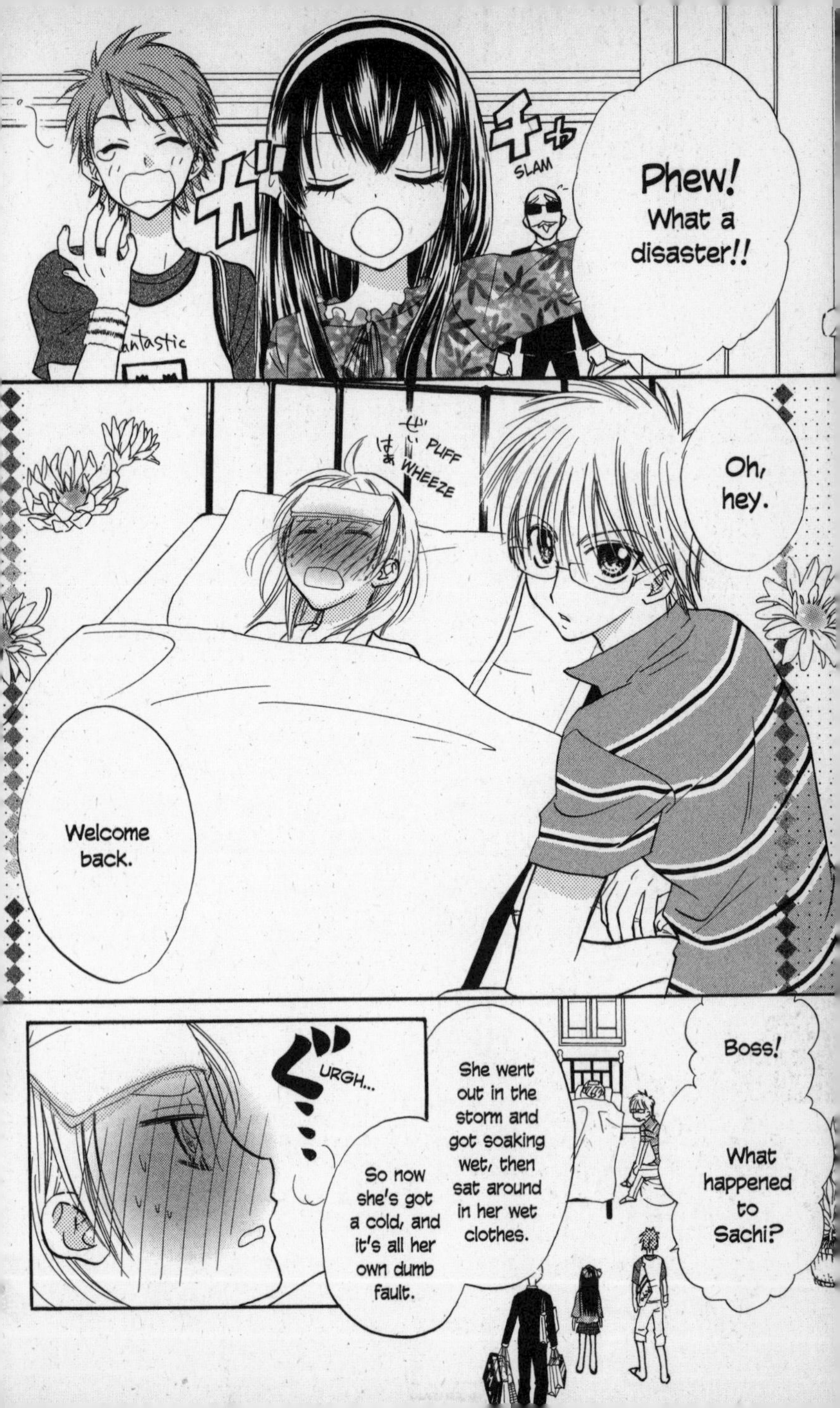

ガチャ
SLAM
Phew! What a disaster!!
Oh, hey.
ぜい はぁ
PUFF WHEEZE
Welcome back.
Boss! What happened to Sachi?
She went out in the storm and got soaking wet, then sat around in her wet clothes.
So now she's got a cold, and it's all her own dumb fault.
ぐ...
URGH...

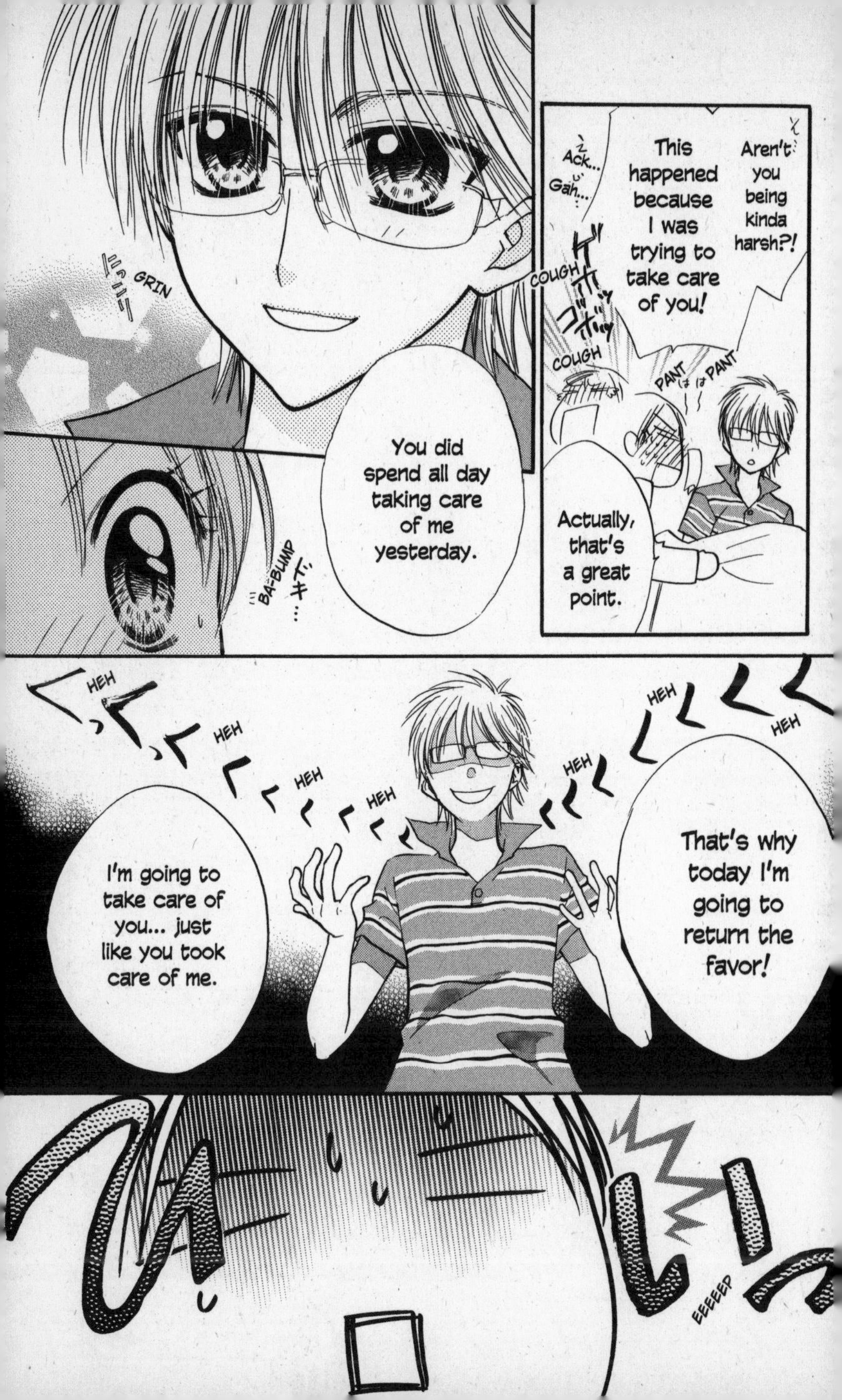
Aren't you being kinda harsh?!
This happened because I was trying to take care of you!
Ack... Gah...
COUGH
COUGH
PANT PANT
Actually, that's a great point.
GRIN
You did spend all day taking care of me yesterday.
BA-BUMP
HEH
HEH
HEH
That's why today I'm going to return the favor!
HEH
HEH
HEH
I'm going to take care of you... just like you took care of me.
EEEEEP

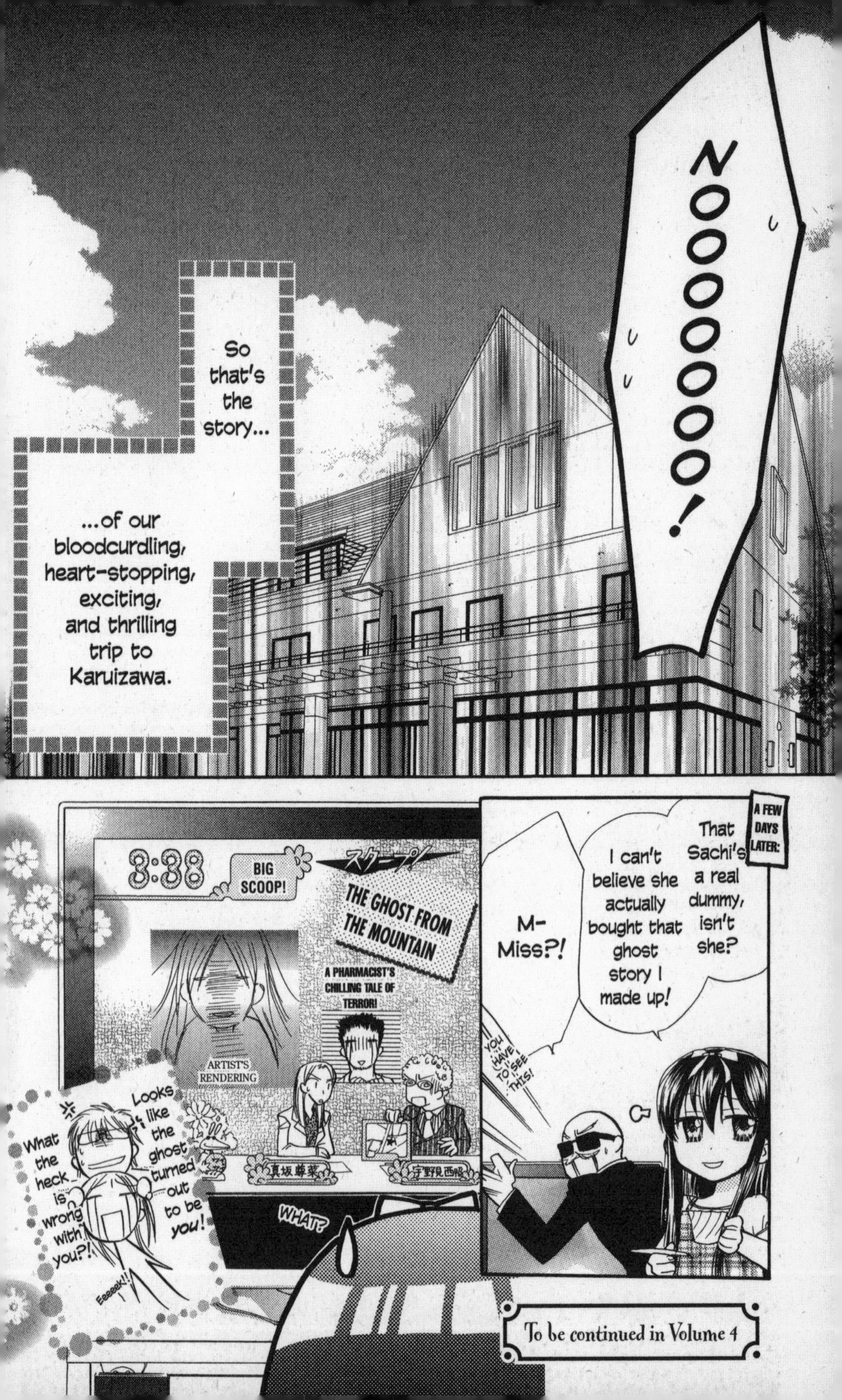
NOOOOOOOO!
So that's the story...
...of our bloodcurdling, heart-stopping, exciting, and thrilling trip to Karuizawa.
A FEW DAYS LATER:
That Sachi's a real dummy, isn't she?
I can't believe she actually bought that ghost story I made up!
M-Miss?!
YOU HAVE TO SEE THIS!
3:38
BIG SCOOP!
THE GHOST FROM THE MOUNTAIN
A PHARMACIST'S CHILLING TALE OF TERROR!
ARTIST'S RENDERING
Looks like the ghost turned out to be you!
What the heck is wrong with you?!
WHAT?
Eeeeek!!
To be continued in Volume 4

How to Treat Your Main Character—
Four-Eyed Prince–Style!

My heroines tend to be predisposed to being miserable as it is, but poor Sachi's the most miserable out of all of them. It's really too bad, 'cause "sachi" also means "happiness" in Japanese, you know!

Random Phone Conference #1 (This is a good example of one of our typical meetings.)

I presented the name to my superiors.

My supervisor, N-san

Mizukami

Oh yeah? What'd they think?

Hey...

that sounded like something Sachi would say!!

Yeah, I guess it did.

I guess that makes me "sachi" (happy) then!

And that was how we ended that phone call.

Random Phone Conference #2 (This was about Chapter 8.)

When it comes to Lily, all she has to do is apologize once and the prince will forgive her. But Sachi would have to apologize 100 times before he would forgive her. That's how big a difference there is between the two of them.

That's so harsh!

Poor Sachi!

What a nice boss she is!

You should at least make Lily have to apologize twice, if Sachi has to apologize 100 times!

That'd be practically the same as it already is...

Well, I *thought* she was nice, anyway...

We ended the meeting on that note.

Good luck, Sachi! Hang in there!!

About the Bonus Story:
Pretty-boy Hater

From the start I've always wanted to come up with bonus stories
that were completely different from *Four-Eyed Prince*.
That's how I wound up with the following story. I've been coming up
with one bonus story for each volume of *Four-Eyed Prince*
and writing them bit by bit from 2005 to 2006. I've tried to come
up with a new and fresh idea every time... so I hope I've managed to
create stories that my readers have enjoyed! ♫

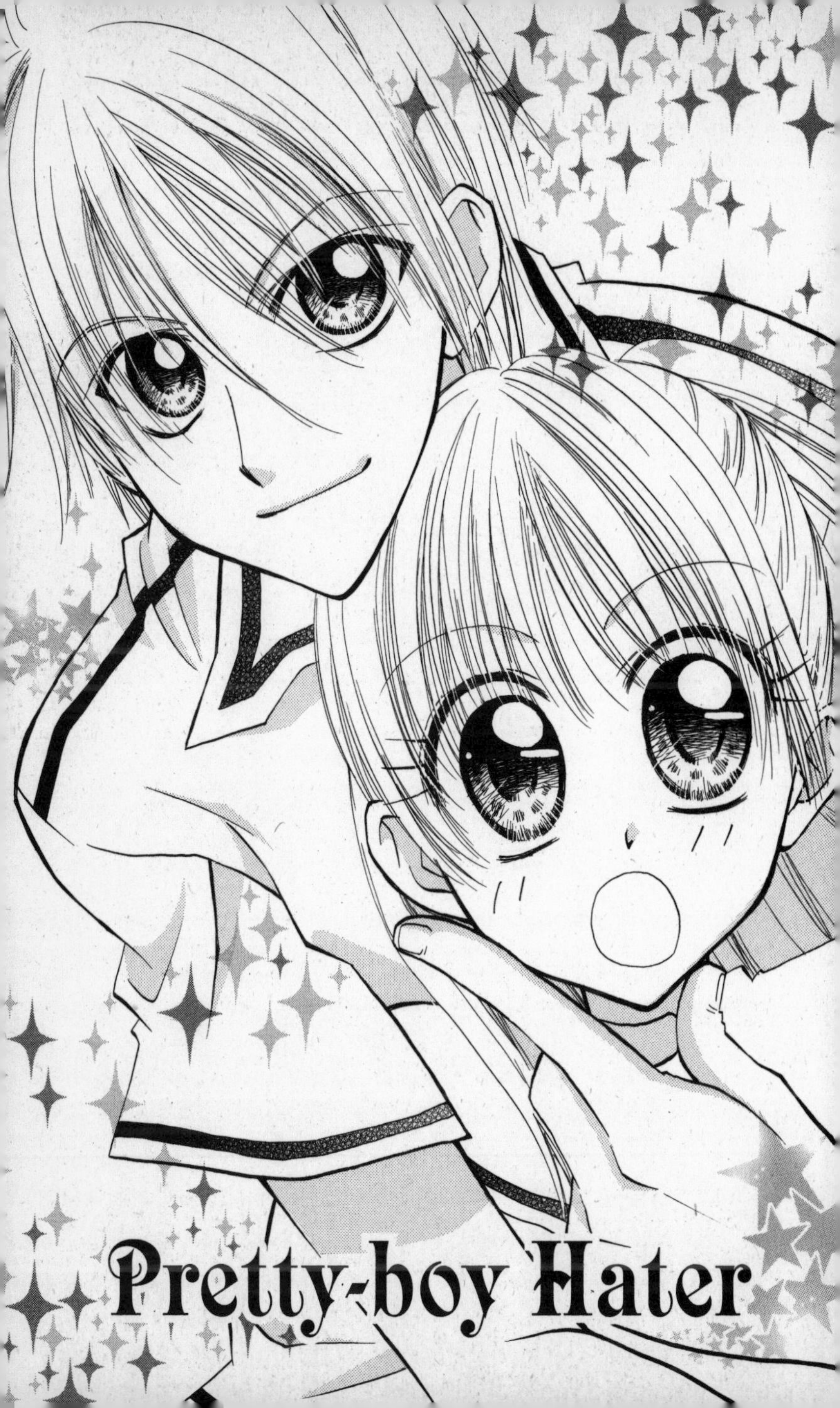
Pretty-boy Hater

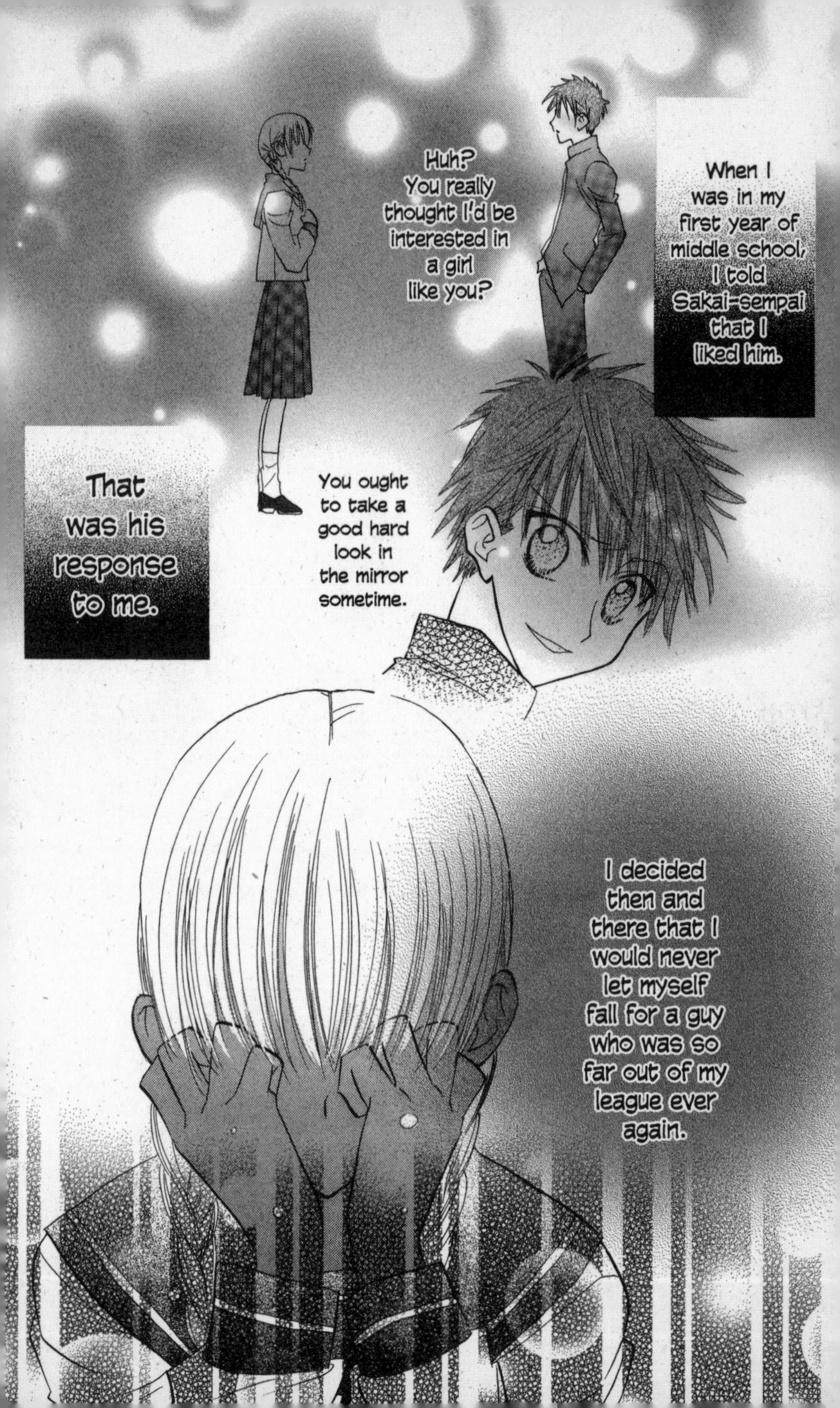
When I was in my first year of middle school, I told Sakai-sempai that I liked him.
Huh? You really thought I'd be interested in a girl like you?
You ought to take a good hard look in the mirror sometime.
That was his response to me.
I decided then and there that I would never let myself fall for a guy who was so far out of my league ever again.

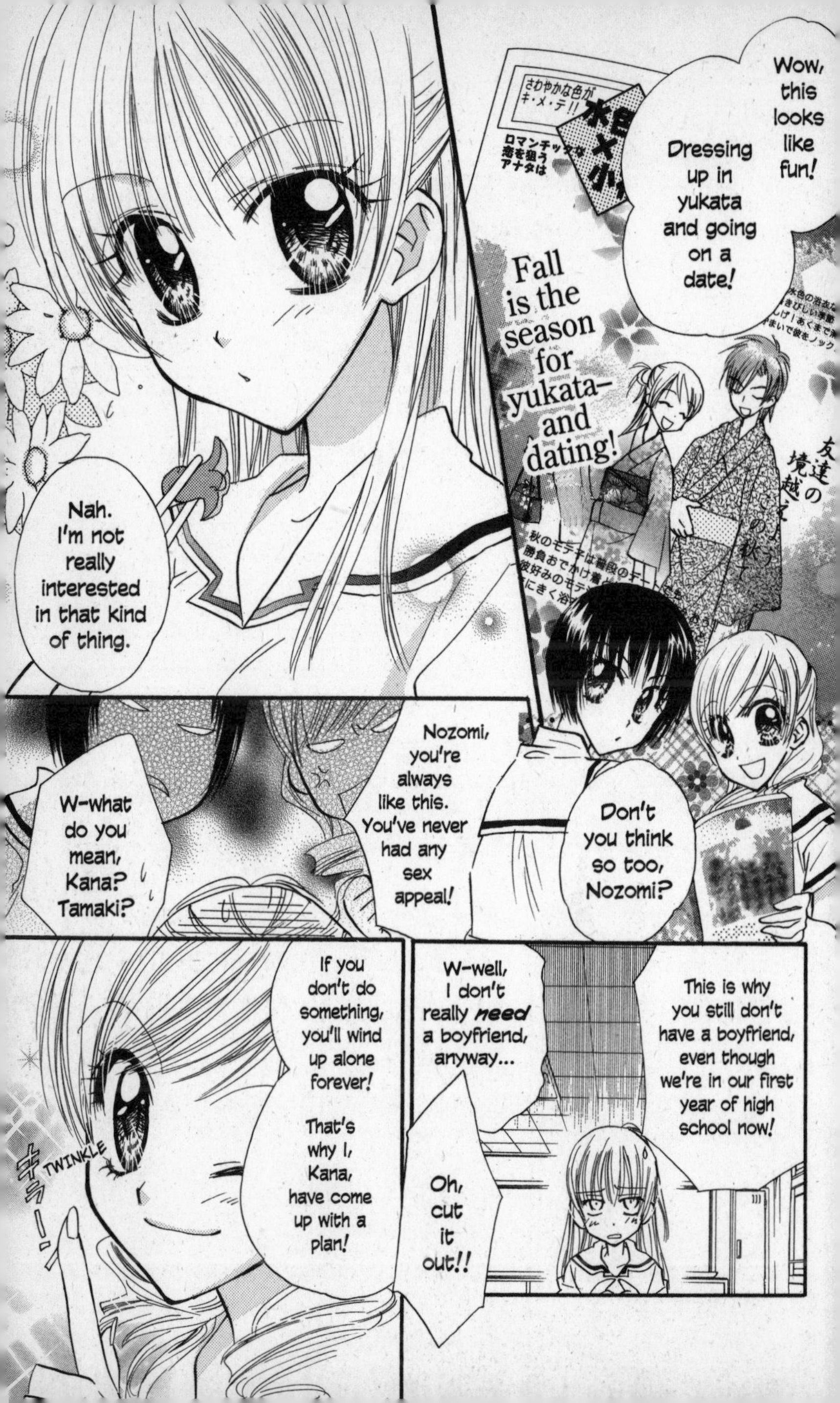
さわやかな色がキ・メ・テ!!
ロマンチックな恋を狙うアナタは
Fall is the season for yukata—and dating!
Wow, this looks like fun!
Dressing up in yukata and going on a date!
Don't you think so too, Nozomi?
Nah. I'm not really interested in that kind of thing.
Nozomi, you're always like this. You've never had any sex appeal!
W-what do you mean, Kana? Tamaki?
This is why you still don't have a boyfriend, even though we're in our first year of high school now!
W-well, I don't really *need* a boyfriend, anyway...
Oh, cut it out!!
If you don't do something, you'll wind up alone forever!
That's why I, Kana, have come up with a plan!
TWINKLE

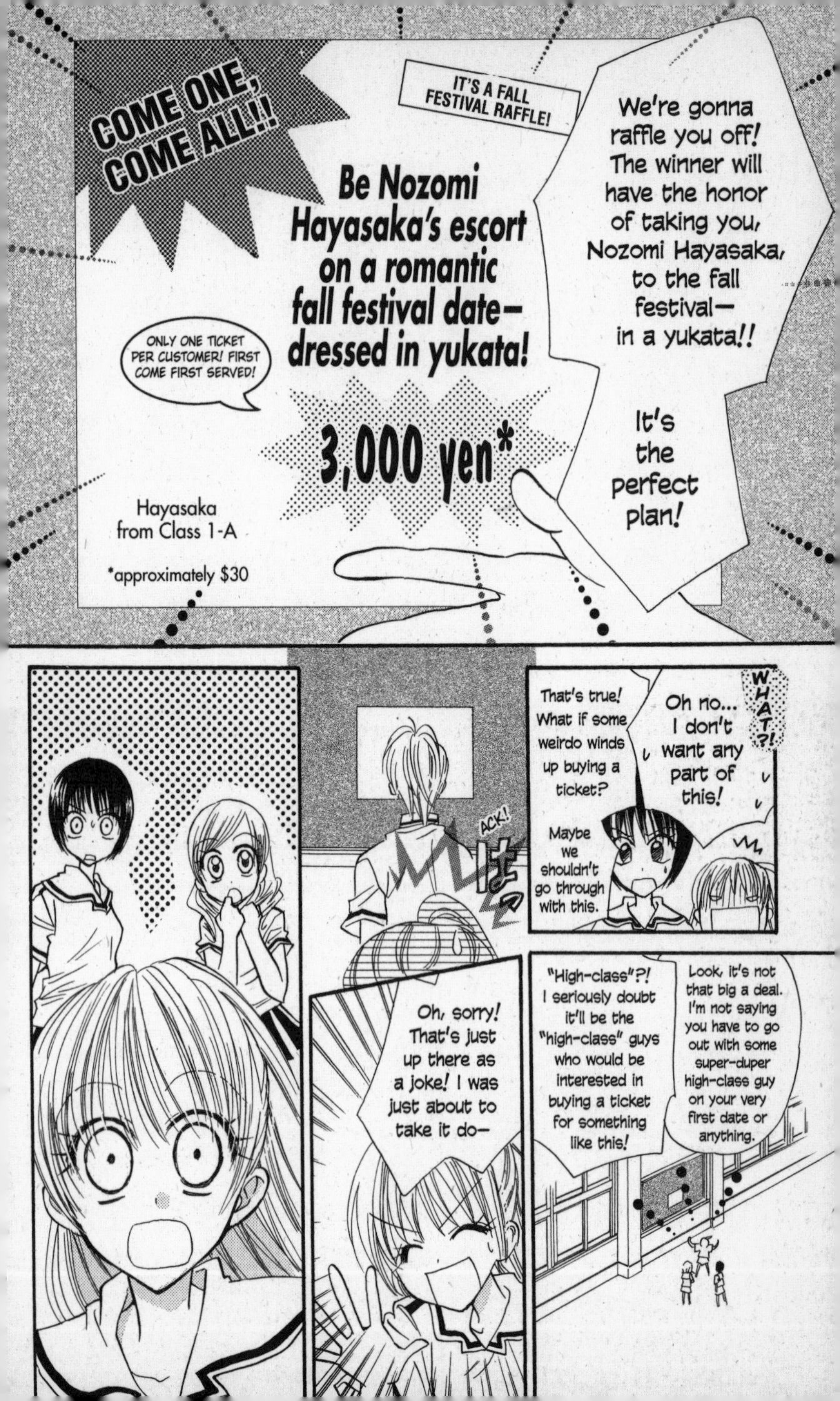
We're gonna raffle you off! The winner will have the honor of taking you, Nozomi Hayasaka, to the fall festival— in a yukata!!
It's the perfect plan!
IT'S A FALL FESTIVAL RAFFLE!
COME ONE, COME ALL!!
Be Nozomi Hayasaka's escort on a romantic fall festival date— dressed in yukata!
ONLY ONE TICKET PER CUSTOMER! FIRST COME FIRST SERVED!
3,000 yen*
Hayasaka from Class 1-A
*approximately $30
WHAT?!
Oh no... I don't want any part of this!
That's true! What if some weirdo winds up buying a ticket?
Maybe we shouldn't go through with this.
Look, it's not that big a deal. I'm not saying you have to go out with some super-duper high-class guy on your very first date or anything.
"High-class"?! I seriously doubt it'll be the "high-class" guys who would be interested in buying a ticket for something like this!
ACK!
Oh, sorry! That's just up there as a joke! I was just about to take it do—

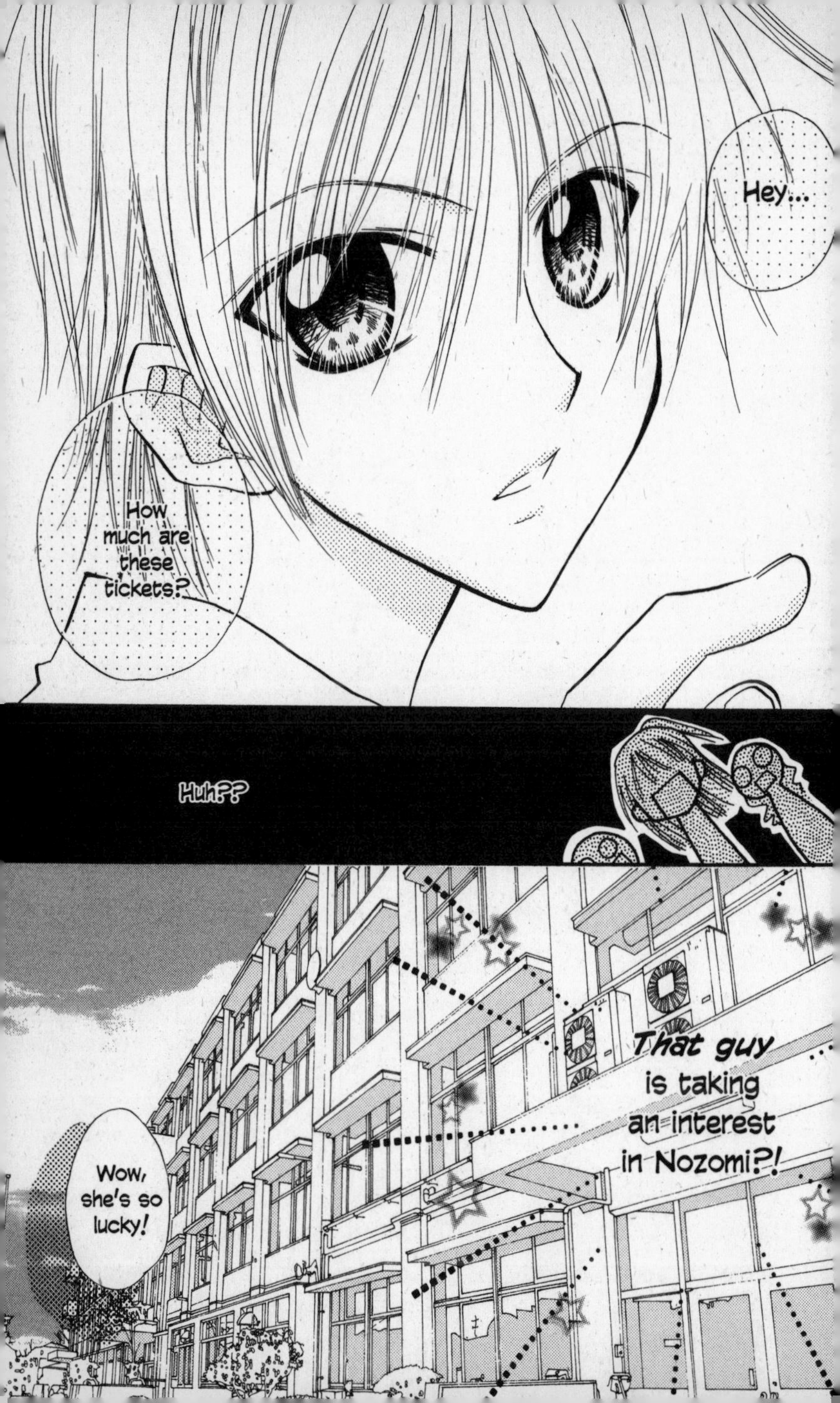
Hey...
How much are these tickets?
Huh??
That guy is taking an interest in Nozomi?!
Wow, she's so lucky!

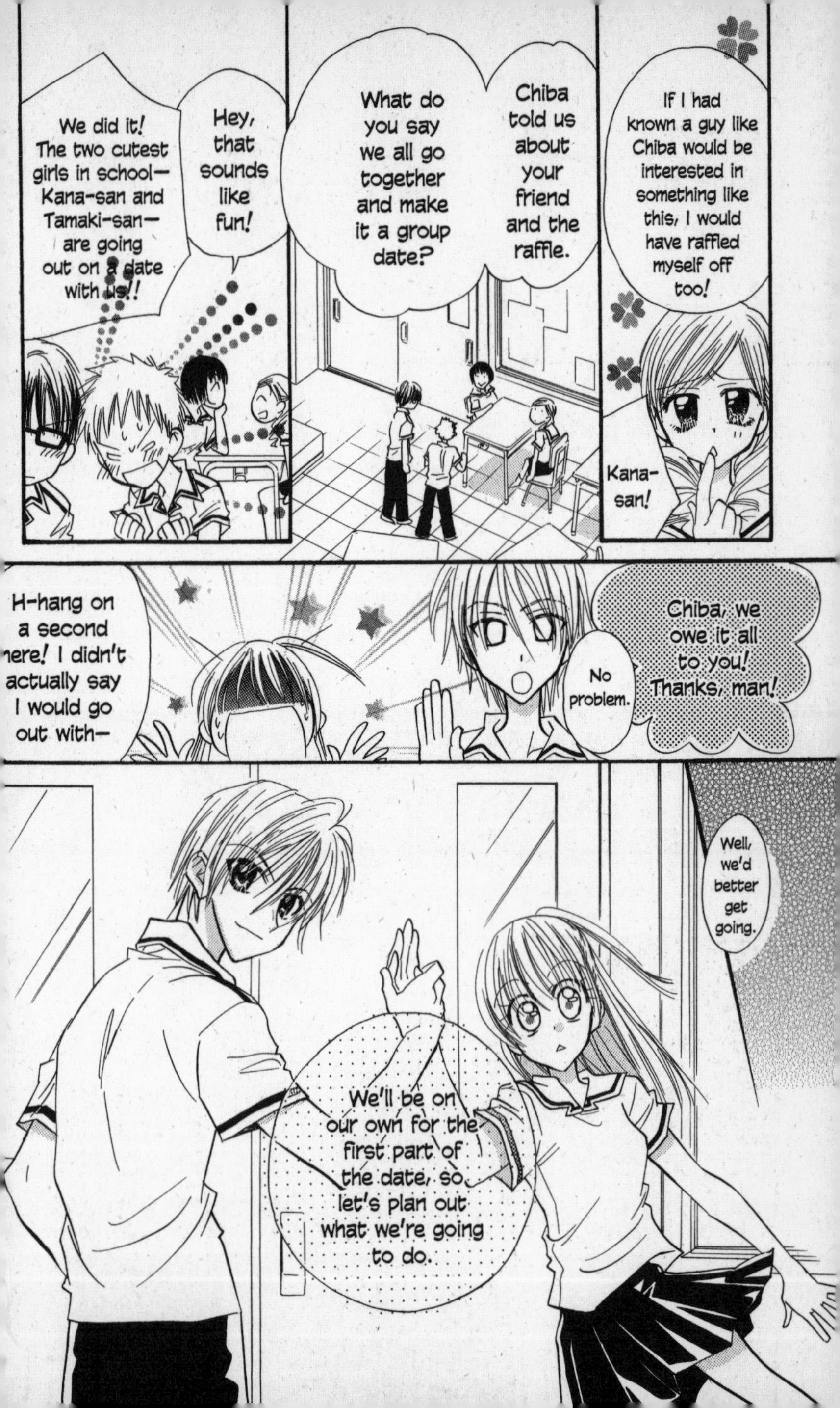
If I had known a guy like Chiba would be interested in something like this, I would have raffled myself off too!
Kana-san!
Chiba told us about your friend and the raffle.
What do you say we all go together and make it a group date?
Hey, that sounds like fun!
We did it! The two cutest girls in school—Kana-san and Tamaki-san—are going out on a date with us!!
Chiba, we owe it all to you! Thanks, man!
No problem.
H-hang on a second here! I didn't actually say I would go out with—
Well, we'd better get going.
We'll be on our own for the first part of the date, so let's plan out what we're going to do.

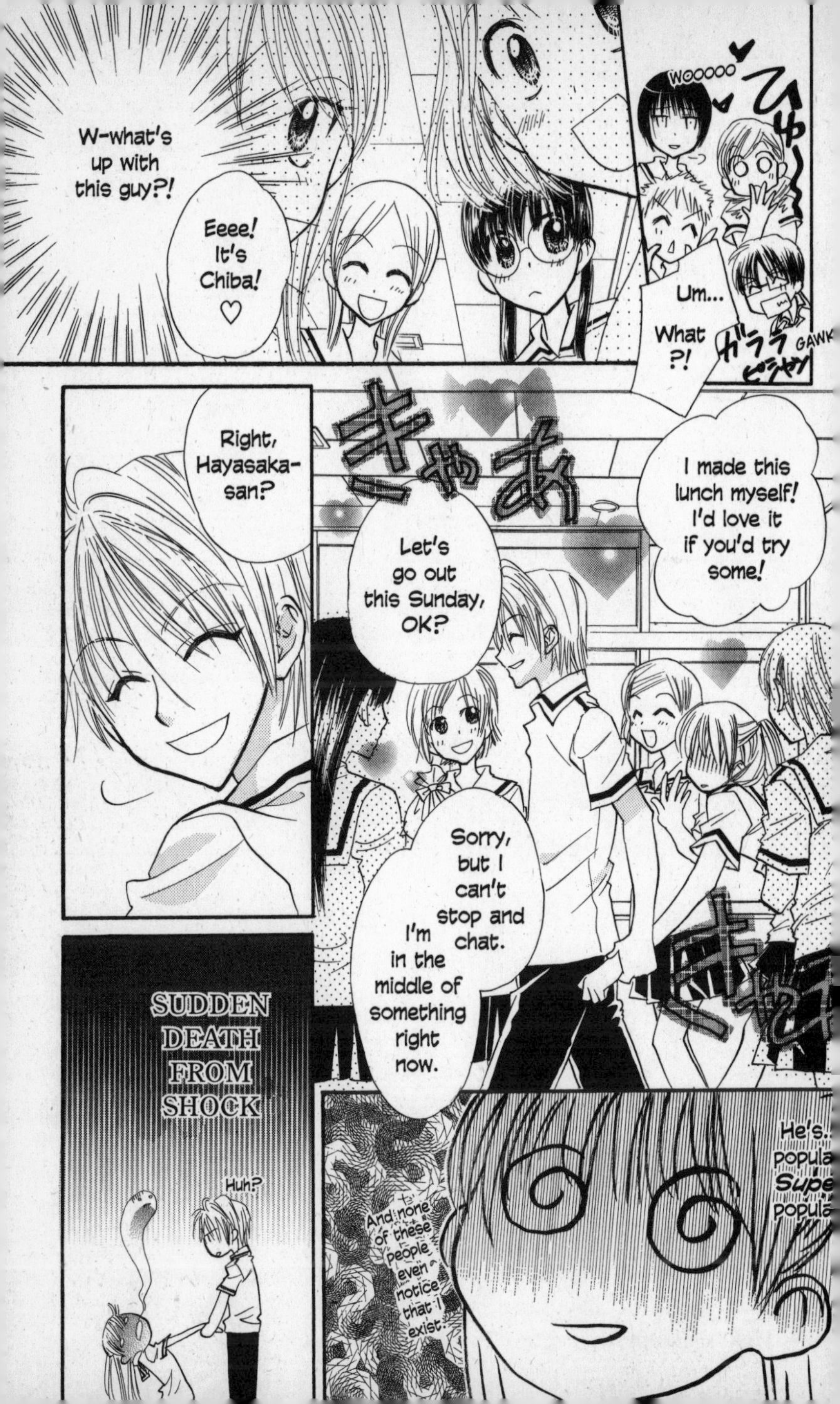
WOOOOO
Um...
What?!
GAWK
Eeee! It's Chiba! ♡
W-what's up with this guy?!
I made this lunch myself! I'd love it if you'd try some!
Let's go out this Sunday, OK?
Sorry, but I can't stop and chat.
I'm in the middle of something right now.
Right, Hayasaka-san?
He's..
popula
Supe
popula
And none of these people even notice that I exist.
SUDDEN DEATH FROM SHOCK
Huh?

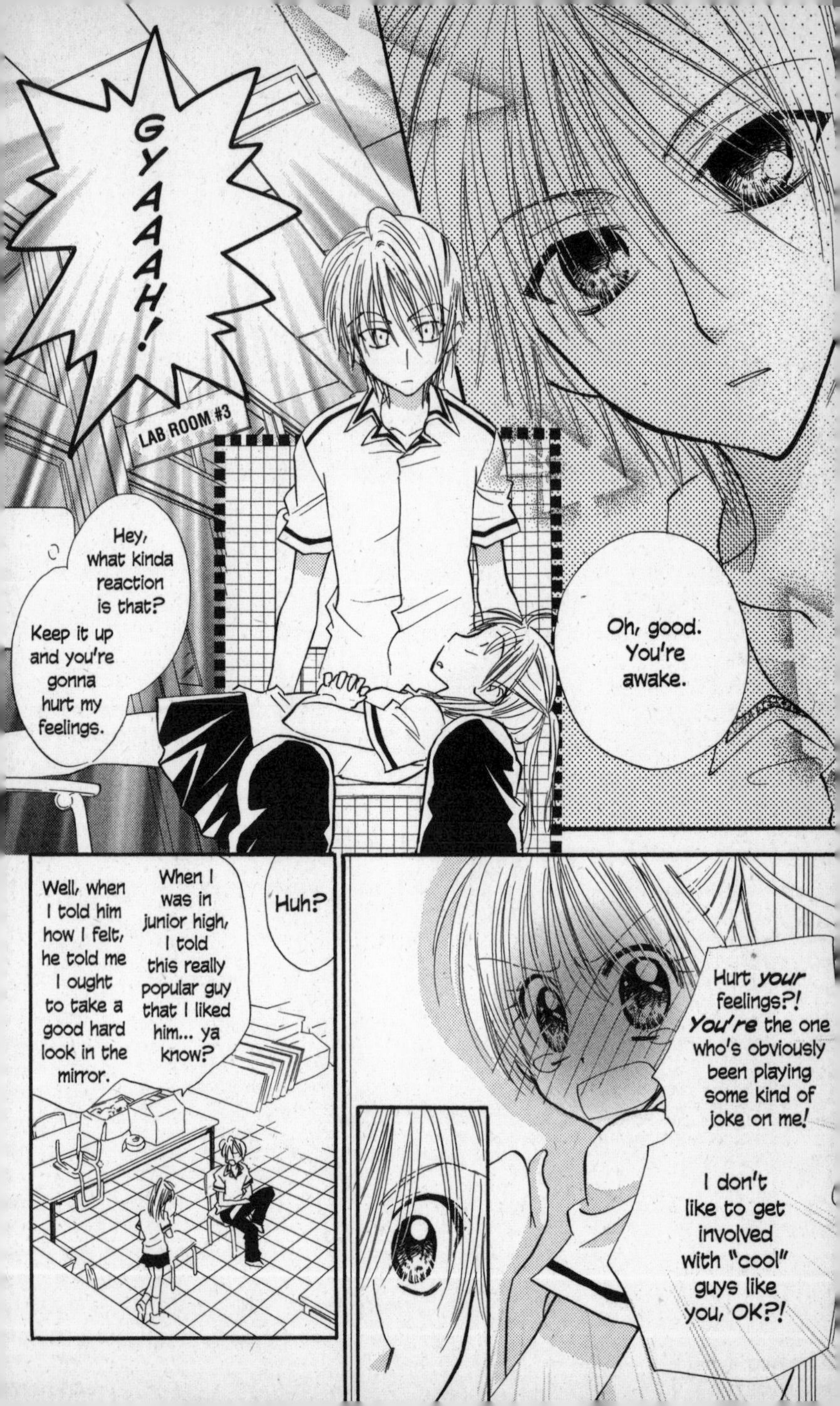
Oh, good. You're awake.
GYAAAH!
LAB ROOM #3
Hey, what kinda reaction is that?
Keep it up and you're gonna hurt my feelings.
Hurt *your* feelings?! *You're* the one who's obviously been playing some kind of joke on me!
I don't like to get involved with "cool" guys like you, OK?!
Huh?
When I was in junior high, I told this really popular guy that I liked him... ya know?
Well, when I told him how I felt, he told me I ought to take a good hard look in the mirror.

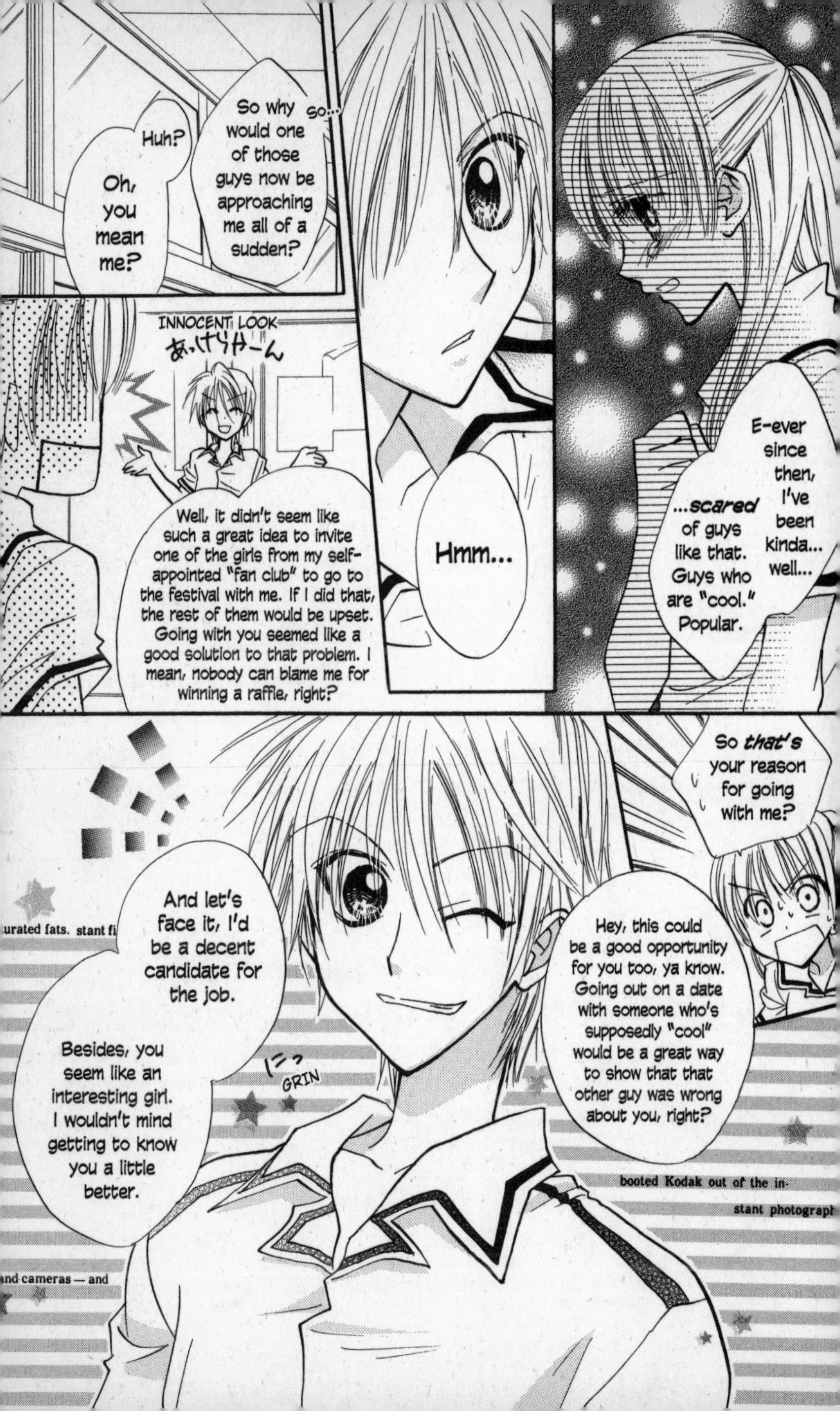

E-ever since then, I've been kinda... well...
...*scared* of guys like that. Guys who are "cool." Popular.
Hmm...
So...
So why would one of those guys now be approaching me all of a sudden?
Huh?
Oh, you mean me?
INNOCENT LOOK
あっけらかーん
Well, it didn't seem like such a great idea to invite one of the girls from my self-appointed "fan club" to go to the festival with me. If I did that, the rest of them would be upset. Going with you seemed like a good solution to that problem. I mean, nobody can blame me for winning a raffle, right?
So *that's* your reason for going with me?
Hey, this could be a good opportunity for you too, ya know. Going out on a date with someone who's supposedly "cool" would be a great way to show that that other guy was wrong about you, right?
And let's face it, I'd be a decent candidate for the job.
Besides, you seem like an interesting girl. I wouldn't mind getting to know you a little better.
にっ
GRIN
urated fats. stant fi
booted Kodak out of the in-
stant photograph
nd cameras — and

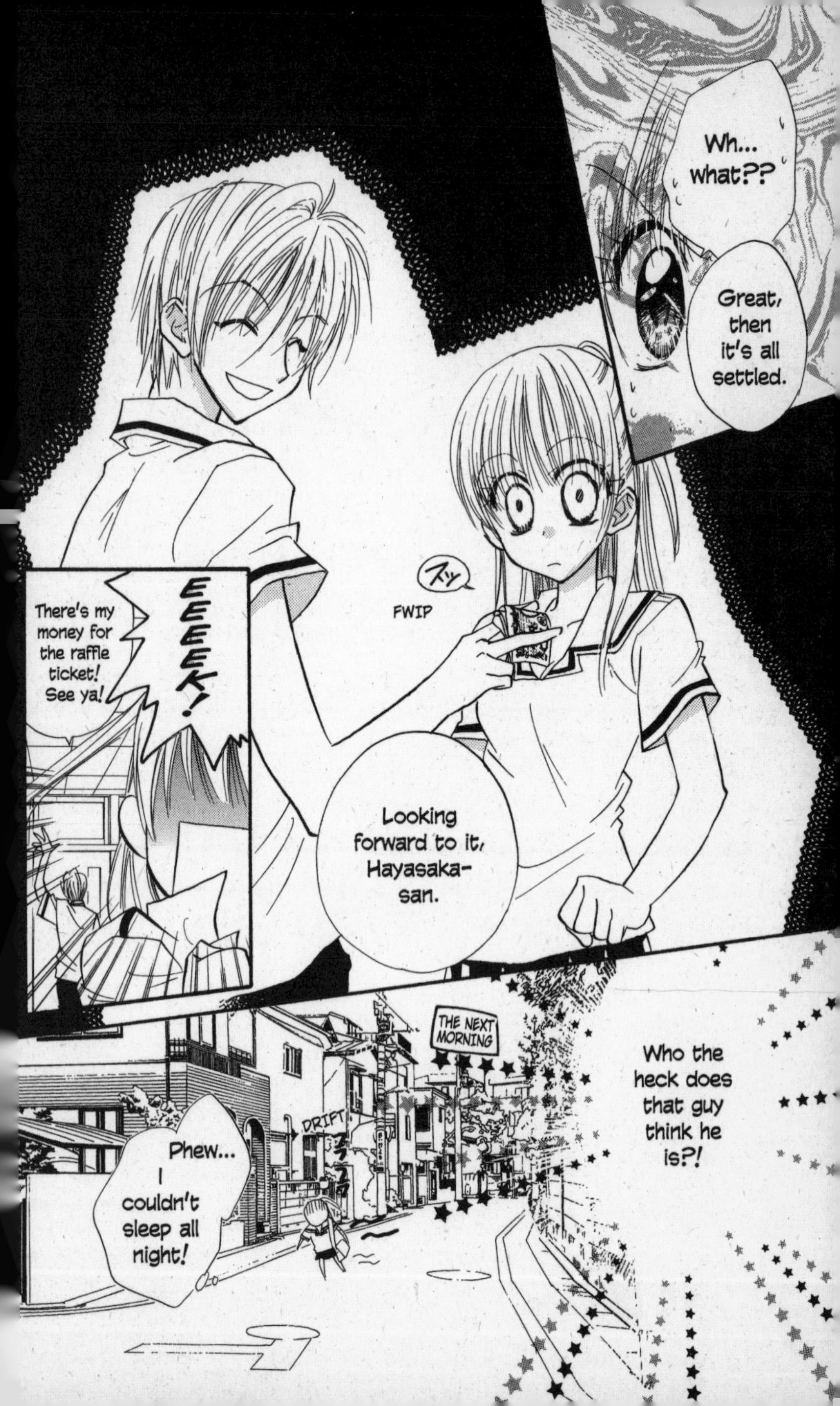
Wh... what??
Great, then it's all settled.
ズッ
FWIP
Looking forward to it, Hayasaka-san.
EEEEK!
There's my money for the raffle ticket! See ya!
THE NEXT MORNING
Who the heck does that guy think he is?!
DRIFT
Phew... I couldn't sleep all night!

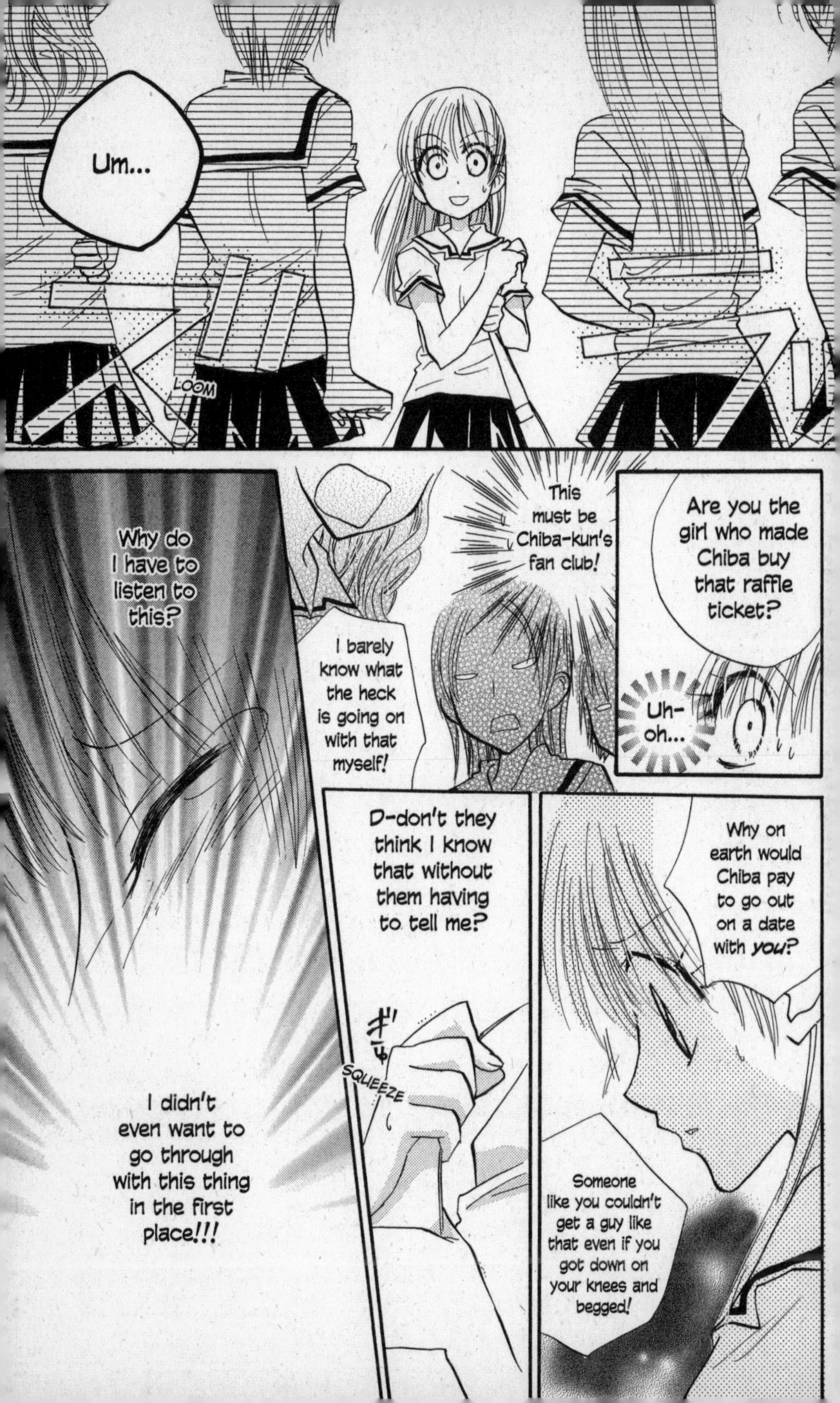
Um...
LOOM
Are you the girl who made Chiba buy that raffle ticket?
Uh-oh...
This must be Chiba-kun's fan club!
I barely know what the heck is going on with that myself!
Why on earth would Chiba pay to go out on a date with *you*?
Someone like you couldn't get a guy like that even if you got down on your knees and begged!
D-don't they think I know that without them having to tell me?
ギュ
SQUEEZE
Why do I have to listen to this?
I didn't even want to go through with this thing in the first place!!!

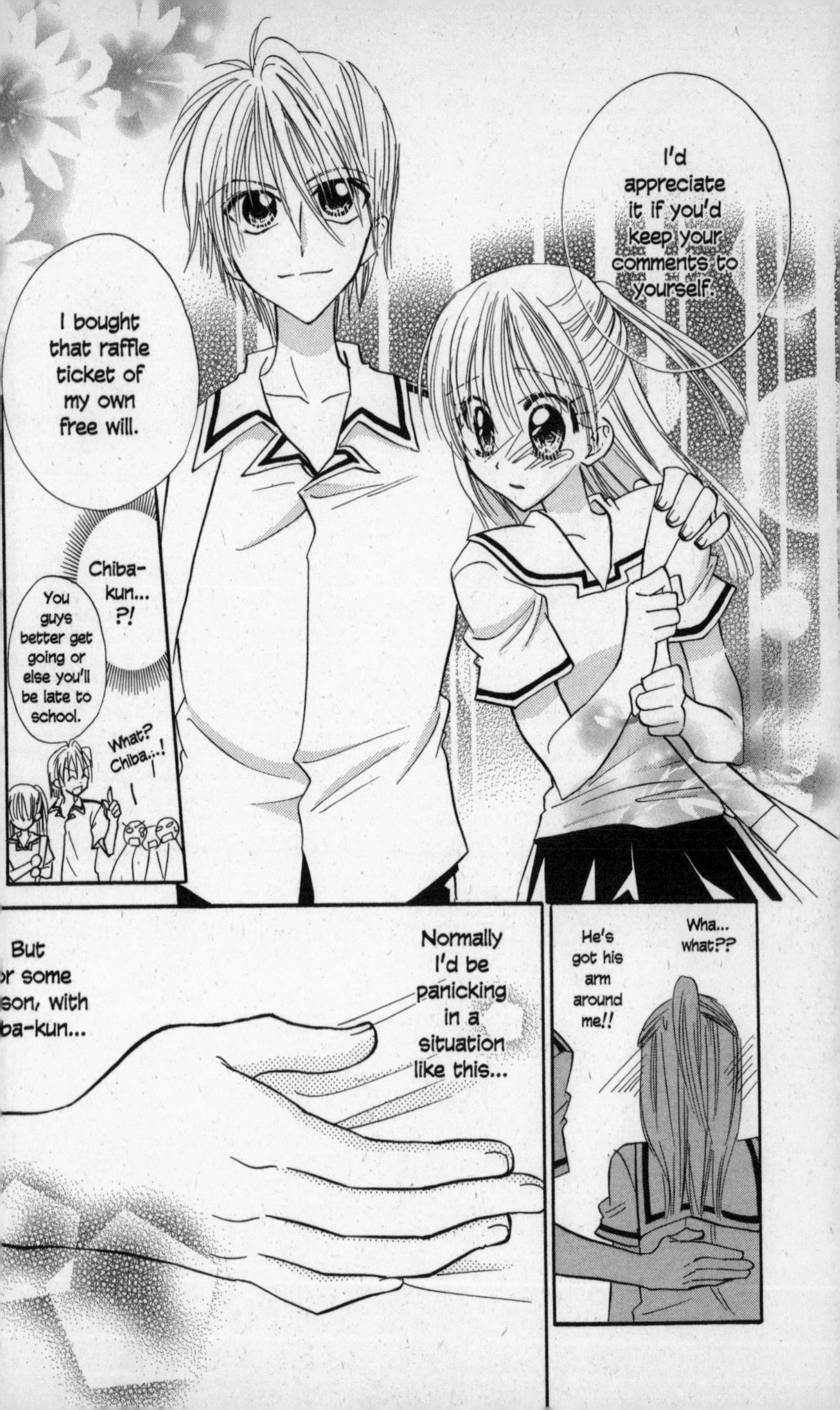
I'd appreciate it if you'd keep your comments to yourself.
I bought that raffle ticket of my own free will.
Chiba-kun...?!
You guys better get going or else you'll be late to school.
What? Chiba...!
Wha... what??
He's got his arm around me!!
Normally I'd be panicking in a situation like this...
But
r some
son, with
ba-kun...

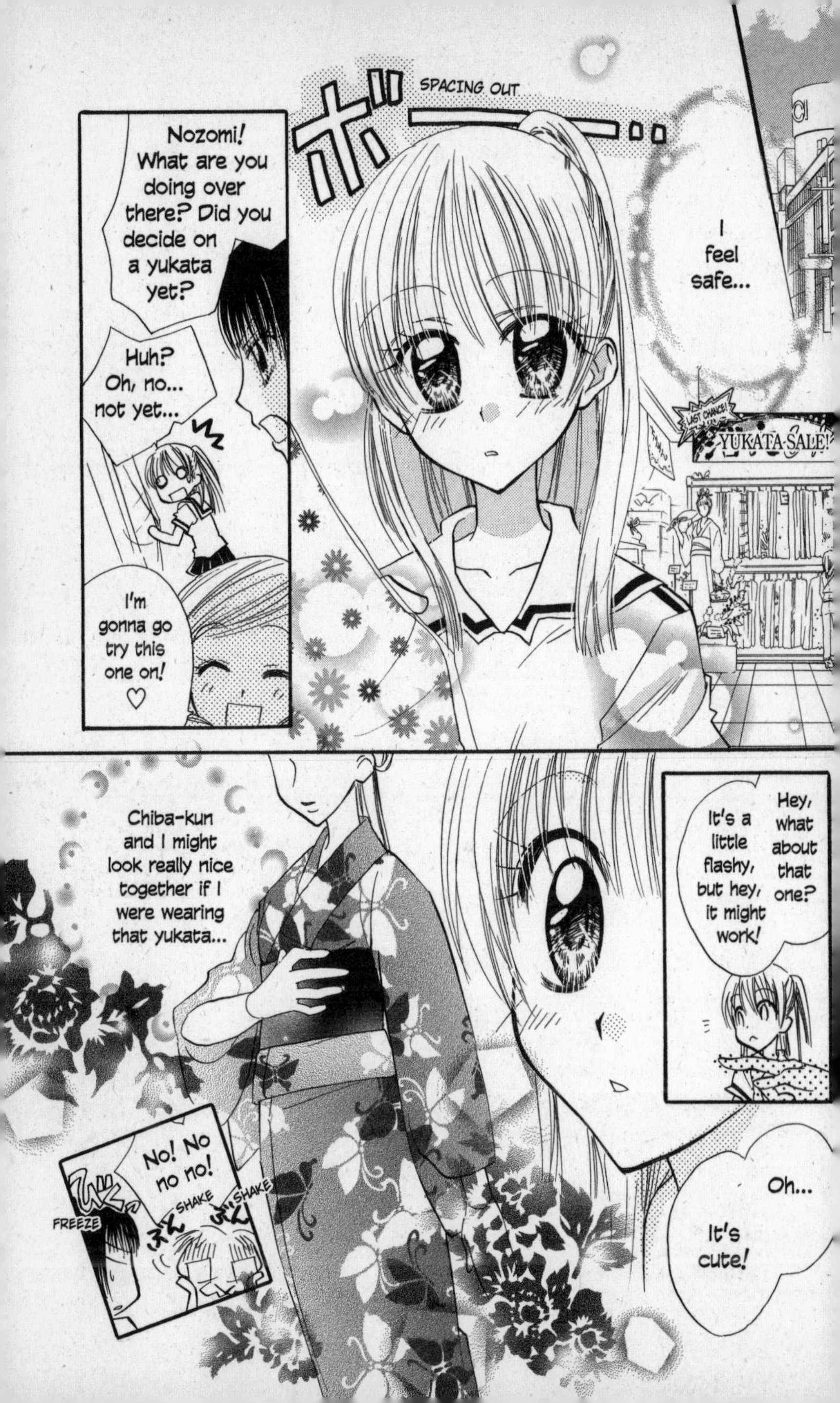

SPACING OUT
I feel safe...
LAST CHANCE!
YUKATA SALE!
Nozomi! What are you doing over there? Did you decide on a yukata yet?
Huh? Oh, no... not yet...
I'm gonna go try this one on! ♡
Hey, what about that one?
It's a little flashy, but hey, it might work!
Oh...
It's cute!
Chiba-kun and I might look really nice together if I were wearing that yukata...
No! No no no!
FREEZE
SHAKE
SHAKE

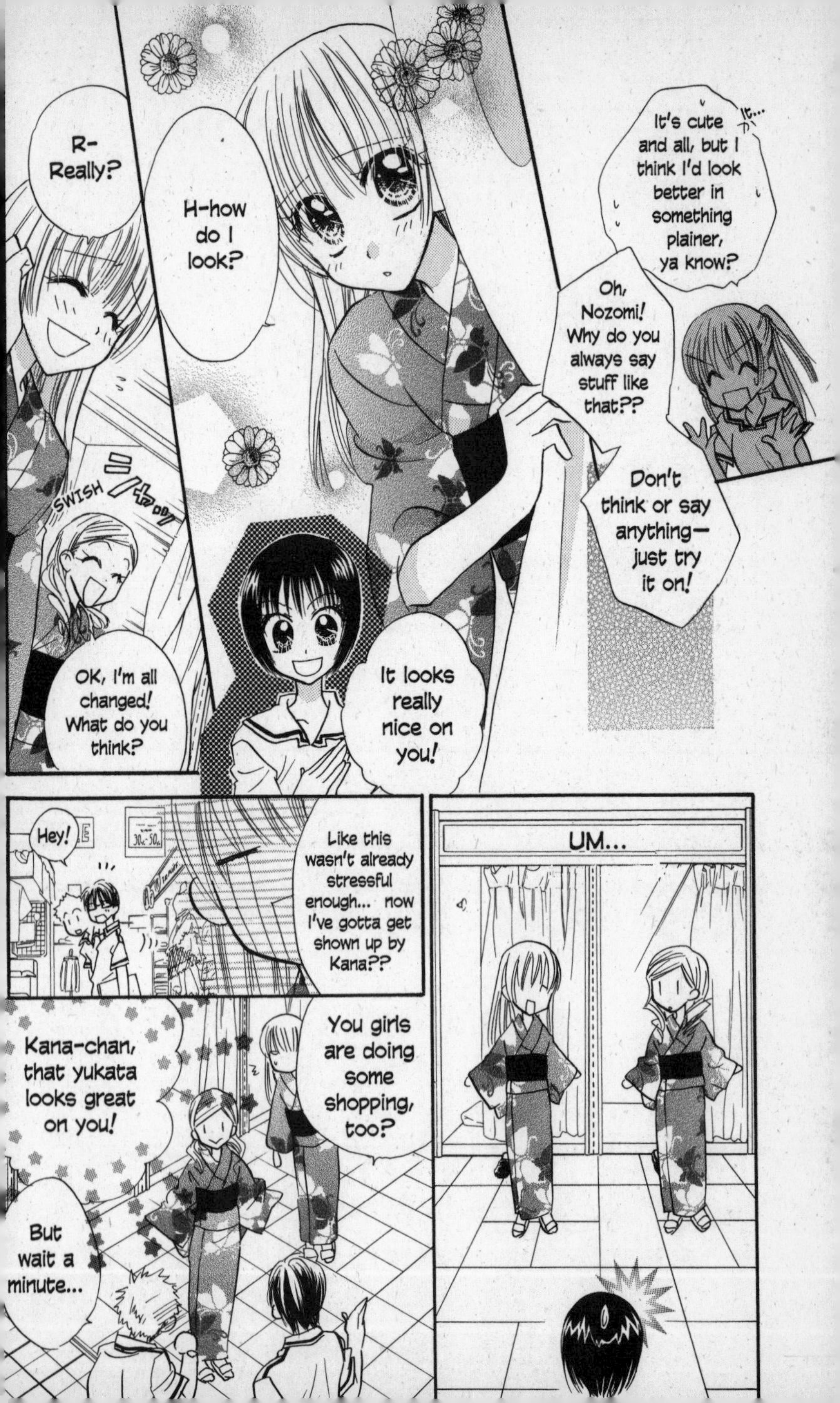

It's cute and all, but I think I'd look better in something plainer, ya know?
It...
Oh, Nozomi! Why do you always say stuff like that??
Don't think or say anything—just try it on!
H-how do I look?
It looks really nice on you!
R- Really?
SWISH
OK, I'm all changed! What do you think?
UM...
Like this wasn't already stressful enough... now I've gotta get shown up by Kana??
Hey!
You girls are doing some shopping, too?
Kana-chan, that yukata looks great on you!
But wait a minute...

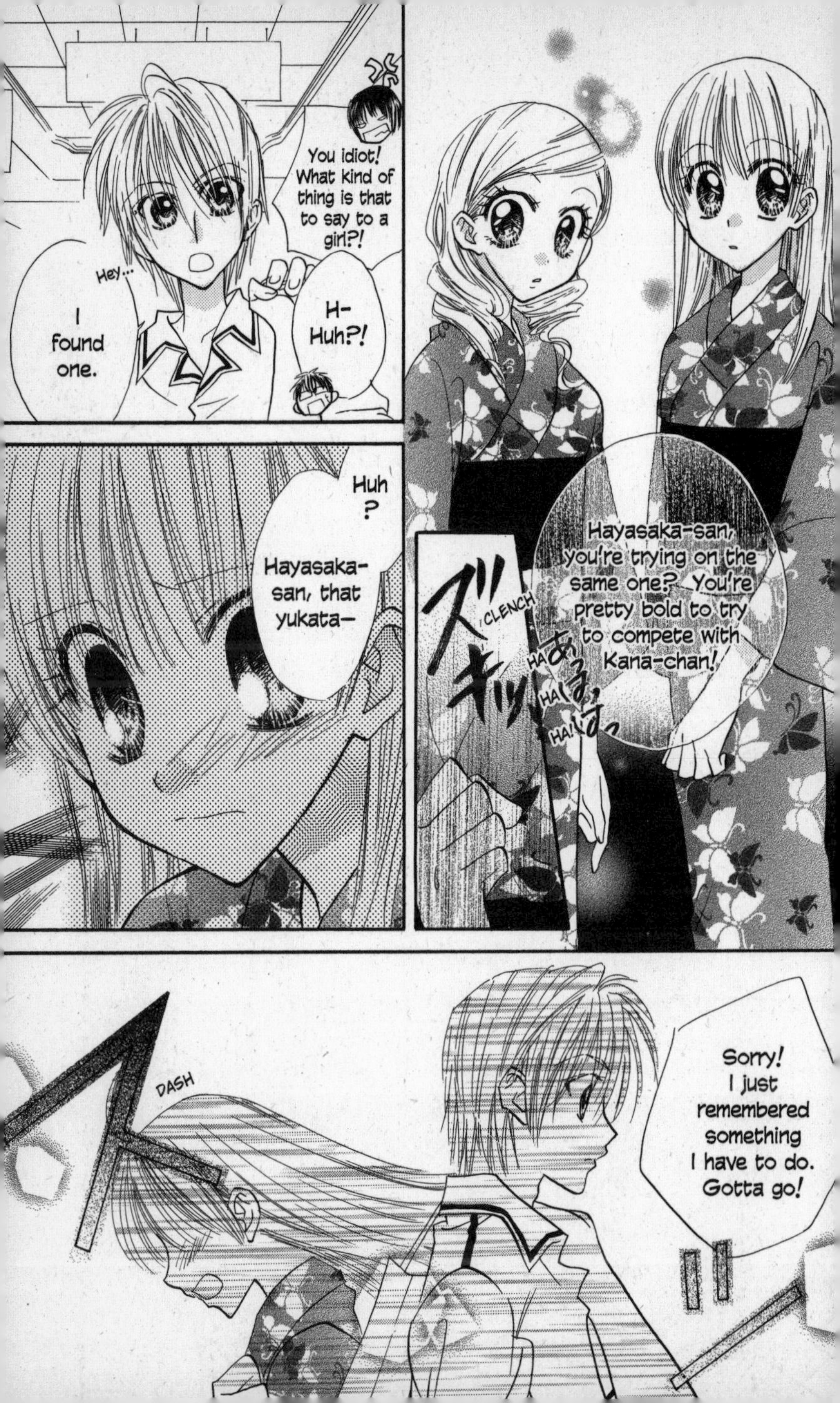
Hayasaka-san, you're trying on the same one? You're pretty bold to try to compete with Kana-chan!
CLENCH
HA HA HA!
You idiot! What kind of thing is that to say to a girl?!
H-Huh?!
Hey...
I found one.
Huh?
Hayasaka-san, that yukata—
Sorry! I just remembered something I have to do. Gotta go!
DASH

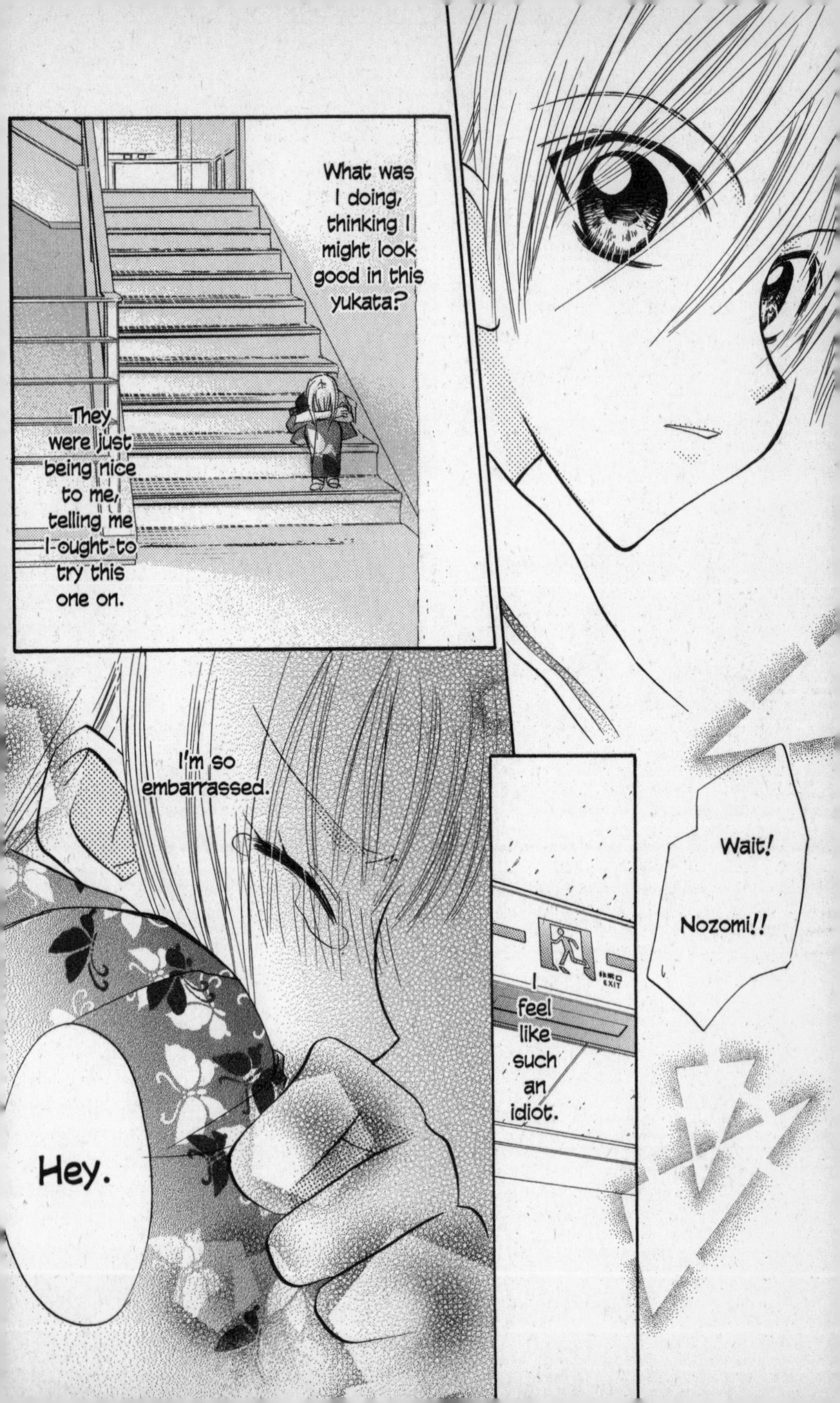
What was I doing, thinking I might look good in this yukata?
They were just being nice to me, telling me I ought to try this one on.
I feel like such an idiot.
Wait!
Nozomi!!
I'm so embarrassed.
Hey.

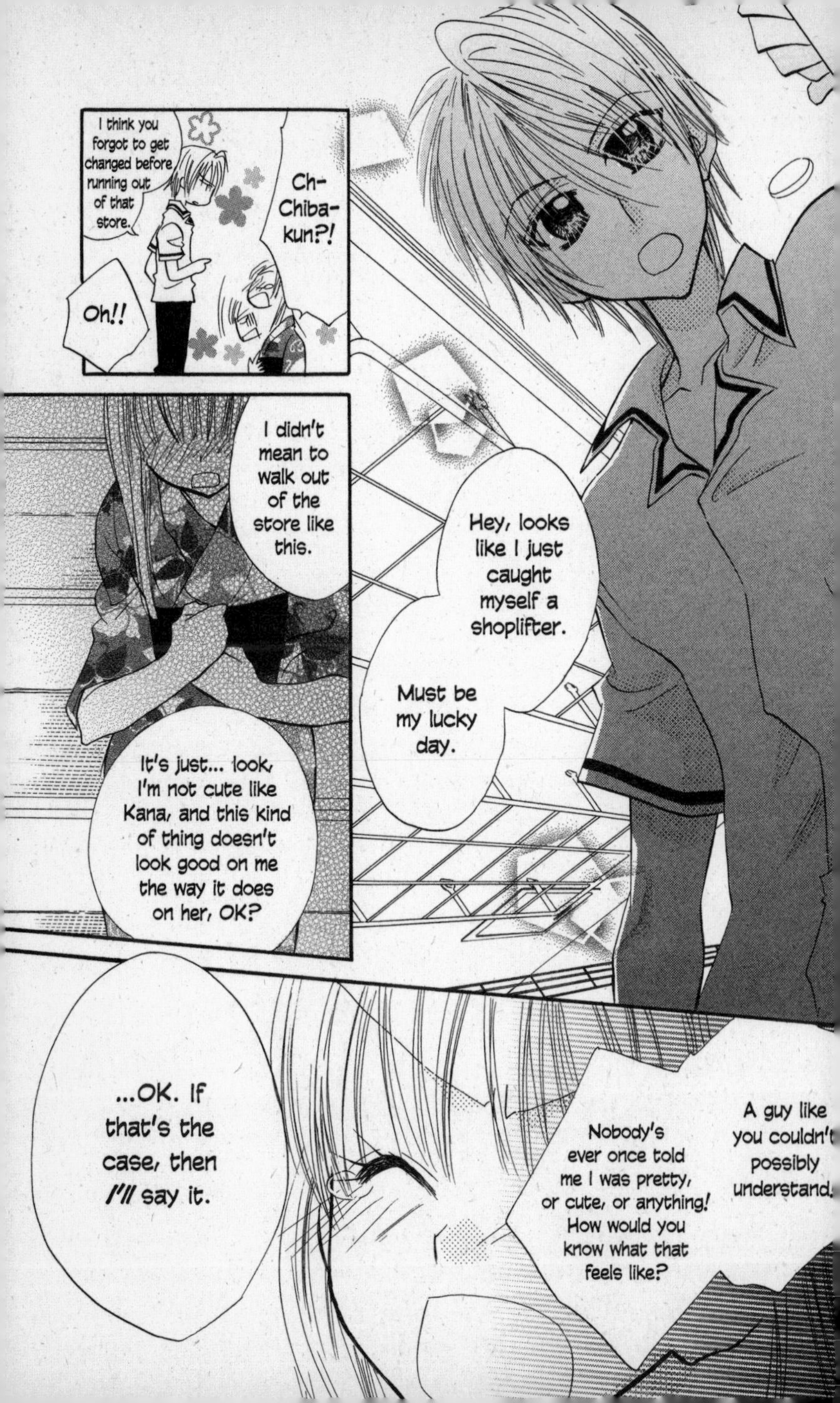
Hey, looks like I just caught myself a shoplifter.
Must be my lucky day.
Ch-Chiba-kun?!
I think you forgot to get changed before running out of that store.
Oh!!
I didn't mean to walk out of the store like this.
It's just... look, I'm not cute like Kana, and this kind of thing doesn't look good on me the way it does on her, OK?
A guy like you couldn't possibly understand.
Nobody's ever once told me I was pretty, or cute, or anything! How would you know what that feels like?
...OK. If that's the case, then *I'll* say it.

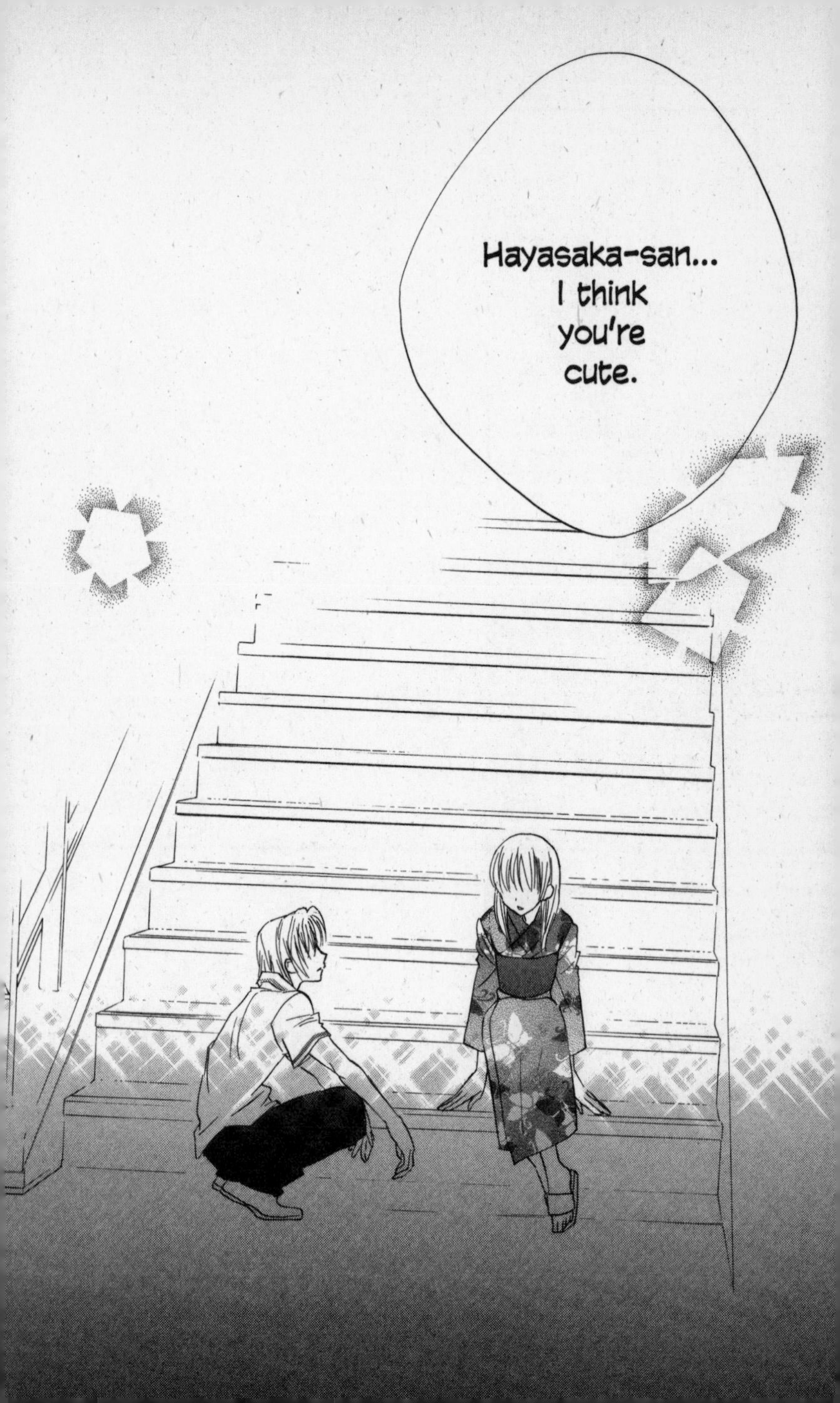
Hayasaka-san... I think you're cute.

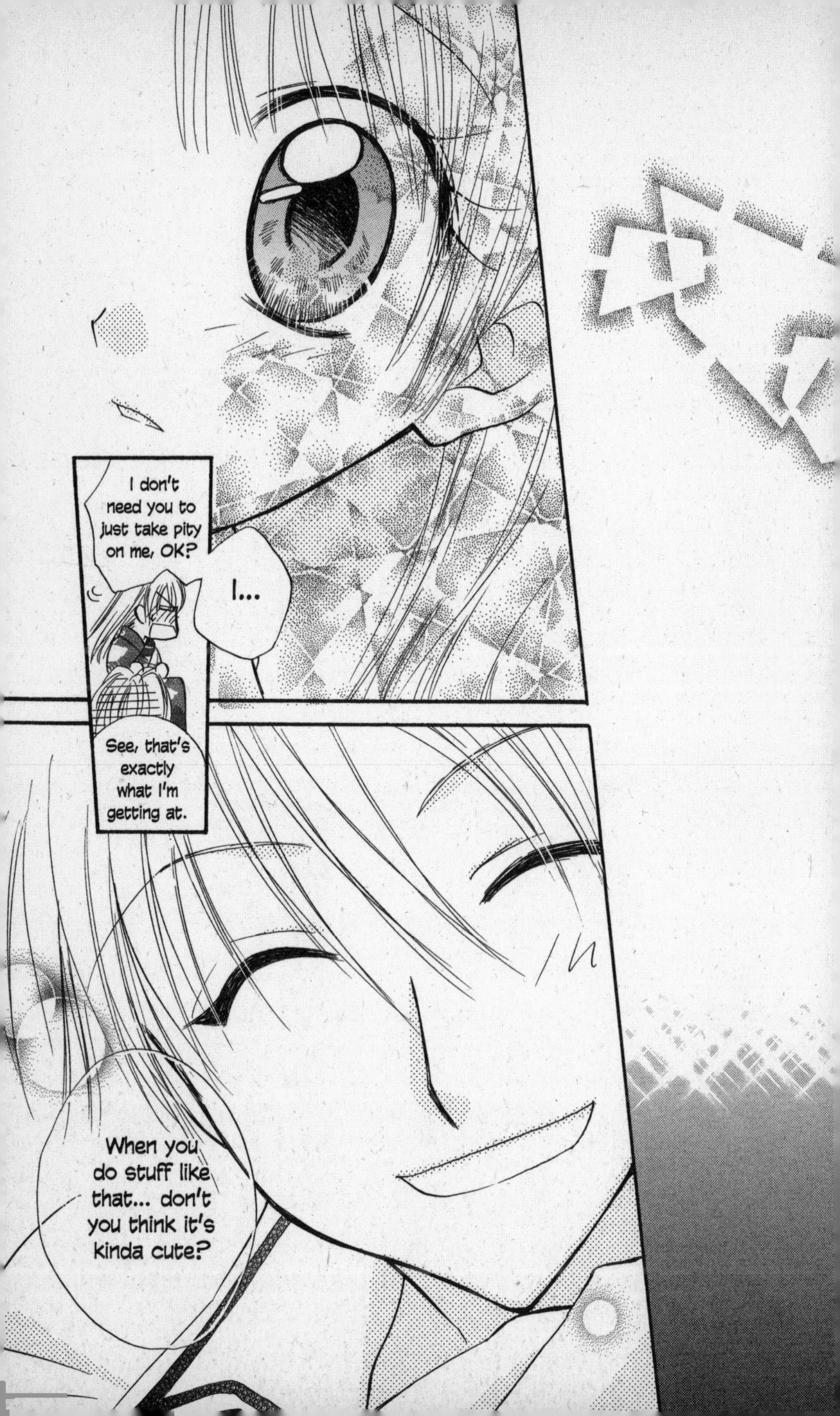
I...
I don't need you to just take pity on me, OK?
See, that's exactly what I'm getting at.
When you do stuff like that... don't you think it's kinda cute?

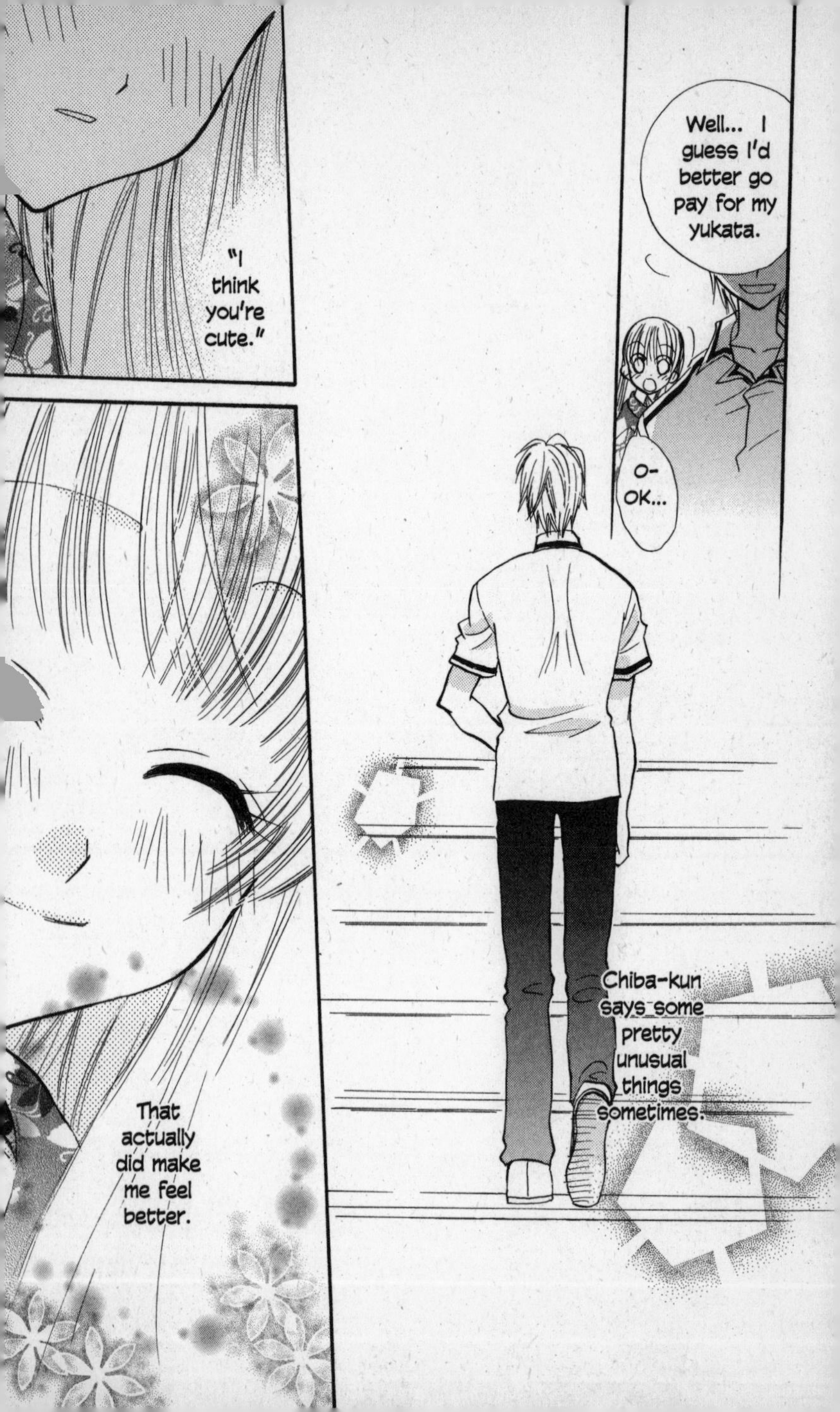
Well... I guess I'd better go pay for my yukata.
O-OK...
Chiba-kun says some pretty unusual things sometimes.
"I think you're cute."
That actually did make me feel better.

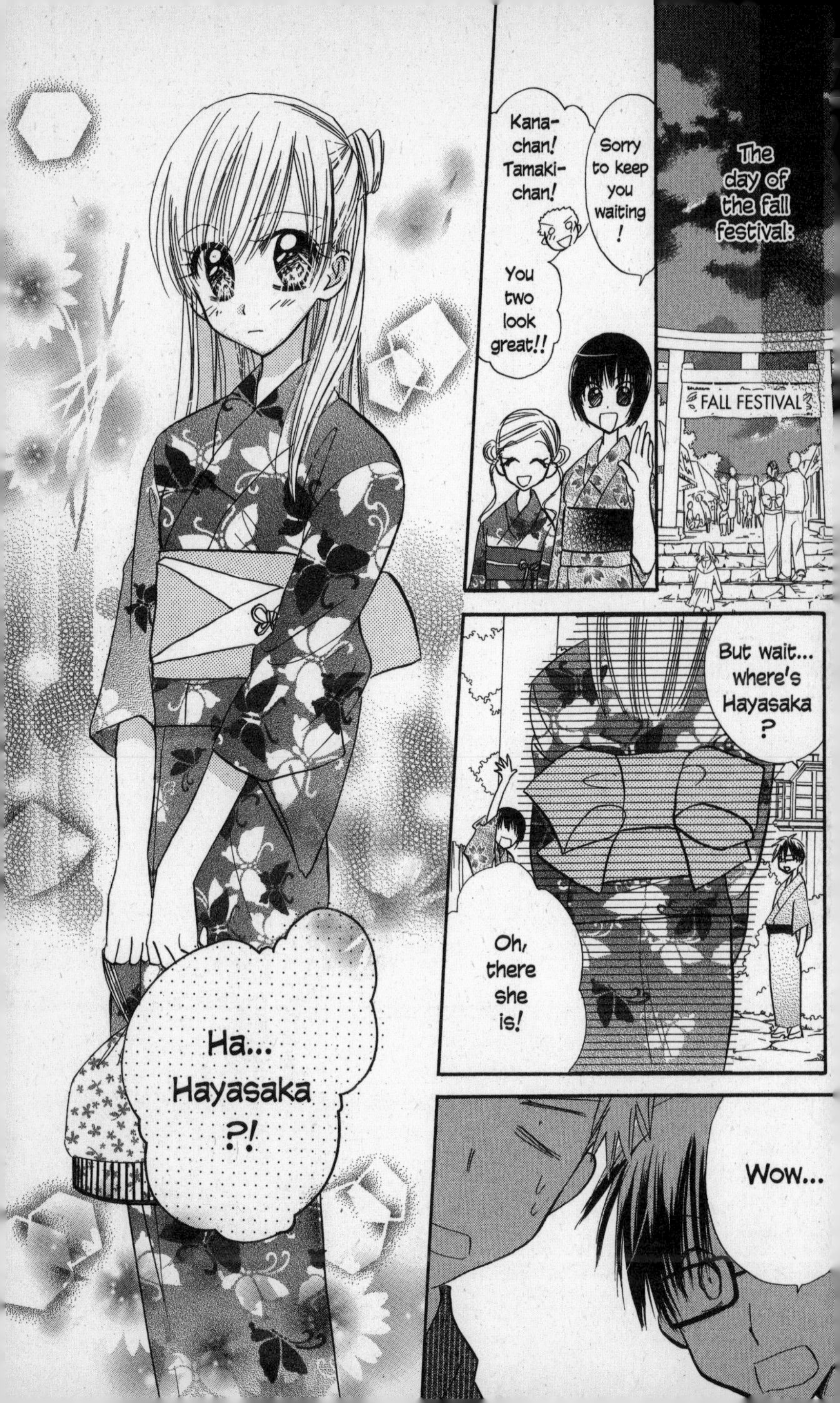
The day of the fall festival.
FALL FESTIVAL
Sorry to keep you waiting!
Kana-chan! Tamaki-chan!
You two look great!!
But wait... where's Hayasaka?
Oh, there she is!
Wow...
Ha... Hayasaka?!

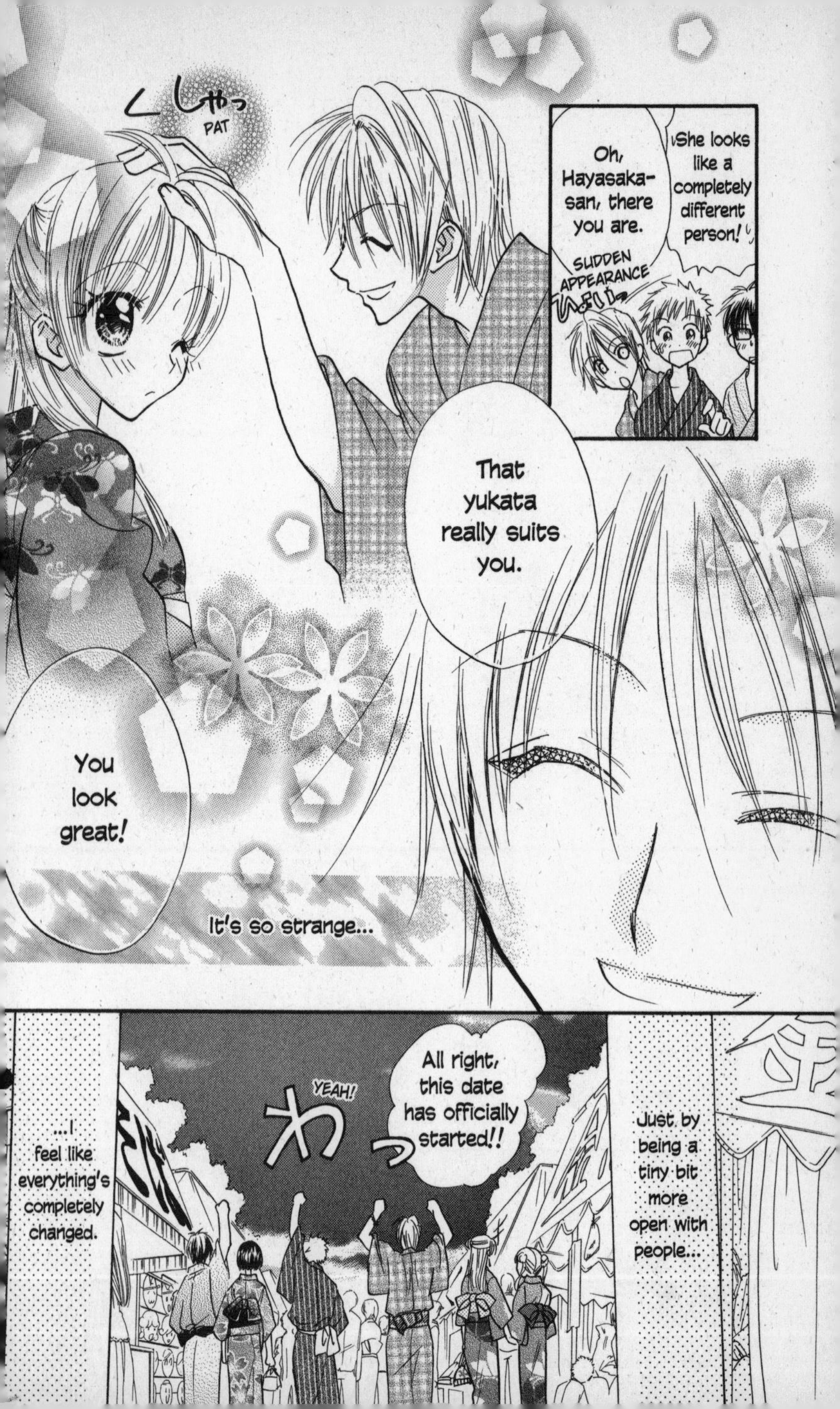

She looks like a completely different person!
Oh, Hayasaka-san, there you are.
SUDDEN APPEARANCE
くしゃっ
PAT
That yukata really suits you.
You look great!
It's so strange...
Just by being a tiny bit more open with people...
All right, this date has officially started!!
わっ
YEAH!
...I feel like everything's completely changed.

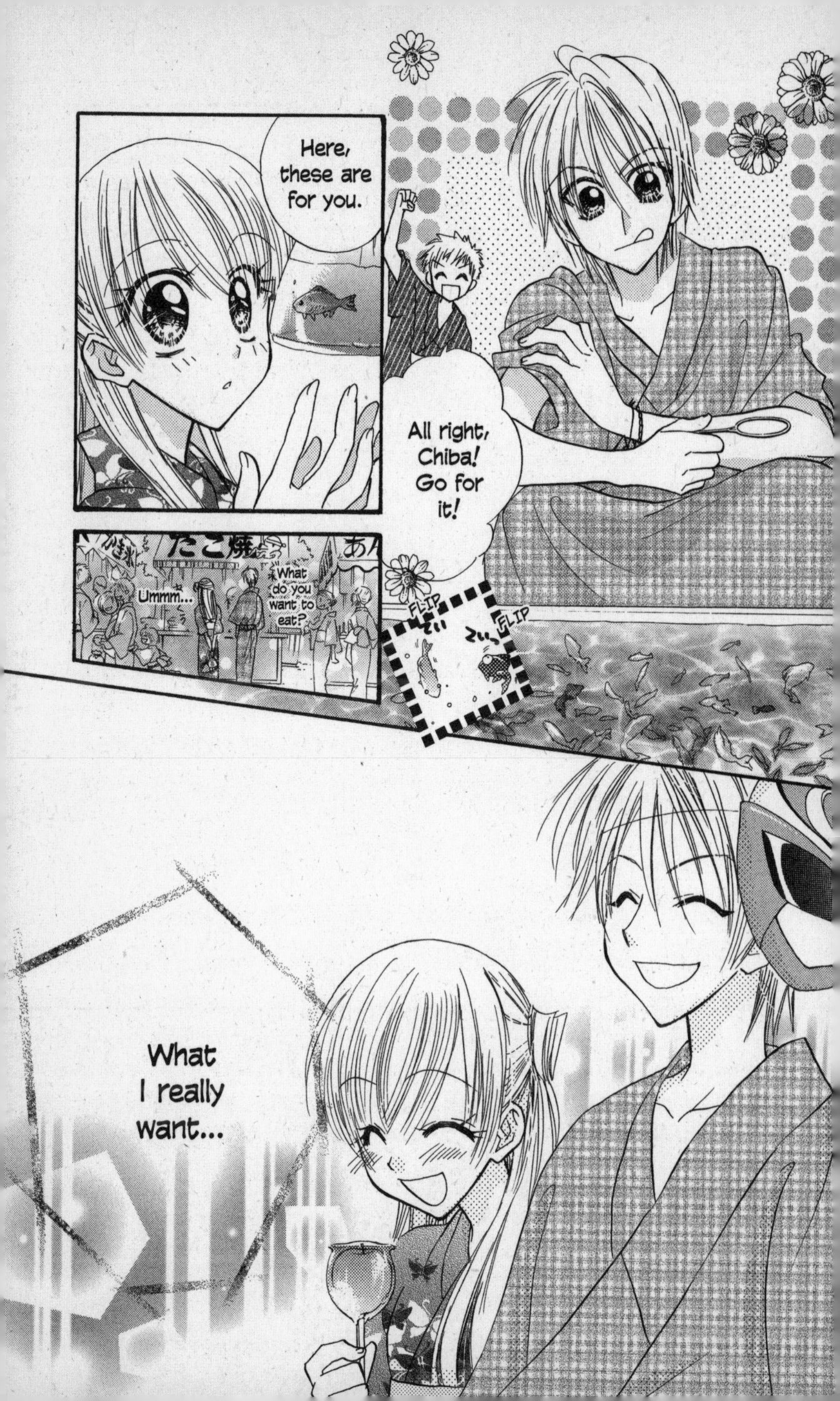
All right, Chiba! Go for it!
FLIP
FLIP
Here, these are for you.
What do you want to eat?
Ummm...
What I really want...

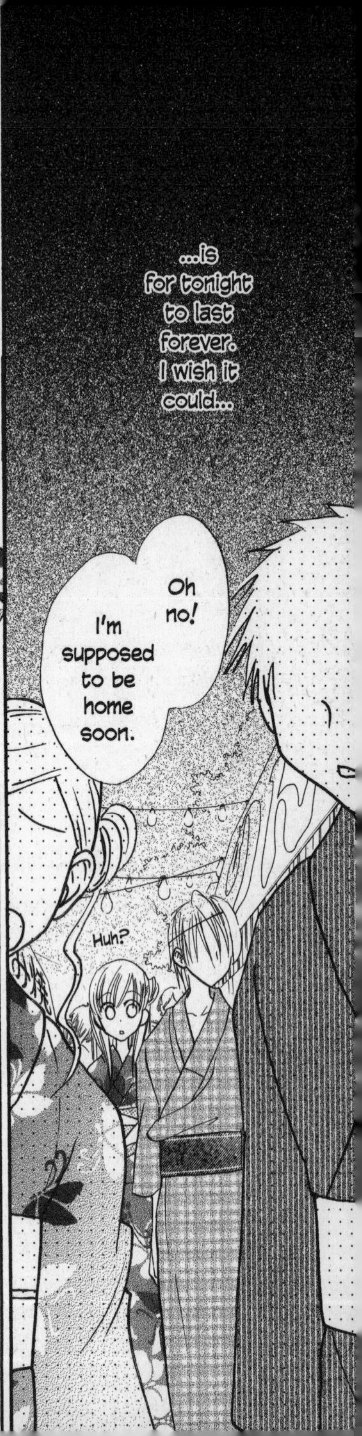
...is for tonight to last forever. I wish it could...
Oh no! I'm supposed to be home soon.
Huh?

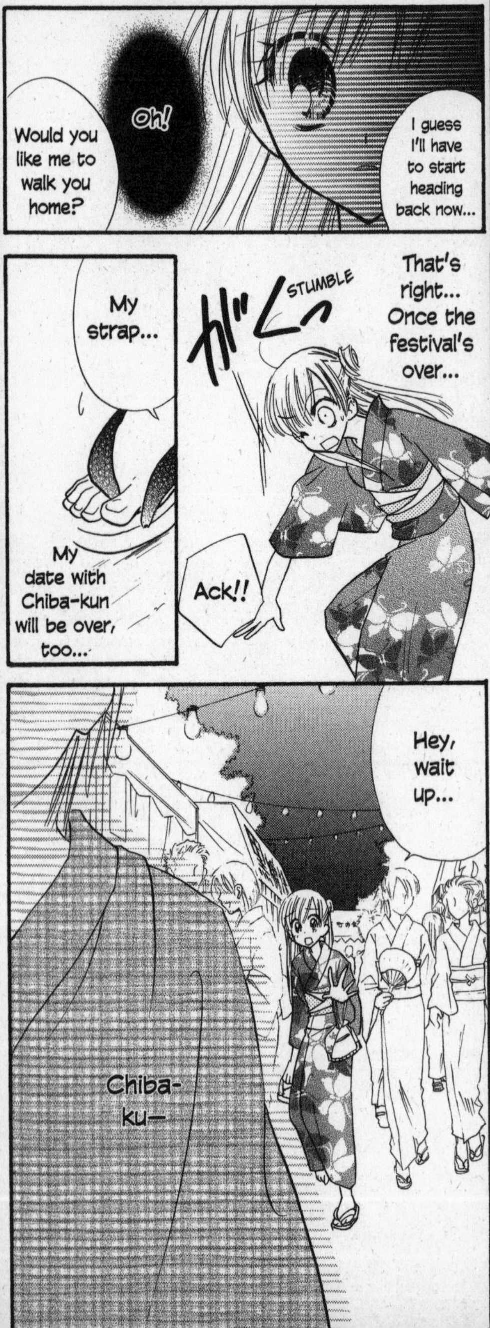
I guess I'll have to start heading back now...
Oh!
Would you like me to walk you home?
That's right... Once the festival's over...
STUMBLE
Ack!!
My strap...
My date with Chiba-kun will be over, too...
Hey, wait up...
Chiba-ku—

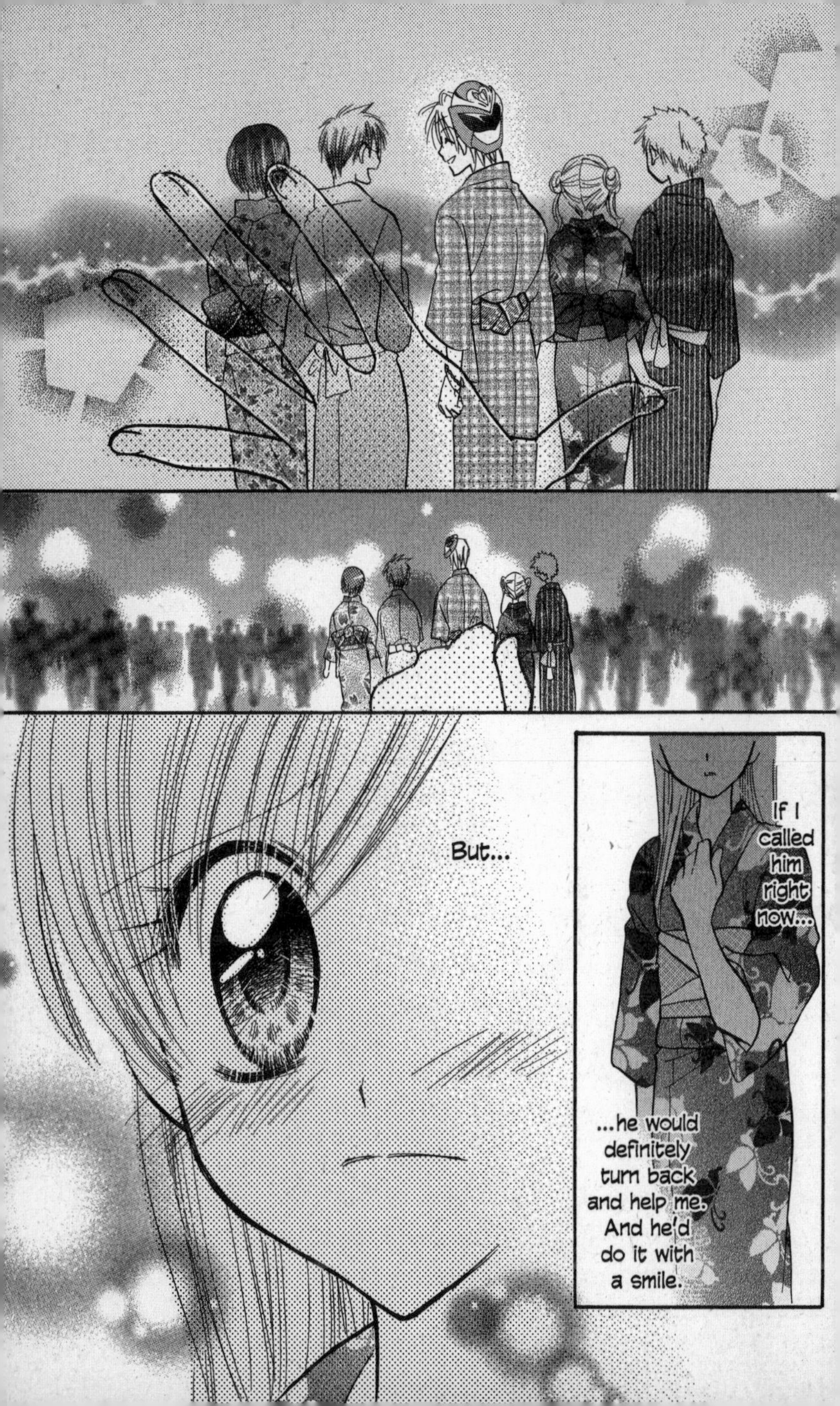
If I called him right now...
...he would definitely turn back and help me. And he'd do it with a smile.
But...

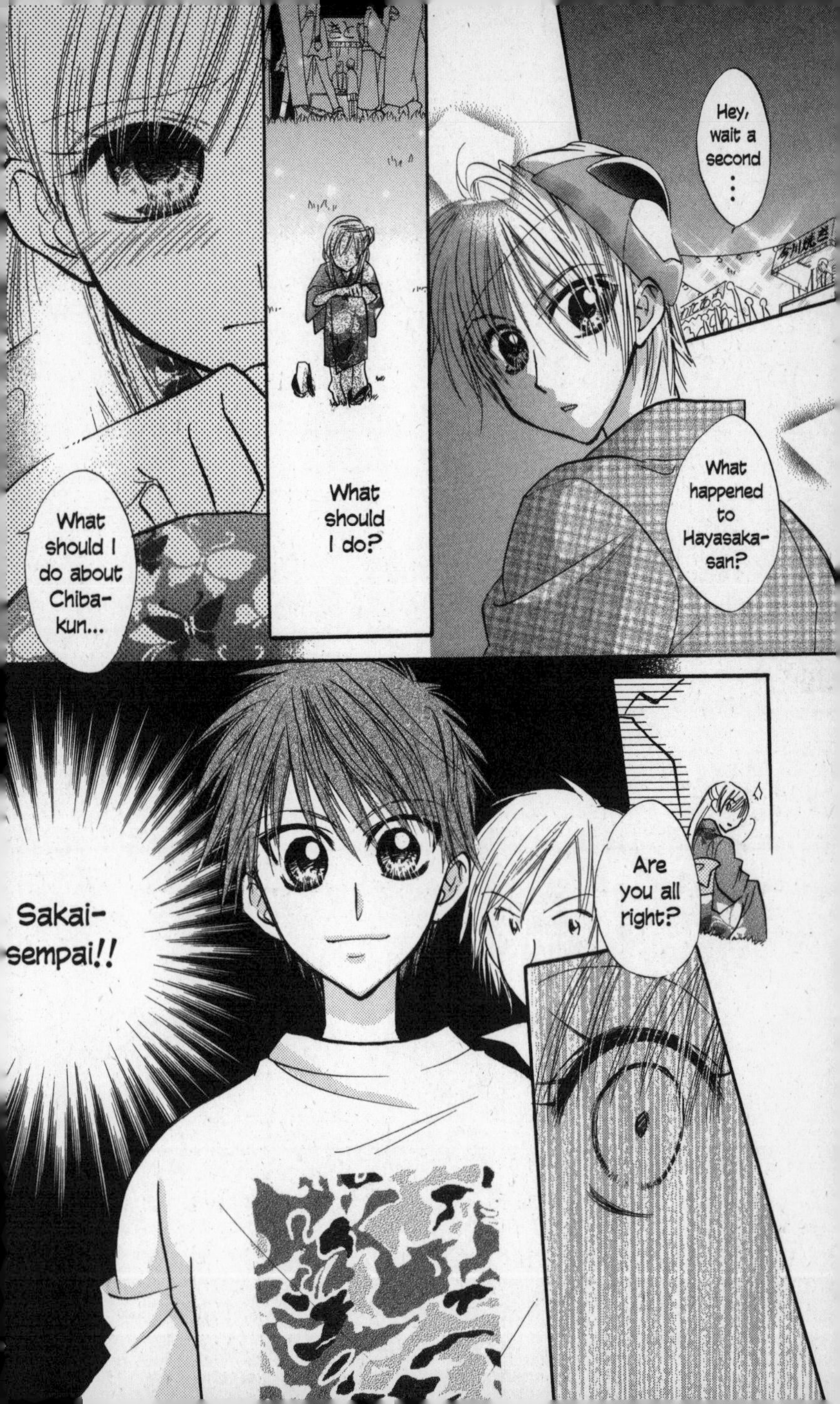
Hey, wait a second ...
What happened to Hayasaka-san?
What should I do?
What should I do about Chiba-kun...
Are you all right?
Sakai-sempai!!

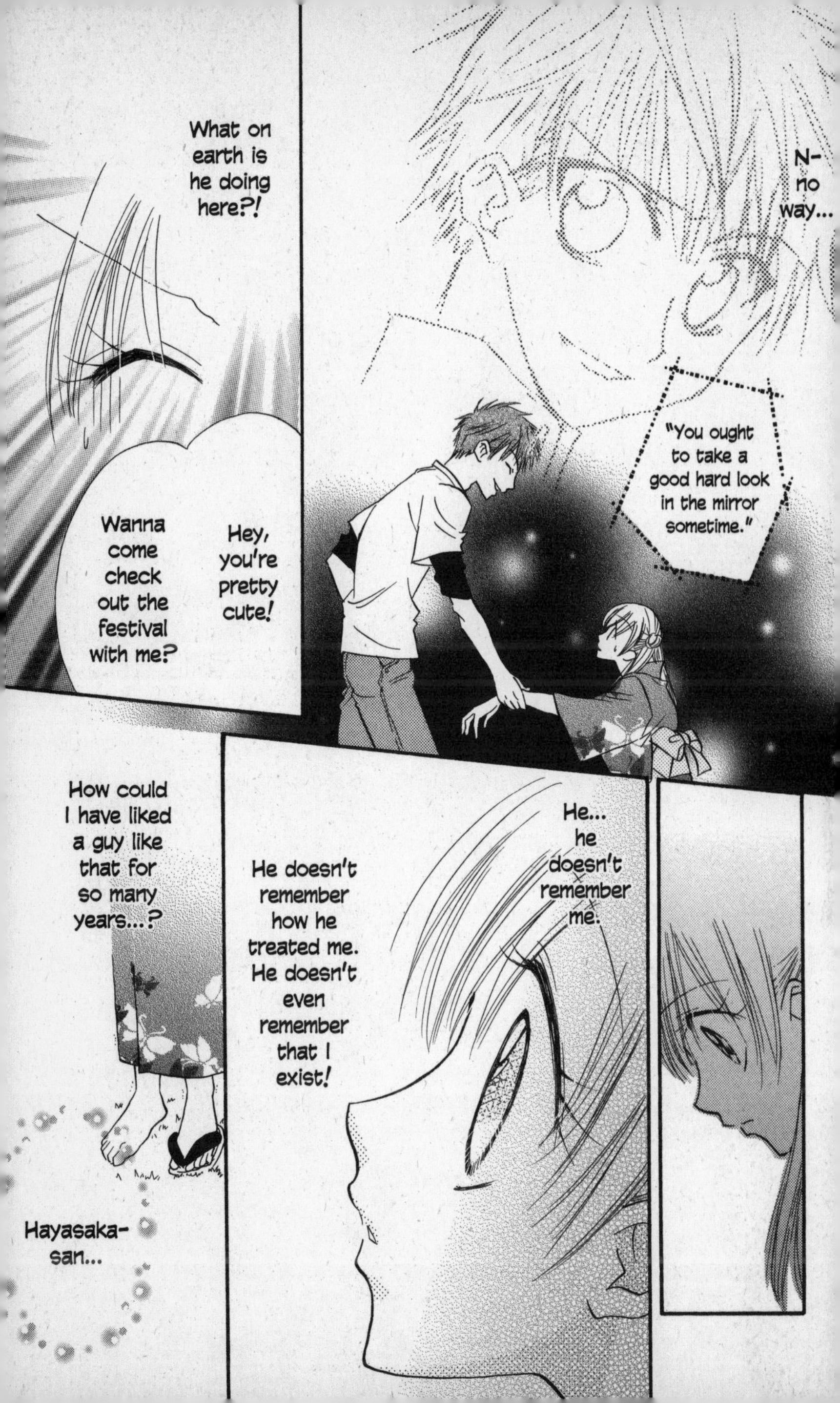
N-no way...
"You ought to take a good hard look in the mirror sometime."
What on earth is he doing here?!
Hey, you're pretty cute!
Wanna come check out the festival with me?
He... he doesn't remember me.
He doesn't remember how he treated me. He doesn't even remember that I exist!
How could I have liked a guy like that for so many years...?
Hayasaka-san...

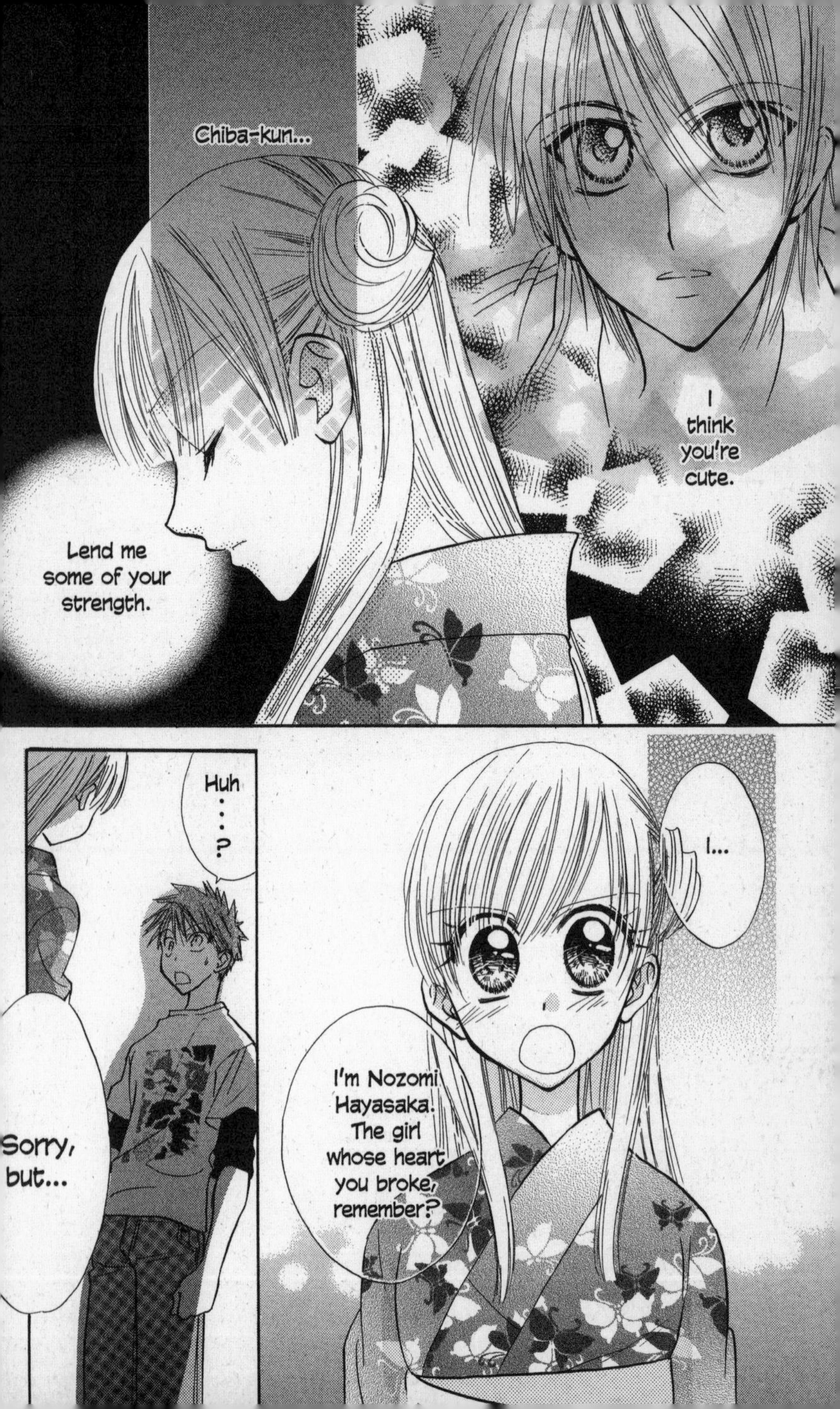
I think you're cute.
Chiba-kun...
Lend me some of your strength.
I...
I'm Nozomi Hayasaka! The girl whose heart you broke, remember?
Huh...?
Sorry, but...

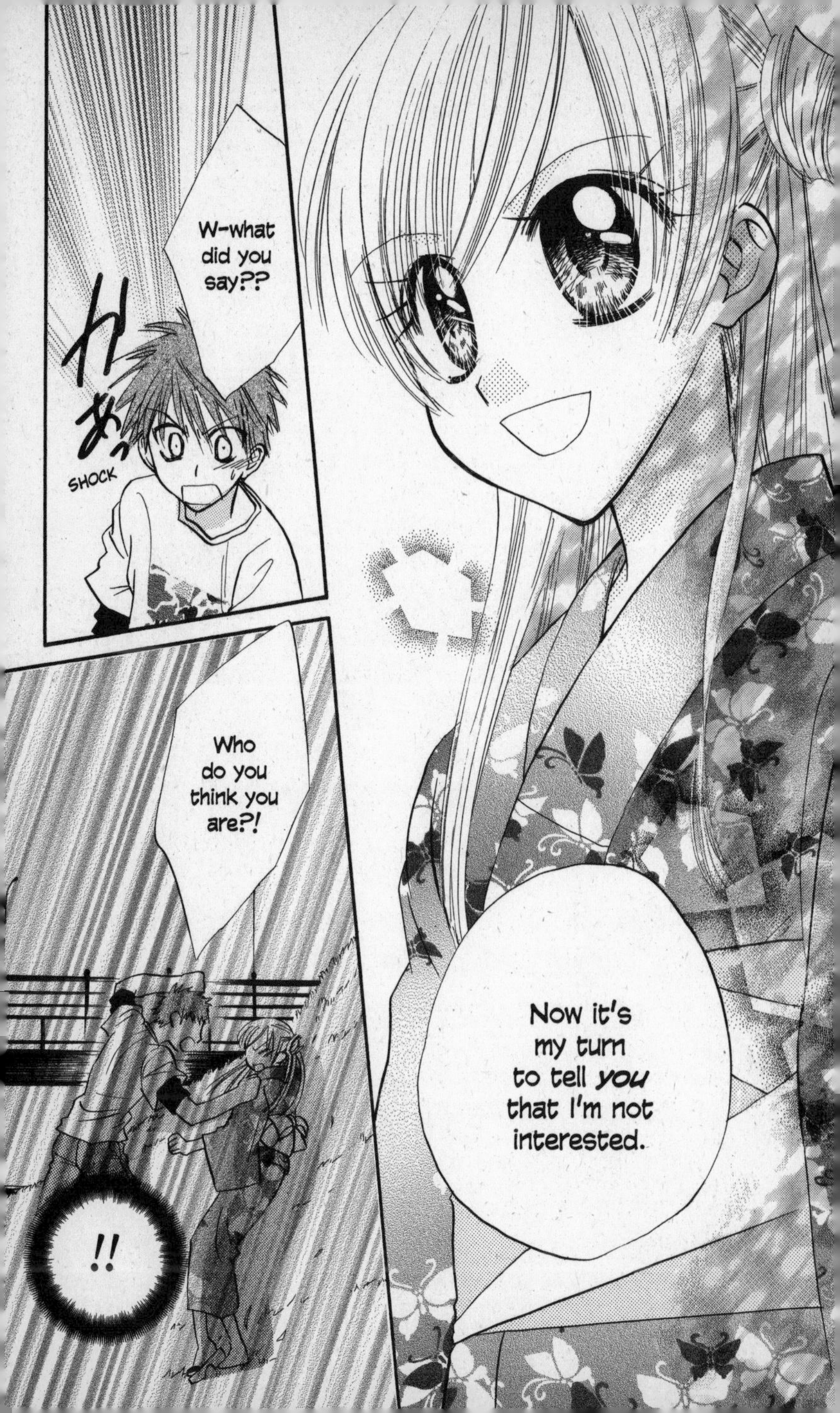

Now it's my turn to tell *you* that I'm not interested.
W-what did you say??
わあっ
SHOCK
Who do you think you are?!
!!

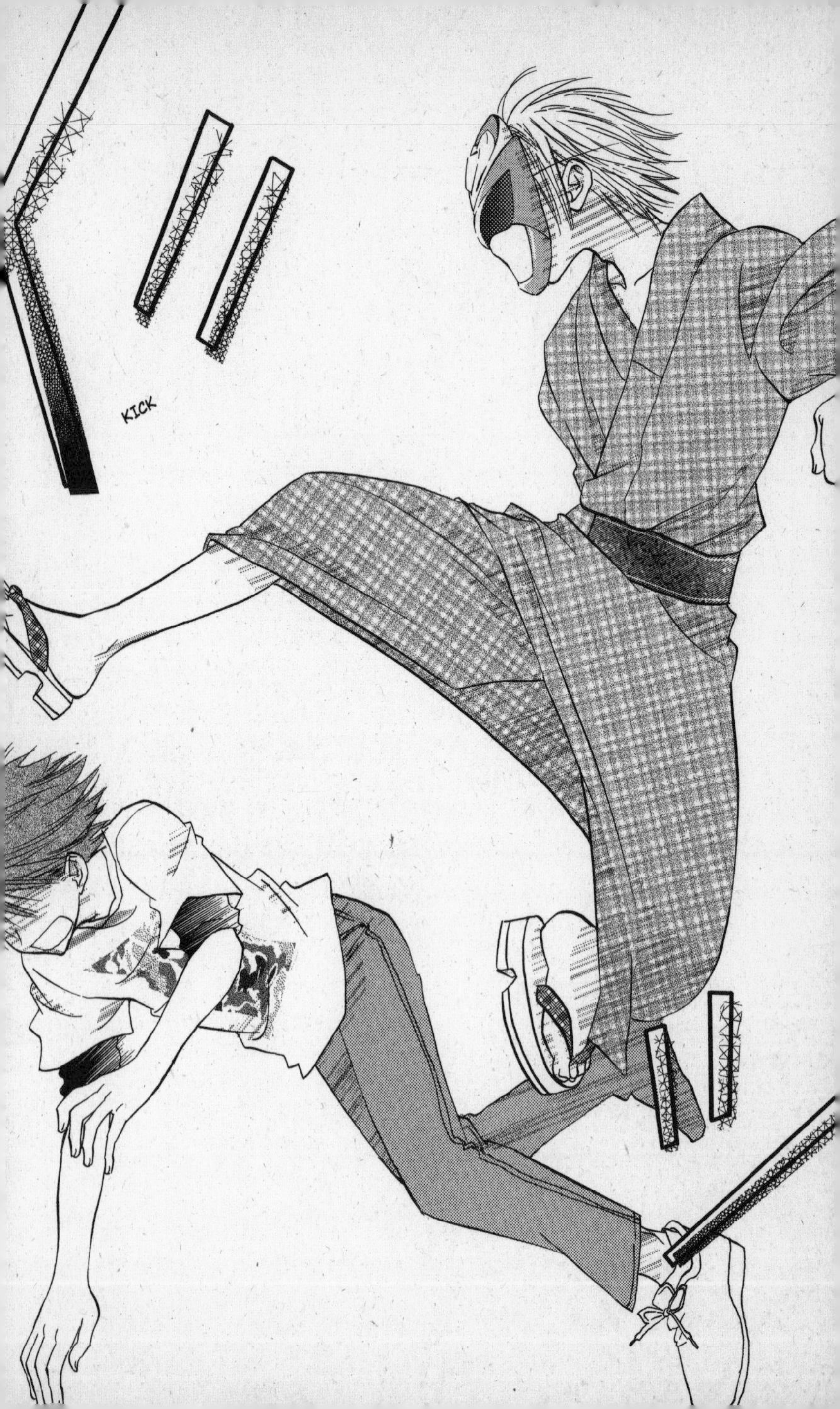
KICK

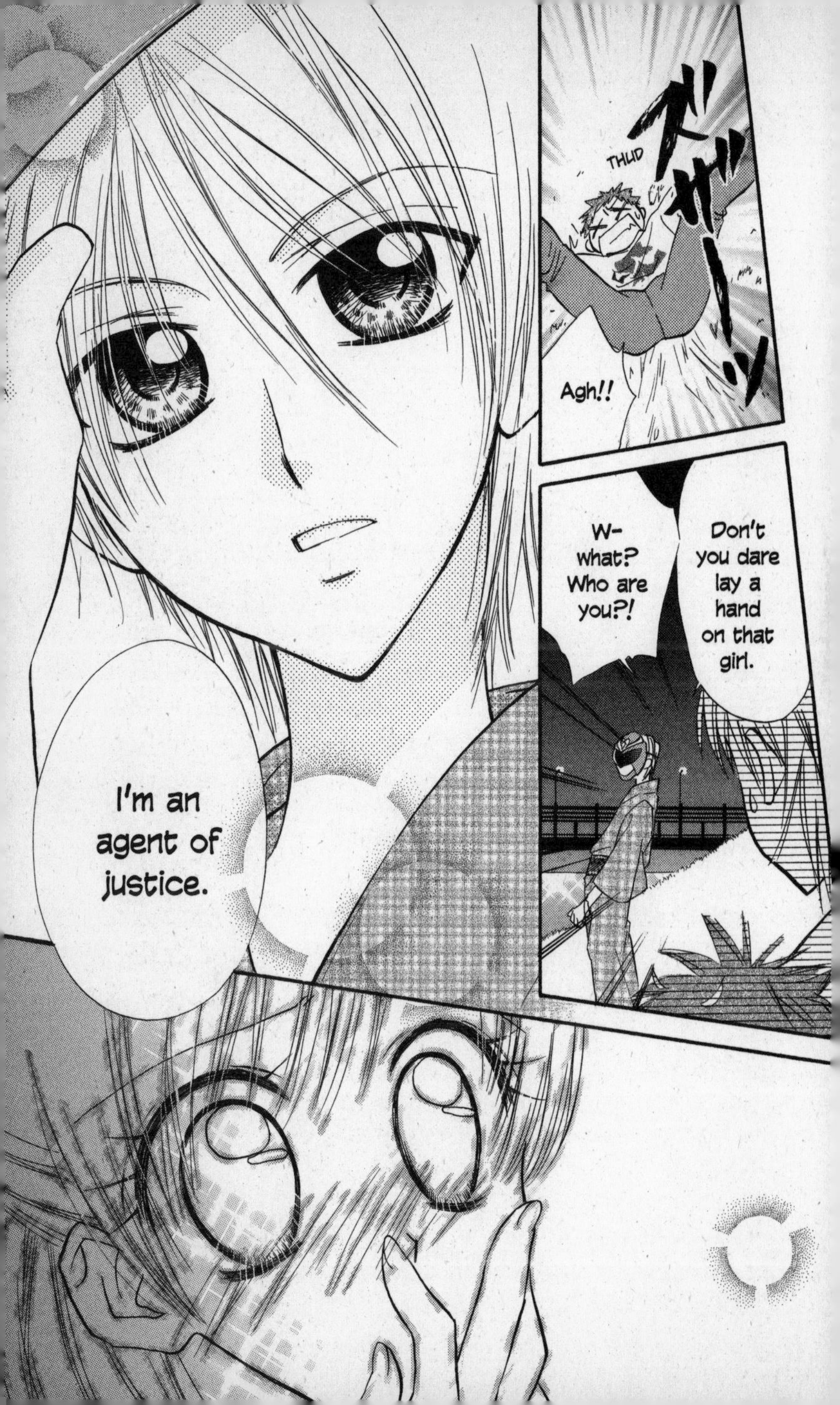
THUD
Agh!!
Don't you dare lay a hand on that girl.
W-what? Who are you?!
I'm an agent of justice.

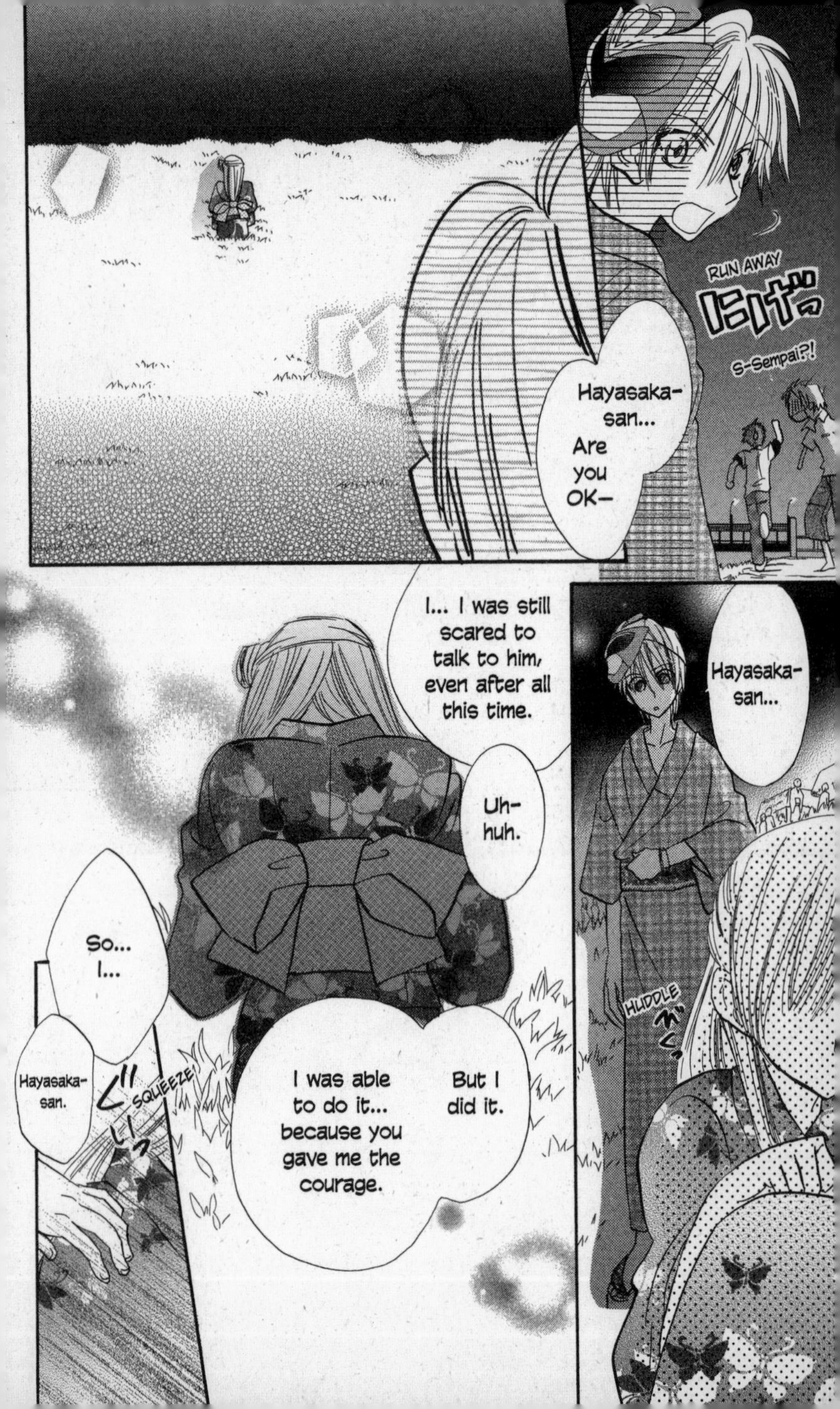
RUN AWAY
にげっ
S-Sempai?!
Hayasaka-san... Are you OK—
Hayasaka-san...
HUDDLE
I... I was still scared to talk to him, even after all this time.
Uh-huh.
But I did it.
I was able to do it... because you gave me the courage.
So... I...
Hayasaka-san.
SQUEEZE

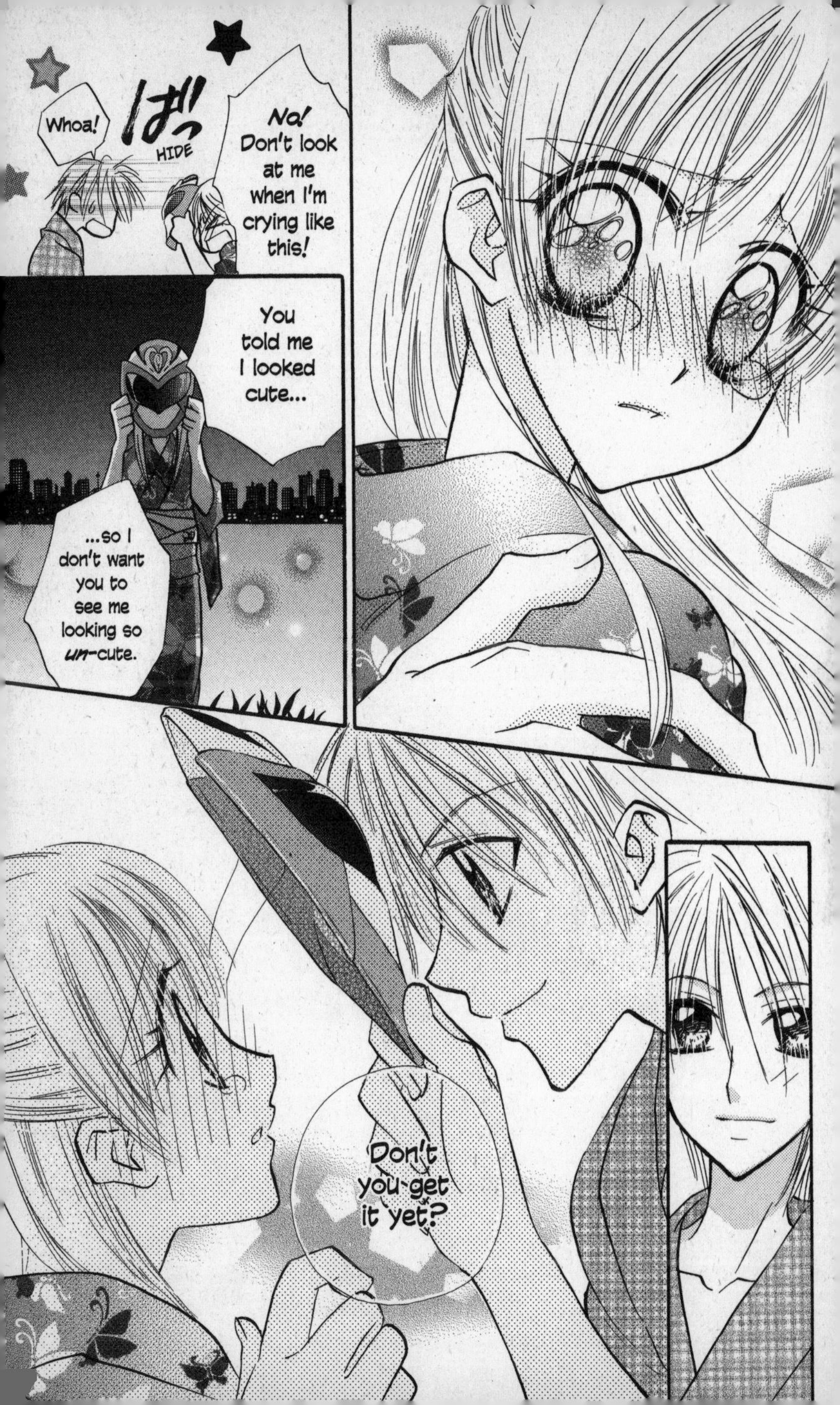
No! Don't look at me when I'm crying like this!
ばっ HIDE
Whoa!
You told me I looked cute...
...so I don't want you to see me looking so un-cute.
Don't you get it yet?

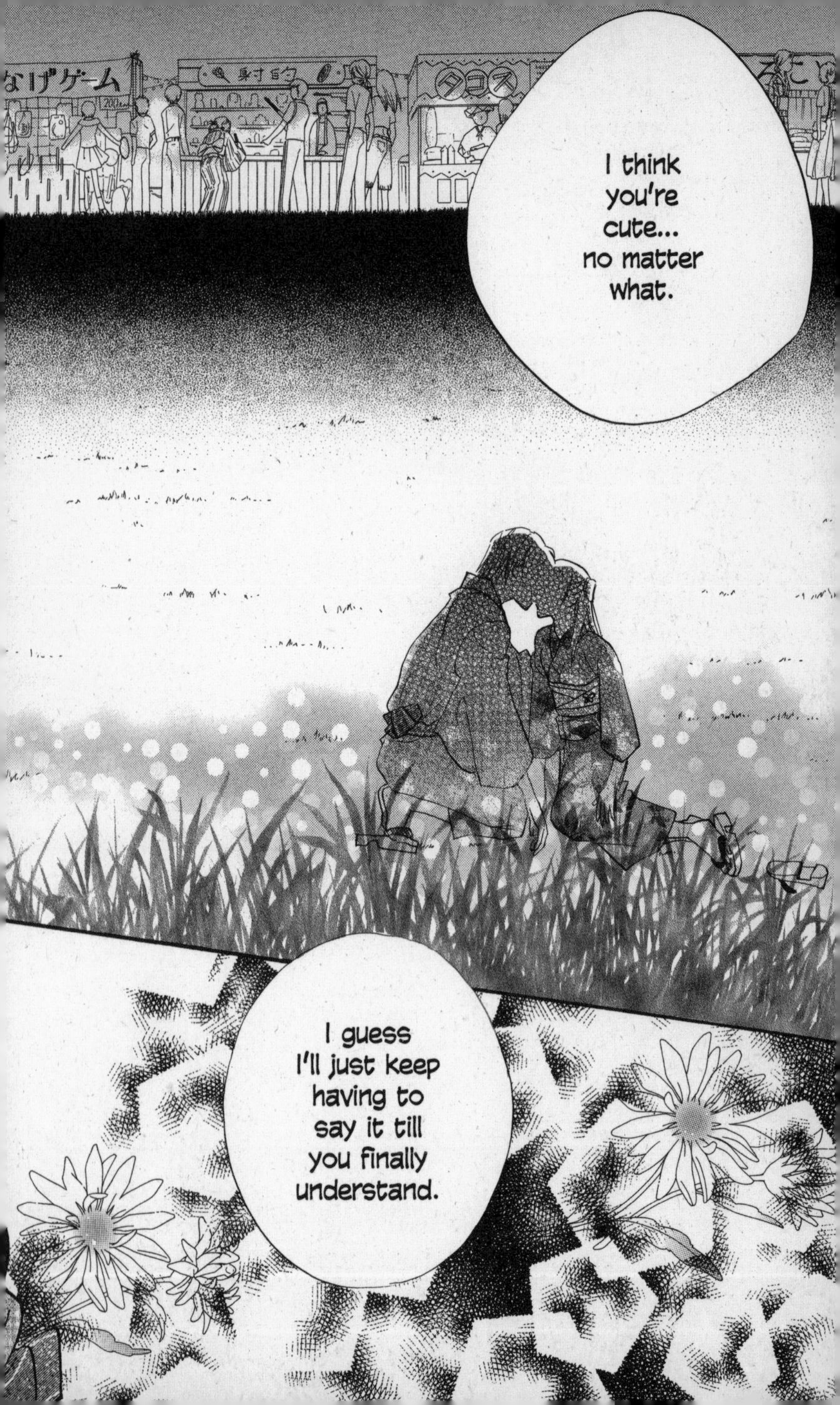
I think you're cute... no matter what.
タコス
なげゲーム
I guess I'll just keep having to say it till you finally understand.

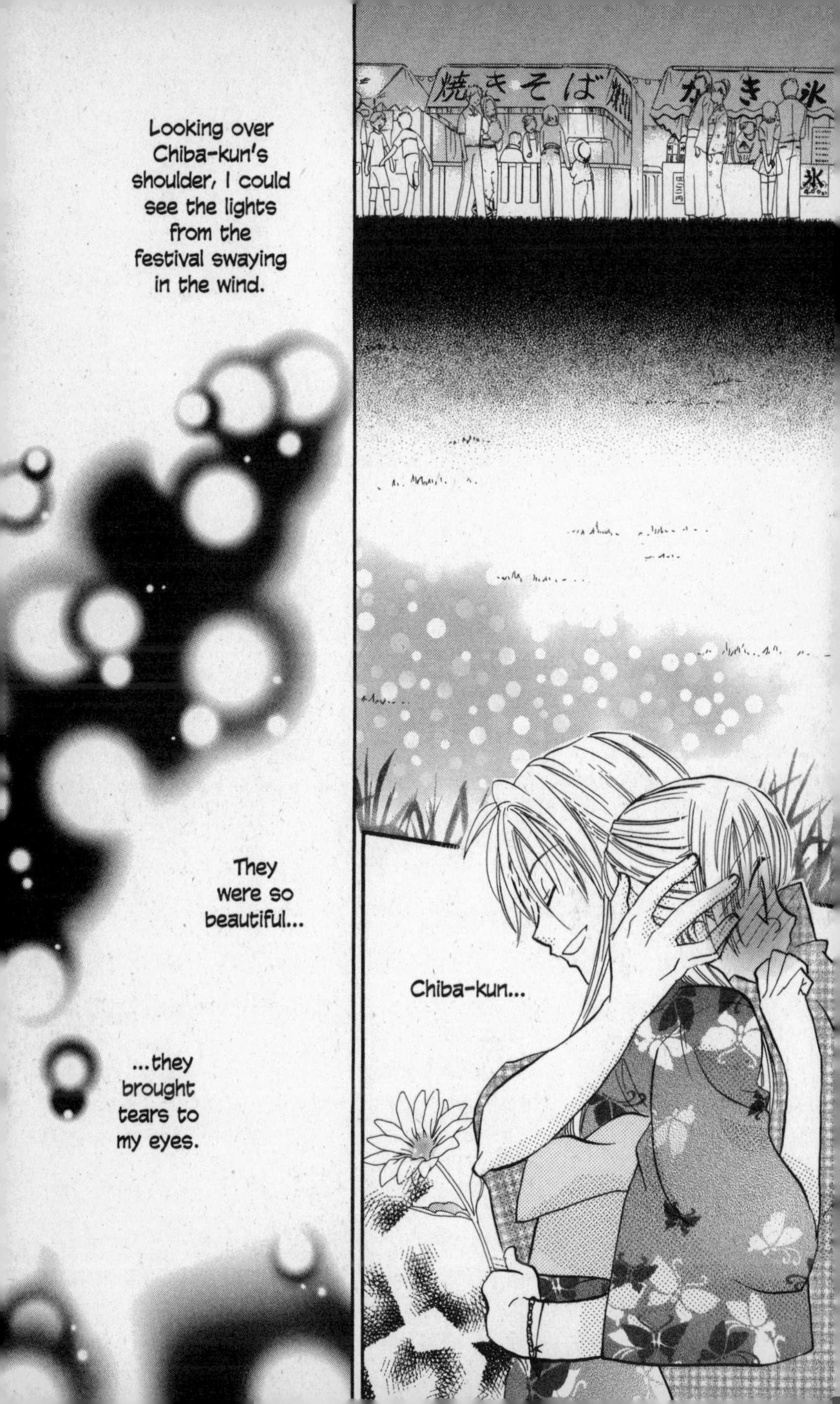
焼きそば
かき氷
氷
Chiba-kun...
Looking over Chiba-kun's shoulder, I could see the lights from the festival swaying in the wind.
They were so beautiful...
...they brought tears to my eyes.

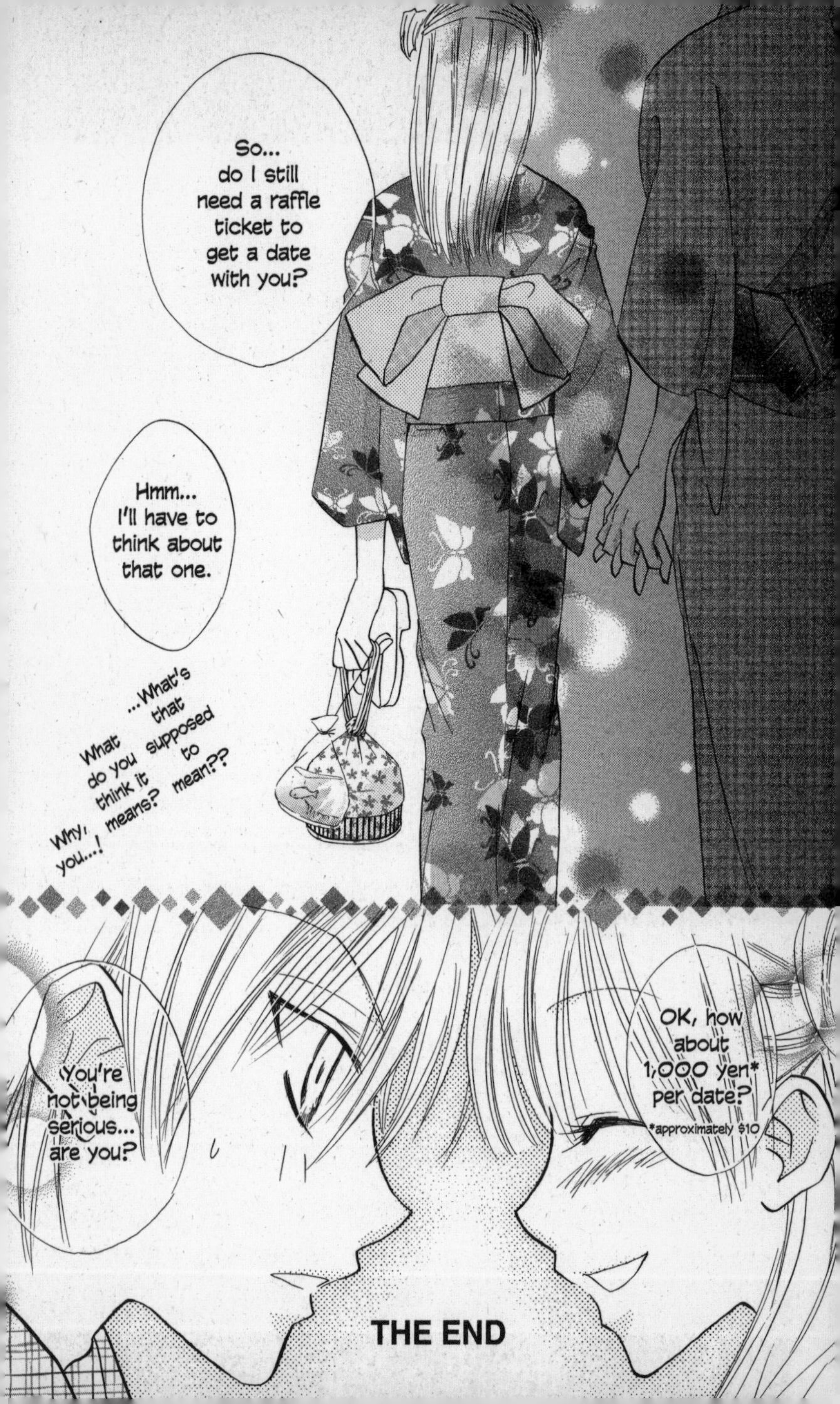

So... do I still need a raffle ticket to get a date with you?
Hmm... I'll have to think about that one.
...What's that supposed to mean??
What do you think it means?
Why, you...!
OK, how about 1,000 yen* per date?
*approximately $10
You're not being serious... are you?
THE END

An Endnote

I hope you're all looking forward to the next volume!

Four-Eyed Prince

is moving slowly but surely along, and I'm hoping I'll be able to continue writing it as peacefully and quietly as possible!

Well, I'll be seeing you again in the next volume!

My dog, Eve, moved on to heaven recently, so I've been sad lately.

But my parents' cats have been doing their best to support me and help me get through it.

SAKURA さくら

KOTONE ニとね

★Special Thanks★
Ichiri·H
Miki·F
Hiromi·H   Naho·Y
Misa·T   Yuko·M

& Editor N & ke Editor T
& my Family
Friends
& You!

Translation Notes

Japanese is a tricky language for most Westerners, and translation is often more art than science. For your edification and reading pleasure, here are notes on some of the places where we could have gone in a different direction, or where a Japanese cultural reference is used.

Onēkei, page 2

This is a popular fashion style in Japan. People who want to follow the "onēkei," or "big sister," fashion trend will have dyed brown hair and tanned skin. They also wear brand-name clothes and accessories.

Bentō, page 16

"Bentō" is the Japanese word for "lunch box"—but Japanese lunch boxes are somewhat different than the lunch boxes we have in the West, which are mainly marketed to and used by children. Japanese bentō are used by adults as well as children, and are typically comprised of two small boxes that stack on top of each other to store two tiers' worth of food in small, separated compartments. Bentō-making is something of an art, with girls often making highly decorative bentō lunches for boys they like. Many mothers also invest a lot of time and effort into making bentō lunches for their children–even to the point of arranging the food to create pictures or creatively slicing or molding food to form various shapes.

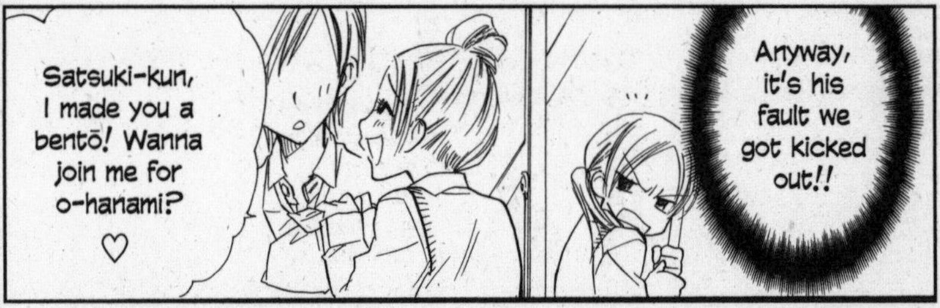
...
Anyway, it's his fault we got kicked out!!
Satsuki-kun, I made you a bentō! Wanna join me for o-hanami? ♡

O-hanami, page 16

This is the Japanese tradition of "flower-viewing." When the sakura (or cherry blossoms) start to bloom in April, it is a long-held Japanese tradition to pack a bentō lunch and eat outside while viewing the beautiful flowers. Sakura only bloom for about two weeks during the Japanese spring, which is why many people make sure to participate in o-hanami at some point before the blooms wither and fall.

Bathwater, page 67

In Japan, it is common for families to draw one bath and then bathe in turns, thereby sharing one tub's worth of bathwater among all members of the family. Of course, each person makes sure to shower thoroughly first so that they are already clean before entering the bath and taking a long, relaxing soak in the water. When they are done, they can place a cover over the bath to keep the water warm for the next family member.

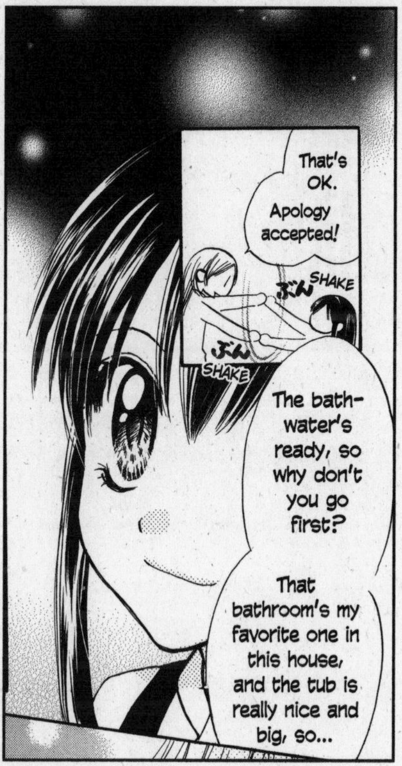
That's OK. Apology accepted!
ぶん SHAKE
ぶん SHAKE
The bath-water's ready, so why don't you go first?
That bathroom's my favorite one in this house, and the tub is really nice and big, so...

Kanashibari, page 90

"Kanashibari" is a Japanese word meaning "sleep paralysis." A person typically experiences paralysis during REM sleep, but someone who is experiencing sleep paralysis will awake from REM sleep only to find themselves unable to move for a short period of time. Sometimes they may also experience dreamlike hallucinations or a feeling of panic. Many people who experience kanashibari will recall it as simply the continuation of a bad dream.

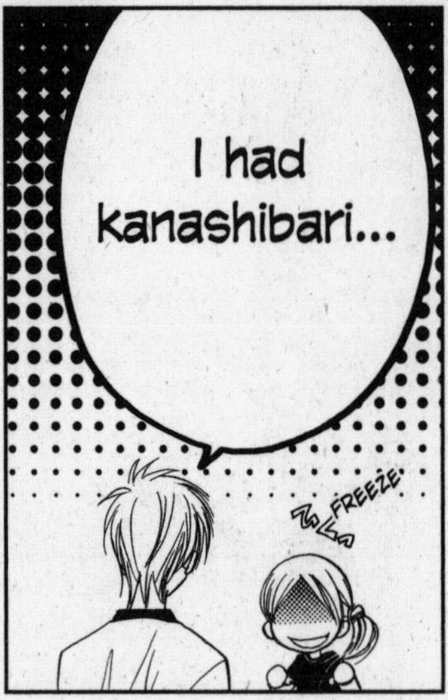
I had kanashibari...
FREEZE

Yukata, page 131

A yukata is a light summer kimono usually made of cotton. Regular kimonos are heavy and warm due to several layers that are worn underneath the kimono itself. However, a yukata is worn without layers beneath and, being made of a lighter fabric, is perfect for warmer weather. They are typically worn to outdoor festivals.

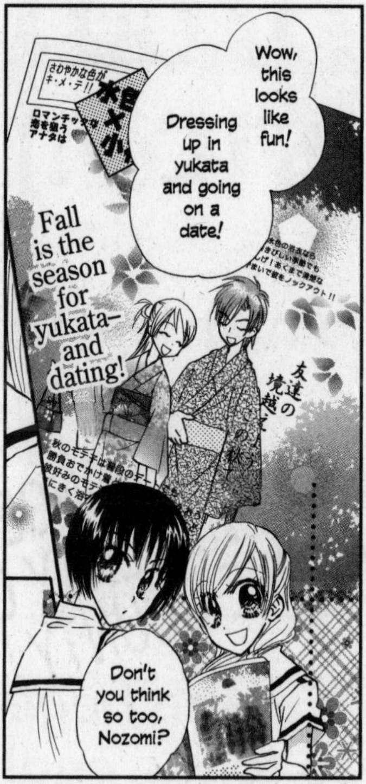

Wow, this looks like fun!
Dressing up in yukata and going on a date!
さわやかな色が キ・メ・テ!!
Fall is the season for yukata—and dating!
Don't you think so too, Nozomi?

TOMARE!

[STOP!]

You're going the wrong way!

Manga is a completely different type of reading experience.

To start at the *beginning*, go to the end!

That's right! Authentic manga is read the traditional Japanese way—from right to left. Exactly the opposite of how American books are read. It's easy to follow: Just go to the other end of the book, and read each page—and each panel—from right side to left side, starting at the top right. Now you're experiencing manga as it was meant to be!